Nonreactive Measures in the Social Sciences

Nonreactive Measures in the Social Sciences

Second Edition

Eugene T. Webb	Stanford University
Donald T. Campbell	Syracuse University
Richard D. Schwartz	Syracuse University
Lee Sechrest	University of Michigan
Janet Belew Grove	Florida State University

Houghton Mifflin Company   Boston
Dallas   Geneva, Illinois   Hopewell, New Jersey   Palo Alto   London

Previously published as *Unobtrusive Measures: Nonreactive Research in the Social Sciences.*

To the memory of Sir Francis Galton

Edgar F. Borgatta, Advisory Editor

Printed in the U.S.A.

Library of Congress Catalog Card Number: 80–50984

ISBN: 0–395–30767–8

Table of Contents

Preface

The revision of *Unobtrusive Measures* did not result from popular demand, nor from want of anything else to do. The decision to go ahead with the revision was made only with difficulty—and obviously not in haste. It grew out of a gradually developing recognition of the opportunity to convey anew, and perhaps more cogently and persuasively, the message intended by the original work. Over the last ten or so years of life of the original volume the question of revision came up among the authors from time to time, but the pressures for revision were not heavy. There was, of course, the opportunity to point to new examples of unobtrusive measures, some arguably better than those in the first book, but that opportunity was only a necessary and not a sufficient condition for a revision. There are new and useful examples in this revision; in particular the work on physical traces, archives, and hardware appears to have advanced considerably and is represented in this volume by substantially expanded chapters. But the numerous new examples made the revision process somewhat aversive both because of the amount of material involved and the necessity for painful decisions about what of the original material to exclude and what portion of the new material to include.

Those familiar with the first edition of the book will note that we have retained, often with little revision, nearly all of the original text pertaining to the methodology and the philosophy of science. Some points have been elaborated and a few new ones have been added, but in the main this second edition is based on an orientation to science and measurement that we consider as useful today as it was 15 years ago. The remainder of the text has been extensively revised with mostly new examples, although we were unable to resist retaining a number of our favorites. Others were retained because they are classics, and still others because the ensuing years have brought nothing better.

Probably the most important force working in favor of a revision was our sense that despite the widespread acceptance of the concept of nonreactive measurement, the practice was still sporadic and undependable. It is our hope that the appearance of *Nonreactive Measures* will stimulate a renewal of interest in and a commitment to the practice of multiple measures not sharing the same sources of error, and that more of these measures will be nonreactive. In addition to new examples of such measures, we believe that some new concepts, or at least concepts new in this application, may be helpful. Various thoughts about unobtrusive measures that we consider "advances" are scattered throughout the text, and a new chapter has been devoted to problems in nonreactive measurement. We considered that chapter a beginning rather than an end, although that comment should not be taken as presaging yet another edition. We hope that some of our more astute readers will be stimulated to carry on some of the conceptual and methodological tasks that are explicit and implicit in the material we present.

Ethical concerns, some related quite directly to issues involved in measuring reactively, have become much more salient since the book was first written, and we attempt to deal with some of these issues in a new chapter on ethics and by somewhat more frequent and careful attention to ethics in the rest of the text. Our chapter is not, however, meant to be a definitive work on ethics, and we have cited literature only very selectively. There are five of us involved now in this volume, and we probably do not even agree completely among ourselves when we get to the boundaries of some ethical issues. We have not tried to be prescriptive in more than a general way, but have regarded it as sufficient for purposes of our work to try to ensure that ethical issues are called to the attention of nonreactive measurers. Until a more august, representative, and authoritative body is able to prescribe specific ethical procedures, we will be satisfied if our readers give careful individual attention to ethical matters and follow the best thinking available in their respective fields.

The change in the title of the book was made only with great reluctance, for we do not want any potential readers to be misled into thinking that the book was a new one—although the revisions have been unusually extensive. Still, we came to realize over the years that the original title was not the best one since it was the nonreactivity of the measures rather than their unobtrusiveness that was of major concern. We were also guided by a sense that our new title put our recommendations into a more accurate and constructive ethical perspective. Nonetheless, the revision is squarely derived from and conceptually consistent with the original.

This second edition could not have been accomplished without the support and encouragement of a number of persons and organizations. The impetus for the revision grew out of encouragement and support for renewed interest in nonreactive measures provided to Lee Sechrest by the Office of Naval Research. Several of the studies cited in this volume were done with support from ONR, and the preparation of Chapter 9 is based directly on work supported by the Navy (ONR Contract N00014-78-C-0469). The authors want to thank Neil Glassman of ONR and H. Wallace Sinalko of The Smithsonian Institution for their personal support and encouragement of these efforts. Miriam Kelty of the National Commission on the Protection of Human Subjects in Biomedical and Behavioral Research was of great help in the drafting of Chapter 5 on ethics; Stephen Withey of the Institute of Social Research is also due thanks for helpful comments and suggestions. Irene Mass was especially helpful in the final stages of manuscript preparation, and the authors owe Russell D. Clark III many thanks for many favors and for being a generally splendid colleague. Jacqueline Rodgers helped in many ways with the tasks of assembling the manuscript, typing, and communicating with publishers, and we thank her. We also want to thank Geoffrey Huck and Rebecca Strehlow, our editors, for support at some very critical moments, and for many helpful suggestions and actions. It may or may not be evident, but we owe gratitude in large quantities to many, many colleagues and students over the years who have encouraged us in our interest in nonreactive measurement and who have provided us with a multitude of examples, some among the finest we know. We could not include all of them in the text, but we are grateful in equal measure for those we did not use.

Finally, all of us, but especially Lee and Janet, want to thank Carol and Bob for their patience and understanding when we most needed it.

Lee Sechrest
Janet Belew Grove

CHAPTER 1

Prologue

This survey directs attention to social science research data *not* obtained by interview or questionnaire. Some may think this exclusion does not leave much. It does. Many innovations in research method are to be found scattered throughout the social science literature. Their use, however, is unsystematic, their importance understated. Our review of this material is intended to broaden the social scientist's currently narrow range of utilized methodologies and to encourage creative and opportunistic exploitation of unique measurement possibilities.

Today, the dominant mass of social science research is based upon interviews and questionnaires. We lament this overdependence upon a single, fallible method. Interviews and questionnaires intrude as a foreign element into the social setting they would describe, they create as well as measure attitudes, they elicit atypical roles and responses, they are limited to those who are accessible and will cooperate, and the responses obtained are produced in part by dimensions of individual differences irrelevant to the topic at hand.

But the principal objection is that they are used alone. No research method is without bias. Interviews and questionnaires must be supplemented by methods testing the same social science variables but having *different* methodological weaknesses.

In sampling the range of alternative approaches, we examine their weaknesses, too. The flaws are serious and give insight into why we do depend so much upon the interview. But the issue is not choosing among individual methods. Rather it is the necessity for a multiple operationism, a collection of methods combined to avoid sharing the same weaknesses. The goal of

1

this monograph is not to replace the interview but to supplement and cross-validate it with measures that do not require the cooperation of a respondent and that do not themselves contaminate the response.

Here are some samples of the kinds of methods we will be surveying in this monograph:

> One investigator wanted to know the relationship between reported and actual beer consumption. He obtained a "front door" measure by asking residents of houses how much beer they consumed each week and a "back door" measure by counting the beer cans in their garbage cans. The back door measure resulted in a considerably higher estimate of beer consumption.
>
> The degree of fear induced by a ghost-story-telling session can be measured by noting the shrinking diameter of a circle of seated children.
>
> Chinese jade dealers have used the pupil dilation of their customers as a measure of the client's interest in particular stones, and Darwin in 1872 noted this same variable as an index of fear.
>
> Library withdrawals were used to demonstrate the effect of the introduction of television into a community. Fiction titles dropped, nonfiction titles were unaffected.
>
> The role of rate of interaction in managerial recruitment is shown by the overrepresentation of baseball managers who were infielders or catchers (high interaction positions) during their playing days.
>
> Sir Francis Galton employed surveying hardware to estimate the bodily dimensions of African women whose language he did not speak.
>
> The child's interest in Christmas was demonstrated by distortions in the size of Santa Claus drawings.
>
> Racial attitudes in two colleges were compared by noting the degree of clustering of blacks and whites in lecture halls.
>
> An enterprising radio reporter in Iowa wanted to know what his audience thought about the various presidential candidates. So, he stationed himself atop the local water tower and called upon his listeners to express their preferences by flushing their toilets as he announced each candidate. He then observed the drop in water level as each candidate's name was called. This "Royal Flush" produced results in accord with later voting.

The methods we will discuss have been grouped into chapters by the characteristics of the data: physical traces, archives, observations. That grouping is merely for the sake of convenience and says nothing of the uses to which the data might be put.

Before examining in detail the arguments for the use of multiple measures and the methodological framework within which they and more traditional measures can be evaluated, it may be well to get right into one of the categories for some concrete examples. Similarly, we will want to consider ethical problems involved in the use of unobtrusive measurement, but that discussion, too, can be postponed until a considerable number of specific examples have been presented.

CHAPTER 2

Physical Traces: Erosion and Accretion

The fog had probably just cleared. The singular Sherlock Holmes had been reunited with his old friend Dr. Watson (after one of Watson's marriages), and both walked to Watson's newly acquired office. The practice was located in a duplex of two physician's suites, both of which had been for sale. No doubt sucking on his calabash, Holmes summarily told Watson that he had made a wise choice in purchasing the practice that he did, rather than the one on the other side of the duplex. The data? The steps were more worn on Watson's side than on his competitor's.

In this chapter we look at research methods geared to the study of physical traces surviving from past behavior. Physical evidence is probably the social scientist's least used source of data, yet because of its ubiquity, it holds flexible and broad-gauged potential.

It is reasonable to start a chapter on physical evidence by talking of Sherlock Holmes. He and his paperbacked colleagues could teach us much. Consider that the detective, like the social scientist, faces the task of inferring the nature of past behavior (Who did the lord of the manor in?) by the careful generation and evaluation of current evidence. Some evidence he engineers (by questioning), some he observes (Does the witness develop a tic?), some he develops from extant physical evidence (Did the murderer leave his eyeglasses behind?). If there are several different types of converging evidence to be weighed, the detective makes a decision on the plausibility of several rival hypotheses. For example:

4

H_1: The butler did it.
H_2: It was the blacksheep brother.
H_3: He really committed suicide.

This chapter discusses only the physical evidence, those pieces of data not specifically produced for the purpose of comparison and inference but available to be exploited opportunistically by the alert investigator. It should be emphasized that physical evidence has greatest utility in consort with other methodological approaches. Because there are easily visible population and content restrictions associated with physical evidence, such data have largely been ignored. It is difficult even to consider a patently weak source of data when research strategy is based on single measures and definitional operationism. The visibly stronger questionnaire or interview looks to be more valid, and it may be if only one measure is taken. In a multimethod strategy, however, one does not have to exclude data of any class or degree solely because it is weak. If the weaknesses are known and considered the data are usable. Rathje (1979) provides a particularly useful discussion of both the limitations of trace measures and the circumstances that warrant their use and interpretation.

Rathje notes that physical traces must be "mapped" onto some physical object, and new traces continually overlay and even eradicate old ones. Traces are even transformed in meaning with successive responses of which they are the result. Thus, the debris from a party provides grounds for inference about what went on, but subsequently the party debris may become a better indicator of habits of waste disposal, for example, the trace is changed if a wine bottle is saved for use as a candleholder. Many behaviors do not produce lasting traces because, for example, the context in which they occur either is not plastic or is too plastic. A heart with initials carved into a sycamore tree may last indefinitely; the same insignia scratched into a cement sidewalk might scarcely be visible, and that inscribed in the sand would disappear with the next wave. On the other hand, Rathje notes that the biases in trace measures at least tend to be unidirectional and predictable: trace measures will scarcely ever underestimate the frequency of behaviors. And, whatever the distortions and biases of trace measures, they are probably not the same as those for survey methods and, hence, remain complementary.

An amusing but instructive caution about the interpretation of trace measures can be found in *Motel of the Mysteries* (Macaulay, 1979), a book well worth reading whether one is a social scientist or not. Macaulay's book is a fantasy based on the proposition that:

> In 1985 a cataclysmic coincidence of previously unknown proportion extinguished virtually all forms of life on the North American continent. On the morning of November 29, an accidental reduction in postal rates on a substance called third- and fourth-class mail literally buried the North Americans under tons of brochures, fliers, and small containers called *Free*. That afternoon, impurities that had apparently hung unnoticed in the air for centuries finally succumbed to the force of gravity and collapsed on what was left of an already stunned population.

The book continues to relate what happens when some 2000 years later excavations uncover the remains of the extinct *Yank* civilization. A previously undistinguished dilettante archeologist falls into an opening and finds himself at the entrance to a room labeled *26* with a small sign reading "Do Not Disturb" hanging from the door handle. The investigating archeologists finally determine that they have stumbled onto an ancient burial ground known as the *Motel Toot'N'C'Mon* and that *26* is one of the sacred burial chambers. The tomb is found to contain a *Great Altar* facing a bed on which one skeleton lies, and in the *Sacred Inner Chamber* there is a *Sacred Sarcophagus* in which there is another skeleton wearing the *Sacred Burial Cap*. Also in the room is the *Sacred Urn* with an attached tank that produced water music. Attached to the *Sacred Urn*, for storage purposes, obviously, there was the *Sacred Collar* adorned with the *Sacred Headband* inscribed with "Sanitized for your protection," and so on. Ultimately several of these finds are turned into museum souvenirs, for example, the "Do Not Disturb" sign and the doorknob become models for a dandy belt buckle. Although *Motel of the Mysteries* is meant to amuse, it should also lead us to question seriously our interpretations of trace measures, for many of which there is certainly more than one plausible hypothesis. Segal (1979), for example, describes the skeleton of a boy of about seven years dead for over 2000 years: His feet are crushed, his shoulders bent out of shape, his head held at a tilt, the result of repeated insult to the brain. Segal's hypothesis? "the product of chronic abuse and mutilation by his elders." (p. 577) We do not doubt that child abuse occurred in the Roman era, but many readers might think of rival hypotheses to explain such a grotesque skeleton.

It may be helpful to discriminate between two broad classes of physical evidence, a discrimination similar to that between the intaglio and the cameo. On one hand, there are the *erosion measures*, where the degee of selective wear on some material yields the measure. Holmes's solution of the stairs on the duplex is an example. On the other hand, there are *accretion measures*, where the research evidence is some deposit of materials. Immediately one thinks of anthropologists working with refuse piles and pottery shards, "kitchen middens," as they are called. The trace measures could be further subdivided according to the number and pattern of units of evidence. We might have two subclasses: remnants, where there is only one or a few indicators of the past behavior available, and series, where there is an accumulative body of evidence with more units, possibly deposited over a longer period of time. For purposes of simplicity, it is easier to consider just the two main divisions of erosion and accretion.

NATURAL EROSION MEASURES

Let us look first at some erosion measures. A committee was formed to set up a psychological exhibit at Chicago's Museum of Science and Industry. The committee learned that the vinyl tiles around the exhibit containing live, hatching chicks had to be replaced every six weeks or so; tiles in other areas of the museum went for years without replacement (Duncan, 1963). A comparative study of the rate of tile replacement around the various museum exhibits could give a rough ordering of the popularity of the exhibits. Note that although erosion is the measure, the knowledge of the erosion rate comes from a check of the records of the museum's maintenance department.

In addition to this erosion measure, unobtrusive observation studies showed that people stand before the chick display longer than they stand before any of the other exhibits. With this additional piece of evidence, the question becomes whether or not the erosion is a simple result of people standing in one location and shuffling their feet, or whether it really does indicate a greater frequency of different people viewing the exhibit. Clearly an empirical question. The observation and the tile erosion are two partially overlapping measures, each of which can serve as a check on the other. The observation material is more textured for studies of current behavior, because it can provide information on both the number of viewers and how long each views the display. The erosion data cannot index the duration of individual viewing, but they permit an analysis of popularity over time and do so with economy and efficiency.

Those readers who have attended American Psychological Association meetings have doubtless observed the popularity of exhibits displaying a live pigeon or monkey (a Skinner-boxed baby also once did well). This observation offers independent evidence for the general principle that dynamic exhibits draw more viewers than static ones. The hypothesis could be tested further by more careful comparison of tile wear about dynamic and static exhibits in the museum, making corrections for their positional distribution. At least part of the correction would be drawn from the previously mentioned research by Melton (1936) on response sets systematically present in museum traffic flow.

The worn floor tiles at the chick exhibit has always been one of our favorite unobtrusive measures, and we suspect a favorite of many others since it is often cited. Alas, technology appears to have overtaken us, for the building supervisor at the museum, Ruben Humphrey, recently told us that three or four years ago the area containing the chick exhibit was remodeled and new floor tiles were put down. The floor tiles have not had to be replaced even once since then and need only to be kept clean and have scuff marks scrubbed off occasionally (R. Humphrey, personal communication, May, 1980). Could we in some manner quantify scuff marks as a substitute for tile wear? Possibly, but that would put the measure in the category of accretions, a discussion to come later.

The wear on library books, particularly on the corners where the page is turned, offers an example of a possible approach that illustrates a useful overlap measure. One of the most direct and obvious ways to learn the popularity of books is to check how many times each of a series of titles has been removed from a library. This is an excellent measure and uses the records already maintained for other purposes. But it is only an indirect measure for the investigator who wants to know the relative amount of reading a series of books get. They may be removed from the library, but not read. It is easy to establish whether or not there is a close relationship between degree of wear and degree of checkouts from the library. If this relationship is positive and high, the hypothesis that books are taken out but selectively not read is accounted for. Note that the erosion measure also allows one to study the relative use of titles that are outside the span of the library withdrawal measure. Titles placed on reserve, for example, are typically not noted for individual use by library bookkeeping. An alternative accretion measure is to note the amount of dust that has accumulated on the books studied.

Mosteller (1955) conducted a shrewd and creative study on the degree to which different sections of the *International Encyclopedia of the Social Sciences* were read. He measured the wear and tear on separate sections by noting dirty edges of pages as markers, and observed the frequency of dirt smudges, finger markings, and underlining on pages. In some cases of very heavy use, ". . . dirt had noticeably changed the color of the page so that (some articles) are immediately distinguishable from the rest of the volume" (p. 171). Mosteller studied volumes at both Harvard and the University of Chicago and went to three libraries at each institution. He even used the *Encyclopaedia Britannica* as a control.

A variation of the erosion method has been suggested by Brown (1960) for studying the food intake of institutionalized patients—frequently a difficult task, if the question is one of overall food consumption of some administrative unit (say, a ward under special treatment conditions compared with a control ward). Brown makes the engagingly simple suggestion of weighing food trucks that enter and garbage trucks that leave. The unit could be varied to be an individual tray of food, the aggregate consignment to a floor or ward, or the total input and output of the hospital. Herbert-Jackson and Risley (1977) have, in fact, done systematic weighing of food before and after meals in order to determine food intake by persons in various programs designed to affect eating habits.

Probably a good deal could be surmised about driving habits and skills from careful examination of the "erosion" of automobiles as they become dented and scraped, as taillights are broken, and as ornaments disappear (Sechrest, 1971). Erosion measures are little used in research, but their potential is evident, and they undoubtedly are used quite often in the informal unobtrusive measurement that we all do.

NATURAL ACCRETION MEASURES

There are large numbers of useful natural remnants of past behavior that can be exploited. We can examine now a few examples of behavior traces that were laid down "naturally," without the intervention of the social scientist.

The detective-story literature, again, is instructive. In a favorite example (Barzun, 1961), a case hinged on determining where a car came from. It was solved (naturally) by studying the frequencies to which the car's radio buttons were tuned. By triangulation of the frequencies, from a known population of commercial station frequencies, the geographic source of the car was learned. Here was a remnant of past behavior (someone setting the buttons orginally) that included several component elements collectively considered to reach a solution. Unimaginatively, most detective fiction considers much simpler and less elegant solutions—such as determining how fast a car was going by noting the degree to which insects are splattered on the windshield.

Radio-dial settings were used in a continuing audience-measurement study, with mechanics in an automotive service department the data gatherers (Anonymous, 1962). A Chicago automobile dealer, "Z" Frank, estimates the popularity of different radio stations by having mechanics record the position of the dial in all cars brought in for service. More than 50,000 dials a year are checked, with less than 20 percent duplication of dials. These data are then used to select radio stations to carry the dealer's advertising. The generalization of these findings is sound if (1) the goal of the radio propaganda is to reach the same type of audience that now comes to the dealership, and (2) a significant number of cars have radios. If many of the cars are without radios, then a partial and possibly biased estimate of the universe is obtained. It is reported, "We find a high degree of correlation between what the rating people report and our own dial setting research" (p. 83).

The same approach could be used to study the selective appeal of different radio stations. Knowing that various shopping centers draw customers from quite discrete economic populations, one could observe dial settings in cars parked in the shopping centers and compare them. As a validation check on the discrimination among the centers, one could (in metropolitan areas) note local tax stickers affixed to the automobiles and compare these with the economic data reported for tax areas by the United States Census.

Dial checking is difficult in public areas because one cannot easily enter the car and make a close observation. And the locking of cars is a selective phenomenon, even if one would risk entering an unlocked car. Sechrest (1971) has reported that a significantly larger proportion of college women lock their cars than do college men. He learned this by checking doors of automobiles parked adjacent to men's and women's dormitories. Foxx and Hake (1977; Hake and Foxx, 1978) were successful in getting odometer readings from the automobiles of students as a way of assessing conservation of gasoline. The students knew that the investigators were checking the locations of their automobiles but did not know that the odometers were being read. All odometers save one could be read from outside the car, and even on that one the last three digits were visible. We would think it foolhardy for an investigator to go around opening car doors to check mileage, and the obvious use of devices such as binoculars and periscopes would be strange, to say the least. However, if odometer readings could be obtained in ways available to ordinary passersby, the method would probably be acceptable.

A warning needs to be inserted about here. Much of what a detective or investigative journalist may do has become unethical or otherwise unpermitted for the social scientist. We later devote a whole chapter, 5, to such problems. A brief rule for now: if individually identifiable data are being recorded, that individual's informed consent is required. The social scientist's goal is almost never to obtain individually identified information, unlike, for example, the investigative journalist or the biographer. When individually identifiable data are collected by the social scientist, they are only intermediary to results in which individuals are rendered anonymous; the only important problem is one of maintaining confidentiality. The beauty of most erosion and accretion measures is that they are collective products in their raw form: the worn floor tiles, the dirtier edges of some articles in public copies of encyclopedias, and so on. On the other hand, the detective's use of the automobile radio button settings of a single car is probably an invasion of privacy denied a social scientist. "Z" Frank's pooled tallies could, however, have been achieved by means precluding individual identification; if not, informed consent would probably have been given in most cases. This book's overall aim is to inspire researchers to get out of the rut of routinized research measures, to brainstorm a wide range of possibilities before narrowing down on the feasible few for the actual research. To this brainstorming challenge, this edition must now add another—to devise ways of collecting data unobtrusively without invading individual privacy.

DuBois (1963) reports on a 1934 study that estimated an advertisement's readership level by analyzing the number of different fingerprints on the page. The set of prints was a valid remnant, and the analysis revealed a resourceful researcher. Compare this with the anthropologist's device of estimating the prior population of an archeological site by noting the size of floor areas (Naroll, 1962). Among the consistently detectable elements in a site are good indicators of the floor areas of residences. When these can be keyed to knowledge of the residential and familial patterns of the group, these partial data, these remnants, serve as excellent population predictors. One of us (Sechrest) was once able to see quite graphically the effects of a typhoon on some poor families in the Philippines since their reconstructed houses were nearly always smaller than their original houses as indicated by the visible marks of the previous corner posts.

The estimable study of McClelland (1961), *The Achieving Society,* displays a fertile use of historical evidence. Most of the data come from documentary materials such as records of births and deaths, coal imports, shipping levels, electric power consumption, and remaining examples of literature, folk tales, and children's stories. We consider such materials in our discussion of archival records, but they are, in one sense, a special case of trace analysis. McClelland further reports on achievement-level estimates derived from ceramic designs on urns, and he indexes the geographic boundaries of Greek trade by archeological finds of vases. Sensitive to the potential error in such estimates, McClelland writes,

> So, rough though it is, the measure of the economic rise and fall of classical Greece was taken to be the area with which she traded, in millions of square miles, as determined by the location of vases unearthed in which her chief export commodities were transported [p. 117].

This measure was related to the need-for-achievement level of classical Greece, estimated from a content analysis of Greek writings.

Another interesting exploitation of traces in the form of art objects are studies (Bolton, 1978; Richards and Finger, 1975) of the way that holding infants and small children has been portrayed down through the ages. From the early paintings of Madonnas with their children to the sculptures of Henry Moore and contemporary photographs, there is a universal tendency for women to cradle their children against their left side. Although even left-handed women hold their babies on the left, there is no such bias to be found in portrayals of men holding children. One of James Dabbs's students did an observational study that confirms both the bias for females and the lack of one for males (Dabbs, personal communication, July, 1980). Salk (1973), who apparently first observed the left-side holding pref-

erence, hypothesized that it arose out of intrauterine conditioning of the infant to its mother's heartbeat, rendering the infant
more quiescent when held near the mother's heart. Another
group of investigators had noted, however, that most infants
show a strong head-turning bias toward the right so that when
carried on the left shoulder, their heads would be facing outward. Ginsberg, Fling, Hope, Musgrove, and Andrews (1979)
found that most of the 80 percent of infants with a right-turning
bias were carried on their mother's left shoulders and most of
those with a left-turning bias were carried on the right. A second study of new-born infants showed that their head-turning
biases predicted quite well how they would be carried at two
to three weeks of age; thus, mothers seemingly adapt to infants
rather than the other way around. How come fathers are so
inept?

Other remnants can provide evidence on the physical
characteristics of populations no longer available for study. Suits
of armor, for example, are indicators of the height of medieval
knights. Physical anthropologists have been able to tell us a
great deal about the appearance and habits of early humans
from the few remains that can be found.

Following the anthropological tradition of refuse study,
several reports suggest that refuse may be used for contemporary as well as historical research. Hughes (1958) observes:

> ... it is by the garbage that the janitor judges, and, as it
> were, gets power over the tenants who high-hat him. Jani-
> tors know about hidden love-affairs by bits of torn-up letter
> paper; of impending financial disaster or of financial four-
> flushing by the presence of many unopened letters in the
> waste. Or they may stall off demands for immediate service
> by an unreasonable woman of whom they know from the
> garbage that she, as the janitors put it, "has the rag on."
> The garbage gives the janitor the makings of a kind of
> magical power over that pretentious villain, the tenant. I
> say a kind of magical power, for there appears to be no
> thought of betraying any individual and thus turning this
> knowledge into overt power. He protects the tenant, but,
> at least among Chicago janitors, it is not a loving protection
> [p. 51].

Janitors do not have an agreed-upon ethical code, but social
scientists do, and their reactions to incriminating, or at least
revealing, garbage should be at the farthest remove from gain-

ing any kind of power at all. Moreover, janitors presumably have implicit consent only to see what is unavoidable in the handling of garbage; social scientists would want to have explicit consent to examine garbage at all. The janitorial example does, nonetheless, provide fuel for the sort of brainstorming about alternative measures that we encourage.

Rathje (1979) has given dignity to the study of garbage by discovering that it really amounts to the study of "contemporary material culture." His own research is entitled *Le Projet du Garbage*. Rathje's work grew out of the interests of the Department of Agriculture in the extent of food wastage, especially in light of an often-voiced opinion that poor people tend to be wasteful. The way to find out is to discover what they throw away. So Rathje's research team arranges to have the contents of garbage cans at specified addresses emptied into labeled plastic bags that are later retrieved at the garbage dump. Rathje's intrepid team then examines and records the contents of each bag.

Are poor people more wasteful of food? No, they actually waste less than their better-off neighbors. And Mexican-Americans waste less food than Anglos. More food is wasted by those who rely heavily on processed foods, such as TV dinners and prepared meals. Surprisingly, more beef and sugar were wasted during times of a well-publicized shortage than during times of plenty, a finding that Rathje takes to be a reflection of "crisis buying." Although Rathje's original work was on garbage, he and his students have since studied many other types of refuse with findings that should intrigue those assiduous enough to look them up.

Rathje's and similar work on other "garbage" projects (*The Christian Science Monitor*, May 13, 1980, p. 4, had a feature story on "urban archeology" that claimed there are about a dozen federally funded projects today) raises some potentially troublesome ethical and human subjects issues. There is the obvious risk of invasion of privacy, the possibility of discovering material in some way incriminating of its former owners, problems in maintaining confidentiality of data, and possible deception. However, the actual problems may be somewhat less severe that they at first seem. Rathje has obtained a legal opinion to the effect that when people put things into their garbage

cans they have abandoned those things and have no further
legal interest in them. A similar opinion was registered in a
rather celebrated case in which an enterprising freelancer collected and examined the garbage and trash of Henry Kissinger.
More recently the same person has been reported sifting
through the garbage cans of former President Nixon (Nobile,
1980). Note that a social scientist would have no likely interest
in the garbage of a single, particular person.

In an extended personal communication, Rathje (May,
1980) told us that he has had no trouble with human subjects
review committees and expects none; one of his projects was
reviewed in an urban university committee in 1979 without any
difficulties. His current work is, however, at the neighborhood
level (census tract—200–500 households, or enumeration district—80–90 households). Within these neighborhoods, on any
given day, households are selected according to a random sampling scheme; and the houses from which collections are to be
made are designated to the collectors, who bag the trash and
put it aboard the trucks for transport to the inspection site.
Prior to doing the collection studies, the residents of homes in
the area are asked to sign consent forms that state that their
garbage may possibly be collected for study at some future
time. Apparently there is no problem in getting agreement
from residents when the purposes of the study are explained.

In Rathje's previous work (in which it was necessary to get
interview data on individual households—73 in all), only one
interviewer and one person in the Sanitary Division knew all
the addresses, but neither could associate his knowledge with
the other's. A third person alone knew the code that would
connect garbage collections with interviews, but, after the coding was done, the codes were destroyed. Ironically, the only
way anyone can now determine even what houses were involved in the study is by the consent forms the 73 householders
originally signed. Paradoxically, the consent forms, designed to
protect respondents, will survive indefinitely to expose their
identities.

Nonetheless, Rathje notes that garbage studies depend ultimately on the integrity of the investigator and his staff and his
supervision of the staff. No matter how garbage is collected and

brought in, it is bound to contain identifying information, such as discarded address labels, greeting cards, cancelled checks, pamphlets with names written on them, and monogrammed clothing. Rathje's student workers must sign a consent form since they could incur risks to health by working on garbage (they are given tetanus shots, lab coats, rubber gloves, and disposable masks). Included on the consent form is an agreement not to engage in close inspection of any material and not to remove material of any kind from the research premises for any purpose.

Rathje himself has made a moral decision that any material that might be found and thought to be linkable to a "victimless" crime would be ignored, but that evidence of any serious crime would obviously have to be reported. Twice recently, body parts were found in plastic bags at the landfill in Tucson, but in both instances it was found that the bags had been transported to the site by private means; still, it was a scare to Rathje and his workers. He believes, in any case, that the best protection he has from an ethical standpoint is the very wide publicity his projects have received in Tucson. He believes that almost no one could be unaware that the garbage studies are being done and that there is some small risk involved in discarding any really incriminating material. The genuine risk is small, however, for in a year Rathje's project examines only 2000 out of about 11,000,000 possible garbage samples!

Sawyer (1961) recounts the problem of estimating liquor sales in Wellesley, Massachusetts. In a city without package stores, the usual devices of observation of purchase or study of sales records are of no help. Sawyer solved the problem by studying the trash carted from Wellesley homes and counting the number of empty liquor bottles.

Rathje and Hughes (1975) were able to compare interview data about beer consumption in homes for which garbage was being studied. As they put it, the front door and back door data did not agree very well. Although interview data estimated beer consumption in only 15 percent of the homes and eight cans per week to be the maximum consumption, the garbage cans indicated beer consumption in 77 percent of homes and 54 percent with more than eight cans discarded per week. In fact, the 54 percent with over eight cans averaged fifteen discarded cans per week. The case for nonreactive measurement is evident.

The duration of the sampling period is a consideration in studying traces of any product in which consumption of a visible unit takes a long time. The study must cover a large enough span to guarantee that a trace of the behavior will appear if, in fact, it did occur. With estimation of whisky consumption, there is the further demand that account be taken of such possibly confounding elements as holidays, birthdays, discount sales in nearby retail stores, and unusual weather. This is particularly true if estimates are being made of the relative consumption of specific types of liquor. A heat wave produces a substantial increase in the consumption of gin, vodka, and rum, while depressing consumption of scotch, brandy, and blended whiskies. Depending upon the area, an unusually high level of entertaining produces consumption of either more expensive or less expensive whisky than usual. The temporal stability of many common products that could be used to measure behavior is quite low.

Investigators besides Rathje have been interested in refuse. Littering is considered a contemporary social problem of at least nagging proportions, and some investigators have studied ways of reducing it (for example, Burgess, Clark, and Hendee, 1971; Chapman and Risley, 1974). One can institute whatever anti-litter procedure one wishes to test and then count, weigh, or, in some other way, estimate the amount of litter, almost certainly a nonreactive measure. However, the problems with litter measures, and with trace measures more generally, are revealed by a court case in the state of Washington (Moody, 1974) in which a man and his wife who had been arrested for littering their campsite were found not guilty by the judge. The problem was that since the litter was not discovered until after they had left the campsite, there was no way of refuting their charge that someone else must have come along after them to do the littering. It is in the nature of trace measures that they permit only inferences about the response that produced the trace.

Litter may not be all bad. After all, litter does at least show that someone was around and that something was going on. An article in a New Orleans paper (*New Orleans States*, Feb. 11, 1970) suggests that the size of the Mardi Gras celebration can be gauged by the amount of trash left by the celebrants. Apparently 1970 was a banner year since the previous year's record was exceeded by about 200 tons.

On a slightly smaller scale, refuse in the form of cigarette butts has proven informative. Holahan (1972) could get some feeling for the social interactions among psychiatric patients by counting the cigarette butts left in the day room. Coffee consumption was also employed as a measure, and both types of unobtrusive measures agreed with data produced by an actual observer. The measures were anonymous by individual, but does the therapeutic setting make all observation acceptable in any case?

Perhaps even more interesting was a study of comparative lengths of cigarette butts discarded in England and the United States. Although the two countries have nearly equivalent cigarette consumption, England has a markedly higher death rate from lung cancer. Sure enough, the English smoke their cigarettes both longer and shorter, the average American butt being 31mm, the English 19mm (Report of the Advisory Committee to the Surgeon General of the Public Health Service, 1959).

A particularly amusing, if fanciful, example of an accretion is the "Rock syndrome." Jelenko (1980) claims that there is a Rock on the campus of Wright State University that is regularly painted by students at an annualized rate of once each 7.02 days. Accretion of paint is 5.08×10^{-3} cm per painting. From these figures Jelenko calculates that in another 7778 years the Rock will have annihilated the gymnasium only 182 meters away. The Rock is, then, clearly an environmental hazard that needs to be dealt with.

Almost as amusing, and illustrating the fact that unobtrusive measurement is not the sole province of scientists, is a news item from the *Los Angeles Times* (April 20, 1980, Part VII, p. 2). A department store executive recounted the case of a tearful bride who returned and wanted credit for an expensive wedding dress because, she claimed, she had been jilted. When store personnel shook out the dress, however, they had rice all over the fitting room.

Dirt can also accumulate and no one seems to like it much, but the way it accumulates can be interesting. Ettlie (1977) was interested in the productivity of workers in woodworking factories and distrusted their reports about the use of various items of machinery. When he checked the accumulation of dust on the machinery, it suggested that his concern was justified. As indicated by *Motel of the Mysteries,* even the accumulation of mail may be a considerable problem, but Palmer and McGuire (1973) used the number of pieces of incoming mail to assess the extent to which psychiatric patients had contact in their communities. We include incoming mail as a trace measure with some hesitation, but it does fit in the sense that all that is known is the quantity and not how it was produced in reality.

Still another accretion phenomenon we have all noticed is graffiti; it can appear almost anywhere, and it seems like once it appears, it grows regularly. Moreover, graffiti (even though the word is plural, it often seems, like sugar, to be comfortable with a singular verb) has a long history, recounted amusingly by Mockridge (1968) in his aptly titled book *The Scrawl of the Wild.* Although most of us are merely amused or annoyed by graffiti, or perhaps indifferent to it altogether, it has been taken seriously by some scholars. "With the collaboration of a number of other persons, we have accumulated some hundreds of wall inscriptions from public toilets" (Kinsey et al., 1953, p. 673). Their findings show a significant difference between men's and women's toilets in the incidence of erotic inscriptions, either writings or drawings. Wales and Brewer (1976) found that the restrooms for females in four high schools actually had more graffiti than did the restrooms for males. The inscriptions produced by, presumably (remember this is a trace measure), the females were predominantly romantic, but those from schools attended by students from higher socioeconomic levels had a higher proportion of erotic content.

Sechrest and Olson (1971) also studied graffiti from institutions thought to differ along socioeconomic lines, viz., trade schools, four-year colleges, universities, and professional schools. To the authors the most striking finding was difference in manifestations of hostility in the four types of schools. There were more hostile graffiti in the trade schools, but the differences in quality were even more striking. Graffitists who attempt hostility in institutions of higher education are stereotypical and unimaginative—uninteresting, too. In the trade schools they really know how to be nasty. On the other hand, as one goes up the educational ladder, there is a regular increase in frequency of inscriptions with homosexual content. We do not know what that means. Sechrest and Flores (1969) found a good bit more homosexual content in graffiti collected in male toilets in the United States than in the Philippines, a country marked by a relatively accepting attitude toward homosexuality.

Graffiti are perhaps the example *par excellence* of the trace response since one does not know who produces them, whether there are a few really mad graffitists doing it all, whether the graffiti arise out of satisfaction or frustration, and so on. Jorgenson and Lange (1975) did find an increase in politically oriented graffiti on a college campus as a national election drew near. One exception to the assertion that we do not know who produces graffiti comes from a study by Rhyne and Ullman (1972), who had observers examine toilet stalls in facilities for males immediately after each use. Apparently about 15 percent of persons making use of the toilet stalls produced some type of graffiti. It really is not just one phantom graffitologist. (Since Rhyne and Ullman's procedure made possible individual identification, especially if the recorder happened to know the person observed, we do not recommend that this study be repeated, even though having it in the record increases our faith in the method.) Incidentally, in a study of self-reported graffiti production, Mankoff (undated) found that 60 percent of the respondents confessed to having written graffiti at some time or other, and 33 percent had used bathroom walls in public buildings for their work. Moreover, there were no reported differences between males and females in tendencies to produce graffiti.

Some of the most careful and astute sifters of traces are good arson investigators, who quite literally have nothing but traces to go on. Consider the following fragments of an account of an investigation of a fire in a small one-story frame house:

> "It didn't start in here," said Fowler, beginning in the small front room. He pointed to the shards of glass left in one window and scattered on the floor. They were blackened,

indicating that a large amount of smoke had entered the
room before the fire did. The room behind the front room
was a little more intensely burned. "We're getting closer,"
said Fowler. They walked through a small alcove into what
had been the kitchen. "Bingo!" said Fowler after one look
in the room. "I'll bet anything somebody set a fire in here."
The remnants of the glass in a window over the kitchen
sink were clear, not black. The glass was melted and
"crazed" . . . This happens only when a fire flares up
quickly and intensely, meaning it was started with a flammable liquid. They bent over the floor together. It was
deeply charred and spongy with water. This indicated that
gasoline or some other flammable liquid had been poured
on the floor to start the fire. In an accidental fire, the floor
hardly burns at all, because a fire, even if it starts there, will
spread up, not out, and will stop burning almost immediately if it has nowhere to go. . . . With the flammable liquid
soaked into the floorboards, the fire had a chance to burn
sideways and down as well. . . . The two investigators in-
spected the wooden cabinets around the sink. Large rolling blisters, called "rolling alligatoring," had formed there,
another indicator that the fire had started with the aid of
an accelerant. In a fire burning without the help of a
flammable liquid, the wood has a flatter, more baked appearance. [And, checking one rival hypothesis] The electricity was disconnected so it could not have been faulty
wiring. (Krajick, 1979, p. 10)

These investigators went on to determine that there was a
likely suspect with a motive—revenge—and took plaster casts
of bootprints in deep mud, found a witness who had seen a blue
van parked with the motor running just before the fire, and
they were able to get photographs of tire tracks. They then
discovered that their prime suspect had been in jail at the time
the fire occurred but that the blue van belonged to a rough
friend of his who had a prior arrest for arson. With the aid of
a search warrant the investigators were able to show that the
tires of the van and the boot soles of the new suspect resembled
the impressions found at the fire scene. However, the impressions were so spongy that it was hard to be sure. The investigators could come up with no further evidence. Although they
were confident they knew the arsonist, no arrests had been
made in the case at the time of the writing.

This tale illustrates two important points quite nicely. First,
imaginative but informed exploitation of traces can produce a

great deal of persuasive information under the right circumstances. But, second, the persuasive interpretation of trace measures will depend upon standards of evidence, some of which may exceed the characteristics of the data. The arson investigation would probably have satisfied virtually anyone that a fire was deliberately set, just as the dog tracks in the mud are incontrovertible evidence of a dog passing (see p. 36). The dog tracks may not be definitive with respect to the identity of the particular dog, and the arson investigators could persuade themselves but not the courts that they knew who made the boot tracks.

The story of the *Shroud of Turin* also provides fascinating glimpses into the methods of detectives of quite another sort. Photomicrographs indicate that one stain is rust, probably left by an old tack; others are most likely blood, and still others are probably serum. One criminologist was allowed to press sticky tape on the shroud to remove dust and other particles; he found pollen similar to samples from the area of the Dead Sea and Palestine. Study of small samples of threads indicate that the shroud is made of linen, commonly used for burials in ancient Palestine, but it also has traces of Middle Eastern cotton, and it is handspun, a practice largely abandoned in Europe with the advent of the spinning wheel in about 1200 A.D. Altogether the Shroud of Turin Research Project involved thirty-five people, a remarkable concentration of effort (Weaver, 1980).

Finally, even the IRS has gotten into unobtrusive measurement. A story in the *Wall Street Journal* (5/20/70) tells of the problem the IRS had with a man in St. Louis who ran a small barbershop and kept few books. Seeking an index of income, the IRS determined the number of towels the barber used and from that information estimated the number of haircuts and shaves given and, hence, income. The tax court refined the estimation a bit in the barber's favor although approving the method generally. The court noted that the IRS overlooked the fact that a shave took three towels to one for a haircut and also did not take into account that the barber did not always charge for trims. The court also disallowed the testimony of the IRS that the barber sometimes used the same towel twice on the grounds that any barber who stuffed a towel full of hair down a customer's neck would not be in business for long.

Experimenter Intervention

The methods discussed so far have all been ones in which the social scientist has taken the data as they come and not intervened in any way to influence the frequency or character of the indicator material. There are conditions under which the social scientist can intervene in the data-production process without destroying the nonreactive gains characteristic of trace and erosion data. One might want to do this, for example, to speed up the incidence of critical responses—a sometimes nagging annoyance with slowly eroding or accreting materials. Or one might want to guarantee that the materials under study were in fact equivalent or equal before they were modified by the critical responses. The essential point is that one's intervention should not impair the nonreactivity of the erosion and trace measures by permitting the subjects to become aware of being tested, nor should the intervention make possible individually identifiable data unless one is prepared to seek individual permission from the persons involved.

Controlled Erosion Measures

John Wallace, our former colleague, once noted that it would be possible to estimate the activity level of children by measuring the rate at which they wear out shoes. It is theoretically possible to start at any point in time with the shoes that children are wearing, measure the degree of wear, and then later remeasure. The difference between the two scores might be a measure of the effect of some experimental variable.

One way to improve the data-gathering process might be to manipulate the recording material so as to make it more receptive to potentially eroding behaviors. One might, for example, provide children with special shoes made to wear out at a faster rate than usual so that activity level could be assessed over briefer periods of time. (Free shoes would increase the proportion of cooperating parents.) With floor tile, for example, surfaces are often coated with substances resistant to wear. Once the coating is worn through, erosion proceeds at a faster rate. For research purposes, it would be desirable to lay uncoated tiles and accelerate the speed with which information is produced.

In other cases, coating of materials may be desirable, either to provide a more permanent measure or to allow one where it otherwise would be impossible. The wear on public statues, reliefs, and so forth may provide an example. Throughout Europe, one may note with interest shiny bronze spots on religious figures and scenes. The rubbing which produced these traces is selective and becomes most visible in group scenes in which only one or two figures are shiny. The new East Wing of the National Gallery of Art in Washington, D.C. has one very sharp corner describing an angle of about 19 degrees, probably as sharp a corner as one is likely to find anywhere. For some reason that corner has come to be regarded as good luck, and people go there to touch and even kiss the corner. The results are clearly evident in a photo of the corner printed in *Washingtonian* magazine (Stein, 1980). Surely someone will periodically rephotograph that corner to document the spread of the stain.

A careful investigator might choose to work another improvement on the floor erosion approach. An important bias is that each footfall is not necessarily an independent event. Once a groove on a stair becomes visible, for example, those who walk on that stair are more likely to conform to the position of the groove than are those who walked before it became visible. This is partly due to the physical condition of the stair, which tends to slide the person's foot into the groove and also possibly due to a response tendency to follow in the footsteps of others. This may be partially controlled in newer settings by placing mats on the steps and noting their wear. The mats could also hide the already eroded grooves.

Bouchard (1976) makes the interesting suggestion that interest in some phenomenon might be assessed by the common practice of posting ads or notices with fringed bottoms on each piece of which is a telephone number. Presumably the more pieces that are removed for reference, the greater the interest. The method would permit a great deal of control by the experimenter and would also permit comparison of the number of phone slips removed and the number of calls actually made. (Tag-takers and telephoners could be kept anonymous except where a sale or contribution was completed, and the research might piggy-back on bona fide notices. But, if to improve experimental control, pseudonotices were employed, with an untruthful "Sorry, already sold" to all callers, ethical boundaries might have been breached, at least, as we judge current standards.)

CONTROLLED ACCRETION MEASURES

Just as with erosion measures, it is sometimes desirable for the researcher to tamper with materials pertinent to an accretion comparison. Noted earlier was a fingerprint study of advertising exposure (DuBois, 1963). Another procedure to test advertising exposure is the "glue-seal record" (Politz, 1958). Between each pair of pages in a magazine, a small glue spot was placed close to the binding and made inconspicuous enough so that it was difficult to detect visually or tactually. The glue was so composed that it would not readhere once the seal was broken. After the magazines had been read, exposure was determined by noting whether or not the seal was intact for each pair of pages, and a cumulative measure of advertising exposure was obtained by noting the total number of breaks in the same issue.

The content restrictions of this method are substantial. It does not provide data for a single page or advertisement, but instead only indicates whether or not a *pair* of pages were exposed to the person's eye. There is no direct evidence whether or not the person even looked at advertisements that appeared on this pair of pages. Nor is the method sensitive to how many people may have been exposed to a given pair of pages. One or more openings yields the same response.

The fingerprint method suffers from fewer restrictions, and it, too, could be improved by an unobtrusive move of the investigator. It is possible to select special paper that more faithfully receives fingerprints, thereby reducing the risk that the level of exposure will be underestimated. The greater fidelity of a selected paper would also improve the ability to discriminate among different fingerprints on the page and, thereby, to determine more accurately the actual number of probable readers of each page. It is clearly impractical and unwise to base a complete study of advertising exposure on fingerprints; it is equally unwise not to consider coincidental methods that yield, as the glue seals do, independent validation data. Clearly, the greater the risk awareness, response set, role evocation, and other variables present to valid comparisons, the greater the demand for independent, nonreactive, and coincidental measures. Note that when properly chosen such measures do not at all invade privacy nor require bothering individuals with requests for permission.

From fingerprints to noseprints—and back to the museum for a final example. The relative popularity of exhibits with glass fronts could be compared by examining the number of noseprints deposited on the glass each day (or on some sample of time, day, month, and so forth). This requires that the glass be dusted for noseprints each night and then wiped clean for the next day's viewers to smudge. The noseprint measure has fewer content restrictions than most of the trace techniques, for the age of viewers can be estimated as well as the total number of prints on each exhibit. Age is determined by plotting a frequency distribution of the heights of the smudges from the floor, and relating these data to normative heights by age (minus, of course, the nose-to-top-of-head correction).

TRANSFORMING THE DATA: CORRECTIONS AND INDEX NUMBERS

The examples provided suggest that physical evidence data are best suited for measures of incidence, frequency, attendance, and the like. There are exceptions. In a closely worked-out theory, for example, the presence or absence of a trace could provide a critical test or comparison. But such critical tests are rare compared to the times when the physical evidence—be it deposit or erosion—is one part of a series of tests.

When dealing with frequency data, particularly when they are in time-series form, it is essential to ask whether or not there are any corrections that may be applied to remove extraneous sources of variance and improve the validity of comparisons.

More so than most classes of data, the type of frequency data yielded by physical materials is subject to influences that can be known (and corrected for) without substantial marginal research effort.

The museum measures of noseprint deposits or tile erosion can serve as examples. We can use these data to answer questions about the popularity of a given exhibit over time. Are the hatching chicks as popular now as they once were? Is there a boom in viewing of giant panda exhibits? The answers to these questions might be of interest in themselves, or we might want them to evaluate the effect of some other variable. We could conceive of a study estimating the effect of newspaper stories on public behavior. Did a story on the birth of a baby leopard in the zoo increase the number of zoo visitors *and* the number of viewers of a leopard exhibit in the natural history museum? The effect may be too transitory for the erosion measure to pick up, but the noseprint deposits could index it. Or do accounts of trouble in a far-off spot increase the number of persons showing interest in museum collections from that area? The museum data might be one more outcropping of an effect that could be tested and used in consort with other measures to evaluate an effect.

In looking at the museum data, we could consider the newspaper-story question as a problem in the effect of an exogenous variable on a time series, and we are compelled to look for other sources of variation besides the story. We know something of the pool from which the critical responses come. Museum attendance varies seasonally (highest in summer, lowest in winter), varies cyclically (up on holidays, weekends, and school vacations) and has had a strong secular movement upward over time. All of these known influences on museum attendance are independent of the newspaper story. They may be partialled out of the total variance of the time series or, in descriptive statistics, be controlled in index numbers. Such corrections, however, are less critical for comparisons across areas. To the degree that these scores can be accounted for—in either inferential or descriptive terms—we achieve more sensitive research. (See further discussion of index numbers on p. 39 ff.)

Auxiliary intelligence exists for most applications of physical evidence data. It may be contained in records kept for other purposes or come from prior knowledge. Consider the problem of estimating advertising exposure by the glue-seal method. In studying a single pair of pages, our only measure is the proportion of pages on which seals are broken. Of course, there are a number of variables known to influence the degree to which magazine pages are opened. The number of pages in the magazine, for example, or the magazine's policy of either clustering or dispersing advertisements throughout its pages, or continuing its most interesting stories as dispersed fragments in the later pages of the issue, will alter responses. Finally, readers of some magazines systematically and predictably read ads more than do readers of other magazines.

Each of these elements should be considered in evaluating the single medium under study. These factors might be combined into a baseline index that states the reasonable exposure expectation for an ad appearing in a very thin issue of Magazine A, with a dispersion strategy of ad placement. The observed score for the given pair of pages can thus be transformed into a number that is in some way related to the expected value.

With more elaborate comparisons than evaluating a single museum exhibit, the problems of extraneous variables and the need for their control in both inference and description become magnified. Keeping with the museum, take the problem of comparing two exhibits located in different sections of the museum. The same information used earlier—the known variation by season, holidays, and so on—is again core intelligence for comparison of the observed physical evidence. The concern becomes one of interactions. At those predictably high and low attendance times, we can expect a significant interaction between the accessibility of the exhibit and the overall level of attendance. The interaction could bias measures of both the number of viewers and the duration of time spent viewing.

We should expect the more accessible exhibit to have a significantly higher marginal lead on noseprints during high attendance periods than during low attendance periods. Some of the interactive difference may come from the greater individual fatigue with large crowds, which might restrict the length of time each visitor spends in the museum. Or the size of the crowds may slow movements so that a number of people with fixed time periods to spend in the museum do not get around as much. Or there may be a population characteristic such that a larger share of peak time visitors are indifferent viewers who lack a compelling interest in the overall content of the museum. They may view either more casually or more erratically.

Corrections must be made for both the main effects and the interactions in such cases, and one way to make them is to include corrections based on known population levels and response tendencies, as well as comparisons across types of target. We could speak of statue rubbings per thousand bypassers, or the rate of floor-tile replacement in a specific display area per thousand summer visitors. These figures are first-line transformations that are valuable. They can become more valuable if enough is known to consider them as the numerator of an index fraction. With the study of past behavior giving the denominator, indexes can be produced for irrelevant variance and make for better comparisons.

Up to this point, we have been talking only of corrections applied to a single measure. Following in the index-number tradition, we can also consider a piece of physical evidence either as one component of an overall index composed of several different classes of data or as an element in a set of physical evidence combined to make an aggregate index.

One might want an overall measure, extending over time, of the completeness with which an institution is being used. This could supplement information on the extent to which it is being attended. In a library, for example, the various types of physical evidence available (dust collection, page wear, card catalogue wear) could be gathered together and each individual component weighed and then combined to produce the overall index. Similarly for museums.

Assume that one wanted to note the immediate impact of an anxiety-producing set of messages on the alleged link between cigarettes and lung cancer. One could, in the traditional way, employ a before-after questionnaire study that measured attitudes toward cigarettes and obtained self-reports of smoking. Or, one could observe. If the anxiety-producing message were embedded in a lecture, at some point toward the middle, it would be possible to observe the frequency of cigarettes lit before, during, and after the mention of the deleterious effects of smoking. Or one could wire a sample of the chairs in the lecture hall and record the amount of squirming exhibited by the auditors at various points. Or following Galton's (1885) suggestion, one could observe the amount of gross body movement in the audience. Or one could note the subsequent sale of books about smoking—ideally framing the setting so that equally attractive titles were available that argued the issue pro and con.

All of these alternatives are viable approaches to studying the effect of the message, with physical evidence an important element because of its ability to measure long-term effects and to extend the physical area of investigation beyond the immediate experimental setting. Depending on the degree of knowledge one had about the messages, the audience, and past effects, it would be possible to construct an index with differential weights for the various component measures of effect. Each of the single measures may be attacked for weakness, but taken cumulatively—as separate manifestations of an hypothesized effect—they offer greater hope for validity than any single measure, regardless of its popularity.

An Overall Evaluation of Physical Evidence Data

The outstanding advantages of physical evidence are its inconspicuousness and anonymity. The stuff of analysis is material that is generated without the producer's knowledge of its use by the investigators. Just as with secondary records, one circumvents the problems of awareness of measurement, role selection, interviewer effects, and the bias that comes from the measurement itself taking on the role of a change agent. Thus, physical evidence is, for the most part, free of reactive measurement effects. It is still necessary to worry over possible response sets that influence the laying down of the data. With erosion measures, this might be so obvious a bias as the tendency for people to apply more pressure to stairs when going up than when going down, or the less obvious tendency to turn right.

With accretion measures, there is the question whether the materials have selectively survived or been selectively deposited. Do some objects have a higher probability of being discarded in public places than others? Or, equally an issue, do some materials survive the intervening events of time better? Archeological research has always faced the problem of the selective survival of materials. Some of this selection comes from the physical characteristics of the material: clay survives, wood usually does not. Other selection comes from the potential value of the material that might be discarded. In writing of the small decorated stamps (seals) used by the ancient Mexican cultures, Enciso (1953) noted, "If any gold or silver was used, the stamps have yet to be found or have been melted long ago. Wood and bone have not survived the ravages of time. This may explain the abundant survival of clay stamps" (p. iv). In Naroll's (1956) phrase, the clay stamps are "durable artifacts." We also discuss this bias in our comments on archival and available records, but it is significant here for the restrictions it places on the content of physical evidence data and thereby the ability to generalize findings.

Any single class of physical evidence is likely to have a strong population restriction, and all physical evidence data are troubled by population problems in general. It is not, for example, easy to get descriptive access to the characteristics of a possible population restriction. One has the remnant of past behavior—a groove or a pile—and it says nothing by itself of those who produced the evidence.

We also must be cautious of physical data because they may vary selectively over time or across different geographical areas. It is possible to get some checks on the character of these restrictions by employing supplementary methods such as the interview or the questionnaire. Some inferences about the character of population bias may come also from a time-series analysis of the data, possibly linking the physical evidence data to time series of other data hypothesized to be selectively contributing to the variance. In a systematic investigation, a careful sampling of both times and locations is possible, and internal comparison of the findings may offer some clues. But the assumption must be that any set of physical evidence is strongly subject to population restrictions, and supplementary information is always required.

Other methods also have population restrictions, and it may be possible to turn the fact of a restriction into an asset.

There are, for example, certain subsets of the population virtually impossible to interview. In such situations, an enterprising investigator should ask whether the population of interest is leaving traces of behavior or material that offer some help in inferring the critical behavior. In this type of problem, the physical evidence is the supplementary data and is used to fill in the population restrictions of other methods used concurrently.

As for the content available to the reach of physical evidence methods, there are substantial limitations. It is not often that an investigator tests a theory so precise in its predictions that the appearance or absence of a single trace is a critical test of the theory. Most of the time, physical evidence is more appropriate for indexing the extent to which an activity has taken place—the number of footfalls, the number of empties tossed aside. Because these activities are influenced by many other variables, we seldom have an absolutely clean expression of some state of being—thus the necessity for corrections and transformations. Yet, if enough information does exist or can be produced, the content restrictions are controllable because they are knowable.

There is the positive gain that the amount of dross in physical evidence is low or negligible. Typically, what is measured is relatively uncontaminated by a body of other material that must be discarded as not pertinent to the research investigation. One can pinpoint the investigation closely enough to eliminate the dross—something not possible in the more amorphous method of conversation sampling, or of observation of "natural" behavior.

Compared with other classes of research methods, we have noted few examples of prior research using physical evidence. This is not through our preference, but because we have been unable to find more. Physical evidence data are off the main track for most social scientists. This is understandable, but still regrettable. The more visible weaknesses of physical evidence should preclude its use no more than should the less visible, but equally real, weaknesses of other methods. If physical evidence is used in consort with more traditional approaches, the population and content restrictions can be controlled, providing a novel and fruitful avoidance of the errors that come from reactivity.

CHAPTER 3

Approximations to Knowledge

Now that some specific examples of unobtrusive measures have been described and some of the context in which they are desirable has been hinted at, it may be well to make a more detailed case for the use of unobtrusive measures and to set forth the methodological issues and problems that are involved. We have entitled this chapter as we have to call attention to our position that our knowledge is always tentative and can only be made incrementally more certain with increasing data or evidence. Unobtrusive measures do not embody truth any more than other measures; they are merely steps, albeit sometimes sizable ones, along the way to it.

OPERATIONISM AND MULTIPLE OPERATIONS

The social sciences are emerging from a period in which the precision of carefully specified operations was confused with operationism by definitional fiat—an effort now increasingly recognized as an unworkable model for science. We wish to retain and augment the precision without bowing to the fiat.

The mistaken belief in the operational definition of theoretical terms has permitted social scientists a complacent and self-defeating dependence upon single classes of measurement —usually the interview or questionnaire. In the 15 years since the first edition of this volume was prepared, we do not think that such dependence has changed much. Yet the operational implication of the inevitable theoretical complexity of every measure is exactly opposite: it calls for a multiple operationism, that is, for multiple measures that are hypothesized to share in the theoretically relevant components but have different pat-

34

terns of irrelevant components (for example, Garner, 1954; Garner, Hake, and Eriksen, 1956; Campbell and Fiske, 1959; Campbell, 1960; Campbell, 1969; Humphreys, 1960).

Once a proposition has been confirmed by two or more independent measurement processes, the uncertainty of its interpretation is greatly reduced. The most persuasive evidence comes through a triangulation of measurement processes. If a proposition can survive the onslaught of a series of imperfect measures, with all their irrelevant error, confidence should be placed in it. Of course, this confidence is increased by minimizing error in each instrument and by a reasonable belief in the different and divergent effects of the sources of error.

A consideration of the laws of physics, as they are seen in that science's measuring instruments, demonstrates that no theoretical parameter is ever measured independently of other physical parameters and other physical laws. Thus, a typical galvanometer responds in its operational measurement of voltage not only according to the laws of electricity but also to the laws of gravitation, inertia, and friction. By reducing the mass of the galvanometer needle, by orienting the needle's motion at right angles to gravity, by setting the needle's axis in jeweled bearings, by counterweighting the needle point, and by other refinements, the instrument designer attempts to minimize the most important of the irrelevant physical forces for his measurement purposes. As a result, the galvanometer reading may reflect, *almost* purely, the single parameter of voltage (or amperage, etc.).

Yet from a theoretical point of view, the movement of the needle is always a complex product of many physical forces and laws. The adequacy with which the needle measures the conceptually defined variable is a matter for investigation; the operation itself is not the ultimate basis for defining the variable. Excellent illustrations of the specific imperfections of measuring instruments are provided by Wilson (1952).

Starting with this example from physics and the construction of meters, we can see that no meter ever perfectly measures a single theoretical parameter; all series of meter readings are imperfect estimates of the theoretical parameters they are intended to measure.

Truisms perhaps, yet they belie the mistaken concept of the "operational definition" of theoretical constructs that continues to be popular in the social sciences, even though the logical positivist philosophy of science that justified it has now been largely abandoned. The inappropriateness is accentuated in the social sciences because we have no measuring devices as carefully compensated to control all irrelevancies as is the galvanometer. There simply are no social science devices designed with so perfect a knowledge of all the major relevant sources of variation. In physics, the instruments we think of as "definitional" reflect magnificently successful theoretical achievements and themselves embody classical experiments in their very operation. In the social sciences, our measures lack such control. They tap multiple processes and sources of variance of which we are as yet unaware. At such a stage of development, the theoretical impurity and factorial complexity of every measure are not niceties for pedantic quibbling but are overwhelmingly and centrally relevant in all measurement applications that involve inference and generalization.

Efforts in the social sciences at multiple confirmation often yield disappointing and inconsistent results. Awkward to write up and difficult to publish, such results confirm the gravity of the problem and the risk of false confidence that comes with dependence upon single methods (Vidich and Shapiro, 1955; Campbell, 1957; Campbell and McCormack, 1957; Campbell and Fiske, 1959; Kendall, 1963; Cook and Selltiz, 1964; Campbell, 1969). When multiple operations provide consistent results, the possibility of slippage between conceptual definition and operational specification is diminished greatly.

This is not to suggest that all components of a multimethod approach should be weighted equally. Prosser (1964) has observed: ". . . but there is still no man who would not accept dog tracks in the mud against the sworn testimony of a hundred eye-witnesses that no dog had passed by" (p. 216). Components ideally should be weighted according to the amount of extraneous variation each is known to have and, taken in combination, according to their independence from similar sources of bias.

Interpretable Comparisons
and Plausible Rival Hypotheses

In this monograph we deal with methods of measurement appropriate to a wide range of social science studies. Some of these studies are comparisons of a single group or unit at two or more points in time; others compare several groups or units at one time; others purport to measure but a single unit at a single point in time; and, to close the circle, some compare several groups at two or more points in time. In this discussion, we assume that the goal of the social scientist is always to achieve interpretable comparisons, and that the goal of methodology is to rule out those plausible rival hypotheses that make comparisons ambiguous and tentative.

Often it seems that absolute measurement *is* involved, and that a social instance is being described in its splendid isolation, not for comparative purposes. But a closer look shows that absolute, isolated measurement is meaningless. In all useful measurement, an implicit comparison exists when an explicit one is not visible. "Absolute" measurement is a convenient fiction and usually is nothing more than a shorthand summary in settings where plausible rival hypotheses are either unimportant or so few, specific, and well known as to be taken into account habitually. Thus, when we report a length "absolutely" in meters or feet, we immediately imply comparisons with numerous familiar objects of known length, as well as comparisons with a standard preserved in some Paris or Washington sanctuary.

If measurement is regarded always as a comparison, there are three classes of approaches that have come to be used in achieving interpretable comparisons: experimental design, index numbers, and plausible rival hypotheses. The most satisfactory of the three is experimental design. Through deliberate randomization, the *ceteris* of the pious *ceteris paribus* prayer can be made *paribus*. This may require randomization of respondents, occasions, or stimulus objects. In any event, the randomization strips of plausibility many of the otherwise available explanations of the difference in question. It is a sad truth that randomized experimental design is possible for only a portion of the settings in which social scientists make measurements and seek interpretable comparisons. The number of opportunities for its use may not be staggering, but, where possible, experimental design should by all means be exploited. Many more opportunities exist than are used.

Index Numbers

The second approach to comparison, a quite different and historically isolated tradition, is that of *index numbers.* Here, sources of variance known to be irrelevant are controlled by transformations of raw data and weighted aggregates. This is analogous to the compensated and counterbalanced meters of physical science, which also control irrelevant sources of variance. The goal of this old and, until recently, neglected social science tradition is to provide measures for meaningful comparisons across wide spans of time and social space. Real wages, intelligence quotients, and net reproductive rates are examples, but an effort in this direction is made even when a percentage, a per capita, or an annual rate is computed. The current interest in a variety of "social indicators" involves many types of index numbers. To be meaningful, most social indicators must be transformed into some sort of an index number.

Interest in index numbers has a history of at least two centuries. Wills (1978), in the course of expounding on the development of the concepts in the Declaration of Independence, gives a fascinating account of eighteenth-century interest in *political arithmetic.* The Marquis de Chastellux wished to discover "an arithmetical measure for the happiness of various epochs in human history" (Wills, 1978, p. 137), and in his works, published in 1772, he speculated that since superstition dampens man's happiness, a measure of public happiness might be arrived at by counting the number of a country's priests. Diderot suggested as a refinement that the consumption of communion wafers in a large city parish be measured since a marked decrease would index a decline in superstition. Madame de Staël thought it should be possible to base an exact science of happiness on statistics for murder, divorce, "and other extreme products of human passion" (Wills, 1978, p. 138), making region by region comparisons possible. Perhaps the most remarkable of all was the work of Sir William Petty in the seventeenth century, for he used a variety of statistical data to calculate what we would now think of as gross national product and concluded that ten million Englishmen were worth twelve to thirteen million Frenchmen!

Thomas Jefferson, as Wills details so engagingly, was much affected by the prospects for quantifying matters of human interest. Jefferson was a vigilant, assiduous, and faithful recording observer. He not only had careful and detailed records of temperatures and rainfall at his farm, but for a seven-year period he had records on dates of first occurrences for 26 natural phenomena including: Asparagus comes first to table, The Red bud, The wood Robin is heard, Fire flies appear, Cherries first ripe, and Wheat harvest begins. Jefferson was much interested in demographics, for he believed that the achievement of happiness for a people rested on procuring and maintaining the right sized population and a preponderance of rural over urban dwellers.

Index numbers cannot be used uncritically because the imperfect knowledge of the laws invoked in any such measurement situation precludes computing any effective all-purpose measures. Furthermore, the use of complex compensated indexes in the assurance that they measure what they are devised for has in many instances proved quite misleading. A notable example is found in the definitional confusion surrounding the labor force concept (Jaffe and Stewart, 1951; W. E. Moore, 1953). Often a relationship established between an overall index and external variables is found due to only one component of the index. A recent instance of a flagrant and harmful index number that has been widely disseminated and cited is the proportion of black infants being born out of wedlock. In 1978 the government's National Center for Health Statistics reported that in 1976 for the first time more than 50 percent of all black births involved unmarried mothers. However, a subsequent analysis, not so widely publicized, indicated that a large proportion of what appeared to be an increase in illegitimacy is accounted for by the fact that married black women are having fewer children with the result that the numerator of the index, the absolute number of illegitimate children, was growing, but the denominator was shrinking. The absolute rate of illegitimacy per 1000 black women had been shrinking for six straight years by 1976. Thus, illegitimacy among blacks is falling, not rising (*Minneapolis Star,* 1978).

Despite these limitations, index numbers, which once loomed large in sociology and economics, deserve more current attention and should be integrated into modern social science methodology (Morgenstern, 1963).

The tradition is relevant in two ways for the problems of this monograph. Many of the sources of data suggested here, particularly secondary records, require a transformation of the raw data if they are to be interpretable in any but truly experimental situations. Such transformations should be performed with the wisdom accumulated within the older tradition, as well as with a regard for the precautionary literature just cited. Properly done, such transformations often improve interpretability even if they fall far short of some ideal (cf. Bernstein, 1935).

A second value of the literature on index numbers lies in an examination of the types of irrelevant variation that the index computation sought to exclude. The construction of index numbers is usually a response to criticisms of less sophisticated indexes. They thus embody a summary of the often unrecorded criticisms of prior measures. In the criticisms and the corrections are clues to implicit or explicit plausible rival interpretations of differences, the viable threats to valid interpretation.

Take so simple a measure as an index of unemployment or of retail sales. The gross number of the unemployed or the gross total dollar level of sales is useless if one wants to make comparisons within a single year. Some of the objections to the gross figures are reflected in the seasonal corrections applied to time-series data. If we look at only the last quarter of the year, we can see that the effect of weather must be considered. A "gain" over the same quarter last year may reflect the unusual lowness of last year rather than a true gain for this year. Systematically, winter depresses the number of employed construction workers, for example, and increases the unemployment level. Less systematically, spells of bad weather keep people in their homes and reduce the amount of retail shopping. Both periodic and aperiodic elements of the weather should be considered if one wants a more stable and interpretable measure of unemployment or sales. So, too, our custom of giving gifts at Christmas spurs December sales, as does the coinciding custom of Christmas bonuses to employees. All of these are accounted for, crudely, by a correction applied to the gross levels for either December or the final quarter of the year.

Some of these sources of invalidity are too specific to a single setting to be generalized usefully; others are too obvious to be catalogued. But some contribute to a general enumeration of recurrent threats to valid interpretation in social science measures.

The technical problems of index number construction are heroic. "The index number should give *consistent* results for different base periods and also with its counterpart price or quantity index. No reasonably simple formula satisfies both of these consistency requirements" (Ekelblad, 1962, p. 726). The consistency problem is usually met by substituting a geometric mean for an arithmetic one, but then other problems arise. With complex indexes of many components, there is the issue of getting an index that will yield consistent scores across all the different levels and times of the components.

In his important work on economic cycles, Hansen (1921) wrote, "Here is a heterogeneous group of statistical series all of which are related in a causal way, somehow or another, to the cycle of prosperity and depression" (p. 21). The search for a metric to relate these different components consistently, to be able to reverse factors without chaos, makes index construction a difficult task. A case in point is provided by the work of Brenner (for example, 1973, 1975), attempting to develop index numbers for both economic conditions and such social ills as mental disorder and crime. Although Brenner believes that his work demonstrates a relationship between economic cycles and the rates of mental disorder and crime, the problems inherent in attempting to correct for all the extraneous factors have brought Brenner's work under intense criticism (for example, Eyer, 1976). But the potential payoff from construction of indexes is great. For good introductory statements of issues in the use of index numbers see Yule and Kendall (1950), Zeisel (1957), and Ekelblad (1962). More detailed treatments can be found in Mitchell (1921), Fisher (1923), Mills (1927), Mudgett (1951), and Morgenstern (1963).

Recently, Ruist (1978), Hoover (1978), and McCarthy (1978) have surveyed a much larger literature for the *International Encyclopedia of Statistics*. However, so far as we are aware, there is as yet no adequate review of the booby traps that lie in wait when one goes beyond looking at a single index for its "direct" informational value and uses series of readings from "the same" index over time or across social units, correlating these with other indexes, or inferring the impact of specific historical events, and so on. No one has done for index numbers what Cronbach (1958) did so well for spurious effects in social perception accuracy scores. His elegant analysis of such "dy-adic" scores has not, so far as we know, been picked up in any social science research methods text, even though the anec-dotes of working statisticians abound with howlers that suc-ceeded in fooling their users for years.

An index number is formed by some combination of other numbers, often by dividing one number by another. Hence, an index number will reflect the values of all the numbers that go to make it up. An index of disposable income per family and an index of savings might be related because both would reflect total income and necessary expenses. To take an obvious case, but one not invariably avoided, indexes of the percent of pupils who are white and the percent who are black in schools will be highly related to each other unless there are sizable numbers of pupils of other ethno-racial designations. The relationship will, of course, be negative. In fact, if index numbers were constructed randomly by pairs, with the restriction that each pair had to have one common element, the two sets of numbers would be likely to be substantially correlated. For example, if Index $A = a/c$ and Index $B = b/c$, A and B might be correlated just because they share the variability in c. Typical situations in which such index series might be constructed would be to rep-resent characteristics of different nations, cities, or census tracts, etc., or situations in which characteristics of some units of interest, perhaps nations, perhaps families, are correlated over time. As an example of the first kind of study, an investigator might be interested in the relationship between size of police force and number of burglaries across a number of cities. Each item of interest would be likely to be indexed by size of population: police officers per 1000 population, and burglaries per 1000 population. The two indexes would thus share city population as a denominator and might have a built-in correlation. We note, however, that Long (1980) has shown that the correlations between index numbers sharing common elements are complexly determined and may take nearly any value. Spurious, artifactual correlations may even stem from measurement error alone when one number, including error, is shared across two indexes. We concur with Long's injunction that any ratio used as an index should make theoretical sense as a ratio. For example, auto accidents per registered vehicle makes sense; auto accidents per number of telephones does not. Ratios that are not rational are probably especially likely to cause problems.

The second type of study would be exemplified by the work of Brenner (1973; 1975), who attempts to show that such forms of personal and social pathologies as mental disorder and crime change over time with economic cycles. The problem that may tend to produce spurious correlations is that, even though two indexes do not share any common elements in terms of the numbers that go to make them up, both may be changing systematically over time. For example, during a period extending from 1882 to 1930, cotton prices were gradually increasing and the number of lynchings in the United States was gradually decreasing (Hovland and Sears, 1940), permitting the erroneous conclusion that lynchings stemmed from the frustrations of low cotton prices. A problem exists with many economic indicators from the very beginning because they often need to be expressed in "constant dollars." Presumably it is the income to be obtained from cotton sales relative to the costs of things that have to be bought that is the important factor in any frustration from prices. Even if prices were expressed in constant dollars but were increasing or decreasing steadily over time, it would be hazardous to assume any causal link between those prices and a similarly changing series. Many things change regularly over time. It has even been demonstrated, as an instance, that suicides have increased regularly with the increasing number of telephones! Probably in the period from 1882 to 1930, the number of deaths attributable to falling off horses decreased, but scarcely in any way attributable to rising cotton prices. The fact that the link between cotton prices and lynchings seems more sensible does not make it truer.

Any time-series analysis must begin with "detrending" of the data, an analytic step that involves determining for each observation the degree to which it deviates from any overall trends. In their analysis of cotton prices and lynchings, for example, Hovland and Sears (1940) ran straight lines through the data for cotton prices and lynchings, plotted separately and determined whether each data point fell above or below the line (which had been drawn to a least squares fit). It was these "detrended" data that they then analyzed, and for which they found the negative relationship between cotton prices and lynchings. The process of detrending is, however, often not so simple, and Mintz (1946) showed that the use of straight lines did not deal at all well with the trends in either cotton prices or lynchings, and when he used more appropriate procedures, the negative correlations largely disappeared.

There can also be perturbations in time series that result from specific features of data systems. Some months have more weekends than others, and those months will have more crimes. Numerator data tend to be collected and corrected over shorter time periods than denominator data. Crimes, for example, are usually counted and reported by months, but population data are not likely to be corrected more than yearly, if that often. Thus, if there is an abrupt increase in estimated city population every January, the drop in crime rate between December and January will be greater than would be expected on the basis of true seasonality. The reporting of 1980 census data will result in corrections in many indexes, probably mostly in the denominators, with the result that there may be a good many discontinuities in many common indexes between 1980 and

1981. To some extent these problems may be avoided by the use of a "moving average" that expresses each data point as a departure from a longer period of which it is the center. If data are reported monthly, the moving average might be calculated for successive 12-month periods. Various other corrections are possible. Since the amplitude of fluctuations is often proportional to absolute level (for example, burglary rates will be more variable during seasons when burglary rates are high), logarithmic transformation prior to seasonal correction is usually preferable with raw data consisting of frequency counts. Even so, seasonal corrections probably very often undercorrect and produce subtle forms of correlated error. At the very least in a time-series analysis, the analysis should be run separately for each element in the index.

Erroneous inferences due to *part-whole correlation* may emerge if the correlation between an index and its correction base becomes of interest and is calculated. A common instance is an index of gain accompanied by an interest in whether people at different original levels gain differentially. Since a gain may be defined as $G = Post\text{-}measure - Premeasure$, a big spurious negative correlation between gain and original level is inevitable, leading to the erroneous conclusion that, the worse off people were originally, the more they will have improved. An analogous positive correlation arises when an element is correlated with a total of which it is a part; for example, the correlation between students' grade point averages in their majors will be correlated with their overall grade point averages in part because the former is part of the latter. If the elements have some degree of independent variability, the spuriousness will diminish with an increasing number of elements. Thus, the briefer the course of study in the major and the longer the course of study outside the major, the lower the built-in correlation.

These warnings should not be taken as discouraging the use of index numbers altogether, but as a caution against their unthinking and indiscriminant use and interpretation. They have a long and generally honorable history and probably as long a future, perhaps one whose prospects can be improved.

Plausible Rival Hypotheses

The third general approach to comparison may be called that of *plausible rival hypotheses*. It is the most general and least formal of the three and is applicable to the other two. Given a comparison that a social scientist wishes to interpret, this approach asks what other plausible interpretations are allowed by the research setting and the measurement processes. The more of these, and the more plausible each is, the less validly interpretable is the comparison. Platt (1964) and Hafner and Presswood (1965) have discussed this approach with a focus in the physical sciences.

A social scientist may reduce the number of plausible rival hypotheses in many ways. Experimental methods and adequate indexes serve as useful devices for eliminating some rival interpretations. A checklist of commonly relevant threats to validity may point to other ways of limiting the number of viable alternative hypotheses. For some major threats, it is often possible to provide supplementary analyses or to assemble additional data that can rule out a source of possible invalidity.

Backstopping the individual scientist is the critical reaction of fellow scientists. Where plausible rival hypotheses are missed, colleagues can be expected to propose alternative interpretations. This resource is available even in disciplines that are not avowedly scientific. J. H. Wigmore, a distinguished legal scholar, showed an awareness of the criteria of other plausible explanations of data:

> If the potential defect of Inductive Evidence is that the fact offered as the basis of the conclusion may be open to one or more other explanations or inferences, the failure to exclude a single other rational inference would be, from the standpoint of *Proof,* a fatal defect; and yet, if only that single other inference were open, there might still be an extremely high degree of probability for the Inference desired. . . . The provisional test, then, from the point of view valuing the Inference, would be something like this: *Does the evidentiary fact point to the desired conclusion . . . as the inference . . . most plausible or most natural out of the various ones that are conceivable?* [1937, p. 25].

The culture of science seeks, however, to systematize the production of rival plausible hypotheses and to extend them to every generalization proposed. While this may be implicit in a field such as law, scientific epistemology requires that the original and competing hypotheses be explicitly and generally stated.

Such a commitment could lead to rampant uncertainty unless some criterion of plausibility were adopted before the rival hypothesis was taken as a serious alternative. Accordingly, each rival hypothesis is a threat only if we can give it the status of a law approximately as credible as the law we seek to demonstrate. If it falls much short of that credibility, it is not then "plausible" and can be ignored.

Even in a "true" experimental comparison, an infinite number of potential laws could predict this outcome, but do not let this logical state of affairs prevent us from interpreting the results. Instead, practical uncertainty comes only from those unexcluded hypotheses to which we, in the current state of our science, are willing to give the status of established laws: these are the plausible rival hypotheses. While the north-south orientation of planaria may have something to do with conditioning, no interview studies report on the directional orientation of interviewer and interviewee. And they should not.

For those plausible rival hypotheses we give the status of laws, the conditions under which they would explain our obtained result also imply specific outcomes for other sets of data. Tests in other settings that attempt to verify these laws may enable us to rule them out. In a similar fashion, the theory we seek to test has many implications other than that involved in the specific comparison, and the exploration of these is likewise demanded. The more numerous and complex the manifestations of the law, the fewer singular plausible rival hypotheses are available, and the more parsimony favors the law under study.

Our longing is for data that prove and certify theory, but such is not to be our lot. Some comfort may come from the observation that this is not an existential predicament unique to social science. The replacement of Newtonian theory by relativity and quantum mechanics shows us that even the best of physical science experimentation probes theory rather than proves it. Modern philosophies of science as presented by Popper (1935; 1959; 1962), Quine (1953), Hanson (1958),

Kuhn (1962), and Campbell (1966; 1969; 1974) make this point clear.

Before listing some of the most common sources of invalidity, it will be helpful to alert the reader to our occasional use of a distinction between internal and external validity. For our present purposes, focused on measurement and comparison in a broad range of contexts, internal validity asks whether or not a difference exists at all in any given comparison. It asks whether or not an apparent difference can be explained away as some measurement artifact. External validity deals with the problem of generalization: To what other populations, occasions, and measures may the observed finding be generalized. We find the distinction useful, but we are aware that at deeper levels and from other perspectives the boundary of the distinction shifts or disappears. In consideration of experimental design, for example, internal validity has been described as hinging on whether or not in a given instance the experimental treatment has made a difference (Campbell and Stanley, 1963/1966). Thus a genuine difference attributable to a change-agent other than the experimental treatment is a challenge to the internal validity of an experiment. Here, as in our first edition, such a problem is a matter of the external validity of a measurement. For experimental validity, Cook and Campbell (1979) have reviewed the criticisms of the external-internal validity distinction and present an expanded typology.

SOURCES OF INVALIDITY OF MEASURES

In this section, we review frequent threats to the valid interpretation of a difference—common plausible rival hypotheses. They are broadly divided into three groups: error that may be traced to those being studied, error that comes from the investigator, and error associated with sampling imperfections. This section is the only one in which we draw illustrations mainly from the most popular methods of current social science. For that reason, particular attention is paid to those weaknesses that create the need for multiple and alternate methods.

In addition, some other criteria such as the efficiency of the research instrument are mentioned. These are independent of validity but important for the practical research decisions that must be made.

Reactive Measurement Effect: Error from the Respondent

The most understated risk to valid interpretation is the error produced by the respondent. Even when he or she is well intentioned and cooperative, the research subject's knowledge that he is participating in a scholarly search may confound the investigator's data. Four classes of this error are discussed here: awareness of being tested, role selection, measurement as a change agent, and response sets.

1. The guinea pig effect—awareness of being tested. Selltiz and her associates (1959) make the observation:

> The measurement process used in the experiment may itself affect the outcome. If people feel that they are "guinea pigs" being experimented with, or if they feel that they are being "tested" and must make a good impression, or if the method of data collection suggests responses or stimulates an interest the subject did not previously feel, the measuring process may distort the experimental results [p. 97].

Guinea pig effects have been called "reactive effect of measurement" and "reactive arrangement" bias (Campbell, 1957; Campbell & Stanley, 1963/1966). It is important to note early that the awareness of testing need not, by itself, contaminate responses. It is a question of probabilities, but the probability of bias is high in any study in which a respondent is aware of his or her subject status.

Although the methods to be reviewed here do not involve "respondents," comparable reactive effects on the population may often occur. Consider, for example, a potentially nonreactive instrument such as the movie camera. If it is conspicuously placed, its lack of ability to talk to the subjects doesn't help us much. The visible presence of the camera undoubtedly changes behavior and does so differentially, depending upon the labeling involved. The response is likely to vary if the camera has printed on its side "Los Angeles Police Department" or "NBC" or "Foundation Project on Crowd Behavior." Similarly, an Englishman's presence at a wedding in Africa exerts a much more reactive effect on the proceedings than it would on the Sussex Downs.

A specific illustration may be of value. In the summer of 1952, some graduate students in the social sciences at the University of Chicago were employed to observe the numbers of blacks and whites in stores, restaurants, bars, theaters, and so forth on a south side Chicago street intersecting the black-white boundary (East 63rd). This, presumably, should have been a nonreactive process, particularly at the predominantly white end of the street. No questions were asked, no persons stopped. Yet, in spite of this hopefully inconspicuous activity, two merchants were agitated and persistent enough to place calls to the university, which somehow got through to the investigators; how many others tried and failed cannot be known. The two calls were from a store operator and the manager of a currency exchange, both of whom wanted assurance that this was some university nosiness and not a professional casing for subsequent robbery (Campbell and others, unpublished). An intrusion conspicuous enough to arouse such an energetic reaction may also have been conspicuous enough to change behavior; for observations other than simple enumerations the bias would have been great. But even with the simple act of nose-counting, there is the risk that the area would be differentially avoided. The research mistake was in providing observers with clipboards and log sheets, but their appearance might have been still more sinister had they operated Veeder counters with hands jammed in pockets.

The present monograph argues strongly for the use of archival records. Thinking, perhaps, of musty files of bound annual reports of some prior century, one might regard such a method as totally immune to reactive effects. However, were one to make use of precinct police blotters, going around to copy off data once each month, the quality and nature of the records would almost certainly change. In actual fact, archives are kept indifferently, as a low-priority task, by understaffed bureaucracies. Conscientiousness is often low because of the lack of utilization of the records. The presence of a user can revitalize the process—as well as create anxieties over potentially damaging data (Campbell, 1967). When records are seen as sources of vulnerability, they may be altered systematically. Accounts thought likely to enter into tax audits are an obvious case (Schwartz, 1961), but administrative records (Blau, 1955) and criminal statistics (Kadish, 1964) are equally amenable to this source of distortion. The selective and wholesale rifling of records by ousted political administrations sets an example of potential reactive effects, self-consciousness, and dissembling on the part of archivists.

These reactive effects may threaten both internal and external validity, depending upon the conditions. If it seems plausible that the reactivity was equal in both measures of a comparison, then the threat is to external validity or generalizability, not to internal validity. If the reactive effect is plausibly differential, then it may generate a pseudo difference. Thus, in a study (Campbell and McCormack, 1957) showing a reduction in authoritarian attitudes over the course of one year's military training, the initial testing was done in conjunction with an official testing program, while the subsequent testing was clearly under external university research auspices. As French (1955) pointed out in another connection, this difference provides a plausible reactive threat jeopardizing the conclusion that any reduction has taken place even for this one group, quite apart from the external validity problems of explanation and generalization. In many interview and questionnaire studies, increased or decreased rapport and increased awareness of the researcher's goals or decreased fear provide plausible alternative explanations of the apparent change recorded.

The common device of guaranteeing anonymity demonstrates concern for the reactive bias, but this concern may lead to validity threats. For example, some test constructors have collected normative data under conditions of anonymity, while the test is likely to be used with the respondent's name signed. Making a response public, or guaranteeing to preserve privacy, will influence the nature of the response. This has been seen for persuasive communications, in the validity of reports of brands purchased, and for the level of antisocial responses. There is a clear link between awareness of being tested and the biases associated with a tendency to answer with socially desirable responses.

There are several fairly common ways in which investigators attempt to reduce the reactivity of their measures, of which the promise of anonymity is one. Investigators may assure subjects that the information they give is for important scientific purposes and that they should, therefore, be truthful. Even when data are not collected under the promise of anonymity, almost always the promise of confidentiality is made. Questionnaires on a single topic often contain "filler" items that are not to be scored but that are thought to reduce somewhat the awareness of the subject of the true purpose of the questionnaire. Unobtrusive measures are but among a fairly extensive variety of measurement procedures addressed to the same problem, ample testimony to the widespread recognition that there is a problem.

The considerations outlined above suggest that reactivity may be selectively troublesome within trials or tests of the experiment. Training trials may accommodate the subject to the task, but a practice effect may exist that either enhances or inhibits the reactive bias. Early responses may be contaminated, later ones not, or vice versa (Underwood, 1957).

Ultimately, the determination of reactive effect depends on validating studies—few examples of which are currently available. Behavior observed under nonreactive conditions must be compared with corresponding behavior in which various potentially reactive conditions are introduced. Where no difference in direction of relationship occurs, the reactivity factor can be discounted.

One procedure for which a good bit of information is currently being developed is the randomized response technique (Boruch and Cecil, 1979) by means of which a randomizing device seen only by the respondent keeps the interviewer from knowing which particular question is being answered by the respondent but which permits a statistical estimation of true responses for groups. An example of the type of finding emerging is that if female college students are queried about their participation in various sexual activities, the estimates of the frequency of such activities is higher from the randomized response technique than from direct questionnaire data (Fidler and Kleinknecht, 1977).

In the absence of systematic data, we have little basis for determining what is and what is not reactive. Existing techniques consist of asking subjects in a post-test interview whether they were affected by the test, were aware of the deception in the experiment, and so forth. While these may sometimes demonstrate a method to be reactive, they may fail to detect many instances in which reactivity is a serious contaminant. Subjects who consciously dissemble during an experiment may do so afterward for the same reasons. And those who are unaware of the effects on them at the time of the research may hardly be counted on for valid reports afterwards.

The types of measures surveyed in this monograph have a double importance in overcoming reactivity. In the absence of validation for verbal measures, nonreactive techniques of the kind surveyed here provide ways of avoiding the serious problems faced by more conventional techniques. Given the limiting properties of these "other measures," however, their greatest utility may inhere in their capacity to provide validation for the more conventional measures.

2. Role selection. Another way in which the respondent's awareness of the research process produces differential reaction involves not so much inaccuracy, defense, or dishonesty, but rather a specialized selection from among the many "true" selves or "proper" behaviors available in any respondent.

By singling out an individual to be tested (assuming that being tested is not a normal condition), the experimenter forces upon the subject a role-defining decision—What kind of a person should I be as I answer these questions or do these tasks? In many of the "natural" situations to which the findings are generalized, subjects may not be forced to define their role relative to the behavior. For other situations, they may. Validity decreases as the role assumed in the research setting varies from the usual role present in comparable behavior beyond the research setting. Orne and his colleagues have provided compelling demonstrations of the magnitude of this variable's effect (Orne, 1959; Orne, 1962; Orne and Evans, 1965; Orne and Scheibe, 1964). Orne has noted:

> The experimental situation is one which takes place within context of an explicit agreement of the subject to participate in a special form of social interaction known as "taking part in an experiment." Within the context of our culture

the roles of subject and experimenter are well understood
and carry with them well-defined mutual role expectations
[1962, p. 777].

Looking at all the cues available to the respondent attempting
to puzzle out an appropriate set of roles or behavior, Orne
labeled the total of all such cues the "demand characteristics of
the experimental situation." A study by Orne and Evans (1965)
showed that the alleged antisocial effects induced by hypnosis
can be accounted for by the demand characteristics of the research setting. Subjects who were not hypnotized engaged in
"antisocial" activities as well as did those who were hypnotized.
The behavior of those not hypnotized is traced to social cues
that attend the experimental situation and are unrelated to the
experimental variable.

The probability of this confounding role assumption varies
from one research study to another, of course. The novelty of
a test-taking role may be selectively biasing for subjects of
different educational levels. Less familiar and comfortable with
testing, those with little formal schooling are more likely to
produce nonrepresentative behavior. The act of being tested is
"more different." The same sort of distortion risk occurs when
subject matter is unusual or novel. Subject matter with which
the respondent is unfamiliar may produce uncertainty of which
role to select. A role-playing choice is more likely with such new
or unexpected material.

Lack of familiarity with tests or with testing materials can
influence response in different ways. Responses may be depressed because of a lack of training with the materials. Or the
response level may be distorted as the subject perceives himself
or herself in the rare role of expert.

Both unfamiliarity and "expertness" can influence the
character as well as the level of response. It is common to find
experimental procedures that augment the experting bias. The
instruction that reads, "You have been selected as part of a
scientifically selected sample . . . it is important that you answer
the questions . . ." underlines in what a special situation and
what a special person the respondent is. The empirical test of
the experting hypothesis in field research is the extent of "don't
know" replies. One should predict that a set of instructions
stressing the importance of the respondent as a member of a

"scientifically selected sample" will produce significantly fewer "don't knows" than an instruction set that does not stress the individual's importance.

Although the "special person" set of instructions may in-crease participation in the project and thus reduce some con-cern on the sampling level, it concurrently increases the risk of reactive bias. In science as everywhere else, one seldom gets something for nothing. The critical question for the researcher must be whether or not the resultant sampling gain offsets the risk of deviation from "true" responses produced by the expert-ing role.

Not only does interviewing result in role selection, but the problem or its analogues may exist for any measure. Thus, in a study utilizing conversation sampling with totally hidden mi-crophones (a study that could raise serious ethical problems), each social setting elicits a different role selection. Conversation samples might thus differ between two cities, not because of any true differences, but rather because of subtle differences in role elicitation of the differing settings employed.

3. Measurement as change agent. With all the respon-dent candor possible, and with complete role representative-ness, there can still be an important class of reactive effects—those in which the initial measurement activity introduces real changes in what is being measured. The change may be real enough in these instances and invalidly generalized to other settings not involving a pretest. This process has been deliber-ately demonstrated by Schanck and Goodman (1939) in a classic study involving information-test taking as a disguised persua-sive process. Research by Roper (cited by Crespi, 1948) shows that the well-established "preamble effect" (Cantril, 1944) is not merely a technical flaw in determining the response to the question at hand, but that it also creates attitudes that persist and that are measurable on subsequent unbiased questions. Crespi reports additional research of his own confirming that even for those who initially say "don't know" processes leading to opinion development are initiated.

The effect has been long established in the social sciences. In psychology, early research in transfer of training encoun-tered the threat to internal validity called *practice effects:* the exercise provided by the pretest accounted for the gain shown on the post-test. Such research led to the introduction of control groups in studies that had earlier neglected to include them. Similarly, research in intelligence testing showed that dependable gains in test-passing ability could be traced to experience with previous tests, even where no knowledge of results had been provided. (See Cane and Heim, 1950, and Anastasi, 1958, pp. 190–191, for reviews of this literature.) Similar gains have been shown in personal "adjustment" scores (Windle, 1954).

Limitations on measurement because the act of measurement changes the phenomenon or object are not unique to social science. In fact, measurement in the physical and natural sciences often produces a permanent change in the object being measured. Theologians, archeologists, historians, scientists, and many other persons appear to have a considerable interest in verifying the authenticity of the Shroud of Turin, a possible relic of Christ. One useful piece of information would be the actual age of the shroud. Unfortunately, the physical chemistry procedures that would be required to determine its age would result in the destruction of a portion of the shroud, and authorities have been unwilling to permit that. One scientist has claimed recently, however, that the age of the shroud could be estimated conservatively within a range of 150 years, using a piece of fabric no larger than a square centimeter, which would provide enough material to repeat the test several times. (A fascinating *National Geographic* article by Weaver [June, 1980] recounts in detail the attempts of theologians and scientists to authenticate the origins of the shroud.) Many assessment tasks involve such limitations. Engineers could not do an actual test of the load carrying capacity of a bridge because the test would destroy it. Assessing physiological and anatomical changes in laboratory animal specimens often requires destroying them so that one cannot, for example, do longitudinal studies of anatomical changes subsequent to brain injuries.

Although actual change in characteristics stemming from measurement operations is likely to be directly proportional to the intrusiveness of measurement, the possibility of analogous artifacts in unobtrusive measures must be considered. Suppose one were interested in measuring the weight of women in a secretarial pool, and their weights were to be the dependent variable in a study on the effects of a change from an all-female staff to one including men. One might, for this purpose, put free weight scales in the women's restroom, with an automatic recording device inside. However, the recurrent availability of knowledge of one's own weight in a semisocial situation would probably act as a greater change agent for weight than would any experimental treatment that might be under investigation. A floor-panel treadle would be better, recording weights without providing feedback to the participant, possibly disguised as an automatic door-opener.

4. Response sets. The critical literature on questionnaire methodology has demonstrated the presence of several irrelevant but lawful sources of variance. Most of these are probably applicable to interviews also, although this has been less elaborately demonstrated to date. Cronbach (1946) originally summarized this literature, and evidence continues to show its importance (Wiggins, 1973).

Respondents will more frequently endorse a statement than disagree with its opposite (Sletto, 1937). This tendency differs widely and consistently among individuals, generating the reliable source of variance known as acquiescence response set (Cronbach, 1946). Although Rorer (1965) and Block (1965) have dissented from this point of view, the ubiquitous presence of direction-of-wording effects—in varying degrees depending on content—seems clearly demonstrated for a wide variety of scales, including their own, when the effect is examined in the correlations between traits (Campbell, Siegman, and Rees, 1967).

Another idiosyncracy, dependably demonstrated over varied multiple-choice content, is the preference for strong statements versus moderate or indecisive ones. Sequences of questions asked in very similar format produce stereotyped responses, such as a tendency to endorse the righthand or the lefthand response, or to alternate in some simple fashion. Furthermore, decreasing attention produces reliable biases from the order of item presentation.

Response biases can occur not only for questionnaires or public opinion polls, but also for archival records such as votes (Bain and Hecock, 1957). Still more esoteric observational or erosion measures face similar problems. Take the example of a traffic study.

Suppose one wanted to obtain a nonreactive measure of the relative attractiveness of paintings in an art museum. One might employ an erosion method, such as the relative degree of carpet or floor-tile wear in front of each painting. Or, more elaborately, one might install invisible photoelectric timers and counters. Such an approach must also take into account irrelevant habits which affect traffic flow. There is, for example, a general right turn bias upon entering a building or room. When this is combined with time deadlines and fatigue (Do people drag their feet more by the time they get to the paintings on the left side of the building?), there probably is a predictably biased response tendency. The design of museums tends to be systematic, and this, too, can bias the measures. The placement of an exit door will consistently bias the traffic flow and thus confound any erosion measure unless it is controlled. (For imaginative and provocative observational studies on museum behavior see Robinson, 1928; Melton, 1933a; Melton, 1933b; Melton, 1935; Melton, 1936; Melton, Feldman, and Mason, 1936.) (Note the age of these studies. Surely it is time for studies of behavior in contemporary museums.)

Each of these four types of reactive error can be reduced by employing research measures that do not require the cooperation of the respondent and that are "blind" to him. Although we urge more methodological research to make known the degree of error that may be traced to reactivity, our inclination now is to urge the use of compensating measures that do not contain the reactive risk.

Error from the Investigator

To some degree, error from the investigator was implicit in the reactive error effects. After all, the investigator is an important source of cues to the respondent, and he or she helps to structure the demand characteristics of the interview. However, in these previous points, interviewer character was unspecified. Here we deal with effects that vary systematically with interviewer characteristics and with instrument errors mostly independent of respondents.

   5. Interviewer effects. It is old news that the characteristics of the interviewer can contribute a substantial amount of variance to a set of findings. Interviewees respond differentially to visible cues provided by the interviewer. Within any single study, this variance can produce a spurious difference. The work of Katz (1942) and Cantril (1944) early demonstrated the differential effect of the race of the interviewer, and that bias has been more recently shown by Athey and his associates (1960). The bias does seem limited to race-sensitive issues, and then it operates in both directions, for example, white interviewers with black respondents and black interviewers with white respondents (Schuman and Converse, 1971). Riesman and Ehrlich (1961) reported that the age of the interviewer produced a bias, with the number of "unacceptable" (to the experimenter) answers higher when questions were posed by younger interviewers.

   Religion of the interviewer is a possible contaminant (Robinson and Rohde, 1946; Hyman et al., 1954), as is his or her social class (Riesman, 1956; Lenski and Leggett, 1960). Benney, Riesman, and Star (1956) showed that one should consider not only main effects, but also interactions. In their study of age and sex variables they report: "Male interviewers obtain fewer responses than female, and fewest of all from males, while female interviewers obtain their highest responses from men, except for young women talking to young men" (p. 143). These findings are amplified by an observational study of transactions in banks that revealed different times required for transactions depending on sex of teller and sex of customer (Larwood, Zalkind, and Legault, 1975). Generally transactions involving female customers were longer, and that was especially the case when tellers were male. On the other hand, transactions between female tellers and male customers were shortest. Probably it is the case that the teller has greatest control over transaction time. One of Dabbs' (personal communication, 1980) students has reported the same effect for library transactions. For a generally useful discussion of various effects on responses in interviews, see Sudman and Bradburn (1974).

The evidence is overwhelming that a substantial number of biases can be introduced by an interviewer (see Hyman et al., 1954; Kahn and Cannell, 1957). In fact, bias may be introduced even by the tone of voice in which a question is asked. In a study of reporting of health-related matters, a rising tone of voice elicited more symptoms than a falling tone but also produced greater reported interest in the interview (Cannell, et al., 1977). Other investigators have found that even slight differences in the wording of questions or the order in which they are presented may lead to significant differences in the outcome of a survey (Turner and Krauss, 1978). Some of the major biases, such as race, are relatively easily controlled; other biases, such as the interaction of age and sex or specific question order effects, are less easily handled.

If we heeded all the known biases, without considering our ignorance of major interactions, there could no longer be a simple survey. The understandable action by most researchers has been to ignore these biases and to assume them away. The biases are lawful and consistent, and all research employing face-to-face interviewing or questionnaire administraion is subject to them. Rather than flee by assumptions, the experimenter may use alternative methodologies that let him flee by circumvention.

6. Change in the research instrument. The measuring (data-gathering) instrument is frequently an interviewer, whose characteristics, we have just shown, may alter responses. In panel studies, or those using the same interviewer at two or more points in time, it is essential to ask: To what degree is the interviewer or experimenter the same research instrument at all points of the research?

Just as a spring scale becomes fatigued with use, reading "heavier" a second time, interviewers may also measure differently at different times. Their skill may increase. They may be better able to establish rapport. They may have learned necessary vocabulary. They may loaf or become bored. They may have increasingly strong expectations of what a respondent "means" and code differently with practice. Some errors relate to recording accuracy, while others are linked to the nature of the interviewer's interpretation of what transpired. Either way, there is always the risk that the interviewer will be a variable filter over time and experience.

Even when the interviewer becomes more competent, there is potential trouble. Although we usually think of difficulty only when the instrument weakens, a difference in competence between two waves of interviewing, *either increasing or decreasing,* can yield spurious effects. The source of error is not limited to interviewers, and every class of measurement is vulnerable to wavering calibration. Suicides in Prussia jumped 20 percent between 1882 and 1883. This clearly reflected a change in recordkeeping, not a massive increase in depression. Until 1883 the records were kept by the police, but in that year the job was transferred to the civil service (Halbwachs, 1930; cited in Selltiz et al., 1959). Archivists undoubtedly drift in recording standards, with occasional administrative reforms in conscientiousness altering the output of the "instrument" (Kitsuse and Cicourel, 1963).

Where human observers are used, they have fluctuating adaptation levels and response thresholds (Holmes, 1958; Campbell, 1961). Rosenthal, in an impressive series of commentary and research, has focused on errors traceable to the experimenter. Of particular interest is Rosenthal's work (1976) on the influence of early data returns upon analysis of subsequent data.

Varieties of Sampling Error

Historically, social science has examined sampling errors as a problem in the selection of respondents. The person or group has been the critical unit, and our thinking has been focused on a universe of people. Often a sample of time or space can provide a practical substitute for a sample of persons. Novel methods should be examined for their potential in this regard. For example, a study of the viewing of bus advertisements used a time-stratifed, random triggering of an automatic camera pointed out a window over the bus ad (Politz, 1959). One could similarly take a photographic sample of bus passengers modulated by door entries as counted by a photo cell. A photo could be taken one minute after the entry of every twentieth passenger. For some methods, such as the erosion methods, total population records are no more costly than partial ones. For some archives, temporal samples or agency samples are possible. For voting records, precincts may be sampled. But for any one method the possibilities should be examined.

We look at sampling in this section from the point of view of restrictions on reaching people associated with various methods and the stability of populations over time and areas.

7. Population restrictions. In the public-opinion-polling tradition, one conceptualizes a "universe" from which a representative sample is drawn. This model gives little or no formal attention to the fact that only certain universes are possible for any given method. A method-respondent interaction exists— one that gives each method a different set of defining boundaries for its universe. One reason so little attention is given to this fact is that, as methods go, public opinion polling is relatively unrestricted. Yet even here there is definite universe rigidity, with definite restrictions on the size and character of the population that can be sampled.

In the earliest days of polling, people were questioned in public places, probably excluding some 80 percent of the total population. Shifting to in-home interviewing with quota controls and no callbacks still excluded some 60 percent—perhaps 5 percent inaccessible in homes under any conditions, 25 percent not at home, 25 percent refusals, and 5 percent through interviewers' reluctance to approach homes of extreme wealth or poverty and a tendency to avoid fourth-floor walkups.

Under modern probability sampling with callbacks and household designation, perhaps only 15 percent of the population is excluded: 5 percent are totally inaccessible in private residences (those institutionalized, hospitalized, homeless, transient, in the military, mentally incompetent, and so forth), another 10 percent refuse to answer, are unavailable after three callbacks, or have moved to no known address. A 20 percent figure was found in the model Elmira study in its first wave (Williams, 1950), although other studies have reported much lower figures. Ross (1963) has written a general statement on the problem of inaccessibility, and Stephan and McCarthy (1958), in their literature survey, show from 3 to 14 percent of sample populations of residences inaccessible.

Also to be considered in population restriction is the degree to which the accessible universe deviates in important parameters from the excluded population. This bias is probably minimal in probability sampling with adequate callbacks, but great with catch-as-catch-can and quota samples. Much survey research has centered on household behavior, and the great mass of probability approaches employ a prelisted household as the terminal sampling unit. This frequently requires the enlistment of a household member as a reporter on the behavior of others. Since those who answer doorbells overrepresent the old, the young, and women, this can be a confounding error.

When we come to more demanding verbal techniques, the universe rigidity is much greater. What proportion of the population is available for self-administered questionnaires? Payment for filling out the questionnaire reduces the limitations a bit, but a money reward is selectively attractive—at least at the rates most researchers pay. A considerable proportion of the populace is functionally illiterate for personality and attitude tests developed on college populations.

Not only does task demandingness create population restrictions, differential volunteering provides similar effects, interacting in a particularly biasing way when knowledge of the nature of the task is involved (Capra and Dittes, 1962; Rosenthal and Rosnow, 1975). Baumrind (1964) writes of the motivation of volunteers and notes: "The dependent attitude of most subjects toward the experimenter is an artifact of the experimental situation as well as an expression of some subjects' personal need systems at the time they volunteer" (p. 421).

The curious, the exhibitionistic, and the succorant are likely to overpopulate any sample of volunteers. How secure a base can volunteers be with such groups overrepresented and the shy, suspicious, and inhibited underrepresented? The only defensible position is a probability sample of the units to which the findings will be generalized. Even conscripting sophomores may be better than relying on volunteers.

Returning to the rigidity of sampling, what proportion of the total population is available for the studio test audiences used in advertising and television program evaluation? Perhaps 2 percent. For mailed questionnaires, the population available for addressing might be 95 percent of the total in the United States, but low-cost, convenient mailing lists probably cover no more than 70 percent of the families through automobile registration and telephone directories. The exclusion is, again, highly selective. If, however, we consider the volunteering feature, where 10 percent returns are typical, the effective population is a biased 7 percent selection of the total. The nature of this selective-return bias includes a skewing of the sample in favor of lower middle-class individuals drawn from unusually stable, "happy" families (Vincent, 1964).

There are still probably more households with television in the United States than there are households with telephones or baths, as we estimated to be the case in the first edition. A 1976 estimate was that 90 percent of households now have a telephone (cited in Tuchfarber and Klecka, 1976), and now about 92 percent (Withey, personal communication, 1980) but most of those without phones are at the bottom of the socioeconomic scale. Among subscribers a substantial proportion are not to be found in a telephone directory, and that proportion is probably growing. Some of those not listed will be new subscribers; Cooper (1964) found that 12 percent of subscribers were too recent to be in a directory. Cooper also found that 6 percent of subscribers had unlisted numbers, a figure that is now about 20 percent (Groves and Kahn, 1979). The unlisted problem can be defeated by a system of random-digit dialing, albeit at a considerable increase in cost over dialing listed numbers. Still, as Tuchfarber and Klecka (1976) have demonstrated, by using computers to generate numbers and by developing highly standardized procedures, the cost of telephone interviews can be kept far below the cost of face-to-face interviewing. Although as many as 50 percent of dialings may be met with busy signals and "not-at-homes," Tuchfarber and Klecka note that with adequate call-back procedures response rates in the range of 90–95 percent can be achieved. Of course, the procedures required to make telephone interviewing by random-digit dialing successful are not inexpensive, but it is probably less expensive than other method of interviewing.

Of considerable interest are Tuchfarber and Klecka's findings in Cincinnati that a sample obtained by random-digit dialing corresponded closely in demographic characteristics to a random sample drawn by conventional means. Poor people and black people were not underrepresented in the telephone sample, and there was only a slight skew in favor of highly educated persons. One group that was somewhat underrepresented was Appalachian whites. The design of the study permitted a comparison of rates of crime victimization and attitudes toward crime as estimated by telephone interviewing and face-to-face interviewing of a randomly selected sample. Random-digit dialing resulted in slightly higher victimization rates for personal crimes and considerably higher rates for all household crimes. Such results are taken as evidence of the likely superiority of telephone interviewing for obtaining crime victimization data on the grounds that people are not likely to report crimes that did not occur. Attitude data also showed almost complete congruence between the two survey methods. Apparently telephone interviewing can produce good data, and when the sample is based on random-digit dialing, it may not be as biased as has been assumed.

Sampling problems of many kinds are certainly acute for the research methods considered in the present monograph. Although a few have the full population access of public opinion surveys, most have much more restricted populations. Consider, for example, the sampling of natural conversations. What are the proportions of men and women whose conversations are accessible in public places and on public transport? What is the representativeness of social class or role?

8. *Population stability over time.* When comparisons over time are the focus, the stability of a population restriction is more important than the magnitude of the restriction. Examine conversation sampling on a bus or streetcar. The population represented differs on dry days and snowy days, in winter and spring, and by day of the week. These shifts would in many instances provide plausible rival explanations of shifts in topics of conversation. Sampling from a much narrower universe would be preferable if the population were more stable over time, as, say, conversation samples from an employees' restroom in an office building. Comparisons of interview survey results over time periods are more troubled by population instability than is generally realized, because of seasonal layoffs in

many fields of employment, plus status-differentiated patterns of summer and winter vacations. An extended discussion of time sampling has been provided by Brookover and Back (1966).

9. *Population stability over areas.* Similarly, research populations available to a given method may vary from region to region, providing a more serious problem than a population restriction common to both. Thus, for a comparison of attitudes between New York and Los Angeles, conversation sampling in buses and commuter trains would tap such different segments of the communities as to be scarcely worth doing. Again, a comparison of employees' washrooms in comparable office buildings would provide a more interpretable comparison. Through the advantage of background data to check on some dimensions of representativeness, public opinion surveys again have an advantage in this regard.

Any enumeration of sources of invalidity is bound to be incomplete. Some threats are too highly specific to a given setting and method to be generalized, as are some opportunities for ingenious measurement and control. This list contains a long series of general threats that apply to a broad body of research method and content. It does not say that additional problems cannot be found.

An Interlude: The Measurement of Outcroppings

The population restrictions discussed here are apt to seem so severe as to traumatize the researcher and to lead to the abandonment of the method. This is particularly so for one approaching social science with the goal of complete description. Such trauma is, of course, far from our intention. While discussion of these restrictions is a necessary background to their intelligent use and correction, there is need here for a parenthesis forestalling excessive pessimism.

First, it can be noted that a theory predicting a change in civic opinion, due to an event and occurring between two time periods, might be such that this opinion shift could be predicted for many partially overlapping populations. One might predict changes on public opinion polls within that universe, changes in sampled conversation on commuter trains for a much smaller segment, changes in letters mailed to editors and the still more limited letters published by editors, changes in purchase rates of books on relevant subjects by that minute universe, and so on. In such an instance, the occurrence of the predicted shift on any one of these meters is confirmatory and its absence discouraging. If the effect is found on only one measure, it probably reflects more on the method than on the theory (for example, Burwen and Campbell, 1957; Campbell and Fiske, 1959). A more complicated theory might well predict differential shifts for different meters, and, again, the evidence of each is relevant to the validity of the theory. The joint confirmation between pollings of high-income populations and commuter-train conversations is much more validating than either taken alone, just because of the difference between the methods in irrelevant components.

The "outcropping" model from geology may be used more generally. Any given theory has innumerable implications and makes innumerable predictions that are unaccessible to available measures at any given time. The testing of the theory can only be done at the available outcroppings, those points where theoretical predictions and available instrumentation meet. Any one such outcropping is equivocal, and all types available should be checked. The more remote or independent such checks, the more confirmatory their agreement.

Within this model, science opportunistically exploits the available points of observation. As long as nature abhorred a vacuum up to 33 feet of water, little research was feasible. When manufacturing skills made it possible to represent the same abhorrence by 76 centimeters of mercury in a glass tube, a whole new outcropping for the checking of theory was made available. The telescope in Galileo's hands, the microscope, the induction coil, the photographic emulsion of silver nitrate, and the cloud chamber all represent partial new outcroppings available for the verification of theory. Even where several of these are relevant to the same theory, their mode of relevance is quite different and short of a complete overlap. Analogously, social science methods with individually restricted and non-

identical universes can provide collectively valuable outcroppings for the testing of theory.

The goal of complete description in science is particularly
misleading when it is assumed that raw data provide complete
description. Theory is necessarily abstract, for any given event
is so complex that its complete description may demand many
more theories than are actually brought to bear on it—or than
are even known at any given stage of development. But theories are more complete descriptions than obtained data, since
they describe processes and entities in their unobserved as well
as in their observed states. The scintillation counter notes but
a small and nonrepresentative segment of a meson's course.
The visual data of an ordinary object are literally superficial.
Perceiving an object as solid or vaporous, persistent or transient, involves theory going far beyond the data given. The raw
data, observations, field notes, tape recordings, and sound movies of a social event are but transient superficial outcroppings of
events and objects much more continuously and completely
(even if abstractly) described in the social scientist's theory.
Tycho Brahe and Kepler's observations provided Kepler with
only small fragments of the orbit of Mars, for a biased and
narrow sampling of times of day, days, and years. From these
he constructed a complete description through theory. The
fragments provided outcroppings sufficiently stubborn to force
Kepler to reject his preferred theory. The data were even sufficient to cause the rejection of Newton's later theory had Ein-
stein's better fitting theory then been available.

So if the restraints on validity sometimes seem demoraliz-
ing, they remain so only as long as one set of data, one type of
method, is considered separately. Viewed in consort with other
methods, matched against the available outcroppings for theory
testing, there can be strength in converging weakness.

The Access to Content

Often a choice among methods is delimited by the relative
ability of different classes of measurement to penetrate into
content areas of research interest. In the simplest instance, this

is not so much a question of validity as it is a limitation on the utility of the measure. Each class of research method, be it the questionnaire or hidden observation, has rigidities on the content it can cover. These rigidities can be divided, as were population restrictions, into those linked to an interaction between method and materials, those associated with time, and those with physical area.

10. Restrictions on content. If we adopt the research strategy of combining different classes of measurement, it becomes important to understand what content is and is not feasible or practical for each overlapping approach.

Observational methods can be used to yield an index of black-white amicability by computing the degree of "aggregation" or nonrandom clustering among mixed groups of blacks and whites (Campbell, Kruskal, and Wallace, 1966). This method could also be used to study male-female relations, or army-navy relations in wartime when uniforms are worn on liberty. But these indexes of aggregation would be largely unavailable for Catholic-Protestant relations or for Jewish-Christian relations. Door-to-door solicitation of funds for causes relevant to attitudes is obviously plausible but available for only a limited range of topics. For public opinion surveys, there are perhaps tabooed topics (although research on birth control and venereal disease has shown these to be fewer than might have been expected). More importantly, there are topics on which people are unable to report but which a social scientist can reliably observe.

Examples of this can be seen in the literature on verbal reinforcers in speech and in interviews. (For a review of this literature, see Krasner, 1958, as well as Hildum and Brown, 1956; Matarazzo, 1962a). A graphic display of opportunistic exploitation of an "outcropping" was displayed by Matarazzo and his associates (1964). They took tapes of the speech of astronauts and ground communicators for two space flights and studied the duration of the ground communicator's unit of speech to the astronauts. The data supported their expectations and confirmed findings from the laboratory. We are not sure if an orbital flight should be considered a "natural setting" or not, but certainly the astronaut and his colleagues were not overly sensitive to the duration of individual speech units. The observational method has consistently produced findings on the effect of verbal reinforcers unattainable by direct questioning.

It is obvious that secondary records and physical evidence are high in their content rigidity. The researcher cannot go out and generate a new set of historical records. He or she may discover a new set, but will always be restrained by what is available. We cite examples later that demonstrate that this weakness is not so great as is frequently thought, but it would be naive to suggest that it is not present.

11. Stability of content over time. The restrictions on content just mentioned are often questions of convenience. The instability of content, however, is a serious concern for validity. Consider conversation sampling again: if one is attending to the amount of comment on race relations, for example, the occurrence of extremely bad weather may so completely dominate all conversations as to cause a meaningless drop in racial comments. This is a typical problem for index-making. In such an instance, one would probably prefer some index such as the proportion of all race comments that were favorable. In specific studies of content variability over time, personnel-evaluation studies have employed time sampling with considerable success. Observation during a random sample of a worker's laboring minutes efficiently does much to describe both the job and the worker (R. L. Thorndike, 1949; Ghiselli and Brown, 1955; Whisler and Harper, 1962).

Public opinion surveys have obvious limitations in this regard, which have led to the utilization of telephone interviews and built-in dialing recorders for television and radio audience surveys (Lucas and Britt, 1950; Lucas and Britt, 1963). By what means other than a recorder could one get a reasonable estimate of the number of people who watch *The Late Show?*

12. Stability of content over area. Where regional comparisons are being made, cross-sectional stability in the kinds of contents elicited by a given method is desirable.

Take the measurement of interservice rivalry as a research question. As suggested earlier, one could study the degree of

mingling among men in uniform, or study the number of bar-
room fights among men dressed in different uniforms. To have
a valid regional comparison, one must assume the same incidence of men wearing uniforms in public places when at liberty. Such an assumption is probably not justified, partly
because of past experience in a given area, partly because of
proximity to urban centers. If a cluster of military bases are
close to a large city, only a selective group wear uniforms off
duty, and they are more likely to be the belligerent ones. Another comparison region may have the same level of behavior
but be less visible.

The effect of peace is to reduce the influence of the total
level of the observed response, since mufti is more common.
But if all the comparisons are made in peacetime, it is not an
issue. The problem occurs only if one elected to study the problem by a time-series design that cuts across war and peace. To
the foot-on-rail researcher, the number of outcroppings may
vary because of war, but this is no necessary threat to internal
validity.

Sampling of locations, such as bus routes, waiting rooms,
shop windows, and so forth, needs to be developed to expand
access to both content and populations. Obviously, different
methods present different opportunities and problems in this
regard. Among the few studies that have seriously attempted
this type of sampling, the problem of enumerating the universe
of such locations has proved extremely difficult (James, 1951)
Location sampling has, of course, been practiced more systematically with preestablished enumerated units such as blocks,
census tracts, and incorporated areas.

OPERATING EASE AND VALIDITY CHECKS

There are differences among methods that have nothing to
do with the interpretation on a single piece of research. These
are familiar issues to working researchers and are important
ones for the selection of procedures. Choosing between two
different methods that promise to yield equally valid data, the
researcher is likely to reject the more time-consuming or costly
method. Also, there is an inclination toward those methods that

have sufficient flexibility to allow repetition if something un-
foreseen goes wrong, and that further hold potential for producing internal checks on validity or sampling errors.

13. Dross rate.   In any given interview, a part of the conversation is irrelevant to the topic at hand. This proportion is
the dross rate. It is greater in open-ended, general, free-
response interviewing than it is in structured interviews with
fixed-answer categories; by the same token, the latter are potentially the more reactive. But in all such procedures, the great
advantage is the interviewer's power to introduce and reintro-
duce certain topics. This ability allows a greater density of relevant data. At the other extreme is unobserved conversation
sampling, which is low-grade ore. If one elected to measure
attitudes toward Russia by sampling conversations on public
transportation, a major share of experimental effort could be
spent in listening to comparisons of hairdressers or discussions
of the Yankees' one-time dominance of the American League.
For a specific problem, conversation sampling provides low-
grade ore. The price one must pay for this ore, in order to get
a naturally occurring response, may be too high for the experimenter's resources.

14. Access to descriptive cues.   In evaluating methods, one
should consider their potential for generating associated validity checks, as well as the differences in the universes they tap.
Looking at alternative measures, what other data can they produce that give descriptive cues on the specific nature of the
method's population? Internal evidence from early opinion
polls showed their population biases when answers about prior
voting and education did not match known election results and
census data.

On this criterion, survey research methods have great advantages, for they permit the researcher to build in controls
with ease. Observational procedures can check restrictions only
for such gross and visible varables as sex, approximate age, and
conspicuous ethnicity. Trace methods such as the relative wear
of floor tiles offer no such intrinsic possibility. However, it is
possible in many instances to introduce interview methods in

conjunction with other methods for the purpose of ascertaining population characteristics. Thus, commuter-train passengers, window shoppers, and waiting-room conversationalists can, on a sample of times of day, days of the week, and so on, be interviewed on background data, probably without creating any serious reactive effects for measures taken on other occasions.

15. Ability to replicate. The questionnaire and the interview are particularly good methods because they permit the investigator to replicate his own or someone else's research. There is a tolerance for error when one is producing new data that does not exist when working with old. If a confounding event occurs or materials are spoiled, one can start another survey repeating the procedure. Archives and physical evidence are more restricted, with only a fixed amount of data available. This may be a large amount—allowing split-sample replication—but it may also be a one-shot occurrence that permits only a single analysis. In the latter case, there is no second chance, and the materials may be completely consumed methodologically.

The one-sample problem is not an issue if data are used in a clear-cut test of theory. If the physical evidence or secondary records are an outcropping where the theory can be probed, the inability to produce another equivalent body of information is secondary. The greater latitude of the questionnaire and interview, however, permit the same statement and provide, in addition, a margin for error.

SCORES AS HYPOTHESES:
A METAPHOR

We suggest here that any "score" on any measure is susceptible to a variety of explanations, one of which will usually be that it represents an accurate representation of a person or object's standing on a trait or dimension of interest. For example, an IQ score of 125 may be taken to represent the hypothesis that the person to whom it is attached is "bright." The radar reading of 78 miles per hour represents the hypothesis that the motorist is speeding. The six cigarettes in the ashtray suggest that the previous occupant of the room was "nervous." In each case there are rival hypotheses which would account for the score, and the rivals are more or less plausible depending upon a variety of factors.

Consider the IQ score of 125. How else might it be explained other than by the brightness of the test subject? Several possibilities come to mind:

The subject had been coached on the test.
The examiner made a serious error in arithmetic.
The subject was extremely ingratiating and the examiner was lenient.
The subject had taken the test several times previously.
The examiner was the subject's mother.

Now all these explanations are possible, and some of them may be plausible in a given case. What wise and careful psychologists try to do, of course, is to render the hypotheses rival to intelligence implausible by the manner in which the test is conducted: arithmetic is checked, examiners are trained to be objective, previous testing is looked for, and mothers are not allowed to report findings on their own children. These usual procedures tend to make the IQ score relatively robust against most rival explanations. Exactly the same strategies are adopted by experimenters to protect their findings against hypotheses that the findings are the result of miscalculations, experimenter bias, and so on. In addition, the socialization processes of science help to protect against the hypothesis that any given set of results might have been faked.

The radar speed score is not so easily protected against plausible rivals, it seems. A recent controversy in the traffic court in Miami has forced a reevaluation of the use of radar, and speed indicators are now thought susceptible to such plausible rival hypotheses as: the radar detected a stationary house or tree, the radar detected some surface of the patrol car in which it was mounted, the radar detected a truck moving up on a smaller vehicle, or the radar simply detected the wrong car in a string of cars. Radar is now under wide attack as a mechanism for detecting speeding violations, and new equipment may have to be designed and built before the plausible rival hypotheses can be laid to rest.

The cigarette butts in the ashtray pose other problems. Could there have been two people in the room? At least check to see whether all six cigarettes are the same brand. Was the ashtray cleaned before the room was occupied? Might the person actually have entered the room much earlier than was originally supposed? Did an absent-minded but quite relaxed person actually light a new cigarette with another left burning and thus produce what appears to be an indicator of heavy smoking? There may, in such cases, be no way of actually rendering all the rival hypotheses implausible, and the measurer—or detective—may be left with the job of selecting among the hypotheses on some other basis, for example, consistency with other information.

If measures are regarded as embodying hypotheses, the careful and alert scientist will often be led to plan measurement operations in such a way as to reduce the number of plausible rival hypotheses to as few as possible and, perhaps, to collect supplementary data which would cast doubt on those remaining as threats to his or her favorite.

Everyman the Unobtrusive Measurer

George A. Kelly (1955) thought it interesting to examine the implications of regarding every person as his or her own scientist. Kelly did not think that scientists do anything so very special that everyone else does not do. Scientists form ideas (hypotheses) about the way things work, they run tests (experiments) to see whether their ideas are right, and they incorporate the findings into their ways of looking at things (theories) and go on to their next hypothesis. That, Kelly thought, is just about how everyone conducts his or her life.

Similarly, everyone engages constantly in a variety of measurement operations not much different from those of scientists. With respect to physical measurement, ordinary people often even use versions of the same instruments that scientists use, for example, thermometers, clocks, tape measures, litmus paper, speed or extent of chemical reactions, and so on. In contrast, ordinary people scarcely ever have available the customary measuring instruments of the social and behavioral scientists, for example, questionnaires and surveys. Probably when operating in the realms of social and behavioral science, ordinary people make use primarily of two measurement approaches, simple self-report and unobtrusive measures.

For many purposes self-report measures will do: Where are you going? Is that a mild cigar? Doctor, is it anything serious? Still, in a great many circumstances, ordinary people know that responses to direct inquiries are not to be trusted: What time did you get home last night? Do you love me? How do I look? Is this a good brand? Are you an honest tradesman?

What then do ordinary people do when they have need of information? They supplement direct self-reports with unobtrusive measures. Rogers and Hammerstein, the marvelous song writing team, had a canny insight into the nature of unobtrusive measurement:

> Don't throw bouquets at me,
> Don't please my folks too much,
> Don't laugh at my jokes too much,
> People will say we're in love.

> Don't sigh and gaze at me,
> Your sighs are so like mine.
> Your eyes mustn't glow like mine,
> People will say we're in love.

> Don't start collecting things;
> Give me my rose and my glove.
> Sweetheart, they're suspecting things.
> People will say we're in love.

The richness of the imagery is remarkable, and as will become clear later, several important types of unobtrusive measures are alluded to in the lyrics.

We are confident that such unobtrusive measurement is characteristic of us all. Moreover, at some level we are all aware of it, and we often attempt to control the image we present to those who would assess us. A young woman meeting her sweetheart's parents for the first time will be trying to create a particular impression (Goffman, 1959), and the parents will be trying to penetrate the obvious by less obvious measures. Hodgkinson (1971) discovered that some maitre d's apparently can predict the size of the tips they will receive from gauging the quality of the footwear worn by customers, and bank loan officers can size up prospective borrowers in only a few seconds. Money doth make careful measurers of us all.

Probably the feature that most distinguishes social scientists from ordinary people as they go about their measurement tasks is the self-consciousness of the social scientists about what they are doing. Like Moliere's character who never knew that he had been speaking prose, most ordinary people never know that they are engaging in unobtrusive measurement. The awareness of social scientists probably does make them somewhat more systematic about the assessment effort, so that they end up with, for example, veritable numerical counts of responses rather than impressions about how often something happened. But the processes are the same. Distrusting deliberate (and possibly self-serving or otherwise biased) reports, all of us, if we are wise, try to supplement our measuring capacities by identifying and observing responses not so susceptible to these biases.

So long as we maintain, as social scientists, an approach to comparisons that considers compensating error and converging corroboration from individually contaminated outcroppings, there is no cause for concern. It is only when we naively place faith in a single measure that the massive problems of social research vitiate the validity of our comparisons. We have argued strongly in this chapter for a conceptualization of method that demands multiple measurement of the same phenomenon or comparison. Overreliance on questionnaires and interviews is dangerous because it does not give us enough points in conceptual space to triangulate. We are urging the employment of novel, sometimes "oddball," methods to give those points in space. The chapters that follow illustrate some of these methods, their strengths and weaknesses, and their promise for imaginative research.

CHAPTER 4

Archives I: The Running Record

> Possibly a wife was more likely to get an inscribed tablet
> if she died before her husband than if she outlived him.

The tablet cited here is a tombstone, and the quotation is from Durand's (1960) study of life expectancy in ancient Rome and its provinces. Tombstones are but one of a plethora of archives available for the adventurous researcher, and all social scientists should now and then give thanks to those literate, record-keeping societies that systematically provide so much material appropriate to novel analysis.

The purpose of this chapter is to examine and evaluate some uses of data periodically produced for other than scholarly purposes, but which can be exploited by social scientists. These are the ongoing, continuing records of a society, and the potential source of varied scientific data, particularly useful for longitudinal studies. The next chapter looks at more discontinuous archives, but here the data are the actuarial records, the votes, the city budgets, and the communications media that are periodically produced, and paid for, by someone other than the researcher.

Besides the low cost of acquiring a massive amount of pertinent data, one common advantage of archival material is its nonreactivity. Although there may be substantial errors in the material, it is not usual to find masking or sensitivity because the producers of the data know they will be studied by some social scientist. This gain by itself makes the use of archives attractive if one wants to compensate for the reactivity that riddles the interview and the questionnaire. The risks of error implicit in archival sources are not trivial, but, to repeat our litany, if they

78

are recognized and accounted for by multiple measurement techniques, the errors need not preclude use of the data.

More than other scholars, archeologists, anthropologists, and historians have wrestled with the problems of archival data. Obviously, they frequently have little choice but to use what is available and then to apply corrections. Unlike the social scientist working with a contemporaneous problem, there is little chance to generate new data that will be pertinent to the problem and circumvent the singular weakness of the records being employed.

Naroll (1962) recently reviewed the methodological issues of archives in his book *Data Quality Control.* His central argument focuses on representative sampling. Do archeologists with their thousand-year-old pottery shards, or historians with a set of two-hundred-year-old memoirs, really have a representative body of data from which to draw conclusions? This is one part of "Croce's Problem." Either one is uncertain of the data when only a limited body exists, or uncertain of the sample when so much exists that selection is necessary.

Modern sampling methods obviate the second part of the problem. We can know, with a specified degree of error, the confidence we can place in a set of findings. But the first part of Croce's problem is not always solvable. Sometimes the running record is spotty, and we do not know if the missing parts can be adequately estimated by a study of the rest of the series. That is one issue. But even if the record is serially complete, the collection of the secondary sources impeccable, and the analysis inspired, the validity of the conclusions must rest on assumptions of the adequacy of the original material.

There are at least two major sources of bias in archival records—selective deposit and selective survival. They are the same two concerns one meets in dealing with physical-evidence data. Durand's study of the ancient Roman tombstones illustrates the selective-deposit concern. Does a study of a properly selected sample of tombstones tell us about the longevity of the ancient Romans, or only of a subset of that civilization? Durand, as noted, suggests that the timing of a wife's death may determine the chance of her datum (CCCI–CCCL) being included in his sample. It is not only the wives who die after their husbands who may be underrepresented. There is, too, a possible economic or social-class contaminant. Middle- and upper-class Romans were more likely to have tombstones (and particularly those that survived until now) than those in the lower reaches of Roman society. This bias is a risk to validity to the degree that mortality rates varied across economic or social classes—which they probably did. The more affluent were more likely to have access to physicians and drugs, which, given the state of medicine, may have either shortened or lengthened their lives. It is to Durand's credit that he carefully suggests potential biases in his data and properly interprets his findings within the framework of possible sampling error.

This same type of sampling error is possible when studying documents, whether letters to the editor or suicide notes. We know that systematic biases exist among editors. Some try to present a "balanced" picture on controversial topics regardless of how unbalanced the mail. With the study of suicide notes, the question must be asked whether suicides who do not write notes would have expressed the same type of thoughts had they taken pen in hand. Any inferences from suicide notes must be hedged by the realization that less than a quarter of all suicides write notes. Are both the writers and nonwriters drawn from the same population?

The demographer cannot get new Romans to live and die; the psychologist cannot precipitate suicides. And therein is the central problem of historical data. New and overlapping data are difficult to obtain from the same or equivalent samples. The reduction of error must come from a close internal analysis that usually means fragmenting the data into subclasses and making cross-checks.

An alternative approach is feasible when reports on the same phenomenon by different observers are available. By a comparative evaluation of the sources, based on their different qualifications, inferences may be drawn on the data's accuracy (Naroll, 1960; Naroll, 1961). In examining an extinct culture, for example, one can compare reports made by those who lived among the people for a long period of time with reports from casual visitors. Or there can be a comparison of the reports from those who learned the indigenous language and those who did not. For those items on which there is consensus, there is a higher probability that the item reported is indeed valid. This consensus test is one solution to discovery of selective deposit or editing of material. It does not eliminate the risk that all surviving records are biased in the same selective way; what it does do is reduce the plausibility of such an objection. The greater the number of observers with different qualifications, the less plausible the hypothesis that the same systematic error exists.

Sometimes selective editing creeps in through an administrative practice. Columbus kept two logs—one for himself and one for the crew. Record keepers may not keep two logs, but they may choose among alternative methods of recording or presenting the data. Sometimes this is innocent, sometimes it is to mask elements they consider deleterious. In economic records, bookkeeping practices may vary so much that close attention must be paid to which alternative record system was selected. The depreciation of physical equipment is an example. Often deliberate errors or record-keeping policy can be detected by the sophisticate. At other times, the data are lost forever (Morgenstern, 1963).

One more example may serve. A rich source of continuing data is the *Congressional Record*, that weighty but sometimes humorous document that records the speeches and activities of Congress. A congressman may deliver a vituperative speech that looks, upon reflection, to be unflattering. Since proofs are submitted to the congressman, he can easily alter the speech to eliminate his peccadillos. If naive readers of the *Record* set out to analyze material from it, they might be misled in thinking that the material is spontaneous, when it is in fact studied.

A demurrer is entered. Even if the data were originally produced without any systematic bias that could threaten validity, the risk of their selective survival remains. It is no accident that archeologists are pottery experts. Baked clay is a "durable artifact" that cannot be digested and decays negligibly. Naroll (1956) comments that artifacts survive because they are not consumed in use, are indifferent to decay, and are not incorporated into some other artifact so as to become unidentifiable.

Discrete and durable, they remain as clues, but partial clues; other evidence was eaten, rotted, or reemployed. Short of complete destruction, decay by itself is no problem. It only becomes one when the rate and distribution of decay is unknown. If known, it may become a profitable piece of evidence—as Libby's (1963) work with radiocarbon dating shows.

For the student of the present, as well as of the past, the selective destruction of records is a question. Particularly in the political area, the holes that exist in data series are suspect. Are records missing because knowledge of their contents would reflect in an untoward way on the administration? Have the files been rifled? If records are destroyed casually, as they often are during an office move, was there some bias in determining what would be retained and what destroyed that would affect the research comparison?

When estimating missing values in a statistical series, one is usually delighted if all but one or two values are present. This gives confidence when filling in the missing cells. If the one or two holes existing in the series have potential political significance, the student is less sanguine and more suspicious of his or her ability to estimate the missing data.

We argue rather strongly for greater attention to archives as a source of data for a wide variety of purposes. Certainly not all archival analysis falls squarely into the category of unobtrusive measurement since a good bit of it involves issues very unlikely to be reactive in any case. For example, Cooper (1973) studied season of birth in relation to occupation for eminent persons listed in *Who's Who,* scarcely a topic likely to be reactive and biased even if done from self-report. Soldiers would not be reluctant to report that they were born in the period from mid-summer to late autumn, and musicians would not prevaricate about having been born in late autumn to middle spring. The cost of doing such a study from archives is only a fraction of what would be required to do it another way. (Incidentally, given that information in *Who's Who* is self-reported, any reactivity will occur in the original archiving and not in the later use of the data.) A recent study by Holmes, Curtright, McCaul, and Thissen (1980) studied recovery from hysterectomies, deaths reported in obituaries, and tournament performances of professional golfers as a function of biorhythms (no relationships found), again, not unusually reactive data sets, but ones retrievable archivally at a fraction of the cost that would be involved in collecting new data. Moreover, archival data are often highly convenient to work with since they are so frequently contained in a single, or small set of, resource(s). Consequently, in this chapter, we will make reference to a wide range of archival studies, a good many of which may not reflect so much the advantages of low reactivity as low cost and high convenience.

In fact, for some types of studies, archives represent the only feasible method of study. Simonton (1975) was able to exploit archival data on creativity as a function of developmental and production oriented periods in history over 127 "generations" (20-year periods) of European history. For their study of the conceptual complexity of revolutionary leaders, Suedfeld and Rank (1976) were forced to rely upon archival materials. Perhaps Welch (1978) who wanted to answer the question "What's the best spot in the country for a woman?" might have been able to obtain survey data from 30 cities with populations over 1,000,000, but from a practical standpoint it is unlikely. By exploiting archives to answer questions having to do with female employment, women in managerial positions, women elected to office, and so on, Welch was able to reach some conclusions about where women are treated the best (Washington, D.C., San Jose, and Denver) and worst (Kansas City, Tampa, and Atlanta).

Archival data do at times involve issues of a high degree of sensitivity. Some newspapers, for instance, publish the names and addresses of persons being divorced, charged with passing worthless checks, arrested, and so on. One might study residential patterns for such persons, or sex differences, or unusualness of names, and so on, and arrive at conclusions rather different from those that might be the end result of more direct efforts, such as community surveys. Surveys of Air Force promotion policies would probably not reveal any racial biases, whereas Butler (1976) showed that black enlisted personnel took consistently longer to be promoted even when matched with white personnel for education, ability test scores, and occupational specialty.

Archives are ubiquitous and numerous, and we all appear in them, usually in many of them. Important issues of confidentiality of information are raised when there is a possibility of open access to archives and when various data sets can be linked. Pileggi (1976), in an article entitled "Secrets of a Private Eye," begins with the statement of a private investigator: "The secret is there are no secrets. I can get information about anyone . . . for a couple of dollars in fees and a 13-cent stamp." (The quotation can be dated to a fairly narrow period of time.) A routine request from the Motor Vehicle Department (New York) for a copy of a driver's license is said to yield, potentially, the following information: height, weight, eye color, and, if it is a chauffeur's license, a picture, whether the license has ever been revoked or suspended, whether eye-glasses are required for driving, whether a hearing aid is needed, whether the person is physically handicapped, whether the person has been confined in a mental institution or ever been convicted of a felony. Information about ownership of an automobile is easily obtained along with the owner's address, driver's license number, and date of birth. A uniform Commercial Code form filed with a county clerk will produce a great deal of information about anyone who has ever applied for a loan anywhere in the country. Commercial information services exist, and they can supply information about birth certificates, marriage licenses, death notices, liquor license applications, state police accident reports, and so on. Unlisted telephone numbers can be tracked down through the tax collector, and an easily available household directory lists telephone numbers by street address as well as numerically. Pileggi discovered that the most difficult place to get information is from a hospital, but even there unscrupulous investigators may beat the system by claiming to be physicians and then moving fast. Articles such as Pileggi's raise quite legitimate concerns about confidentiality and ethics, and those who work with archival data should take as much care as any other investigators to protect their research subjects, and perhaps even the families of those subjects, from invasions of privacy, threats to personal dignity, and other ethical breaches.

The problems just referred to involved obvious misuse of data files, but problems in maintaining confidentiality can arise in legitimate use of data banks by social scientists. A major problem arises from the possibility of individuals being identifiable even if specific identifiers are removed from the data. If, to take a somewhat obvious example, a small town has only three physicians, and a student drug user is identified as the 16-year-old son of a physician, confidentiality will have been destroyed. The problems of maintaining confidentiality if data sets are really small may be insurmountable, but Campbell, Boruch, Schwartz, and Steinberg (1977) and Boruch and Cecil (1979) present a number of useful suggestions for enhancing confidentiality with data sets of reasonable size. In most cases social scientists would have relatively little interest in data sets so small that confidentiality could not be preserved at all. A second confidentiality problem arises when one wishes to determine the relationships between variables in two confidential files. A typical example would be the desire of an investigator to determine the extent of criminal records among persons seeking treatment for venereal disease: obviously both files would be confidential. Even if data from both files were printed out without identifiers, there still might be a possibility of breaching confidentiality, a risk that would increase with increasing amounts of information listed. Again, Campbell et al. and Boruch and Cecil present potential methods for protecting confidentiality, for instance, by mutually insulating confidential files through mechanisms not requiring reporting of individual data. In the example of attempting to link venereal disease and criminal records, an investigator might provide police officials with five lists of ten persons each, all of whom would have been treated for venereal disease, and five more lists of ten persons each constituting a comparison group not treated. The police could then provide the mean number of arrests for persons on each list, along with a measure of variability, and they could also recode the lists in such a way that only the designation of Group A vs. Group B would be retained. Confidentiality might even be further enhanced if the police randomly deleted one name from each list so that the investigators would not even be sure just which nine of the ten original persons were being reported on. We think it important to know that confidentiality can, under most circumstances, be protected in using archival data.

ACTUARIAL RECORDS

Birth, marriage, death. For each of these, societies maintain continuing records as normal procedure. Governments at
various levels provide massive amounts of statistical data, ranging from the federal census to the simple entry of a wedding in
a town-hall ledger. Such formal records have frequently been
used in descriptive studies, but they offer promise for hypothesis-testing research as well.

Take Winston's (1932) research. He wanted to examine the
preference for male offspring in upper-class families. He could
have interviewed prospective mothers in affluent homes or fathers in waiting rooms. Indeed, one could pay obstetricians to
ask, "What would you like me to order?" Other measures, nonreactive ones, might be studies of adoption records, the sales of
different layette colors (cutting the data by the class level of the
store), or the incidence of "other sex" names—such as Marion,
Shirley, Jean, Jerry, Jo.

But Winston went to the enormous data bank of birth
records and manipulated them adroitly. He simply noted the
sex of each child in each birth order. A preference for males was
indicated, he hypothesized, if the male-female ratio of the last
child born in families estimated to be complete was greater
than that ratio for all children in the same families. There was,
in fact, a considerably higher proportion of last-born male than
female children; these families quit while they thought they
were ahead. More recently Markle (1974) has found that adults
living in Tallahassee, Florida, express a preference for male
children that would result in about 116 male births for every
100 females. Westoff and Rindfuss (1974) show, however, that
the effect of sex preselection, if it were possible, would be very
limited in the United States. Mark Twain (Neider, 1959) noted,
quite independently of being a male, that his birth was of some
consequence since he increased the population of his birthplace
by 1 percent, something not accomplished by many of the
greatest men in history, not even Shakespeare! Twain specu-
lates that he could have done it of anyplace, even London.

With the detail present in birth records, Winston was able
to aggregate his upper-class sample of parents by the peripheral

data of occupation, and so forth. The same auxiliary data can be employed in any study to serve as a check on evident population restrictions—a decided plus for detailed archives. Recall, as an instance, the richness of the information sources cited by Pileggi (1976) as of interest to private investigators.

Winston's study also illustrates the time-sampling problem. For the period studied, and because of the limitation to upperclass families, Winston's measure is probably not contaminated by economic limitations on the absolute number of children, a variable that may operate independently of any family sex preference. Had his study covered only the 1930s, or were he making a time-series comparison of economically marginal families, the time factor could offer a substantial obstacle to valid comparison. The argument for the existence of such an economic variable would be supported if a study of the 1930s showed no sex difference among terminal children but did show significant differences for children born in the 1940s.

Economic conditions are only one of the factors important to errors due to timing. Wars, depressions, and acts of God are all events which can pervasively influence the comparisons of social science data. The subjective probability of their influence may be awkward to assign, yet the ability to control that influence through index numbers and other data transformations is a reasonable and proper practice.

There are many demographic studies of fertility levels in different societies, but Middleton (1960) showed a shrewd understanding of archival sources in his work. He developed two sets of data: fertility values expressed in magazine fiction, and actuarial fertility levels at three different time periods. For 1916, 1936, and 1956, he estimated fertility values by noting the size of fictional families in eight American magazines. A comparison with the population data showed that shifts in the size of fictional families closely paralleled shifts in the true United States fertility level.

Middleton had a troublesome sampling problem. Since only a small number of magazines continued publication over the period from 1916 to 1956, was the group of eight long-term survivors a proper sample? This durable group may not have been representative, but it was quite proper. The very fact that these eight survived the social changes of the 40 years argues that they probably reflected the society's values (or those of a sufficiently large segment of the society to keep the magazine economically alive) more adequately than those which failed. The issue was not one of getting a representative sample of all magazines, but, instead, of magazines which printed material that would have recorded more faithfully the pertinent research information.

Most fertility studies are concerned with the desire or plans for children, but Matejcek (1970) was interested in the effects on children of having been unwanted. In 1958 abortion was made legal in Czechoslovakia, but the law did not permit abortion under just any conditions, and a fair proportion of women who applied for abortions were denied them. It was possible to identify and follow up, in 1970 and subsequently, the entire population of 313 children born in 1961–63 to women who were denied abortions upon both initial application and an appeal. Comparisons with matched control groups were made on a wide variety of archival measures from schools, health centers, and so on. Such a study could not be done in the United States because of the privacy of abortion information.

Christensen (1960) made a cross-cultural study of marriage and birth records to estimate the incidence of premarital sex relations in different societies. He simply checked off the time interval between marriage and birth of the first child—a procedure that showed marked differences in premarital conception, if not in activity among cultures. His study illustrates some of the problems in cross-cultural study. The rate of premature births may vary across societies, and it is necessary to test whether this hypothesis can explain differences. Data on the incidence of premature births of later-born children in each society permit this correction. A population problem to be guarded against in these cross-cultural studies, however, is the differential recording of births, marriages, and the like. There are many societies in which a substantial share of marriages are not formally entered in a record-keeping system, although the parties initially regard the alliance to be as binding as do those in other societies where records are more complete. The incidence in Mexico of "free-union" marriages is both extensive and selective—more prevalent among working classes than other groups (Lewis, 1961).

Some countries, most notably Denmark, keep remarkably complete records of a wide variety of phenomena of societal interest, this making possible many types of studies not easily accomplished in the United States. Mednick and his associaes have, for example, been able to carry out sophisticated studes of the genetics of schizophrenia and of crime because of the careful and complete way births, including twin births, are recorded in Denmark and the equally careful recordings of cases of mental disorder and crime (see, for example, Mednick, Schulsinger, Higgins, and Bell, 1974; and Mednick and Christiansen, 1977). Many persons may not realize that official records in the United States are often not kept especially well. The reasons are varied, but an important one is expressed pithily in a comment by an old India hand warning a friend about taking government statistics too seriously:

> The government is very keen on amassing statistics. They collect them, add them, raise them to nth power, take the cube root and prepare wonderful diagrams. But what you must never forget is that every one of these figures comes in the first instance from the *chowty dar* (village watchman), who just puts down what he damn pleases (Stamp, 1929, pp. 258–59).

The quotation may be old, but the warning is not outdated. Not so long ago there was a controversy in one state over the contention that there had been 5000 excess deaths attributable to contamination from a nuclear power facility. Ultimately, however, it seemed more likely that county clerks simply did not get around to recording many deaths until a calendar change had occurred. Of course, the United States has a much larger, more diverse, and more dispersed population than Denmark, and that creates problems of enormous size and complexity. Record keeping in the United States could profitably be improved, but it would not be an easy task.

Simple marriage records alone were used by Burchinal and Kenkel (1962) and Burchinal and Chancellor (1962). The records were used as a handy source by Burchinal and Kenkel to study the association between religious identification and occupational status. The records provided a great body of data from which to work but also posed a sampling question: are men about to be grooms a good base for estimating the link between religion and occupation? The small cadre of confirmed bachelors is excluded from the sample universe, and, depending upon the dates of the records studied, there can be an interaction between history and groomdom.

Another study by Burchinal and Chancellor (1963) took the complete marriage and divorce records of the Iowa Division of Vital Statistics for the years 1953 and 1959. From these records, the authors compared marriages of same-religion and mixed-religion pairs for longevity. As might be expected, they found mixed marriages to be significantly shorter-lived than same-religion ones. Of the mixed marriages, those partners who described themselves as Protestants without naming a specific affiliation showed the highest divorce rate. Such findings as these are, of course, quite susceptible to changing social customs and mores, but systematic archival studies may be of great value in tracking those very changes.

By studying dispensations for cousin marriages recorded in Roman Catholic Church archives, Freire-Maia (1968) estimated inbreeding in United States, Canadian, and Latin American Catholic populations. The records enabled estimations of the frequencies of marriages between first cousins, first cousins once removed, and second cousins, which in turn permits calculation of a coefficient of inbreeding sufficiently exact to make reasonable the comparison of large areas. Inbreeding was highest in Latin America and lowest in the United States.

Of all the marriage-record studies, probably none is more engaging than Galton's (1870/1960) classic on hereditary genius. Galton used archival records to determine the eminence of subjects defined as "geniuses" and additional archives to note how their relatives fared on eminence. Few scientists have been so sensitive as Galton to possible error in drawing conclusions, and, in a section on occupations, he notes that many of the judges he studied postponed marriage until they were elevated to the bench. Even so, their issue of legitimate children was considerable. In Stein and Heinze's (1960) summary: "Galton points out that among English peers in general there is a prefer-

ence for marrying heiresses, and these women have been pecu-
liarly unprolific" (p. 87). And on the possible contaminant of the
relative capacities of the male and female line to transmit
ability:

> ... the decidedly smaller number of transmissions along
> the female line suggests either an "inherent incapacity in
> the female line for transmitting the peculiar forms of abil-
> ity we are now discussing," or possibly "the aunts, sisters,
> and daughters of eminent men do not marry, on the aver-
> age, so frequently as other women." He believes there is
> some evidence for this latter explanation [p. 89].

Galton (1872) even used longevity data to measure the efficacy
of prayer. He argued that if prayer were efficacious, and if
members of royal houses are the persons whose longevity is
most widely and continuously prayed for, then they should live
longer than others. Data showed the mean age of death of
royalty to be 64.04 years, men of literature and science 67.55
years, and gentry 70.22 years. There has even been an experimental test of prayer, for Joyce and Welldon (1965) did a double-blind test of the efficacy of prayer in restoring the health of
seriously ill people. Prayer did not prove to be efficacious. Galton's data are consistent with the hypothesis that it is praying,
rather than being prayed for, that is conducive to longevity.

One of the most persistent and intriguing facts about longevity is that wherever there are data, women outlive men. It
has often been suggested that the longer life expectancy of
women may be attributable to the fact that in general they are
less exposed to the stresses of the work world than are men.
However, a study by the Teacher's Insurance Annuity Association (Participant, 1972) showed that whether women were receiving annuity benefits as retired staff members or as wives of
retired staff members, their mortality rates at all ages were the
same. Males of just about all mammalian species have shorter
life expectancies than females, perhaps, some have speculated
(Daly and Wilson, 1978), because males are genetically pro-
grammed to be more active and take more risks in breeding.
Other data indicate that the females of just about all species
outlive males, even among houseflies! (Trivers, 1972.)

Some years ago various investigators began to notice what
they thought was a consistent tendency for persons to die at

such times as to suggest that the timing of death might be affected by psychological factors. Thus, some alleged that death often occurred in relation to anniversaries of stressful or emotionally powerful events (for example, Fischer and Dlin, 1972). Of particular interest has been the birthdate-deathdate phenomenon, purporting to be a regular tendency for frequency of deaths to decline in the months just preceding people's birthdays and then to rise in the months just subsequent (for example, Alderson, 1975; Phillips, 1972; Phillips and Feldman, 1973). More recent reanalyses (Schutz and Bazerman, 1980) of previously published data, however, have cast doubt on the birthdate-deathdate phenomenon as well as on hypotheses relating delayed death to national elections and a religious holiday (Yom Kippur). Some people, palmists for instance, believe that people die when their time has come, but Wilson and Mather (1974) measured the "lifelines" on the palms of corpses and found no relationship between the length of the line and age at death. And, continuing this somewhat macabre topic, we note that Walters and Markley (1975) used death records to study the "Transylvania effect;" homicides and suicides are not more frequent during the time of a full moon. In fact, a careful review of the literature on the moon-behavior problem concludes that there is probably no effect of the moon on human behavior although, admittedly, not all behaviors (for example, amorous ones) have been explored (Campbell and Beets, 1978). Sudden death from heart attacks may result from stresses in life. Exploiting the excellent records on cardiac deaths kept in Sweden, Rahe and Lind (1971) were able to show that persons suffering such deaths had experienced a substantial increase in psychosocial stress factors in the last six months of their lives. A recent Canadian study (Rabkin, Matthewson, and Tate, 1980) showed that a remarkably large proportion of sudden cardiac deaths among males occur on Mondays (stresses of the new week or excesses of the past weekend?). Dabbs' (personal communication, 1980) students, incidentally, observed that people are more inclined to sleep on buses on Mondays and that there is more conversation on Fridays.

Durkheim's pioneering study of suicide (1951) shows an active exploration of archival source possibilities. He concluded that "the social suicide rate can be explained only sociologically" (p. 299) by relating suicide levels to religion, season of the year, time of day, race, sex, education, and marital status, doing all of this for different countries. All of these variables were obtained from available archives, and their systematic manipulation presaged the morass of cross-tabulations that were later to appear in sociological research.

Another study employing death records is Warner's (1959) work, *The Living and the Dead*. Death and its accoutrements in Yankee City were the subject of this multimethod research. Warner consulted official cemetery documents to establish a history of the dead and added interviewing, observation, and trace analysis as aids to his description of graveyards. "Their ground and burial lots were plotted and inventory was taken of the ownership of the various burial lots, and listings were made of the individuals and families buried in them" (p. 287).

His findings are of interest for what they say of response tendencies in the laying down of physical evidence. Here the response tendencies, and the way in which they vary across social-class groups, become the major clues to the analysis. Warner found the social structure of Yankee City mirrored (if this be the proper verb) in the cemetery; he found evidence on family organization, sex and age differentiation, and social mobility. For example, the father was most often buried in the center of the family plot, and headstones of males were larger than those of females. In some cases, Warner found that a family that had raised its social status moved the graves of their relatives from less prestigious cemeteries to more prestigious ones.

Tombstones would be an interesting source of data for comparative analysis of different cultures. In matriarchal societies, for example, is the matriarch's stone substantially larger than the husband's? Does the husband get a marker at all? What are the differences in societies with extended versus nuclear family structures?

Warner's findings tie in with Durand's (1960) study of ancient Rome. In both studies, the relative dominance of the male was demonstrated by the characteristics of the tombstones.

A more recent commentary on tombstones comes from Crowald (1964), who wandered through Moscow's Noyo-Devich cemetery, noting the comparative treatment of old czarists and modern communists. After noting that over Chekhov's grave a cherry tree is appropriately blooming, he states:

> ... the cemetery also tells a quieter, more dramatic tale. Climbing out of some weedy grass is the washboard-sized marker of Maxim Litvinov, once a Stalin foreign minister and the wartime Soviet envoy to America. His mite of a marker reminds what happened to those who fell from Stalin's favor [p. 12].

Just as in ancient Rome, the timing of a wife's death makes a difference in the nature of the tomsbstone. Here, this potential contaminant is used as a piece of evidence.

> Novo-Devich does show, too, that things have changed in Russia since Stalin. For example, there is the great marble monument to Rosa Kaganovich. She was the wife of Lazar Kaganovich, the Stalin lieutenant booted from power in 1957 by Premier Nikita S. Khrushchev. Kaganovich is in full disgrace, but he fell after Stalin died. So his wife, who died in 1961, still got her big place in the cemetery. Fresh flowers decorate her marble [p. 12].

These objects are just big and small pieces of stone to the uninformed, but to the investigator who possesses intelligence on those buried and relates it to the stones, the humble and grandiose memorials are significant evidence.

Birth is to death as marriage is to divorce. The latter, too, is archived and can be so investigated. A current trend in that area of jurisprudence is toward the "no fault" divorce, but there are fears that removing any impediments to divorce will result in an unwanted increase in divorce rates. Nebraska adopted a no fault divorce law, and Mazur-Hart and Berman (1977/1979) treated the move as an interrupted time series and examined divorce rates before and after. No fault had little effect on divorce rates although it may have increased divorce rates somewhat among black couples and temporarily for couples over 50 and those married longer than 25 years.

Birth records also represent a potentially rich archival source for a variety of investigations. For example, what is in a name? Fads and fashions, but probably also ethnicity and social class, and, perhaps to the discerning eye, a host of social trends. The Office of the New York City Health Commissioner keeps track of names given to babies and publishes a list of the most popular names. In 1979 (*New York Times,* April, 1980), the most popular names for boys were Michael, David, Jason, Christopher, John, Joseph, Anthony, James, Robert, and Daniel. (What happened to William?) The most popular names for girls were Jennifer, Jessica, Nicole, Melissa, Michelle, Lisa, Elizabeth, Maria, Christine, and Danielle. Save for Maria, both lists seem awfully Anglo-Saxon for a city as ethnically diverse as New York. Maria had been fourth on the list in 1964 (when Lisa and Michael were both number one). The list will bear watching. The name Maria tells us something, and we will want to watch it over the next few years to determine whether it is increasing or decreasing in relative frequency. Many proud parents used to manifest family pride by passing down a name to a son, who would then become "junior" or the II, III, or IV, and so on. A study of birth certificates has shown that the practice has been more common on the eastern seaboard than in the rest of the country. Records over the past century suggest that the practice was once common only in the white property owning and professional classes but has now spread to the white working class and to the black population. In general, however, the practice is on the decline (Taylor, 1974).

Frequently, one has a choice among different archival sources, and a useful alternative are directories, whether of residents, association members, or locations. Ianni (1957–1958) elected to use city directories as the primary source of data in his study of residential mobility. An analysis of these directories over time allowed him to establish the rates of mobility, and then relate these mobility indexes to the acculturation of ethnic groups.

It is obviously a tedious task to perform such an analysis, and the work includes a high amount of dross. If possible, such mobility levels might be more efficiently indexed by access to change-of-address forms in the post office. But the question here becomes one of population restriction. Is the gain in efficiency that comes from use of change-of-address forms worth the possible loss in completeness of sampling? The answer comes, of course, from a preliminary study of evaluating the two sources of data for their selective characteristics.

Telephone directories are, of course, a gold (both yellow

and white) mine of information about the communities they so
literally describe. Ethnicity of communities would be easily
determined, foods and other products held necessary or desirable could be discovered, types of recreation likely to be engaged in would be revealed, and the directory might even help
one to locate oneself with respect to latitude. Reed (1976) has
shown that the definition of geographic (and cultural) "South"
can be derived from frequency of telephone directory entries
beginning with "Southern" and "Dixie." The telephone directory definition agreed well with other definitions based on
different criteria, but the two words did seem to have somewhat
different connotations in different communities. Using various
cultural factors, Gastil (1971; 1972; 1976) has identified cultural
regions of the United States that are associated with other phenomena of interest. For example, the southern cultural region
is associated with low educational levels, high infant mortality,
and high rates of homicide. Are those problems found everywhere they favor "Dixie?"

For some studies, more selective directories are indicated,
and the inclusion of a person in a directory serves as one element in the researcher's discriminations. *Who's Who in America* does not print everbody's name nor does *American Men of
Science.* W. H. Clark (1955/1960) used both of these sources in
his "A Study of Some of the Factors Leading to Achievement
and Creativity with Special Reference to Religious Skepticism
and Belief." Boring and Boring (1948/1963) used *American
Men of Science* to choose the psychologists studied in their
useful article on the intellectual genealogy of American psychologists. Fry (1933/1960) had earlier used *Who's Who in
America* in a study entitled "The Religious Affiliations of American Leaders." (See also Lehman and Witty, 1931/1960).

Fry's work showed that if one depends on the editors of
such directories for selective inclusion, one must also rely on the
individuals listed for complete reporting. All of the problems
associated with self-report are present, for the individual has a
choice of whether or not he will include all data, and whether
he will report accurately. The archive serves as an inexpensive
substitute for interviewing a large sample of subjects stratified
along some known or unknown set of variables. Fry found that

a 1926 religious census showed 3.6 percent of the general population to be Jews, while only .75 percent of the entries in *Who's Who in America* were listed as Jews. Does this mean that Jews are less distinguished, are discriminated against in being invited to appear in the directory, or is there selective reporting by the Jews of their religion? Fry gave a partial answer to the question by a check of another directory—*Who's Who in American Jewry.* He found 432 persons in this directory who had reported no Jewish affiliation in *Who's Who in America,* thereby raising the Jewish percentage to 2.2. By raising the question of another plausible hypothesis for a comparison (3.6 percent of the population compared with .75 percent in the directory), he structured a question which was testable by recourse to a second archival source highly pertinent to the hypothesis.

A recent study of the biographical entries of eminent Jews (in *Who's Who in America*) came to the conclusion that many such persons lacked any strong sense of Jewish identity on the basis of their lack of membership in Jewish organizations and involvement in Jewish causes (Zweigenhaft, 1980). Zweigenhaft's measure of eminence was membership on the boards of directors and trustees of major corporations and foundations, and it may be that Jews are assimilated into such groups only when they downplay their ethnic-religious identity.

Kenneth Clark (1957) used the American Psychological Association's directory in his study of the psychological profession. For any study extending over a long period, the APA directory can be frustrating. As the number of psychologists grew, the detail in the individual listings shrank. Thus, the number of items on which a complete time series could be produced were reduced as tighter and tighter editing took place. The measuring instrument was constant in its content for only a few pieces of information. The change in the number of available categories of information is a detectable shift in the quality of the measure. Other changes, such as increasingly difficult requirements for membership or individuals responding to the greater bulk of the directory by writing more truncated listings, may change the character of the instrument in a less visible way and produce significant differences that are, in fact, only recording artifacts.

Digging into the past, Marsh (1961) obtained the names of 1047 Chinese government officials from the government directories of 1778 and 1831–1879. He then correlated the ranks of the officials with the time required to reach a particular rank and with factors such as age and family background. If there was no differential recording, one may conclude with Marsh that the rich get there faster.

One of the very important advantages of archives is that the data have all been collected by the time one wishes to use them. It would be discouraging in the extreme to think of having to wait around while people's careers unfold in order to determine what the effect of some experience on eminence might be. Although biographical—especially autobiographical —material is scarcely collected in an unobtrusive way, it may be minimally reactive for many purposes since those providing it may have little capacity to foresee the uses to which it might be put. What eminent Jew listing his organizations for *Who's Who* would anticipate that at some time well into the future a social scientist would be checking his memberships in Jewish organizations. And if he did so anticipate, what would he do about it? Lie? Or run right out and join some?

Eisenstadt (1978) defined eminence by the criterion of having had a half page or longer biography in either *Encyclopaedia Britannica* or *Encyclopedia Americana*. He was then able to find support for the hypothesis that such eminence is associated with loss of a parent. Given that Eisenstadt's sample of 699 individuals included writers (36 percent), statesmen (25 percent), philosophers (15 percent), and scientists/scholars (14 percent), and that it spanned the ages from the time of Homer to that of John F. Kennedy, the results can scarcely be held to be an artifact of some elusive temporal, local, or occupationally specific factor. Cooper (1973) indicates that specific field of eminence may be associated with season of birth:

> Soldiers seem to be born mid-summer to late autumn
> Doctors are born early summer to mid-autumn
> Artists arrive in late winter to late spring
> Musicians are born in late autumn to middle spring, the winter months and early spring apparently being a good time to compose musicians, if not music.

   Simonton has been involved in a series of studies of genius, creativity, and success, and his work indicates the exceptional usefulness of various archival sources when they are well exploited. Using data published by Cox (1926) on *The Early Mental Traits of Three Hundred Geniuses*, Simonton (1976) divided the group into persons having been distinguished for their creativity and those distinguished for leadership. In perhaps the most interesting finding, Simonton determined that education bears an inverted U-shaped function to ranked eminence among creators; apparently it is possible to stifle creativity both with too much and too little education. However, for leaders the intelligence-eminence relationship is straightforward: the higher the education, the lower the ranked eminence. Aspirants to leadership should not waste time pursuing advanced degrees! Simonton also found that a father's status had no direct impact on ranked eminence of his son. Another study of 696 of the best-known musical composers in the Western classical tradition (Simonton, 1977a) used a recursive structural equations model to show that eminence as a classical composer is attributable to, among other things, having been born at a time when there were relatively few composers concentrated in small geographic areas, thus yielding a goodly number of role models, but also having begun composing early and living a long time. In general Simonton's work (also Simonton, 1977b) shows that creative eminence is much related to creative productivity; those who do more do best. Surprisingly, in his study of the productivity of ten classical composers over time, Simonton (1977b) found that they were little influenced by such external events as public recognition, war, intranational disturbances, and personal stress.

   A topic much debated in personality in recent years has been the relative importance of trait and situational factors in determining behavior. Simonton (1980) views this problem in the light of historical disagreement about the "great man" theory of the determination of critical social events. Simonton took advantage of the long preoccupation of historians (and the rest of us) with war, and analyzed data for 326 land battles that have been extensively documented in one or more of three military archives. Simonton was able to get data for these battles on various characteristics of the generals (for example, age, battle experience, years of experience, cumulative victories, winning streak status, and tendency to attack), and for such situational factors as army size, home soil advantage, existence of divided command, and heterogeneity of troops involved. Victory was predicted by the generals' years of experience, length of winning streak, and taking of the offensive. Only the existence of a divided command among the situational variables was predictive of victory—clearly a victory for the great men. The cumulative victories of generals were related to their ability to keep their casualties relatively low, but casualty rates were also relatively low for larger armies and those with divided commands. Of no small interest is Simonton's finding that winning streaks of the generals were longer by a good bit than losing streaks; losing generals do not last for long.

POLITICAL AND JUDICIAL RECORDS

An archival record—votes—is the dependent variable for office holders, the absolute criterion measure; but for the social scientist, it is only an indicator. Votes cast by the people determine the politician's most important piece of behavior (staying in office), and votes cast by the legislator are the definitive test of his position and alliances. Obviously voting is not unobtrusive; voters, whether the public or legislators, must cooperate to vote and they know that their votes are being registered. In the case of the general public, the fact that voting is done anonymously might lead to the presumption that voting would be nonreactive. That, however, might depend on the specific use to which the voting records are put. If, for example, one took votes cast as an index of favorable sentiments toward the candidates, some error might be introduced if there were one or more candidates perceived as unlikely to win or as, in some manner, unqualified for the office. Voters might well react to the voting process and vote for an otherwise less favored candidate in order to avoid "throwing their vote away," or voting for a likable candidate not seen as being able to manage the responsibilities of office. Probably a fair number of voters cast their votes as they do out of some considerations of party loyalty, another biasing factor. Obviously, voting by legislators is potentially more reactive since they must vote publicly if their votes are to be known, and their very voting stance may produce a response from the public that would affect their subsequent voting record. Moreover, in recent years, it has become common for various groups to assess voting records of legislators and to issue "scores" based on the special interests of the groups. It is not known whether these assessments have any impact on the legislators, but the possibilities for reactivity exist. On the other hand, it seems likely that a great many votes are taken on issues and in ways that are quite nonreactive to the ultimate purposes for which analyses are to be done, and voting records should not be overlooked as a potentially rich source of information.

In the past the political scientist has had to be content with roll-call votes, since the desultory ayes and nays on voice votes are never traceable to their sources. An empirical question, one on which we can find no research but about which anecdotes abound, is the difference between bills voted on by roll-call and by voice. Certainly political reporters are aware of the many times that voting patterns seem drastically changed when there is a demand for a roll-call vote on a motion previously voted on merely by voice. More recently the opportunities for voting studies in legislative bodies have changed markedly with the advent of the electronic voting machine that publicly registers each vote. Even so, some caution must be exercised. In the 1980 session of the Florida legislature there was one occasion involving a politically sensitive bill on which the votes of two absent legislators were cast by person(s) unknown, something quite contrary to the rules. Still, the opportunities for more detailed and penetrating studies of both legislators and the legislative process should be greatly enhanced by the electronic scoreboards.

In the first edition of this book we reviewed a number of studies of voting behavior and voting statistics and still think that discussion worth the reader's effort to obtain. In the ensuing years, however, we have encountered no instances of dramatic new developments, methods, or findings, and rather than merely repeat the previous discussion, we will review some of the issues and highlight findings.

If one wants to evaluate legislators, say for conservatism or environmental concern, it is usually necessary to select from among a variety of possible bills or motions a few that best tap the dimension of interest. Many issues are, however, sufficiently complex that votes across them may not add up to much. Currently, that is, in 1980, for example, the United States Congress has before it a bill that establishes a huge wilderness area in Alaska. The bill is much desired by many conservationists, but it might, from the standpoint of the energy conscious, severely restrict the development of much needed energy sources. The bill is regarded as a drastic federal intrusion into a state's affairs by some persons, and as a justifiable intervention to protect national as opposed to local interests by others. Some native American groups favor the bill; others oppose it. A vote on the bill could scarcely be considered a very pure measure of level of environmental concern and perhaps even less so of liberalism-conservatism. Moreover, some legislators manage to evade voting on certain critical issues to avoid taking a public stand, thus producing a population restriction. It may be possible to improve voting measures by applying sophisticated psychometric and scaling procedures to them. Gage and Shimberg (1949) picked ten bills to measure progressivism in one Congress and eight for another and were able to construct Guttman scales with high coefficients of reproducibility. One suspects that in the 1980 Congress, a legislator who will vote for the Alaskan wilderness bill will vote for most other environmental protection bills—except, perhaps, for those in his or her home state.

According to many analysts, the current political scene is different from that of even the recent past because of the powerful influence of single-issue groups—groups such as those opposed to gun control, favoring environmental protection, against abortion—that judge politicians on very narrow grounds. These judgments along with strong influence may distort voting patterns considerably. For example, a prominent politician with an almost unblemished liberal voting record has recently been forced to take a public stand against gun control because he is in a difficult senatorial campaign in which he could be defeated on that single issue. Eventually there will be material for fascinating political studies in the effects of the various single-issue movements, but for the moment they probably obscure broader dispositions and trends.

Previous studies of legislative voting have not exploited the fact that there are 50 state legislatures, all but one bicameral, hence 99 state legislative bodies. These numbers would enable the truly assiduous and persistent researcher to assemble large bodies of data bearing on questions about the voting habits of legislators. One study of state legislators, for example, was directed at the determinants of their votes on abortion reform. Religious affiliation was a better predictor of votes than party affiliation, age, or urban vs. rural constituency. Many interesting problems are probably better investigated at the state than at national level in any case.

There have been a number of interesting findings with respect to voting behavior. For example, Gage and Shimberg (1949) found that younger senators are not necessarily more progressive than older ones; senators from the same state do not tend to vote the same; and voting patterns are systematically different between regions of the country. Dempsey (1962) developed a "Loyalty Shift Index" by noting the percentage of party issues that senators voted for or against on roll calls. Using roll-call reports in the House, Riker and Niemi (1962) looked for evidence of congressional coalitions. By noting if members of Congress voted on the winning side, on the losing side, when eligible, or when ineligible, they produced an index of coalitions. Other issues that either have been or feasibly could be investigated include determining variables affecting seniority (MacRae, 1954a), assessing group tension by content analysis of political speeches (Grace and Tandy, 1957), and estimating perceptions of individual job security by the degree to which members of Congress use their franking privilege.

One interesting question about a legislative body is the degree to which it is influenced by public opinion. Obviously, legislators, individually and collectively, claim to be sensitive to public opinion on most issues. They reserve the right to vote against public opinion when conscience demands. Burstein and Freudenberg (1978) thought the opinion of the public concerning the Vietnam war a good matter about which to fashion a study of legislative policy. One advantage of the war issue was that public opinion manifested itself in a number of ways, and another was that public opinion changed over time. An advantage from the standpoint of voting is that it was relatively easy to identify a long series of bills and motions, 91 in fact, that related to the conduct of the war and that could be scaled according to the level of "hawkishness" implied. The data came from bills before the Senate. Independent variables were the content of the bills, war costs, public opinion, and the occurrence of antiwar demonstrations. Content was measured along three dimensions: hawkishness, generosity of funding, and warpowers initiatives granted to the President. War costs were assessed in terms of total battle deaths and incremental cost of the war during each funding year. Public opinion was obtained from polls conducted throughout the war gauging the proportion of people who felt that entry into the war had been a mistake and the proportion approving the way the President was handling the situation. Anti-war demonstrations were indexed from monthly counts published in the *New York Times,* a crude index, as the authors admit, but one probably highly correlated with the actual number. The data were analyzed separately for the period up to and the period subsequent to the Cambodian invasion in 1970.

The findings showed, to begin with, that public opinion that the war was a mistake, the monetary cost of the war, total deaths, and occurrence of demonstrations were all very highly intercorrelated because all four changed regularly and linearly with time. The correlation with time is obvious in the case of total deaths ($r = .93$) since deaths can only increase over time, but the correlation of negative public opinion with time ($r = .99$) is no artifact and shows that public opinion about the wisdom of United States involvement in the war became regularly less favorable over the years. Other analyses showed that all the above variables had significant effect on Senate roll-call outcomes in the direction of decreasing the proportion of hawkish votes, but since the variables were so highly intercorrelated, it was impossible to determine their separate effects. Other analyses did indicate that demonstrations in the months preceding a vote had some impact on the number of dovish votes, but the number of war deaths just before votes did not have an effect. Apparently senators were affected by the way the war was going, not by the outcomes of battles. Still other analyses suggested that 1970 marked a turning point in the way the Senate reacted to the war. Before 1970, funding was not an important dimension in affecting outcomes of votes, but the main hawkishness dimension was important. After 1970, funding became important and the hawkish dimension lost importance. These results seem to indicate that up until 1970 the financial burden of the war was bearable, and the main opposition came from the doves, but after 1970 the costs began to make the distinction between hawks and doves irrelevant. Finally, before 1970 recent demonstrations appeared to decrease hawkish votes, but after 1970 demonstrations preceding a vote seemed to have a small, but opposite effect. The authors interpret their findings in terms of early consciousness-raising effects of demonstrations and later interference with the production of a consensus.

The behavior of the member of Congress can also be used to study persons outside the Congress. It is a common practice for a legislator to insert into the *Congressional Record* newspaper columns that reflect his or her point of view. In a study of political columnists, Webb (1962a; 1963) employed these data for an estimate of liberalism-conservatism among 12 Washington columnists. Individual members of Congress were assigned a liberal-conservative score by evaluations of their voting record published by two opposing groups—the conservative Americans for Constitutional Action and the liberal Committee on Political Action of the AFL-CIO. The two evaluations correlated −.75 for senators and −.86 for House members. Columnists were then ordered on the mean score of the members of Congress who placed their articles into the *Record*.

It would be valuable to supplement such an analysis with a comparative study of how various writers treat the same event. Cogley (1963) suggested this in his verse on the interpretation of the Papal encyclical, *Pacem in Terra:*

> David Lawrence read it right
> Lippmann saw a Liberal light,
> William Buckely sounded coolish,
> Pearson's line was mostly foolish. . .
> To play the game you choose your snippet
> Of Peace on Earth and boldly clip it [p. 12].

The voting records of the people can also be used to measure the effect of experimenter intervention in preelection settings. Among the memorable studies in social science is Gosnell's (1927) field experiment on getting out the votes. Selecting 12 electoral precincts, Gosnell divided them into experimental and control conditions. The experimental precincts were sent a series of nonpartisan messages encouraging registration and voting in a forthcoming election, while the control precincts received only the normal preelection stimulation— generally of a politically partisan nature. The effect of the mail effort was determined by an analysis of registration lists, pollbooks, and census material. Here Gosnell intervened in a "natural" way, established controls, and employed inexpensive archival records as his tellingly appropriate dependent variable. Hartmann's (1936) study of "emotional" and "rational" political campaign pieces also used votes.

Bain and Hecock (1957) further demonstrated the ability to test persuasion principles in a natural laboratory free from the reactive biases of the university research suites. They were interested in the effect of physical position on alternative choices, and found data in the aggregate voting statistics from Michigan elections. Michigan was chosen because of (1) the absence of a law requiring ballots to be burned after the election (an obvious impediment to archival studies of voting behavior) and (2) the systematic rotation of candidates' names on the Michigan ballot. This rotation is practiced in several states and represents an assumption that position on the ballot does indeed have an effect. "Under [California] state law, the incumbent's name goes first on the ballot, and political handicappers give as much as 20 percent edge—greater than the margin of most senatorial victories—to this psychological primacy" (*Newsweek* 1964, p. 28).

Because of the Michigan system of rotation, Bain and Hecock could work an orthogonal analysis, establishing the vote of each candidate and each position on the ballot. The findings supported the assumptions of veteran political hands and the ballot constructors: there was a significant position effect. It would be a provocative study to take this and other naturally occurring possibilities for a position effect (for example, the sale of goods in a supermarket when placed in different shelf patterns), and compare the results with those derived from the traditional experimental laboratory.

Voting is also behavior of interest in relation to the views of the general public. Voting is certainly not an unobtrusive behavior, even though it does occur in secret—only with respect to how, not whether. Moreover, voting is a behavior that is meant to provoke a reaction. Participation in elections is notably low when people are apathetic, that is, when they believe that their votes will not have an effect. Nonetheless, changes in voting patterns over time or differences between geographic areas may reveal subtle attitudinal and other variations not discernible in the individual voter. One of the very substantial advantages in the study of voting is that the number of observations is usually quite large, making detectible even small differences. In off-year and primary elections, only a small share of eligible voters cast ballots, but this selective behavior is not damaging to validity, since the critical variables—election or not election, margin of victories—are posited directly on this selectivity.

Obviously there are many factors that may influence the electorate, including, one hopes, the positions taken by the candidates. It is probably true, however, that the positions candidates take reflect in part their intended constituencies. Sullivan and Uslaner (1978) studied congressional elections and found that in marginal districts the views of candidates tended to diverge from each other, and ultimately the candidate with views closest to those of the constituency tended to win. On the other hand, in noncompetitive districts the incumbent tended to win even if the views of the other candidate were closer to those of the constituency. Whatever the reason, incumbents in safe districts have a lot of latitude and presumably could afford to vote their consciences. Do they? The votes of a judicial body may provide data for other than obvious research. Final votes of the Supreme Court are made public and can be related to public opinion, and so on. Supreme Court votes are to some extent predictable based on mathematical analyses of past voting behavior (Schubert, 1963; Nagel, 1962; Ulmer, 1963), or at least they once were. The Supreme Court, too, changes over time and so does the nature of the cases brought before it. Any comparison over time of the behavior of the court system relative to some legal issue must take account of the variation in issues and arguments before the court.

Many, many groups vote regularly in this country. It is the American way. But their voting behavior is seemingly little studied. Certainly there are many opportunities to study interesting phenomena in less complex settings and in atmospheres less charged with tension than is usually the case in legislatures and courts. For example, there are probably hundreds of union-representation elections every year, and most go unnoticed by social scientists. In one that did not, however, Schriesheim (1978) found that pro-union voting was strongly but negatively correlated with overall job satisfaction ($r = -.64$), but even more strongly with total economic satisfaction ($r = -.74$). Noneconomic aspects of jobs apparently have relatively little to do with why workers join unions ($r = -.38$).

OTHER GOVERNMENT RECORDS

Some government records are orthodox sources for the social scientist. The birth, death, and marriage archives, as we have already seen, can be used for straightforward descriptive work or for less direct applications. Other records have less visible, but equally fruitful, applications. In this section are examples of research that has used power failures, municipal water pressure, parking-meter collections, and the like as research data.

The weather is a reasonable start. Durkheim (1951), as noted above, used weather as one of the variables in his study of suicide. An early investigation by Lombroso (1891/1960) also used archival analysis to note the effect of weather and time of year on scientific creativity. He drew a sample of 52 physical, chemical, and mathematical discoveries and noted the time of their occurrence. His evidence, shaky as it is, showed that 22 of the major discoveries occurred in the spring, 15 in the autumn, 10 in the summer, and 5 in winter. Note that when season is used as a surrogate for weather, quite plausible rival hypotheses immediately offer themselves. For example, in Christian areas of the northern hemisphere, winter is a time for several holidays of great importance. Perhaps major discoveries do not occur so often in the winter because scientists, like other folks, take time off for other things in the winter. On the other hand, is it not possible that spring discoveries stem from hard winter's work?

There may be a season for just about everything. Smolensky (*Science News*, 1980) reports that late summer and early fall are the peak seasons for human sexual activity: most babies are conceived in July, August, and September (a similar pattern occurs for monkeys). Incidences of rape cluster in late summer (data from 1880–84 show the same pattern); venereal disease reflects the same pattern of sexual activity; English data reveal peaks in sales of contraceptives in late July and early August; testosterone peaks in September when sperm counts fall (an indication of increased sexual activity); and girls tend to have their first mentrual periods in late fall or early winter. Although in spring a young man's fancy may turn to love, it is only in summer that he tends to get around to it. Given the fact that weather is everywhere and all the time, it is, perhaps, surprising that so little is known about the specific effects of weather variables on behavior. There have been some studies done, and they produce interesting, if not wholly consistent, findings. Cunningham (1979) has produced a brief review in an introduction to his own work. An early investigator (Dexter, 1904) found very low barometric pressure, excessive humidity, and abnormal winds to be related both to poor student deportment and to increased corporal punishment by teachers. It has been reported that at about that same period of time the Bank of England would not let its bookkeepers work on certain critical sets of records on very foggy days because of the increased probability of errors (Dexter, 1904). Temperature has been found to be related to the occurrence of serious incidents of collective violence, but in a somewhat complex way. In a study of 102 archived instances of riots, Baron and Ransberger (1978) found that frequency of rioting increased with temperatures through the mid-80s but declined beyond that point. (Riot? It's too darned hot!) Actually, rioting was likely to be preceded by several days of increasing temperature with a stable temperature during the disturbance, followed by declining temperature. Other weather factors that have been reported to be related to behavior are: low barometric pressures and suicide (Digon and Bock, 1966); amount of snow and suicide (Lester,

1974); and limited sunshine and high humidity to bad moods (Persinger, 1975). Note again that the interpretation of the above findings is by no means straightforward—low barometric pressures, lack of sunshine, and so on, are likely to be correlated with seasonal changes in activities, work pressures, and many other features of life. If the series of observations extended over only a short time, the findings would be more readily interpretable than if it extended over a long time.

Cunningham (1979) was interested in the effects of weather on emotional well-being and how, then, it might affect altruistic behavior. Previous investigators (Lockard, McDonald, Clifford, and Martinez, 1976; Cialdini, Vincent, Lewis, Catalan, Wheeler, and Darby, 1975) had reported that panhandlers were more successful in spring than in autumn, but no direct connection to a weather variable could be made. Cunningham arranged to have university students approached with a request to complete at least part of a questionnaire as a favor to the experimenter. The students were approached out-of-doors on 36 randomly selected days in spring and summer, and in a second study during winter and early spring. People were likely to be more helpful when the sky was clear and a great deal of sunshine was striking the earth. Temperature was negatively associated with helping in the summer and positively in the winter. Helping was also somewhat more likely when humidity was low and when a breeze was blowing in the summer and on still days in the winter. Since his study was conducted out-of-doors, Cunningham reasoned that the effect might be attributable to momentary comfort of those persons approached. Therefore, he did a second study indoors where comfort was controlled. The second study was one on the size of tips left to waitresses in a restaurant that had windows on two sides. Waitresses were blind to the purposes of the study but did rate their own moods, since size of tip might have been affected by weather but mediated by waitress behavior. However, the results indicated that sunshine was related to percent of check left as tip, as was relative humidity, that is, larger tips were left on more humid days. As might be expected, outdoor temperature and barometric pressure were unrelated to tipping behavior. Waitresses' moods were also better on sunny, warm, dry days, but their mood ratings were obtained before they received any tips, and waitress mood was unrelated to size of tip. Dabbs (personal communication, 1980) reports that one of his students found Sunday School contributions to be somewhat larger on nice days. These and other studies of local climates over relatively brief periods of time help to illuminate our understanding of larger scale studies such as might be done from archived records.

Using quite a different type of record, Mindak, Neibergs, and Anderson (1963) took the ongoing records of parking-meter collections as one index of the effect of a Minneapolis newspaper strike. They hypothesized that one of the major effects of the strike would be a decrease in retail shopping. Since most of the parking meters were located in the downtown shopping area, revenue collection from them was a good piece of evidence on the strike's effect. The data showed marked decreases during the months of the strike, using a control of previous years.

City budgets were the stuff of Angell's (1951) study on the moral integration of American cities. He prepared a "welfare effort index" by computing local per capita expenditures for welfare and combined this with a "crime index" based on FBI data to get an "integration index."

A particularly interesting and novel use of data comes from the study of city water pressure as it relates to television viewing. For some time after the advent of television, there were anecdotal remarks about a new periodicity in water pressure levels—a periodicity linked to the beginning and end of programs. As the television show ended, so the reports ran, a city's water pressure dropped, as drinks were obtained and toilets were flushed. A graphic display of this hypothesis was provided by Mabley (1963), who published a chart showing the water pressure for the city of Chicago on January 1, 1963. This was the day of a particularly tense Rose Bowl football game, and the chart shows a vacillating plateau until the time the game ended, when the pressure level plummets downward. A recent report (*Michigan Daily,* October 31, 1980) indicated that the same effect was found for half-time and end-of-game breaks in Milwaukee at the time of the Super Bowl (a 30-million-gallon effect). A 15-million-gallon effect was found at the conclusion of the Carter–Reagan debate.

Using this approach, one could study the relative popularity of different retirement times. Since a large amount of water is used by many people at bedtime, a comparison of the troughs at 9:00, 9:30, 10:00, and so on could be made. Similarly, a comparison could be made in the morning hours to estimate time of arising. Two problems arise. Do those who retire early use the same amount of water as those who retire late? It is, after all, possible that a smaller number of showers and baths would be taken by those who retire late—particularly in areas with a high number of apartment dwellers. Another difficulty of such a study is comparison across different time areas. Many people end the day by viewing television news. In the metropolitan Chicago area, for example, some three million people watch the 10:00 P.M. newscasts. But the last major television newscast in the eastern areas is at 11:00 P.M. This one-hour variation might influence the times of people going to bed. The water pressure index could help establish whether it did or not. Similarly, it could be used to study the relative amount of attendance paid to entertainment and commercial content of television. The critical point of study in this research would be the water pressure levels at the times of mid-show commercials. The prior decision of viewers to turn the set off at a specified hour would influence the water pressure index for commercials at the beginning and end of shows but should be a minor rival hypothesis for those embedded within the entertainment content of the program.

A similar measure, a more catastrophic one, has been manifest in the United Kingdom. This measure, electric power failures, gives plausibility to the hypothesis that it is commercials (and not earlier decisions to turn the set off) that influence the drops in water pressure. At the time of the introduction of the United Kingdom's commercial television channel, a series of power failures hit the island. Whole areas were blacked out, and it was noticed that the timing of the power failures coincided with the time of commercials on the new television channel. The explanation provided was that viewers left their sets to turn on electric water heaters to make tea. The resulting power surge, from so many heaters plugged in simultaneously, overloaded the capacity of a national power system unequipped to handle such peaks. The commercials remain; new power stations have been built. This measure is a more discontinuous one than water pressure, but it would be of value to compare the water pressure levels with power demands. If the hypothesis is correct, that the English were plugging in water heaters, one should find a higher correlation between the two measures in the United Kingdom (with a small time lag as water precedes power) than in the United States. Another imaginative link between two time series of archival data was provided by De-Charms and Moeller (1962). They gathered the number of patents issued by the United States Patent Office from 1800 to 1950. Relating these to population figures, they prepared a patent production index for 20-year periods over the 150-year span. These data were then matched to findings from a content analysis of children's readers for the same period, with a prime focus on achievement imagery. The matching showed a strong relationship between the amount of achievement imagery in their sample of books and the number of patents per million population.

CRIME AND LEGAL RECORDS

For many reasons there has long been an interest in documenting a wide variety of behaviors, events, and processes related to crime and the response of the legal system. As we shall see, the documentation, or at least the uses made of the documentation, has not always been of a high level of accuracy. Nevertheless the records are extensive, many go back for long periods of time, and, in their best use, they provide fascinating insights into the social order. We can here, in fact, give only the barest sampling of the types of data available and the uses to which they might be put.

How much crime is there? The problem is how to know. There are estimates that only about half of all crime is reported, homicide and auto theft being in all likelihood the most completely reported crimes. Surveys of victims (for example, Law Enforcement Assistance Administration, 1975) suggest that much crime goes unreported, but how capable are victims of defining crime? One study of the ultimate dispositions of 58 cases of "armed robbery" (Vera Institute, 1977) found that such events as a husband taking his wife's paycheck by threatening her with a knife and a man taking his gun to go next door to collect an overdue $10 loan had been charged initially as armed robberies. And, technically, so they were, but they are not exactly what most citizens have in mind when thinking about "crime waves." Eck and Riccio (1979) have shown that relatively small differences in tendencies to report crimes get translated into much larger differences in estimations of crime frequency. Other writers have noted that police have great discretion in taking crime reports, defining the criminal charges, deciding when crimes have been solved, and so on, with the result that very little credence can be placed in official police statistics with respect to amount of crime and whether it is going up or down. How about the newspapers? Davis (1952) analyzed opinions of citizens in Colorado about the amount of crime in their cities in relation to officially reported crimes and newspaper reports of crime. Citizen opinions seemed more closely linked to newspaper crime reports than to actual reported crime, and newspaper crime reports seemed independent of actually reported crime. Simón (1979) has shown that after the heavy media attention paid to the two assassination attempts against President Ford in September of 1975, there was a marked increase in threats against the President as indicated by Secret Service records.

Somewhat more startling are the findings of Phillips (1977; 1978) on the effects of newspaper publicity given to suicides and murders. In the week following a publicized suicide, automobile accident fatalities increase by over nine percent, and the greater the publicity, the greater the increase. Phillips suggests that the increase is most plausibly explained as concealed suicide. Moreover, crashes of noncommercial airplanes increase after either suicide or murder stories in newspapers, again in some proportion to the level of publicity. Accidents involving only the pilot, however, increase only after suicide stories; multiple-victim accidents increase after both suicide and murder stories. Perhaps such news is not fit to print.

Why don't they do something about crime? They do. Every now and again pressures will build up and those with appropriate authority will decide to "crack down" on the criminals. Analysis of available records in the criminal justice system can show how effective the crackdowns are. Several years ago the state of Florida became sufficiently annoyed at armed robbers to pass a law mandating a three-year prison term for any felony committed with the use of a gun. It was later reported that in the first year the law was in place only 12 cases were prosecuted under that law. Perhaps in some manner a good many armed robbers were allowed to "plea bargain" for a lesser charge. Plea bargaining has been regarded by some as representing a soft attitude toward crime that actually encourages more of it. Therefore, plea bargaining itself has been the subject of crackdown efforts. In one midwestern county, a newly elected prosecutor issued a strict policy forbidding plea bargaining in drug cases, in the expectation that drug offenders would end up with the heavy prison sentences he thought they deserved. A subsequent analysis of court records (Church, 1976) showed that removing discretion in charging from prosecutors resulted mostly in a shift of discretion to judges, who came under heavier pressures than ever to reduce sentences or grant probation. Moreover, if judges were unwilling to make concessions on sentences, then offenders were more likely to refuse to plead guilty and, therefore, put the state to the expense of a trial. One of the rationales used to support the practice of plea bargaining is the pressure on courts of large numbers of cases that simply could not be dealt with if everyone insisted on going to trial. Analysis of court records (Heumann, 1975) suggests, however, that the use of plea bargaining is not related to the volume of work facing the courts but rather to the mutual interest that most defendants and courts have in avoiding a trial—defendants because they usually are guilty and have no effective defense and courts because trials are expensive.

One of the most stringent crackdowns ever was the 1973 drug law passed in New York to levy markedly increased penalties on drug offenders. The effects of the law were evaluated by analysis of archived data (Joint Committee on New York Drug Law Evaluation, 1978), and the study is of interest both because of the extensive and imaginative use of indicators, for example, using reported hepatitis cases to index heroin use, and because of the findings about the effects of the crackdown. The law could not be adequately implemented, was ineffective, and cost a lot of money.

Crackdowns may not be particularly effective ways of dealing with crime for any number of reasons, but one likely reason is that a crackdown in any one part of the system may well be accompanied by moderation in some other part. Ross (1976) has studied a number of attempts to crack down on traffic law violators, none of which was effective, and his analysis of court records shows that if the police arrest more people, the courts let more go, and if the penalties become too heavy, the police will not arrest or the courts will not convict, and so on. However, not all efforts to intervene with traffic violators are necessarily ineffective. A special program at an Air Force base singled out airmen involved in injury-producing accidents to be screened with a view to possible discharge as unsuitable for the service or for psychiatric treatment. In addition there was an educational campaign mounted against drinking and driving. Subsequent analysis of accident records (Barmack and Payne, 1961) showed a rather dramatic decrease in frequency of accidents during a time when no such decrease was occurring nationally or in the state in which the base was located, no such decrease was occurring at another nearby base, and no change in policy activity was detectable.

Perhaps locking up criminals has a deterrent effect on crime or at least yields the benefit of incapacitating them. Conventional wisdom says yes, but the data are not so positive. A study by a National Academy of Sciences panel (Blumstein, Cohen, and Nagin, 1978) that relied on a wide range of archived data about crime, which were analyzed by means of complex statistical models, indicated that deterrence is a fairly weak and somewhat uncertain consequence of punishment, and incapacitation, while certain, is likely to be a very expensive way to deal with rising crime rates.

Could crime be reduced by any softer approach? Denmark liberalized its laws concerning pornography in the mid-1960s with the result that child molestation decreased substantially, but some other apparent decreases in sex crimes may have resulted from decreased propensities for reporting such crimes (Kutchinsky, 1973). In a notably good instance of the value of complementary data sets, Kutchinsky was able to show that attitude surveys suggested changes in public attitudes toward some sex crimes were consistent with the hypotheses that they were less likely to be reported, that is, the public became more tolerant. No such attitude change occurred for child molestation.

Another indication that a nonpunitive approach to producing compliance with the law may be effective is provided by the work of Schwartz and Orleans (1967). They surmised that taxpayers might be more honest with their income tax reports if they were reminded of their obligations as citizens to pay their fair share of taxes. On the other hand, citizens might also pay more if they were reminded of the penalties for being carelesss. The intervention devised by Schwartz and Orleans was to interview taxpayers just prior to income tax filing time, with alternative interviews being structured to remind them of the obligations imposed by citizenship to pay taxes and the benefits to society of a tax system or to remind them of the penalties awaiting those who inaccurately make out their tax reports. Households were selected and assigned randomly to interview conditions, with the study being carried out in neighborhoods populated with taxpayers likely to be itemizing deductions. The problem remaining was to get the critical outcome measures: income declared, deductions claimed, and taxes paid. The IRS does not give out such data on its taxpayers, but it was willing to provide data for groups of taxpayers, and Schwartz and Orleans were able to get data for their experimental groups. The upshot of their study was that the interview did not make a difference in amount of taxes paid, *but,* the "punitive" interview resulted in higher reported income *plus* higher claimed deductions; hence, the same amount of taxes. This study is a classic case of the potential reactivity of the interview.

The obvious interest of the public and of governmental institutions in crime has resulted in voluminous archives of every imaginable kind. One investigator (Miller, 1979) interested in determining how many Americans have arrest records has concluded that the only conceivable way some previous estimates based on FBI files could have been produced was to sample file drawers to determine about how many records there are per drawer, multiply by the number of drawers per cabinet, and then measure the linear feet of file cabinets. How many arrest records are there? Perhaps as many as 45,000,000! On the other hand, that investigator also concluded that any

estimate would be likely to have a large unknown error component because of the difficulty in purging files when people die,
emigrate, have multiple identities, and so on. Zeisel (1973) has
also shown that important biases can enter into the use of archived data: at one time the FBI was knowingly using a substantially biased statistic to support its claim that much criminal
recidivism could be blamed on the softness of federal courts
toward criminals. Still, these archives do exist and can be usefully exploited by the wary and wise.

Many records, probably especially those having to do with
the law, are considered highly sensitive if not confidential. Consequently, it is often difficult to get access to them. Archer and
Erlich (1980) wanted to know whether a crime wave in a California county had resulted in an increase in sales of handguns.
California law requires registration of handguns, but one
agency that kept such records regarded them as confidential
and would not let the investigators examine them. However,
the agency did agree to weigh stacks of the records in order to
provide an estimate of purchases per month. Fortunately for
methodology, the investigators discovered that there was another agency that kept the same records and that did not regard
them as confidential. Thus the investigators were able to compare weight data with actual counts, and the correspondence
was quite close. As Archer and Erlich point out, the weight
method might be generally useful, but the differential attitudes
of the two agencies toward their records is also instructive.

One more note of some interest about archived crime data:
since the early 1970s, the National Crime Survey program has
been doing criminal victimization and attitude surveys in many
American cities. These attitude data on such matters as crime
trends, fear of crime, neighborhood problems, and police performance may eventually prove valuable to researchers able to
take advantage of the existence of highly comparable data
across cities and time.

THE MASS MEDIA

Among the most easily available and massive sources of
continuing secondary data are the mass media. The variety,

texture, and scope of this enormous data pool have been neglected for too long. In this section, we present a selected series
of studies that show intelligent manipulation of the mass media.
We have necessarily excluded most content analyses and focused on a few which illustrate particular points.[1]

It is proper to start this section by citing Zipf, who sought
order in diverse social phenomena by his inventive use of data
that few others would perceive as germane to scientific inquiry.
In a model study, Zipf (1946) looked at the determinants of the
circulation of information. His hypothesis was that the probability of message transfer between one person and another is inversely proportional to the distance between them. (See also
Miller, 1947; Stewart, 1947; Zipf, 1949.) Without prejudice for
content, he made use of the content of the mass media as well
as sales performance. How many and how long were out-of-
town obituaries in the *New York Times?* How many out-of-town
items appeared in the *Chicago Tribune?* Where did they origi-
nate? What was the sales level in cities besides New York and
Chicago of the *Times* and *Tribune?* To this information from
and about the mass media, Zipf added other archival sources.
He asked the number of tons of goods moved by Railway Express between various points, and checked on the number of
bus, railroad, and air passengers between pairs of cities. All of
these were appropriate outcroppings for the test of his hypothesis on inverse proportionality, and in all cases the data conform,
more or less closely, to his prediction.

As yet newspapers and magazines, the print media, provide the only dependable archives for study since television,
radio, movies, and so on, the visual and auditory media, are
either not so dependably archived or else archives are not readily available to those who might want to study them. Both newspapers and magazines may be exploited for the study of
short-lived events, for the study of events that are continuing
(the Iranian hostage "crisis" and its handling in the media may
one day make a fascinating study), or for the monitoring of
trends. When Mao Tse-tung died, it provided an opportunity to
determine the political climate in China, for his death occa-

[1]For general treatment of content analysis, see Berelson (1952); Pool
(1959); North et al. (1963).

sioned an outpouring of obituaries written by a wide variety of persons. Chai (1977) did a content analysis of obituary notices on Mao with the intent of determining the degree of support for the moderates. An index devised by dividing the total number of antirightist symbols by the total number of words proved useful in demonstrating that the military did not strongly prefer moderates over radicals and that the cities were more radical than the provinces.

The media, of course, concentrate on what is of current interest, and that concentration makes it possible to track many phenomena and index the growth and decline of public interest in them. Simón (1979) has commented on the capacity to track the course of fads by the attention paid them by the media. In his paper Simón shows how reports of UFO sightings were influenced by motion picture portrayals of extraterrestial beings and their equipment. The number of English-language science fiction films was markedly higher in the 1950s and 1960s, when the UFO sightings began and peaked, than in previous decades, and UFO reports are remarkable for their resemblance to motion picture portrayals.

The public record characteristic of the newspaper also allows linguistic and lexical analysis. If verbal behavior is really expressive, then one should be able to study a public figure's (for example, a president's) position on issues by studying verbatim transcripts of speeches, press conferences, and other public utterances. Those instances involving stumbles in syntax, or which are prefaced by a string of evasive dependent clauses, may be symptomatic of trouble areas. Interesting, however, is the suggestion that President Eisenhower may deliberately have employed impenetrable syntax as a way of rendering obscure a position he did not want to reveal (Will, 1980). Once we suggested that press conference questions that receive unusually long or short replies might indicate significant content areas. Ray and Webb (1966), however, showed that the length of President Kennedy's responses was closely related to the length of questions asked.

Obviously presidents and other public figures differ greatly in speech style, and any analysis directed toward diagnosing their concern with particular issues would have to take stylistic variations into account. On the other hand, style itself might be examined as of interest in its own right. The speeches of Woodrow Wilson have been studied about as thoroughly as imaginable, providing fascinating indicators of Wilson's personal style. Although quite unfriendly in tone and clearly overdone, Hale's early (1920) analysis of Wilson's speech mannerisms and "affectations" such as alliterations is provocative. Runion's (1936) analysis of Wilson's speeches was more objective, less provocative, but still commanding of interest. For example, the average length of Wilson's sentences was 29.26 words—his style was not Hemingway's. Eisenhower's awkward style of extemporaneous public speech has often been regarded as rather directly reflective of his personal style, although as noted above, caution must be exercised in making any direct interpretations. Barber (1972) has made extensive use of archived material in his analysis of presidential character. On Eisenhower, for example, Barber says, "Ike's very bumbling appears to have made him seem more 'sincere,' . . . Not above letting professional advertising men tell him what to do in his campaigns, Eisenhower as President kept editing warm words out of his speeches" (p. 161). Donley and Winter (1970) examined the inaugural addresses of American presidents from 1905 to 1969, eleven in all, employing the familiar methodology required to score content for need-Achievement and need-Power. The results were thought to be in substantial agreement with the consensus judgments of historians and political scientists concerning the administrations of the presidents involved. An interesting note was that the four presidents who had had attempts made on their lives were higher in both need-Achievement and need-Power than the other seven presidents.

Perhaps a somewhat lower level of journalism is imagined in the reporting of society news, but James (1958) found it useful evidence of community social structure. Although engagement and wedding announcements in newspapers clearly represent a biased sample of such events, they are often rich in detail, especially in smaller cities, and permit many interesting analyses. Clark, Grove, and Sechrest (1980) have been studying newspaper accounts of weddings with respect to such variables as: religious affiliation, inclusion of the groom in the wedding picture, educational level of bride and groom, number of persons in the wedding party, the location chosen for a honeymoon, occupations of bride and groom, marital status of the parents of bride and groom, judged attractiveness of bride, and length of the announcement. Among the early findings are that fundamentalist church affiliation is associated with inclusion of both bride and groom in the published wedding picture, and rated attractiveness of the bride is associated with her education—these findings being perhaps true only in Tallahassee, Florida. Incidentally, we cannot remember having seen a picture of a racially mixed couple in any wedding announcement, nor, for that matter, even an announcement of a marriage detectably mixed. When that begins to occur, it should be noted.

In Tallahassee the newspaper has a policy of publishing all wedding announcements it receives, along with photographs if they are furnished. It is no big deal to get into the Tallahassee paper. Seemingly, it is a big deal to get one's wedding announced in the *New York Times* (Levy, 1980), which is estimated to publish only about one of every four announcements it *receives,* most New Yorkers undoubtedly deciding not even to try. It is reported that in 1947, one half of all "lead" weddings featured either a bride or groom or both from the Social Register, and 57 percent of lead weddings were performed in Episcopalian churches although only 2.5 percent of the paper's coverage area was of that denomination. It was not until 1954 that the *Times* decided to run a photo of a black bride. Today, according to Levy, a *Times* wedding announcement is still a "barometer" of social standing, with use of a photo and amount of space being useful quantifiers.

When citizens write letters to the editors of newspapers or magazines, those citizens become, for as long as files are kept, immortalized. Analysis of letters to editors might show something of the concerns of the public and could certainly be compared to the results of polls. One study that made just such a comparison (Sikorski, Roberts, and Paisley, 1967) found that public concerns over such matters as the Vietnam War and race relations were mirrored in letters to the editor in about the same way as in polls. On the other hand, Grey and Brown (1970) concluded that letters to the editor tell as much about the editor as about the citizenry. Only a small proportion of all letters get published, and those that do are not selected at random. Letters are often instigated by an editorial or by some other letter, and most letters appear to be against something rather than for it. With respect to the latter observation, Saks and Ostrom (1973) studied the differential frequency of signing of letters pro- and antipolice following a police shooting of a black, juvenile burglary suspect and police reaction to several campus demonstrations and disturbances. For both instances antipolice letters were considerably more likely to be signed than propolice letters. The authors consider two explanations tenable, one being that failure to sign has a protective function when revelation of identity might lead to scorn or hostility, and the second is that failure to sign might reflect the person's conception of him or herself as a member of a silent majority.

Much work exists on the political bias of the media. A content analysis of press bias during political campaigns is as predictable as the campaigns themselves. There are many ways in which bias may be manifested: amount of space, attention to negative as opposed to positive events, choice of adjective descriptors, and so on. Westley, et al. (1963) is a good example of a study of bias in news magazines. A fine, relatively unused source of information pertaining to potential bias is photographs. The element of editorial selectivity which is a contaminant in some other studies, for example, of letters to the editor, becomes the center of analysis. Editors have a large pool of photographs of a candidate from which to pick, and the one they eventaully choose is a revealing piece of intelligence. One of the writers has noted this in American political campaigns, and Matthews (1957) has suggested that it is a phenomenon that might be studied across societies. Writing of the British press, he states:

> They [photographs] can be made to lie . . . as Lord Northcliffe was one of the first to discover. When he was using the *Daily Mail* to try to get Asquith out as Prime Minister and Lloyd George in, he once issued this order: "Get a smiling picture of Lloyd George, and underneath put the caption 'Do It Now,' and get the worst possible picture of Asquith and label it: 'Wait and See'" [p. 165].

A television interviewer told Malcolm X, the late Black Nationalist leader, that he was surpised at how much Malcolm smiled.

The black leader said that newspapers refused to print smiling pictures of him. During the political career of Richard Nixon, there were many charges that the press deliberately chose to publish pictures that showed him at his worst, for example, emphasizing his "five o'clock shadow." Was there any change over time?

As in all these studies of the running record, there is the opportunity for time-series analysis. One might well be able to learn whether a medium is changing in its posture to a candidate and determine approximately when the change occurs. The selective practice has been so prevalent over time that it is likely to have little "instrument decay" (Campbell and Stanley, 1963/1966) to invalidate time-series analysis.

But do photographs lie? In a most interesting article on the use of photographs as documents, Jackson (1978) reminds us of the McCarthy hearings concerning the photograph of G. David Shine that had been provided by McCarthy in an attempt to demonstrate a relationship between two persons in time. However, when Attorney Joseph Welch recovered the original print, it had other people in it and gave clear evidence of a totally different relationship among the persons involved. More recently the *Washingtonian* (June, 1979) published three versions of a photograph of Senator Ted Kennedy leaving a meeting. One photograph was clearly devised to make it appear that he was leaving in the company of a very attractive, young, blond woman; the second photograph showed only the senator, and the third photograph included a wide enough angle to make it evident that the senator was, in fact, (well almost certainly) leaving in the company of another male dignitary, a clergyman, and that the young woman was in a completely different party. What makes the photographs especially interesting is that they had all been published in successive editions of the *Washington Star*. Interestingly, the complete, uncropped photo was published only in the *Washingtonian*.

Becker (1978) asks the question, "Do photographs tell the truth?" in a particularly useful and provocative discussion. He concludes that photographic documents tell nothing more than that they exist as photographs. To interpret the photographs, to know what they really mean, one must have additional information about the circumstances of their making and the intent of those presenting them. Becker shows that the approach taken by Campbell and Stanley (1963/1966) in detailing threats to the validity of experiments is applicable to the study and interpretation of photographic documents. Another *Washingtonian* article (Goulden, 1979) shows two pictures of Senator Kennedy and his wife, Joan. One taken in 1976 clearly shows that she was wearing a wedding ring; a second one, taken in the fall of 1979 just as clearly shows that she is not wearing a wedding ring. Presumably the difference is meant to suggest something, but what? Were the photographs a fair sample of her ring-wearing behavior at each time? Does failure to wear a wedding ring in 1979 mean anything in relation to wearing one in 1976, or has the custom of wearing such rings generally declined?

Even the most vitriolic critics of television commercials will admit that the media themselves are a force within the society for socialization of the young and attitude change of the old. Thus, they justify study. G. A. Steiner (1963) demonstrated the salience of television for a national United States sample by showing the extreme alacrity with which sets are repaired. Before television, it had been said that a cigarette was the object so compelling that deprivation would cause one to walk out in a snowstorm. This energy allocation is also inferred in the advertising slogan, "I'd walk a mile for a Camel." Over the past several years great concern has been expressed over the potential vulnerability of young TV viewers, what with the constant commercial messages urging purchase of expensive, flashy toys, sugar-laden foods, and so on. Fortunately, recent studies suggest that parents are by no means pushovers when it comes to acceptance of pleas to purchase, and in any case, children seem to see through commercial messages somewhat better than had been thought (Rubenstein, 1978). Still, studies of the content and style of children's TV commercials might be rewarding.

Sports Media

A subcategory of media that has been of wide interest is sports publications, including the sports pages of newspapers. One of the characteristics of many types of sporting activites is that they are documented so thoroughly, with the consequence that the archives are voluminous. Moreover, there is a high degree of interest in keeping the records as accurately as possible and in detecting and correcting errors when they are found. The idea of rewriting history to make it conform to ideology, as was portrayed in Orwell's *1984,* is probably at least imaginable to most people and meets either cynical amusement or mild disdain. But would even Orwell have dared to suggest that there might be a time when baseball history could be rewritten because a ruling group might wish that the Los Angeles Dodgers had won the 1978 World Series? Truly sports are different. Some of them even march to the cadence of a different drummer. Grauer (1973) found that the New York Stock Exchange is characterized by daily flurries of activity at the beginning and end of every trading session, with the midday period being rather slow. On the other hand, National Football League records show that more plays are run in the second quarter, followed closely by the fourth, then the third, and first. In effect, football games have two deadlines to stimulate increased activity.

Grusky (1963b) wanted to investigate the relationship between adminstrative succession and subsequent change in group performance. One could manipulate leaders in a small group laboratory, but, in addition, one can go, as Grusky did, to the newspapers for more "natural" and less reactive intelligence. From the sports pages and associated records, Grusky learned the performance of various professional football and baseball teams, as well as the timing of changes in coaches and managers. Does changing a manager make a difference, or is it the meaningless machination of a front office looking for a scapegoat? It does make a difference, and this old sports writer's question is a group-dynamics problem, phrased through the stating of two plausible rival hypotheses. In another study, Grusky (1963a) used baseball record books to study "The Effects of Formal Structure on Managerial Recruitment." He learned that former infielders and catchers (high-interaction personnel) were overrepresented among managers, while former pitchers and outfielders (low-interaction personnel) were underrepresented.

One of the hazards often perceived by baseball managers is the trading of a player who will then come back to haunt his old team with especially good performances. Does that occur? Kopelman and Pantaleno (1977) found the evidence for the

hypothesis to be weak over an entire sample of 47 traded players, but there was some support for it among players traded for
the first time, those who had been with their teams a long time,
those who were young, and those with high ability. Stronger
results were obtained for players characterized by two or more
of the listed characteristics.

Another strongly held conviction in sports is that the home
team usually has an advantage. Schwartz and Barsky (1977)
looked at the outcomes of 1880 major-league baseball games,
182 professional football games, 542 professional hockey games,
and 1485 college basketball games, surely a data set that would
be difficult to match in any other field. Sure enough, the home
teams had an advantage, but more for indoor than outdoor
sports. In fact, the outcome of games was as much related to
homefield advantage as to the average ability of a team's players
(teams are, of course, relatively well matched for ability anyway). The home field advantage was more related to offensive
than defensive performance, and it could not be explained by
player fatigue of the visitors nor by lack of familiarity with the
playing area. Rather, it seems generally attributable to the social support of the home audience. Perhaps not so incidentally,
their study of records of a Canadian ice hockey league led
Russell and Drewry (1976) to conclude that crowd size may be
positively related to aggression by players in the game. Aggression increased over the three periods of the games, but it did
not increase over the season.

Those involved in sports contests are often called upon to
explain the outcomes. In the case of coaches, those explanations
may be thought worth publishing in the sports pages. Woodhouse (1978) was interested in studying some of the ideas of
Weiner, et al. (1972) about attributions for success and failure,
but in a real-life setting. Noting that football coaches are often
quoted on the sports pages, Woodhouse identified 450 college
football games that had taken place in 12 southeastern states,
that had been written up in one or more of 12 newspapers, and
that involved direct quotes from one or both coaches in the
news story. After categorizing the responses according to an
appropriate scheme, Woodhouse found that coaches did, as expected, show a strong tendency to attribute success to internal
factors and failure to external factors, with both team or player

ability and team or player effort being often cited as factors in winning. Task difficulty was likely to be cited as a factor after a losing performance. Luck was not often resorted to as an explanation for game outcome by these coaches, but coaches with past records showing them to be winners were likely to mention their good luck after wins, but not losses, and were more likely to mention handicaps such as injuries afflicting their losing opponents. Noblesse oblige. Coaches with losing records were not so magnanimous. Lau and Russell (1980) also studied newspaper attributions for 33 different sporting events and found, as they expected, that winners attributed their successes to their own, stable characteristics ("We're good!), and losers attributed their poor outcomes to external factors beyond their control.

Of course, there are different types of wins, and there were some differences in attributions in Woodhouse's study, depending on whether the outcome of the game was as anticipated and whether the margin of victory or defeat was narrow or large. Tannenbaum and Noah (1959) were interested in the vocabulary of sports outcomes and analyzed the verbs that appeared in sports headlines. They asked how many runs in baseball equal a "romp" or how many points in football equal "rolls over." In addition to providing descriptive information on the empirical limits of such verb usage, they demonstrated a home-town bias. The one-run margin might yield either "Sox Edged 8–7" or "Sox Bludgeon Yankees 8–7." That sports vocabulary is so highly elaborated is a reflection of the principle observed by Zipf (1946) that any phenomenon which must be talked about frequently will be associated with a proportionally large vocabulary. When a sports section must carry the outcomes of dozens of sports events every day, an extensive vocabulary is required to produce any variety at all.

What makes some sports participants better than others, and what makes participants better at some sports than others? Some years ago Worthy (1974) began to study athletic performance in relation to eye color (pigmentation), and he has made considerable use of archived sports information as well as of other archival sources. Worthy claims that persons with dark eyes are generally better at sports activities that involve speed and fast reaction time; light-eyed persons are better at activities that place less emphasis on speed and permit self-pacing. For example, Worthy claims that dark-eyed baseball players do relatively better at hitting (a reactive activity), and light-eyed players do relatively better at pitching. Subsequently, Worthy has used archived information on flying speeds of birds, information recorded by ornithologists presumably interested in accuracy and not reactive to other concerns, to show that light-eyed birds have generally slower flying speeds than dark-eyed birds, and that birds of prey are more likely to be dark-eyed than are birds that feed on seeds, grubs, and so on. Even fruitflies show the relationship between eye color and speed! Worthy's work has been extended to the study of children by Gary and Glover (1976). His work has not, however, gone unchallenged, and Jones and Hochner (1973) found mixed results suggesting that eye color is not a sufficient explanation of sports performance. They found that black (dark eyed) baseball players were better hitters than whites, but black pitchers were also better pitchers. White basketball players were better free-throw shooters than blacks but were not worse off in field goal accuracy, the latter presumably being a reactive activity. Jones and Hochner found that black basketball players shoot relatively more often than they assist in comparison to white players, and they also rebound more often, findings Jones and Hochner think are consistent with their opinion that black-white differences reflect differences in approach to the game rather than differences in reactive vs. self-paced abilities. Note, however, that Jones and Hochner were studying performance in relation to race rather than eye color. Recently, Tedford, Hill, and Hensley (1978) have found that dark-eyed Caucasians of both sexes have faster reaction times than light-eyed Caucasians, the difference being larger for well-practiced responses.

One final note on a sport of a different sort. Optimism is a central element in Griffith's (1949) original and adroit research on horse players. The newspapers supplied the odds, results, and payoffs of 1386 horse races run in the spring and summer of 1947. His hypothesis is worth quoting:

> If the psychological odds equaled the a posteriori [odds] given by the reciprocal of the percentage [of] winners, the product of the number of winners and their odds would equal the number of entries at each odd group after correc-

> tion of the odds had been made for loss due to breakage
> and take. If the product exceeds the number of entries, the
> psychological odds were too large; if the product is less
> than the number of entries, the odds were too small [p.
> 292].

The results, which should receive some distribution beyond the archives of the *American Journal of Psychology,* suggest that long shots and favorites are overbet, while not enough money is put on horses with middle-range odds. Now if one could only find a dark-eyed horse running at middle-range odds!

Analysis of Literary and Other Treasures

Since the advent of print, it has been possible to store up the folklore, fantasies, and other imaginative productions of the storytellers of society. More recently it has become possible to record, via film and videotape, even those productions meant for visual, rather than strictly verbal, enjoyment. If one assumes that such productions reflect in some degree the times and place of which they are a part, then careful analysis of them may be revealing of important and perhaps subtle social phenomena and trends.

In one of the early and still more interesting analyses of movies, Wolfenstein and Leites (1950/1970) explored them for clues to the American psyche, and with some fascinating, if as yet unreplicated, insights. One of the more interesting observations had to do with the characteristically American theme of the "good-bad girl". A frequently encountered movie character is the basically wholesome girl who is, through circumstances not of her doing, in a situation that makes her appear quite wicked. A critical development in the movie, then, is to unmask her so that the hero will see her for the very fine person she truly is. Wolfenstein and Leites believe that the good-bad girl epitomizes the American conflict between the attractions of profane love and the value of sacred love. The French, on the other hand, frequently have as central characters in their movies the bad-good girl, who in the end, wins the hero despite the pain he will suffer. Thus, French movies portray the breaking down of the ideal image of woman. The authors go on to suggest that love never truly ends in American films; if it does, it was not true love and was based on a false premise. We have already mentioned the study by DeCharms and Moeller (1962) of patents and achievement imagery in children's readers, and there have been many other studies of achievement imagery in literature as related to indicators of economic development at the national level. More recently, however, McClelland (1975) has analyzed children's readers for the occurrence of content related to affiliative and power motives, but he also analyzed best-selling novels and hymns for the same content. He then showed that periods of time characterized by high need-Power and low need-Affiliation were likely to be followed by war after 15 or 20 years. Conversely, low need-Power and high need-Affiliation were likely to be followed by peace. McClelland's method provided accurate predictions for 12 out of 13 cases.

Middleton (1960), mentioned earlier, did a longitudinal study of the fertility values in magazine fiction, linking them to actuarial fertility data. This research suggests that media, if carefully selected, can serve as a mirror of society's values—or at least of some selective elements within the society. Thus, even though there is no objective indicator against which to judge it, Brown's (1978) finding that over a 74-year period the advice given in marriage advice columns in women's magazines gave evidence of increasingly egalitarian marital roles is of interest. Brown, incidentally, cited the second sentence in this paragraph as justification for his study. Perhaps, then, of even greater interest is the study by Scully and Bart (1973) on the portrayal of women in gynecological textbooks over a period of time ranging from 1943 to 1972. The textbooks were clearly written from a male's point of view and showed disappointingly little evidence of having been influenced by research findings on female sexuality.

Race relations have also been approached by way of literary analysis. Schulman (1974) selected 20 biographical and historical books written in the 1960s by both white and black authors and studied the ways in which interactions between persons of different races had been portrayed. The findings were diverse, but among them were that males of both races are more dominant over women of their own race than over women of another race and that both men and women are warmer in interactions with members of their own race and with members of the opposite sex.

Even cartoons may be grist for the mill of the literary analyst. How are psychologists, psychiatrists, and other psychologically oriented personnel differentiated by the society? One can ask people of course, and one should. But of value, too, is a study of what the mass media contain on the question. Ehrle and Johnson (1961) plucked 4760 cartoons, all of which pictured psychological personnel, from six different consumer magazines. Their evidence suggests no substantial differentiation among the groups. This finding could be further tested by observing psychologists at cocktail parties and noting how often they are asked, "now how is a psychologist different from a psychiatrist?" Or one could ask the psychologists to relate their cocktail party experiences.

MULTIPLE CONFIRMATION

Ray (1965) has written of multiple confirmation through different sources of published material, noting as an example, "values of Hitler's Germany were compared with those of other countries by content analyses of plays (McGranahan and Wayne, 1948), songbooks (Sebald, 1962), handbooks for youth organizations (Lewin, 1947), speeches (White, 1949), and the press (Lasswell, 1941)."

In what is virtually a tour de force in the exploitation of multiple sources of information and inference, Sales (1973) set out to test the hypothesis that people tend to become more authoritarian when under threat. Reasoning that the great depression of the 1930s was a source of strong and continuing threat in comparison to the more comfortable years of the 1920s, Sales looked for reflections of authoritarianism in the two time periods. Since authoritarians are said to admire power and strength, Sales examined comic strips from the two decades. Of 20 comic strips that made their initial appearance in the 1920s, only two stressed the power of the main character; by way of contrast, 12 of 21 started during the 1930s stressed the power of the protagonist. Another authoritarian characteristic, cynicism, was also more prevalent in the 1930s as indicated by an analysis of magazine articles from major periodicals. Superstition was greater in the 1930s if the number of books published on astrology may be taken as an indication, and authoritarian submission was suggested by the fact that only eight state legislatures had passed laws requiring loyalty oaths during the 1920s, but 17 did so in 1930s. There also appeared to be more books published in the 1920s that were critical of the United States. Authoritarians are supposed to be disinclined to self-examination of their inner thoughts and motives, and publication of both magazine articles and books on psychoanalysis and psychotherapy decreased fairly dramatically from the 1920s to the 1930s. Moreover, statistics from American public high schools showed a drop in the number of students studying psychology between the two decades. Although the available statistics indicated a decline in crime in the 1930s, the percentage of the city budget devoted to the police force increased in both New York City and Pittsburgh. Herbert Hoover made virtually no reference to crime during his 1928 election campaign, but in 1932, he devoted a whole speech to the problem, although crime rates had not gone up at all. Court records of Allegheny County, Pennsylvania, showed that some criminals were also treated more harshly in the 1930s, for the average sentence bestowed upon rapists in the 1920s was 3.4 years, but in the 1930s it was 4.7 years.

Sales also believed that the period from 1959 to 1964 was a relatively low threat time, and that 1967–1970 could be characterized as high threat—for example, crime rates were much higher, civil disturbances were much more frequent, inflation was on the rise, there were more labor disputes, American men were being killed in Vietnam, and drug usage was increasing rapidly during the later time period. Public opinion polls also showed a rise in anxiety in the college population and a rise in the fears of the citizenry about the future of the nation. There was also an increase in the number of registered "attack" dogs (German Shepards, Dobermans, Great Danes) and a drop in the registrations of "lap" dogs as indicated by the American Kennel Club. During the high threat years there were more heavyweight boxing championship fights and there were more persons making their living by boxing according to census data. Total gate receipts from boxing also went up. Subscriptions to a conservative periodical, the *Christian Beacon,* were also far higher in the later, high threat period.

One can only admire the diligence and imagination displayed by Sales and be impressed by the consistency of the reported data.

THE STUDY OF INSTITUTIONS

The use of archival data is not limited to the study of groups of persons. A variety of records can also be exploited to study human institutions. The more interesting examples are studies of cities, but courts, police departments, legislative bodies, and many other institutions could be studied from archived data in the public domain. By using the media, even corporations, department stores (advertising), and many other private institutions could be studied.

Of all the studies using available records, few can measure up to E. L. Thorndike's (1939) work on the goodness of cities. Aware that "only the impartial study of many significant facts about cities enables us to know them" (p. 147), Thorndike gathered 37 core pieces of information about each of 310 United States communities. To develop his "goodness scale," he combined these to produce 297 characteristics for each city. And this in the era before computers! Examples of Thorndike's measures are infant death rate, percentage of sixteen- and seventeen-year-olds attending school, average salary of high-school teachers, and per capita acreage of public parks.

Thorndike went further and gathered ratings of the cities from various occupational groups. He noted that "thoughtful people realize that popular opinions about cities, are likely to err" (p. 142). How far they are likely to err (using his statistical data as criteria) is demonstrated by these findings: infrequency of extreme poverty correlates .69 with Thorndike's overall goodness of cities, but –.18 for the judgments of clergymen and social workers; the infant death rate (reversed) correlates .82 with the aggregate statistical index, but .03 with businessmen's ratings of the cities. Few could read this report and not reap methodological profit.

Obviously cities change over time, and Thorndike's list might not be an especially useful guide today for anyone looking to relocate. Fortunately, some more recent lists are available. The Midwest Research Institute (1970) assembled data for 65 U.S. cities with populations of 500,000 or greater, the measures including economic, political, environmental, health, education, and social variables. For example, the environmental variables included an air pollution index, percent dilapidated houses, number of sunshine days, and number of hot and number of cold days. The political variables included newspaper circulation, proportion of population registered to vote, salaries of municipal workers, crime rate, and average welfare payments. The results of the analysis showed cities in the Northwest, West, and Midwest to rank relatively high.

Still more recently, Louis (1975) set out, for some strange reason, to discover the *worst* American city, a goal perhaps unattainable since he limited his analysis to 50 cities. Louis used archived data from the Uniform Crime Reports, Vital Statistics of the United States, the Census Bureau, *Who's Who*, the Environmental Protection Agency, the American Library Directory, and *Leahy's Hotel-Motel Guide* to get information on 24 variables. The worst (among the 50) American city turned out to be Newark. The best? Seattle, by a narrow margin over Tulsa and San Diego.

Persons working overseas are often interested in knowing the level of development of cities with which they are not familiar. An analogous concern in this country would be to know the level of sophistication of a city in which one was offered a job. McKendry and Parco (1967) worked on the problem in the Philippines, approaching it by means of a Guttman scale. The items employed were such things as whether a community had a municipal building (nearly all did), a resident physician (fewer did), electricity (still fewer), a bank, piped water, and finally, such telling discriminators at the high end of the scale as a hospital, a public phone, a park, and a hotel. On the whole the scale worked quite well.

Some years ago one of the authors encountered a column by the humorist Goodman Ace entitled "How to Tell a City." The problem was, Ace averred, that in the good old days one could tell whether a place was really a city by whether it had a major league baseball team, but the growth of the country has outstripped the supply of major league teams, and there may be cities without teams. Therefore, Ace proposed a scale which included such items as the following: a main street shopping area without an Army-Navy store (1 point); taxicabs with meters (1 point); no one tells you how far it is from someplace else (1 point); it has a symphony orchestra (1 point) and no one tells you about it (2 points). The 1979 *World Almanac* provides data on several characteristics of U.S. cities, presumably provided originally by the cities themselves. Kansas City, Chicago, and Los Angeles do not report having symphony orchestras, and New York reports only having a place for one to play. Newark, Louisville, San Jose, and Birmingham all get one point.

It would also be useful to have some unobtrusive indicators of the mood of a city, and a list of potential indicators of urban unrest was once prepared for Washington, D.C. The list included damage to street lights, defacement of public buildings, sales records of militant publications, requests to authorities for increase in street lighting, sales of door locks, enrollment in gun handling courses, and incidence of false fire alarms. The latter is interesting because in their study of conflict between fire fighters and ghetto dwellers, Shaver, Schurtman, and Blank (1975) found that false alarms were quite well predicted by a linear combination of six variables: nearby vacant lots, nearby open, abandoned buildings, nearby schools, nearby playgrounds, heavily traveled streets (negative), and nearby stores with windows providing a view of the alarm box (negative). False alarms were associated geographically with areas in which fire fighters were likely to be harrassed by people.

Universities and their individual departments can be and have been studied by way of archived information. Many people wonder what are the best universities and departments in which to study, and survey data do exist (Cartter, 1966; Roose and Anderson, 1970). Of greater interest here is a study of British, Canadian, and U.S. departments of psychology in terms of citations of articles published by their faculty members. The *Social Science Citation Index* provides a convenient way of obtaining such information, and Endler, Rushton, and Roediger (1978) did an analysis of citations and found that Stanford's psychology department was at the top in terms of both total number of citations and mean number of citations per faculty member. Stanford had been ranked number one also in the 1970 Roose-Anderson survey.

DATA TRANSFORMATIONS AND
INDEXES OF THE RUNNING RECORD

Of all the different classes of data treated in this monograph, none has so great a need for transformation as those cited in this chapter. Because the data are drawn from continuous records which typically extend over long periods of time, all the extraneous events of history are at work to threaten valid research comparisons.

Perhaps the most obvious of these is the change in the size of the population. The population increase has meant that the absolute values of actuarial and allied data are relatively useless for comparative purposes. In studies employing election records, for instance, the absolute number of votes cast provides an inadequate base for most research purposes. Beginning with the election in 1864, in 21 of 29 presidential elections the winning candidate received more votes than the winning candidate in the previous election. The 39 million votes for Ford in 1976 would have won any election except the one in 1976, Nixon's in 1972, and Johnson's in 1964. Similarly, the absolute number of entries associated with population level has changed over time. This secular trend in the data is often best removed. Thus, Ianni (1957-1958) had to construct a relative index of residential mobility over time, and DeCharms and Moeller (1962) transformed patent production to an index tied to population.

Time also works its effect by a change in the composition of a critical group. The number of members of the House of Representatives may stay relatively stable over a long time period, but the characteristics of these members of Congress change—and, in changing, produce a set of rival hypotheses for some investigator's explanation of a research comparison. A reapportionment of the House (to reflect population distribution more adequately) can mean substantial changes in the aggregate voting behavior of the House, influencing the decisional setting for all members of Congress, both those there before the change and the new members.

With known changes in composition, it may be necessary to segregate research findings by time periods in which relatively homogeneous external conditions held. This is a grosser correction than the more continuous correction possible for data linked to population. Even with population, though, the only thoroughly reliable data—the census totals—are produced only once every ten years. The accuracy of intervening estimates, whether from the Census Bureau itself or the highly reliable *Sales Management* magazine, are high but still imperfect.

The frailty of individual sets of records, which is discussed below, has caused investigators to employ indexes which combine several different types or units of information. The adequacy of such combinations rests, of course, on the degree to which the component elements are adequate outcroppings of the research hypothesis, as well as the degree to which appropriate weights can be assigned to the elements. Setting these questions aside, however, it is apparent that combined indexes must be employed when an investigator lacks a theory so precise and subtle as to predict a single critical test, or, when the theory's precision is adequate, no data exist for the critical test. For E. L. Thorndike's (1939) purpose in studying cities, there was no acceptable alternative to transforming such data as park area and property values into indexes. And for MacRae (1954b) and Riker and Niemi (1962) the unstable nature of a single vote by a congressman forced the construction of indexes of samples of votes, which were hopefully a less ephemeral source for comparisons. MacRae needed a "liberal index," Riker and Niemi, an "index of coalitions." Because the individual unit was highly suspect as a sampling of the critical behavior under study, the sampling had to be expanded. There occurs, too, the attendant questions of how the units are to be stated, weighted, and combined.

One of the major gains of the running record, then, is the capability to study a hypothesis as external conditions vary over time. Such analysis demands that the investigator consider all possible transformations before making comparisons, and also decide whether indexes will provide a more stable and valid base for hypothesis testing. This requirement is not as pronounced in the discontinuous archival records cited in the chapter that follows nor among the observational and physical-evidence methods.

ARCHIVES ARE WHERE YOU FIND THEM

Undoubtedly many things are never archived, but the total quantity of material that is in some way recorded and stored is staggering. What is needed are researchers who know where to look and what to do with what they find. We cannot begin to provide a list of archives, but we do want to note here some of the types of official data that are available, more as a stimulant to readers to look even further afield than as suggestions for specific investigations.

The federal government, of course, collects and stores large amounts of data of all kinds, nearly all of which is available in one form or another under the Freedom of Information Act. A great deal of information collected by the government is published and is readily available. One of the most interesting and useful government publications is the *Statistical Abstract of the United States.* This yearly publication contains information on almost every aspect of our society, and the fact that the information is published yearly makes it very easy to study trends over time. Very little of the information in the *Abstract* is cross-classified, leaving much to the imagination of a hard-working researcher. *The World Almanac* is published yearly and distributed through major newspapers. It has been published yearly since 1886 and contains an extraordinary variety of information, some patently trivial, but some potentially exploitable for interesting purposes. Does it mean anything that the number of poodles registered with the American Kennel Club decreased substantially from 1976 to 1977? Why does Portland have only two buildings taller than 300 feet when Minneapolis has nine? Newspapers also report regularly on many phenomena of potential interest to social scientists. The *Washington Post,* for example, publishes a weekly business section that provides information on economic indicators. The number of passengers in the three airports serving Washington, D.C. was down by more than 100,000 from a week in March of

1979 to the same week in 1980. Washington, D.C. gained about 5000 gas meters from 1979 to 1980, and the housing-cost index increased by about 13 percent over the year. The *Post* also regularly publishes "best seller" lists for books separately for Washington, D. C. and the nation. Books with political themes, whether fiction or nonfiction, almost always sell better in Washington. Where else? Obviously many other archives could be listed, but any interested investigator can locate them if his or her level of awareness is increased sufficiently to notice them. They are there.

OVERALL EVALUATION OF RUNNING RECORDS

It should be obvious that we prize the potential for historical analysis contained in running records.

> The best fact is one that is set in a context, that is known in relation to other facts, that is perceived in part in the context of its past, that comes into understanding as an event which acquires significance because it belongs in a continuous dynamic sequence ... (Boring, 1963, p. 5).

If a research hypothesis, particularly for social behavior, can survive the assaults of changing times and conditions, its plausibility is far greater than if it were tested by a method that strips away alien threats and evaluates the hypothesis in an assumptive, one-time test. Validity can be inferred from a hypothesis' robustness. If the events of time are vacillating, as they usually are, then only the valid hypothesis has the intellectual robustness to be sustained, while rival hypotheses expire.

One pays a price in such time-series analysis, the necessary price of uncertainty. We again agree with that gentle stylist Boring (1963): "The seats on the train of progress all face backwards; you can see the past but only guess about the future" (p. 5). A hypothesis might not hold for anything but the past, but if the present is tested, and a new, possibly better, hypothesis produced, those same running records are available, as economical as ever, for restudy and new testing.

For all the gains, however, the gnawing reality remains that archives have been produced for someone else and by someone else. There must be a careful evaluation of the way in which the records were produced, for the risk is high that one is getting a cut-rate version of another's errors. Udy (1964) wrote of ethnographic data:

> Researchers who use secondary sources are always open to the charge that they are cavalier and uncritical in their use of source materials, and cross cultural analysis—particularly when large numbers of societies are used with information taken out of context—is particularly vulnerable to such criticism (p. 179).

At the beginning of this chapter, we detailed the operating questions of selective deposit and selective survival of archives. Both these contaminants can add significant restrictions to the content and contributing populations of the archival materials. In the discussion of individual research studies, we have noted how roll-call votes, marriage records, reports of congressional speeches, letters to the editor, crime reports, and other records are all subject to substantial population or content restrictions in their initial recording. To a lesser degree, the selective survival of records can be a serious contaminant, and in certain areas, such as politics, it is always a prime question.

Those contaminants that threaten the temporal and cross-sectional stability of the data are controllable through data transformation and indexing methods—if they can be known. Happily, one of the more engaging attributes of many of these records is that they contain a body of auxiliary data that allows the investigator good access to knowledge of the population restrictions. We have noted this for the absentee contaminant in congressional voting and the selective choice of cases in judicial proceedings. With the actuarial material on birth, marriage, and death, it is often possible to find within the records, or in associated data series such as the census, information that will provide checks on the extent to which the research population is representative of the universe to which the findings are to be generalized.

If the restrictions can be known, it is possible to consider the alternative of randomly sampling from the body of records, with a stratification control based on the knowledge of the population restriction. This is feasible for many of the records we have mentioned because of their massiveness. Indeed, even if no substantial population contaminants exist, it is often advisable to sample the data because of their unwieldy bulk. Since usually they can be divided into convenient sampling units, and also frequently classified in a form appropriate for stratification, the ability to sample archival materials, particularly those in a continuous series, is a decided advantage for this class of data. The sampling of observations, or of traces of physical evidence, is markedly more difficult.

The population restrictions are potentially controllable through auxiliary intelligence; the content restrictions are more awkward. For all the varied records available, there may still be no single set, or combination of sets, that provides an appropriate test of an hypothesis.

Something of this content rigidity is reflected in Walter Lippmann's (1955) discussion of the "decline of the west." Lippmann writes of the turn of the century when

> The public interest could be equated with that which was revealed in election returns, in sales reports, balance sheets, circulation figures, and statistics of expansion. As long as peace should be taken for granted, the public good could be thought of as being immanent in the aggregate of private transactions (p. 16).

Yet many of the studies reported in this chapter have revealed the power of insightful minds to see appropriate data where associates only see "someone else's" records. There is little explicit in patent records, city water pressure archives, parking meter collection records, or children's readers to suggest their research utility. It required imagination to perceive the application, and a willingness to follow an unconventional line of data collection. Imagination cannot, of course, provide data if none are there. Our thesis is solely that the content limitations of archival records are not as great as the social scientist bound by orthodoxy thinks.

There is no easy way of knowing the degree to which reactive measurement errors exist among running archival records. These are secondhand measures, and many of them are contaminated by reactive biases, while others are not. The politician voting on a bill is well aware that his action will be noted by others; he may not be aware that an observer in the gallery made a note of the tic in his left eye when his name was called to vote. The records contributed by the person or group studied —the votes, the speeches, the entries written for directories— are produced with an awareness that they may be interpreted as expressive behavior. Thus, those errors that come from awareness of being tested, from role elicitation, from response sets, and from the act of measurement as a change agent are all potentially working to confound comparisons. With other data, such as the reports of presidential press conferences and census figures, the investigator has the additional bias of possible interviewer error passed along.

For data collected by a second party, by someone other than the producer (birth and death records, weather reports, power failures, patents, and the like), the risk of awareness, role, or interviewer contaminants is present but low. The main problem becomes one of instrument decay. Has the record-keeping process been constant or knowably variant over the period of study? Suicides in Prussia jumped 20 percent between 1882 and 1883. It may be that response sets on the part of the record-keepers, or a change in administrative practice, threatens valid comparisons across time periods or geographic areas. To know of this variation is extremely difficult, and it represents one of the major drawbacks to archival records.

In summary, the running archival records offer a large mass of pertinent data for many substantive areas of research. They are cheap to obtain, easy to sample, and the population restrictions associated with them are often knowable and controllable through data transformations and the construction of indexes. But all content is not amenable to study by archival records, and there is an ever-present risk that reactive or other elements in the data-producing process will cause selective deposit or survival of the material. Against this must be balanced the opportunity for longitudinal studies over time, studies in which one may test a hypothesis by subjecting it to the rigor of evaluation in multiple settings and at multiple times.

CHAPTER 5

Overt Ethics for Covert Measurement

The first edition of *Unobtrusive Measures* was completed at a time when concerns about ethics of research in the social and behavioral sciences were only beginning to be brought to the fore, and, although the book is sprinkled with reminders about ethical problems, they now sound much more like urgings toward good manners than serious ethical prescriptions. By the time of publication of *Unobtrusive Measures* there were clear signals that ethical problems of a most serious nature were going to be posed. Milgram (1963) had initiated his series of articles on obedience to authority and had been smartly challenged by Baumrind (1964). The work of Berkun, et al. (Berkun, Bialek, Kern, and Yagi, 1962) on effects of stress on performance had created a considerable furor because of the powerful stress that was created in young soldiers. In the 1980s, sensitivity to ethical issues and general ethical principles underlying research are taught in university courses and in continuing education programs. Since the first edition of this book, considerable attention has been focused on ethics in research. One example is the recent *Ethics in Social and Behavioral Research* by Diener and Crandall (1978), a general and comprehensive treatment of ethical issues. Also, the National Commission for the Protection of Human Subjects of Biomedical and Behavioral Research, established by legislation in 1974, has published several sets of recommendations and explanatory and exploratory essays and studies in a series of reports and appendices. The summary reports and recommendations have been published in the *Federal Register*. The complete reports and appendices are available from the National Technical Information Service.

144

WHAT ARE THE ETHICAL ISSUES
IN UNOBTRUSIVE MEASUREMENT?

There are many ethical issues that may be raised in the context of a research enterprise, but there are two major issues that are especially likely to be encountered in research involving unobtrusive measurement. There is, first, the issue of privacy, which is likely to become problematic because for so many unobtrusive measures the very measurement procedures employed are meant to evade the awareness of the person and, hence, threaten to jeopardize private concerns. The second issue is informed consent from those participating as subjects in research, an issue again arising out of the inherent nature of many nonreactive measures since they are meant to be carried out without awareness or even cooperation of the research subject. To the extent that either the right to privacy or the necessity for informed consent, both aspects of the ethical principle respect for persons, is regarded as inviolate, use of nonreactive measures may be ruled out. We will argue that neither is inviolate, but that both place limits on what may ethically be done in the name of nonreactive measures.

RIGHT TO PRIVACY

Privacy is a value held dear by most Americans, perhaps to a greater extent than by many other people. Smith (1976) notes, for example, that Russians seem to place much less value on privacy than Americans, and they do not, in fact, even have a word for privacy in their language. In the United States privacy is codified as a "right" (Privacy Act of 1974), and there are legal remedies for violations (invasions—the words are suggestive of offense) of privacy. In addition, however, privacy is, if not a right, at least a strongly supported privilege in the codes of ethics of (probably) most national academic organizations involved in social and behavioral research (for example, see American Psychological Association, 1973; American Sociological Association, 1971; American Association of Public Opinion Research, 1979; American Anthropology Association, 1980).

It is, however, easier by far to insist that privacy be respected than to specify just what privacy means and whether there are any limits on it. We think that there is a continuum represented by the situations in which behavior might possibly be observed, and at one end of the continuum privacy certainly could not be said to be violated, and at the other end it just as certainly is violated. In between there is an area in which it is difficult to draw very distinct boundaries and in which much will depend, as does so much of any ethical system, on individual judgments (perhaps in some cases on "situation ethics").

At one end of the continuum there is the public behavior of public figures. There can be no objection, for example, to linguistic analysis of the speeches of politicians, to analysis of their gestures in videotaped performances, and the like. Media figures must endure the omnipresent paparazzi with their cameras and must expect that their every move may be observed and reported by some paid observer or another or even by unpaid observers operating from occasionally malicious motives. High ranking politicians inebriated anywhere they can be seen are fair game, or so it seems. Less public persons apparently may lay claim to some slight degree of privacy even in public places, for example, making public the names of men arrested in the company of prostitutes is probably widely regarded as a breach of justifiable privacy. A mayor of Boston once did publicize the names of prominent citizens who were delinquent in their real estate taxes by means of a large billboard, but public pressure forced him to end the practice quickly.

The privacy problem for nonpublic figures centers around their presumed lack of awareness that they might be being observed at all, even though in a public place. A citizen might well scratch himself while in the aisle of a market, but he would not expect that note be taken of that fact and recorded in some logbook. Would the subjects in Sechrest and Flores's (1971) study of leg jiggling in coffee shops and bars have been offended had they known that strangers were taking note of their scarcely conscious behavior, and was it a violation of their privacy? Most such observations are harmless enough and they do not raise any very serious ethical problems, although we caution that specific instances need to be considered carefully by individual investigators.

Clearly in a middle position on the continuum are public places that, because of their particular nature, may be regarded as momentarily private or which, again because of their particular nature, are regarded as socially and psychologically private, even though they are in a strict sense public. An example of the former place is the secluded area of a park or field where no observers are visible. If persons engaged in personal matters, whether of the heart or the pocketbook, are seen by observers hiding themselves or by observers at a distance using binoculars, those persons may with justice feel that their privacy has been invaded. One of the less attractive habits of the notorious paparazzi is to use telephoto lenses in order to get pictures of celebrities in states of undress under what they would certainly consider private conditions. We could not condone such invasions of privacy for research purposes (their use for legal purposes is up to the courts).

There are some places in which most persons clearly expect that their behavior will be unregarded, even if the place is in a real sense public; it is a place in which the fiction of privacy is to be maintained. It is this set of expectations that was the basis for the furor over the work of Humphreys (1970) and Middlemist, Knowles, and Matter (1976). Both research projects were carried out in "public" toilets, but people do not enter public toilets with the expectation that their behavior will be of any interest to anyone else in the establishment; their expectation is likely to be that their behavior will be studiously ignored. One of the features of public toilets that makes them tolerable is the understanding that other people will not take advantage of the opportunity to look or listen. Even in the case of the research by Humphreys on the behavior of homosexuals in a public toilet, the homosexuals, while expecting to be noticed, were not expecting to be noticed in the way that they were.

Actually each of the two investigations just mentioned involved an exacerbating feature that compounded the simple ethical problem of making observations of private behavior in public places. Humphreys copied down the auto license numbers of participants in homosexual activities and later obtained their home addresses from the Department of Motor Vehicles and sent an interviewer to their homes on the pretext of interviewing them on unrelated matters but so as to get a variety of personal information from them. In the Middlemist, et al. study the investigators used a periscope device so as to be able to determine the mean length of flow of urine both with and without an observer being apparent. Both exacerbating procedures undoubtedly contributed very heavily to the extent of criticism directed to the investigators in the two studies. We do emphasize, however, that both studies were carried out for serious scientific purposes with no thought of demeaning anyone, that both studies appear to have been carried out with ample safeguards for protecting subjects, and that in neither case has any evidence of harm to any subject ever been made public. The ethical controversy has involved principles, not consequences.

At the extreme of the invasion of privacy continuum is "spying" on private behavior. Although never much employed by scientific investigators, there have been instances in which persons in obviously private settings have been subjected to surveillance, one of the most astounding instances being the hiding of observers under beds in students' rooms to eavesdrop on conversation (Henle and Hubble, 1938). Although such spying has its place in some parts of the criminal justice system, it cannot be accepted as legitimate in science today. Even in the context of justice, such behavior has been questioned, as demonstrated in the issues raised by the "Abscam" cases of 1980.

We reiterate that we are not sure just where lines should be drawn, and we probably would not even agree completely among ourselves. Where the recording of behavior requires no special stimulus augmenting devices nor such undue intimacy as might be involved in slipping up on people without their awareness, and when the behavior is occurring in places that everyone would agree are psychologically as well as legally public, there should be no serious ethical objection. Otherwise, ethical objections might be raised with individual differences in sensitivity (or squeamishness) being determinant until a clear intrusion on privacy is achieved.

When Is Privacy Violated?

Suppose a museum wished to know what its patrons really thought of and had to say about its exhibits and therefore concealed a recording device within certain key exhibits to record comments during visiting hours. At least if the museum were reasonably busy and if reasonable precautions were taken, it would be possible to record spontaneous conversation while still guaranteeing anonymity to those being recorded. Would the guarantee of anonymity protect the right of privacy? Note that although museum conversations occur in public places, they often occur without the expectation that they are, in fact, public. In a study of the production of graffiti by college students (Rhyne and Ullman, 1972), observers checked toilet stalls after each use to determine whether any graffiti had been produced by the previous user. Does that violate privacy? There has thus far been no objection on grounds of invasion of privacy when graffiti are recorded from walls after their production. How is the study of anonymous graffiti different from anonymous recorded conversations? In the first place, graffiti may be regarded as being produced specifically for the purpose of being seen, if not for scientific study. Second, the immediacy of conversations, all produced in a few hours, may be troubling in comparison to graffiti produced over a considerable time span.

There may be a more general, and in the long run, more important problem stemming from recording conversations, from videotaping interactions surreptitiously and so forth. Although it may be possible in a specific instance to protect anonymity of individual subjects, widespread surreptitious recording and filming for any purposes would eventually create a social climate of suspicion that might interfere in important ways with the ordinary freedom of social intercourse. Although that concern is more pragmatic than principled, we think it an important one and would discourage surreptitious recording even if individual anonymity could be absolutely guaranteed.

Warning:
Your Privacy May Be Invaded
Under some circumstances it may be possible to warn people that they *may* be subject to concealed observation or recording. For example, one could put a sign at the entrance to a museum indicating that conversations might be recorded. Would that resolve the ethical issue surrounding invasion of privacy? It might, but it would have to be recognized that if the

warning were sufficiently explicit at least some degree of reactivity would be likely. We would not, for example, think it ethical to place such a warning at the entrance to a building and then record conversations in the bathrooms of that building. If patrons were given a sufficient warning, they might well guess that the topic of interest was reactions to exhibits, and that might lead some persons to very deliberate and self-conscious statements, for example, "Hey, if you are listening, I think this is a great exhibit."

Another possibility for some kinds of observations would be to do the observations (or recordings), and then inform people afterwards and ask their permission for use of the material. That was the procedure followed by Allen Funt in producing the popular and long-running TV show *Candid Camera.* Such a procedure is probably acceptable for a commercial enterprise if reasonable precautions are taken, but we are dubious of the use of such a procedure in science. Certainly if any sizable number of persons refused permission, the censoring would jeopardize the proper interpretation of the observed behavior. We are not sure that it is advisable for social scientists to become identified as snoopers even if, after the fact, most people prove not to mind having been snooped on.

We do have something of a paradox here in the fact that social science researchers must abide by ethical principles that do not constrain ordinary citizens. It may be in bad taste for an ordinary citizen to observe (and record) a wide variety of behaviors, but if no law is broken, the citizen's conscience is his or her only guide. Science is characterized by a collective conscience expressed in ethical principles, and adherence to those principles can be enforced, when necessary, by sanctions, even to the point of professional ostracism.

Confidentiality of Information

A subset of privacy issues arises out of assuring that research data are kept confidential once they are collected. Privacy can be violated by the release of information, even that given willingly, as well as by the process of collecting it in the first place. For most research involving most respondents, confidentiality poses no great problems in the social and behavioral sciences. Most research is relatively innocuous, protection of confidentiality is reasonably good, no one is much interested in the data, and no one knows very well what to make of them if confidentiality were breached. That set of circumstances should not lull social scientists into a sense of security, however, for some data are not so innocuous, people feel rather differently even about having innocuous things about them made public, and one cannot always anticipate the uses to which data may be put. Certainly nonreactive measurers should be as careful as, or more careful than, any other researchers in the protection given to the confidentiality of research data.

Nor should it be forgotten that groups, including perhaps entire ethnic groups or cultures, can be damaged by release of information about them. Probably relatively few individuals would like to have their sexual practices made public in great detail, and it may be that ethnic or cultural groups would just as soon not have their sexual practices written up for publication either. Alcoholics Anonymous, to cite a specific example, makes a point of refusing to be studied by social scientists, and we would think it an ethical breach for a participant observer to obtain entry to an AA group for the purposes of describing its membership and functioning. Would it be an ethical breach for a social scientist deceitfully to penetrate a right wing, violence-prone group for the purposes of studying it and publishing the results? We think it probably would be.

There are not absolute rules that can be invoked with respect to the requirement that social scientists maintain the confidentiality of their data files and that they do not publish information that would be damaging to a person or group. For a variety of reasons, we Americans are more concerned about damage to persons than to groups, and scientists should go to the greatest lengths to ensure that individuals are not damaged by breaches of confidentiality concerning information obtained about them in the course of their participation, wittingly or unwittingly, in scientific investigations. (In December 1979, the Supreme Court let stand a $75,000 libel award against a novelist on the basis of what was considered a too thinly disguised portrayal in a novel. Psychologists who too thinly disguise the identities of their research subjects might be the targets of similar suits.) The situation with respect to groups is more complicated in every respect, but clearly there should be compelling reasons to publish scientific data that might bring a group of any kind into disrepute or expose group members to ridicule and scorn. The exact point to draw the line would involve complex considerations concerning the group's degree of cooperation in producing the data, the knowledge of the group of the purposes of the data, the degree of damage and so on. It should be incumbent upon the scientist to present the rationale for any seeming breach.

Interestingly, ethical problems among historians revolve around possible concealment of information rather than unwarranted revelations. The very purpose of history is to expose truth. There would probably be agreement among historians that irrelevant truths need not be revealed, for example the discovery of the true paternity of a public figure might not need to be revealed in a history of economic policies. In general, however, for a historian to conceal a relevant truth would be regarded as "unethical" and "would be fatal" to his or her career (Link, personal communication, 1980). Serious controversies have, in fact, arisen when biographers have been less than frank; but it should be pointed out that these biographers have rarely been historians.

An excellent and comprehensive review of privacy issues and methods for "assuring" privacy has recently been written by Boruch and Cecil (1979). The book should be familiar to every social scientist involved in work in which there is risk of damage or ethical deviation stemming from lapses in confidentiality.

Protection of Personal Dignity

Above all, we think that the issue of protection of privacy comes down to the right of people to whatever personal dignity can be accorded them by scientists who wish to study their behavior and is one aspect of the general ethical principle, respect for persons. That principle incorporates respect for autonomy and protection of persons whose autonomy is temporarily or permanently diminished. It should not be necessary for scientists to diminish the dignity of their subjects in any important way, and if it seems necessary in order to do the research, then perhaps the research should not be done. Since dignity resides in the relationships between people, the researcher should be free of any sense that he or she is assaulting the dignity of a person. There are many behaviors that are considered private, even when they occur in public places, and to make attempts to observe them furtively, even if not surreptitiously, may create a kind of relationship that is conducive to one-sided scorn or contempt. We would tend to discourage the study of such behaviors. We do, on the other hand, conclude with Diener and Crandall (1978) that a great deal of social science research, including most observations most of the time in most public places is inherently harmless and should not be impeded by overly strict interpretations of the right to privacy.

INFORMED CONSENT

The ethical principle, respect for persons, was adopted by the National Commission for the Protection of Human Subjects of Biomedical and Behavioral Research and is implicitly, if not explicitly, part of most codes governing research with humans. It follows that participants in research should be informed of, understand, and consent to their involvement. The consent process, then, has two components: "informed" means that research subjects must be told and must comprehend the nature of the research, its purposes, procedures, the risks that may be entailed, the benefits they might expect to receive, if any, that they are free to withdraw at any time, and the responsible scientist to contact for information about results or for resolution of resultant problems or harms. The voluntary aspect of consent means that research subjects must be in a position to assume willingly the procedures, risks, and benefits of the research. It there is coercion, even subtle coercion, then consent, if offered, may not be considered voluntary. Thus, if students are required by an instructor to participate in an experiment, the voluntary aspect of consent is violated. When students are required to participate in some research projects of their choice, it may be violated less, particularly if there is an alternative to research participation and that alternative is not notably unattractive. Information and voluntariness may vary and reflect levels of respect for persons and their autonomy.

In some social science and behavioral research, however, the direct application of informed consent requirements is troublesome and difficult, not to say occasionally impossible. Sometimes an intervention is not directed toward a specific individual but toward a group. In other cases the intervention cannot be very easily defined, and in some cases there is not intervention at all. Risks are often difficult to assess and to describe. Moreover, and much to the point here, in social and behavioral science it is often highly likely that if subjects are given enough information about a research investigation in order to give informed consent, they will alter their behavior in ways that will affect the outcome of the investigation.

In research involving unobtrusive measures (and field experimentation), there is often no readily identifiable research subject whose consent can be obtained prior to participation in the experiment. Consider, for example, a mini-experiment conducted by a layperson, but resembling many field experiments conducted by social scientists. Bradshaw (1980) noticed that nuns who regularly solicit alms in Grand Central Terminal in New York customarily look rather glum. One day, however, Bradshaw saw one nun smiling brightly and "the activity at her basket seemed unusually brisk." Bradshaw subsequently disguised herself as a nun and positioned herself in the terminal. She spent the first day with a suitably glum visage and collected $143 (not, it would seem, a bad take) and the second day with a smile, which resulted in a total contribution of $186. In Bradshaw's little study, it would have been virtually impossible to identify the "subjects," since all persons coming her way were potential subjects, but they would not have been subjects unless they looked at and took cognizance of her; at that point, they would already have become subjects. Obviously no prior informed consent could have been obtained without, possibly, informing all those persons headed her way that they would encounter a woman in a nun's habit holding out an alms basket. Would it have been possible, let alone reasonable, to have "debriefed" all those persons who made a donation, giving them an opportunity to take their money back? (The donations were actually contributed to the Order of nuns that usually solicited donations in the terminal. Questions might, nonetheless, be raised concerning a possible disrespect engendered by publishing the article.) Many research efforts would involve a similar, and perhaps even worse problem, for example, in observing the number of persons on either side of the court during an intramural basketball game. In some instances, the "subjects" are altogether unknown, for example, in studying the brands of beer cans thrown beside the road in different parts of a community. In this latter case the National Commission would not define the research as involving human subjects since nobody is individually identifiable. Still, if one found that a particular community was characterized by more littering of cheap brands of beer cans, the community could be brought into disrepute.

Another problem that arises in the case of groups or other social entities is that it is not always clear from just whom consent should be obtained and what would constitute consent in a particular instance. For example, suppose one wished to do a study of manifestations of racism in two cities: Should it be necessary to get consent for the study? From whom, then? The mayor? The city council? The entire populace? Suppose there were a referendum on the study in each city, and the vote were 51 percent in favor and 49 percent opposed to the study? Would that, then, constitute consent for the study to be done? The issues would be thorny. In some instances there may be risk of a "tar brush" effect even on those members of a group who do not participate in a study. If, as an instance, a study were done of the number of physicians who cheat on their income tax, and if the findings tended to be adverse, the reputations of honest physicians might still be in some measure diminished. There is no solution to these problems; it is up to individual scientists to display caution and for the scientific disciplines to maintain continuing awareness of how far from the ethical brink it is possible to stray. Institutional Review Boards, established to review ethical aspects of research involving humans, also need to remain sensitive to what is ethically acceptable in their local communities.

Studies of honesty involve still other issues since some of them come close to entrapment. Obviously very few persons would steal or cheat if they were told that they were in an experiment designed to get them to do that very thing. Yet, if subjects are not told that they are in an experiment, and they commit a dishonest act that has been made convenient by an experimenter, they have been enticed into a disreputable behavior almost certainly out of keeping with their mundane daily behavior. Any subsequent pangs of guilt the dishonest subjects might experience or any anxiety about the possibility they might be found out are experimenter induced. Although it would seem unlikely, should any such subject experience a severe reaction, the tenuous ethical position of the experimenter would have been made clear. Fortunately most honesty studies involve infractions so minor or so common that serious negative reactions are unlikely; is there, then, no *principle* involved? One might posit an implicit contract within most societies, and certainly within ours, that people will be honest even in small matters unless there is some overriding reason to behave otherwise. (We would not expect, for example, a hungry, down-and-out person to make any particular effort to determine who might have lost the dollar he or she just found in the street.) Since even small dishonest acts represent some breach of that contract, it may not be unethical for a serious scientist to study such small dishonesties by providing the occasion for their occurrence, providing proper measures are taken to maintain confidentiality and to avoid insults to the dignity of persons involved. Clearly, however, the more serious the dishonesty permitted to occur, the greater the justification that is required for providing the occasion. Serious ethical problems would be posed, for instance, by providing even the occasion on which people might be tempted to steal or otherwise misappropriate $100. We have, on the other hand, observed finders of letters we have "lost" (Sechrest, Grove, and Cosgrove, 1980) tear off uncancelled 15-cent stamps and throw the letters away, and we have not felt any ethical qualms.

There is a stronger implicit social contractual obligation for honesty for some groups of persons than others. Specifically, there are persons who occupy social roles of such a nature that other persons are dependent upon them for honest behavior, and the threshold for ethical dilemma arising out of entrapment may be higher for such persons. Certainly there seems to be a substantially greater tolerance of fairly strong tests of honesty involving nonreactive measurement for such groups. Several years ago, for example, the pecuniary honesty of the police in one city was tested by losing wallets containing money in such ways that they were found by policemen. It was, then, a simple matter to determine whether the wallets were returned. The return rate was reminiscent of a famous pair of headlines in the *Chicago Tribune* back in the 1930s. After an investigative study by reporters, the *Tribune* headlined its story "Half of Chicago Cops Are Crooked!" There was an immediate storm of protest so that the next day the paper published a retraction headlined "Half of Chicago Cops Are Not Crooked." Over the years many professionals and technicians have been subjected to tests of their honesty in ways that have been informative and on occasion disheartening. Short-changing, short weighing, overcharging, and the like have all been studied by means of nonreactive arrangements. An illustrative and recent study (Chicago Tribune Task Force, 1976–1978) was of automobile repair shops presented with a very minor problem that should have cost only a few dollars to repair. Actual repair estimates ranged up to nearly $500 in some shops, although others offered to fix the problem for as little as $8.43! Probably only the sternest adherent of ethics in research would perceive an ethical problem in such tests of the honesty of people and groups committed to public service. Note, however, that the tarbrush operates after such tests, and researchers often meet with protests from members of the occupations so tested.

Federal Legislation and Regulations
Regarding Ethics of Research Involving Humans

The Privacy Act of 1974 provides safeguards against invasion of privacy by requiring that Federal agencies: (1) permit an individual to determine what records pertaining to him or her are collected, kept, used, or disseminated by agencies; (2) prevent dissemination of records without consent of the individual; (3) be vulnerable to civil suit for damages that result from violation of the Act; (4) permit persons to copy, correct, or amend records; (5) collect, maintain, use, or disseminate records of identifiable personal information in a way that assures it is for a necessary and lawful purpose, that the informaton is correct and current, and that adequate safeguards are provided to prevent misuse of information; and (6) allow exemptions from the requirements only when required for important policy reasons as determined by statutory authority.

As well as the right to privacy, the United States has codified the right of citizens to information about the workings of their government. The Freedom of Information Act, passed in 1966 and amended in 1974, provides that "any person" is entitled to access to agency records, except to the extent that a record or part of a record is exempt. Exceptions in roughly nine areas are specified in the Act, including: records that protect national security or foreign policy; records exempted from disclosure by specific statutes; records of a personal and private nature such as welfare, medical, and personnel files; records having financial, commercial, or professional value obtained with an assurance of confidentiality; and certain other records including some investigatory or law enforcement information. The exemptions to the Freedom of Information Act are options to withhold information—they are permissive, not mandatory —and agencies may often make discretionary releases of exempt materials (unless prohibited by law to do so). In addition, every agency is required to publish regulations telling the public how to request information, fees charged, and other procedural matters. Thus, U.S. citizens have access to an extraordinary array of information. This access makes possible a range of nonreactive studies of archival information that would not previously have been possible. On the other hand, for many government servants, the Freedom of Information Act is seen to conflict with the Privacy Act. The act has a broad scope, has generated numerous disputes, and has resulted in more open government. Since the end of the Nixon administration, for example, Henry Kissinger has been engaged in legal battles to maintain the privacy of his notes prepared while he was Secretary of State, with his opponents claiming that the notes fall under the Freedom of Information Act and Kissinger claiming that they are private. Recognizing there are certainly workings of the federal government and its employees that may legitimately be kept confidential, the Privacy Act should not be allowed to become a shield against the Freedom of Information law.

Protection of Research Subjects

The increasingly large role of the federal government in medical, behavioral, and social research has resulted in the formulation of guidelines and regulations to govern research involving humans subjects. During the last decade there has been heightened public interest in whether research subjects are adequately protected, and policies governing such research have been reexamined, revised, and formalized. However, formal review procedures to foster protection of human subjects of research were established in 1953, when the Clinical Center was opened at the National Institute of Health. Issues addressed in a policy document included: how much risk to subjects was justified; what aspects of research must be disclosed to subjects; and the role of group consideration in the resolution of questions surrounding such issues.

For research conducted in nongovernmental institutions that receive federal funds, the federal government has, since 1966, required review at the local institutional level by a duly constituted Institutional Review Board (IRB). That year the Surgeon General stipulated that clinical research and investigation involving humans should be supported only if the judgment of the investigator is subject to prior review by institutional colleagues to assure an independent determination of the protection of the rights and welfare of those involved, of the appropriateness of the methods used to obtain informed consent, and of the risks and potential medical benefits of research. Although the policy clearly pertained to medical research, a "clarification" explicitly extended it to behavioral research. The initial requirement was limited to research supported by the U.S. Public Health Service (PHS).

In 1971 the PHS requirements were adopted by the Department of Health, Education and Welfare (DHEW) in *Institutional Guide to DHEW Policy on Protection of Human Subjects,* and were applicable to research supported by that agency in which human subjects may be at risk. However, the *Institutional Guide* noted that if an institution failed to discharge its responsibilities for the protection of "individuals in its care," whether or not DHEW funds were involved, the Secretary might question whether the institution and individuals concerned should remain eligible to receive future funds from DHEW for activities involving human subjects.

In 1974, regulations were issued for protection of human subjects by DHEW (Federal Register 45 CFR 46). These regulations, amended, currently govern the system of Institutional

Review Boards. The regulations are stated as applicable to DHEW (now Department of Health and Human Services) grants and contracts, but they also quote the National Research Act (PL 93-348), which implies wider applicability to other agencies, and perhaps to all biomedical and behavioral research involving humans conducted or supported by any institution that receives federal funds. IRB review is required to determine whether subjects will be placed at risk, and if so whether: the risks to the subjects are so outweighed by the sum of benefits to the subject and the importance of the knowledge to be gained as to warrant a decision to allow subjects to accept the risks; the rights and welfare of subjects will be adequately protected; legally effective informed consent will be obtained by adequate and appropriate methods. If risks are found the IRB is required to review the conduct of the research at timely intervals. In 1975, amendments placed additional responsibility on the IRB for review of research involving certain subject groups in order to implement recommendations of the National Commission for the Protection of Human Subjects of Biomedical and Behavioral Research. Included in that Commission's mandate was an evaluative study of the IRB system, studies of the consent requirements, a consideration of risk-benefit assessment, a consideration of the boundaries between research and practice, and an identification of ethical principles that should underlie the conduct of biomedical and behavioral research. The Commission was also given an additional charge to study disclosure of research information.

The inclusion of behavioral and social research in the Commission's mandate, as well as in guidelines and regulations governing research with human subjects, has generated considerable controversy. Some claim that behavioral and social research were included without sufficient thought about similarities and differences between those kinds of research and biomedical research, and without careful consideration of whether the same policy should apply to both. Others have argued that a single policy would serve to avoid arbitrary distinctions along disciplinary lines and would acknowledge the interaction between biological and behavioral variables in many studies. This controversy has not been resolved. One option now under consideration is that research characterized by low risk to subjects *not* necessarily undergo mandatory review by the institutional review committee. Examples of low-risk research that might be eligible for expedited review procedures or exempted from the review requirement should be published shortly. Researchers should make sure they keep current about federal policy. Information about policy concerning research with human subjects is available locally from the Institutional Review Board, or from the Office of Protection from Research Risks at the National Institutes of Health in Bethesda, Maryland.

CHAPTER 6

Archives II: The Episodic and Private Record

In the preceding chapter, we outlined the joys and sorrows of those archives on which there is typically a running time record. Here we continue our discussion of archives, but center on those that are more discontinuous and often not a part of the public record. Such data are more difficult to come upon than the public records, unless the investigator is affiliated with some organization producing the material. The insurance sales of a casualty company, the nurse's record on a bedside clipboard, and last year's suicide notes from Los Angeles are more available to the "inside" investigator than they are to the curious outsider. But if these records are more difficult and costly to acquire than public records, they can often provide a gain in specificity of content. The amount of irrelevant dross commonly declines as an investigation is limited to a particular set of privately produced data.

We have already mentioned the risks to validity inherently present in archival records. The main analytic difference between the records mentioned in this and in the earlier chapter is the common inability to make longitudinal analyses of the private data. Sometimes security is the reason, sometimes the data are stored for shorter periods, sometimes financial and labor costs preclude an analysis over time. Whatever the cause, this is a major loss. The best defense against it is to find a related set and combine both—one continuous and the other discontinuous—for a more textured series of comparisons.

Lincoln (1980) provides a very useful discussion of both the advantages and the limitations of the analysis of documents and records as a part of program evaluation. She makes a distinction between records and documents that would often be worth

162

preserving. Specifically, a *record* is "any written statement prepared by an invidual or an agency for the purpose of attesting
to an event or providing an accounting," and a *document* is
"any written (or filmed) material other than a record and which
was not prepared specifically in response to some request from
or some task set by the investigator" (p.4). Examples of records
include: airline manifests, chattel mortgage records, city directories, expense account vouchers, legal notices, military
records, telephone company records, business and trade directories, county plat books, and police records. Examples of documents include: letters, memoirs, diaries, wills, suicide notes,
epitaphs, film scripts, memoranda, propaganda pamphlets, government publications, diplomatic communiques, and medical
histories. Lincoln points out that records are typically analyzed
by processes of aggregation and integration subjected to trend
analysis or simple tracking. Documents, however, usually require content analysis or involve case survey method.

The critical scientific question to be asked concerning
records is whether they can be trusted to be accurate. Lincoln
points to six factors bearing on the accuracy of records:

1. errors introduced by the persons to whom records per-
   tain, whether introduced inadvertently or intentionally
2. errors introduced by data collectors
3. errors introduced by recording or filing mistakes
4. changes in record-keeping systems which make some
   records noncomparable to others
5. errors due to historicity or temporal changes
6. factors that enter into the development of "official sta
   tistics"

As in so many other areas of human enterprise, those proposing
to make use of records should know that it is the buyer who
must beware.

Similarly, Lincoln cites Clark (1967) as a source for critical
questions about the origins and usefulness of documents.

What is the history of the document?
How did it come into my hands?
What guarantee is there that it is what it pretends to be?
Is the document complete, as originally constructed?
Has it been tampered with or edited?

If the document is genuine, under what circumstances and
for what purposes was it produced?
Who was/is the author?
What was he trying to accomplish? For whom was the
document intended?
What were the maker's sources of information? Does the
document represent an eyewitness account, a secondhand
account, a reconstruction of an event long prior to writing,
an interpretation?
What was or is the maker's bias?
To what extent was the writer likely to want to tell the
truth?
Do other documents exist that might shed additional light
on this same story, event, project, program, context?
If so, are they available, accessible? Who holds them?

Since Clark is a historian, some of the questions have that orientation, but, as Lincoln notes, several of them are particularly
appropriate when documents are not ascribed to any particular
author (project reports often are not), when one comes into
possession of a copied paper, or when documents are assembled
from sources who do not wish their identity known (Deep
Throat). Obviously, documents also must be used with considerable caution.

Some of the data in this chapter are episodic in character,
but complete in reporting: many sources do maintain long and
accurate record-keeping systems. The military is one such
source, and Lodge (1963) has conducted a provocative correlational study with United States Navy records. All those who
have learned his results on air crashes tend now, as passengers,
to squint studiously at their pilots' height. Dipping back into the
navy records, Lodge collected reports of 680 jet plane accidents, and then searched other records for the height of the
pilots. He learned that men exceeding the average height of 72
inches had significantly more accidents than their shorter contemporaries. This may be traced to the design of aircraft cock-
pits and the visual angle on instrument panels.

We have divided the sources into three gross classes: sales
records, institutional records, and personal documents. All
three are potential substitutes for direct observation of behavior. This is most obvious with personal documents, where the
unavailability of a source may force the investigator to use
whatever alternatives are available. But sales and institutional

records may work in the same way and can broaden the scope
of an investigation that is primarily based on observation. They
may fill in holes present in an observational series or be used to
produce a broader sampling of the behavior under study.

SALES RECORDS

In a society as oriented to marketing and record keeping
as ours, sales data abound for study of a varied body of content.
Nonetheless, sales data are not without their limitations. For
one thing, sales records may not always be available since some
companies regard them as valuable sources of information to
competitors. One of us was once involved in a study in which
one aim was to determine whether there were any biases in the
brands of beer cans found along roadways. Both retailers and
distributors insisted that there was no way of knowing how
much of each brand of beer was being sold in the community
in question. Odd way to run a business. Sales records may also
not be in a form suitable for the analyses planned, for example,
sales data may not be available by day of week, by season, and
so on. In still other instances, sales data may be misleading
because of constraints of some kind on sales. Hillebrandt (1962)
sought to test the interesting hypothesis that major air crashes
produce passenger anxiety by determining the sales of alcoholic
drinks at Chicago airports in times just before and just after
major crashes. He was unable to use the proposed data, however, because the major Chicago airport, O'Hare, had only recently been completed, and the construction of bars had not
caught up with demand. Thus, there was negligible variance
from day to day in sales, and the small amount that existed
seemed to be based on variations in bartenders' speed, not on
the states of mind of passengers. Currently (that is, in 1980) sales
figures for new American-made automobiles might suggest that
those buying them prefer larger sizes in relation to those who
buy foreign cars. In fact, however, the supply of smaller American-made autos is far below demand; they are not there to
be sold.

As noted above, Hillebrandt (1962) did not get to use bar
sales as a measure. He continued with his study, however, and
used the volume of air passengers. With a complete set of data

over time, he was able to transform the data, correcting for systematic sources of variance irrelevant to his hypothesis. He partialled out the seasonal variation in air traffic, for example, and accounted for the secular changes in traffic level at Chicago's two major airports. The residual material demonstrated that crashes were only a very short-term depressant on travel. Just as with the bar sales, there is some rigidity in his data that tends to blunt comparisons. A certain number of people have no alternative to flying, regardless of how dissettling was a major crash the day before. Some people can do as they please, and there was an account in the *Washington Post* some years back (Morisey, 1970) of the increase in bookings on transatlantic ships (a reported quadrupling) subsequent to a rash of airplane hijackings.

Insurance, a paid-for hedge against risk, is an admirable measure of the effect of disaster. Just as one can examine trip insurance sales and link them to crashes, one can examine the timing of casualty insurance sales and link them to the occurrence of hurricanes or tornadoes. Add to this sales of life insurance (compared to the time of death of close friends or relatives), and one has a three-way index of the general effect of disaster.

These same data could be used to test Zipf's (1946) hypothesis further. Is the amount of casualty insurance taken out inversely proportional to the distance from the disaster? How the mapping of insurance underwriting compares to a meteorological map of tornado probability would be a necessary control. It might be that the hypothesis holds only in areas that have had tornado experience. This would give support to Zipf's hypothesis, but even greater support would come if a significant amount of insurance were written in proximate areas with little or no tornado experience. What, in brief, is the nature of the generalization of effect?

How unlikely a source of research material is the sale of peanuts! Yet, continuing in the vein of study of anxiety or tension, peanut sales are a possibility that should be systematically explored. An anecdotal report appeared in the *Chicago Sun-Times* from the concessionaire in that city's baseball parks. He casually observed that peanut sales after the seventh inning of a game are significantly higher than earlier—but only during a tight game. If the game is one-sided, there is no late-inning increase in peanut purchasing. Is this a sound, nonreactive measure of involvement or tension? It may be, but it illustrates the problems associated with such archival measures—one must pay special heed to rival hypotheses.

One should look at population restrictions. It may be that the finding (if it may be legitimatized as such) on the increase coming only in tight games is an artifact of selective attendance and not tension. There is a hyperbolic curve of attendance in a one-sided game. A substantial number of fans usually arrive late, and another substantial group leave early if the game appears to be already decided. The population potential for peanut purchasing is thereby variable across innings, and the effect of a tight game should be to reduce the early departures and provide a larger base for sales in later innings. For a finer test, a simple correction would be to transform the peanut sales into unit sales per X thousand fans per inning—a transformation possible by clocking turnstile movement in and out.

One other element of population restrictions must be considered. We have examined only the issue of the absolute number of fans available in the park to buy the peanuts. Is there any plausibility to the notion that those who leave early are more or less devoted to peanuts? One might determine this by interview at the exit gate, or by looking for traces of peanut shells in vacated seats.

Sales data can also be used to infer popularity and preference. The impact of Glenn's orbital flight was evidenced by record-breaking sales of the commemorative stamp issued to mark it. Similarly, the sale of commemorative Kennedy stamps and the great demand for Kennedy half-dollars after their issuance, as well as all the special books and the reappearance of *Profiles in Courage* on the best-seller list, provides persuasive evidence, if any were needed, of the man's influence on public thinking. By contrast, the sales of Richard Nixon's post-resignation books have been reported to be low, and on the first day that the Watergate tapes were made available for public listening at the Library of Congress, only 12 people showed up.

Another measure of the popularity of a person is the value of his or her autograph in the commercial market. The supply level must be controlled, of course, making it likely that most autographs would be conservatively valued until their creators are safely incapacitated. Hamilton (1978) produces a book on autographs that is regularly updated, and he provides separate estimates of the values of signatures (S), signed documents or letters (D), handwritten letters (H), autographed quotations (Q), and signed photographs (P). In 1978 the following values were said to prevail:

	S	D	H	Q	P
Elvis Presley	$60	$100	$260	$120	$200
Richard Nixon	$60	$150	$2000		$150
John Hancock	$205	$150	$300		
Winston Churchill	$100	$225	$400		$215
Napoleon	$125	$250	$5000		
Charles Dickens	$50	$110	$200		
Ralph W. Emerson	$35	$50	$150		
Anne Frank	$75	$150	$200	$325	$185
Daniel Webster	$12	$40	$75		
Calvin Coolidge	$25	$85	$400		

We suspect that the values given reflect some intricate relationships between supply and the popularity (or notoriety) of the persons involved. Two largely unknown signers of the Declaration of Independence, Thomas Lynch and Button Gwinnett, have had values of $4000 placed on their signatures, and $100,-000, in the case of Lynch, and $125,000, in the case of Gwinnett, for signed letters. Hamilton makes the point that the signatures of John Wilkes Booth ($500) and Lee Harvey Oswald ($250) are worth more than those of Abraham Lincoln ($300) and John F. Kennedy ($150), the presidents they killed. Leon Czolgosz, the assassinator of President William McKinley, apparently left no signatures behind, but a document signed by him is worth $5000 as compared to $100 in the case of McKinley. Maybe outlaws, except forgers, do not write much. A handwritten letter from William Bonny (Billy the Kid) is said to be worth $8500, and one by Jesse James, $6500.

What more is there to a signature than the cachet of owning one by a well-known person? Graphologists have long insisted that handwriting is revealing, a proposition about which we are considerably dubious. Nonetheless, signatures do change from time to time, and Zweigenhaft (1970) hypothesized that with increasing social status the area covered by a person's signature would be larger. He first showed that the signatures of professors on library sign-out cards were larger than those of students, then showed that professors asked to sign a card wrote larger than did blue collar workers, who in turn had larger signatures than students. Finally, and perhaps most interesting, Zweigenhaft was able to examine the signatures of a professor written in 90 textbooks he had acquired over a period of eleven years extending from undergraduate to post-graduate years. The signatures increased steadily in size with what would appear to be increasing status. The area covered by the boundaries of the signatures grew from about 15 square centimeters as an undergraduate to 70 square centimeters as a faculty member. Could the professor's undergraduate books have been condensed versions or his ink supply limited? Would signature size reflect other than self-ascribed status?

In another paper Zweigenhaft (1977) reports on a series of signature-size studies related generally to the issue of status and self-esteem. Males use up more space when signing library cards than do females, and the difference seemingly is not related to body size. Moreover, the difference does not manifest itself before adolescence. Experimental manipulations designed to increase or decrease self-esteem have an effect on signature size that is consistent with other findings, and students asked to imagine that they are important persons produce larger signatures. Increasing status is also associated with adding a middle initial to one's signature. What's in a name? If not much, then why are there far more Robert Andersons (8) listed in Standard and Poor's as corporate president or board chairman than any other name? [*Standard and Poor's Register of Corporations, Directors and Executives* (1979), (5)5 30, III, 15:2.]

There may be more to a signature than meets the eye. In 1865, Sylvia Ann Howland died, leaving a portion of her estate to her niece, Hetty Robinson, in a will and codicil dated 1863 and 1864, respectively. Hetty Robinson, however, produced a will dated 1862 that not only left her aunt's entire estate to her but that instructed its executioners to ignore all subsequent wills. There ensued a considerable brouhaha that centered on the possibility that the Howland signature on the 1862 will was a forgery. In what is purported to be the first use in law of probabilistic and statistical evidence (Meier and Zabell, 1980), Benjamin Pierce, Professor of Mathematics at Harvard, undertook to show that the 1862 signature was a tracing. The proof consisted of a demonstration that the signature was so highly similar to an undisputed original in the characteristics of 30 downstrokes that the probability of it being an independently produced specimen was vanishingly small. There were available in the Howland papers 42 other signatures for comparison. Meier and Zabell (1980) note some deficiencies in Pierce's reasoning without, however, completely invalidating his argument. Another witness, an engraver, testified for Hetty Robinson concerning the remarkable similarities in signatures left by John Quincy Adams. Hetty ultimately lost her case on other legal grounds, but she died Hetty Robinson Green in 1916, known as one of the most colorful and successful financial wizards of Wall Street, leaving a fortune of $100,000,000.

One possible way of determining the ascribed status of some sets of persons might be to note the number of times their photographs have appeared in various publications. Templer, Austin, and Veleber (1980) have done just that in an attempt to assess the eminence of psychologists. Their method involved simply counting the number of times psychologists' pictures appeared in one or more of 19 introductory psychology textbooks. Freud, Piaget, Skinner, John B. Watson, Maslow, Pavlov, Rogers, and Jung led the list. Surely the textbook producers were, for the most part, recognizing eminence, for were they merely interested in broadening the knowledge of the readers, they would have chosen pictures of psychologists whose faces are less familiar than the likes of Freud, Jung, Skinner, and so on.

The sales and pictorial content of stamps are a useful but unused bit of expressive intelligence. An analysis of the illustrations on stamps may give indications of the state of political opinion in the nation. What does an analysis of illustrations printed during the early years of the Fascist regimes in Germany and Italy show? It has been suggested that stamp illustrations presage aggressive political action. Perhaps somewhere a philatelistic psychologist has prepared this study, using illustrated sets of stamp catalogues by year of issue.

A possible flaw in such analysis is a potential datum for another topic of study. Each nation does not print its own stamps. Many former colonial territories continue, as a cost-saving device, to use secondhand engravings and the printing facilities of the former governing power. The stamp illustration may thereby reflect an economic and not a political decision. But whether or not a former colonial territory still relies on the old power is itself a clue to relations between the two. One could, for example, compare former British and French colonies in Africa. Or compare new nations within what was a single colonial area. Guinea prints her own stamps; Mali buys hers from France. Sechrest has a small collection of maps of the world printed in different countries, and with but one exception, each country rearranges the topography in such a way as to place itself as near the center of the world as possible. Hong Kong, however, loyal to the crown in 1964 at least, placed England in the center and itself off to the side.

The diffusion of information among physicians was the topic of Coleman, Katz, and Menzel's (1957) research. Instead of the more standard, and reactive, tactic of interviewing doctors, they elected to go to pharmacy records for information about which doctors prescribed what drugs when. Sampling at intervals over a 15-month period, they related the physician's adoption of new drugs to his/her social network. Such hard-nosed data can be a useful check on interviewing data, provided the effect of collecting such records does not alter the behavior of the record keepers. This is a very implausible risk with drug prescription, but a reasonable one when dealing with less legally controlled records. The danger is not so much in masking information as it is in improving it. The record keeper may perform a more conscientious job because he/or she knows that the work is being put to some use. If the investigator using such records stresses the greater glory to humanity that will come from the record keeper's cooperation, the investigator may actually be increasing the risk that the instrumentation process will change—thereby threatening the validity of comparisons over time.

The social network variable employed by Coleman, Katz, and Menzel can be measured by methods other than the standard interview or sociogram. To study the extent to which interaction among different departments of a university took place, one could use orthodox procedures. In addition, so humble a document as a desk calendar might be checked. This record can provide information on who lunched with whom, with what degree of frequency, and across what departments. Not everyone notes such engagements (a population restriction), and the desk calendar is not a likely source for learning of other engagements, such as social dinners or meetings so regular that they don't have to be noted (content restrictions). Staying just with the lunch dates, one route to learn the character of the restrictions would be to enlist the aid of waiters in faculty clubs. The reader can conjure up objections to this assistance.

Drug sale records are in common use by pharmaceutical houses to evaluate the sales effort of their detail staff. Both the houses and the detail staff have learned that the verbal statement or the observed enthusiasm of a doctor for a new drug is a highly unstable predictor of what he or she will prescribe. If records are available for checks on self-reports, they should by all means be used. Such checks are particularly useful when the data are produced continuously by the same subjects, for then a correction can be applied to the self-reports. If the assumption can be made that the character of the error is constant over time, it may not be necessary to run both sets of data concurrently.

Something of an analogous correction can be seen with economic forecasters. Firms that employ more than one forecaster are said to compute the response-set characteristic of the forecaster (optimism or pessimism) and apply a secret correction to his or her periodic predictions. This is a rather interesting data transformation, since its existence shows the set rigidity of the forecasters. They, too, know whether they have been over- or underestimating, yet that knowledge does not produce potent enough feedback to overcome the response set. Morgenstern (1963) notes reports of the same type of corrections applied by Soviet planners in the 1930s.

Boring (1961) has detailed how a similar type of response

error was an early cause célèbre in astronomy. Differences in reaction times among astronomical observers became known, and the phrase "personal equation" was coined to describe the bias. In an evolving history, the contaminant existed but was unknown, became known and the cause of study for the purpose of eliminating its biasing effect, and then became the substantive material of a large body of psychological research.

The sale of stocks was used by Ashley (1962) in a study interesting for what it says of positive and negative reward. Isolating firms that announced an unexpected dividend or earnings statement, either up or down, Ashley traced the stock prices following the announcement. An unexpectedly high dividend influenced the price of the stock for about 15 days, while an unexpectedly low dividend or earnings statement had an effect for only about four days. There are other places to measure extinction than in a Skinner box. See, for instance, Winship and Allport's (1943) study on newspaper headlines and Griffith's (1949) research on horse race odds—both studies of optimism-pessimism. Hamilton (1942) has also conducted an interesting content analysis on the rise of pessimism in widely circulated Protestant sermons.

A more common use of sales records (but still surprisingly uncommon) is as a measure of propaganda effectiveness. Within advertising, particularly, there has been extensive writing on the inadequacy of survey methodology to predict the advertiser's major criterion, sales. An excellent annotated bibliography reviewing advertising's effect on sales has been prepared by Krueger and Ramond (1965).

Henry (1958) gives numerous examples of the discrepancies between respondents' reports and sales figures, indicating that the reasons a consumer gives for buying a product cannot be relied upon. A review (Nisbett and Wilson, 1977) of a series of studies of people's cognitions concerning the reasons for their behavior suggests quite strongly that most people most of the time do not have especially good access to their own mental processes, with the consequence that reasons given for any behavior are nearly always suspect. Reactive measurement thus suspect, other methods of consumer preference measurement must be found.

Walbeck (1973) was concerned that mothers in a child nutrition study might not comply in purchasing the nutritional supplement they were to give to their children. Therefore, she provided mothers with discount coupons they could use to buy the supplement and arranged with the local suppliers to return the coded coupons to her for counting. As anticipated, the mothers in the experimental groups more regularly purchased the product than did mothers in the control group. How much more persuasive those results are than would have been the case had she been forced to rely upon self-report alone.

Henry mentions an example of a controlled sales experiment on "shelf appeal." One brand of candy is sold in three types of wrappers, with variables such as shelf position and number of units displayed controlled. The dependent variable is the sales level of the different packages. One such study done in the context of Halloween trick-or-treating showed that overweight children showed a distinct preference for candies wrapped in brightly colored paper, even though they were smaller candies than the plain brown wrapped ones that the children of normal weight went for (Fraser, 1972).

There is an ideal experimental medium for advertising research in direct-mail sales efforts. Lucas and Britt (1963) comment upon a number of studies that have varied such elements as the color of paper, inclusion of various incentives, and stamping a return envelope by hand or by meter. They also cite the example of a department store which might send out a monthly statement to customers containing one of ten variants of an advertisement selling a specific product. The average return per layout would then be determined by subsequent sales. Utility company bills are a similar medium for relating to the public. Some researchers interested in energy conservation have placed pro-conservation messages in with utility bills and then studied energy consumption in subsequent months (Seaver and Patterson, 1976; Seligman and Darley, 1977). One big advantage of such a procedure is that it is relatively easy to develop good comparison groups or areas that do not receive the conservation message.

The large mail-order houses (Sears, Montgomery Ward, and others) regularly conduct controlled experiments on different thematic appeals. This is easily performed by varying the content of the appeal and simply counting the returns attributable to the different sources. In a revealing finding, one of these houses discovered that an advertisement describing a self-riding lawnmower as something of an adult's toy dramatically outsold an appeal that argued its superior functional merits.

Using sales results of a promotional campaign, Blomgren and Scheuneman (1961) found a "scare" approach was less effective for selling seat belts than one that featured a professional racing driver and appealed to masculine control and relaxation.

Nearly 50 years ago, Jahoda-Lazarsfeld and Zeisel (1932) studied the impact of the depression by noting the level of grocery sales. The same measure is used now to evaluate the efficacy of different sales themes. A before-after design was used by the National Advertising Company (1963) to learn the effect of large outdoor signs placed in the parking lots of three shopping centers. They used store audits to determine the sales of products advertised on the signs and then compared these data to sales from a control sample of equivalent stores. Another method of "pretesting" advertising themes is to place treatments of the theme in prominent places within a supermarket and then observe sales. This has been done by comparing sales attributable to a single theme against a control of past sales, and also by employing multiple themes and comparing one against the other. In this latter approach, close attention has been paid to time sampling problems, so as to protect the equivalence of the populations exposed to each version.

One could similarly experiment with vending machines, although we do not know of any such research. By random assignment of the display of experimental cigarette packages to machines, or by systematically varying exhortatory messages over machines, one could employ lever-pulling as the effectiveness measure.

Aside from the commercial applications of such research, direct-mail advertising, vending machines, and the like offer a fine natural laboratory for the study of persuasion. Mindak, Neibergs, and Anderson (1963) used the sales of tickets to parades and to a civic aquatennial as one of their several measures of the effect of a newspaper strike. Roens (1961) reported on the use of different combinations of media to carry the same propaganda theme (for Scott paper), and Berreman's (1940) study of factors affecting the sale of novels found that publicity elements had little effect.

Mailing lists themselves can be interesting. Probably many people have wondered how their names can be spread so widely. The answer, of course, is that mailing lists get bought (and probably begged, borrowed, and stolen) from those who possess them by those who regard them as valuable for use (and probably for eventual resale). Who gets mailing lists from whom? Sechrest and Grove have a study long in progress in which they study the distribution of mailing lists by the simple expedient of varying their names in minor ways, such as different spellings or middle initials, when they respond to potential commercial or other enterprises by mail. It appears that making a charitable contribution will get you on other charity lists but not on commercial lists; you can end up on mailing lists for pornography somewhat innocently, but once on such a list, the spread is fast and far; so is the spread once you are on a commercial list, for example, for "gift house" catalogs. The most interesting thing so far has been that the order over the years of several fruitcakes from a Texas supplier led in early 1980 to a request for a political contribution to the campaign of a Texas presidential candidate. The specific address could have been no coincidence; the evidence was incontrovertible that someone suspected there might be a closet Texan in Florida.

The stuff of commercial persuasion, advertisements proper, has been employed in a number of ways for other purposes. The want ad columns of newspapers have served as economic predictors (Fowler, 1962), and one of our colleagues, Russell D. Clark III, is studying changing patterns of used automobile sales ads by measuring column inches of advertising in a paper that categorizes auto ads according to size of auto. In this case one can get a weekly account of the kinds of automobiles that are being offered for sale by private owners. Despite widespread publicity about energy problems, increasing gasoline prices, and assurances that the public is interested in small cars, Clark has found that in 1977 customers of a car dealer in

Florida were twice as likely to be trading up in car size, and in 1979 the figure was two-and-a-half times. Incidentally, another want ad study (Goldstein, Minkin, Minkin, and Baer, 1978/1979) determined that a policy of offering free newspaper classified ads for found objects increased the number of such ads considerably. Perhaps there are more good sports than at first seems likely— they just do not want to have to pay for the privilege.

Advertisements have also been used to test theories of social change. Assuming that ads reflect values, Dornbusch and Hickman (1959) sampled 816 issues of the *Ladies Home Journal* and analyzed the content of advertising to estimate the degree of "other-directedness" displayed. These data tested Riesman's hypotheses on the history of "other-directedness." Two classes of indexes were employed: (1) endorsements by persons or groups and (2) claims that a product is related to satisfactions in interpersonal relations.

Singh and Huang (1962) made a cross-cultural study of advertising, comparing American and Indian advertising for similarity and relating the findings to socioeconomic and cultural factors. Since they used print advertising, it is important to take account of differential literacy rates in such comparisons. If the advertisers are addressing their messages to literate "prospects" and reflecting the values of those "prospects," the differential literacy rate may interact with magazine readership and prospect status to yield differences between societies that are spurious. This is less a concern with broadcast advertising, although there may be a population restriction in that those who either own or are more available to radio or television receivers vary systematically across countries.

INDUSTRIAL AND INSTITUTIONAL RECORDS

Among the finest work to be found on discussion of multiple methods and the criterion problem is that of the industrial psychologists. One rarely finds such attention to the relative merits of ratings versus observation versus performance versus interviewing versus questionnaires versus tests. Guion (1961) has offered an excellent short treatment of this subject, as have

Ghiselli and Brown (1955) and Whisler and Harper (1962). But these have not supplanted the singular statements on "criteria of criteria" by R.L. Thorndike (1949).[1]

The number of private records marshalled by the industrial psychologists has been impressive. Amount and quality of output are probably the most frequently used behavioral measures and are usually expressed in some transformed score—the number of units produced by a worker or department per unit of time, the amount of sales per unit of time, or the profitability of activity by dollars invested by the firm. The known subjectivity of ratings by supervisors or foremen increasingly moved many of the specialists in this area to pure behavioral measures, but ratings remain because of the difficulty in making behavioral measures comparable.

We review a body of studies with data drawn from the institutional records of companies, schools, hospitals, and the military. A good share of these come from industry, but the overlap with other institutions is marked.

Most writers argue for multidimensional criteria. Ghiselli and Brown (1955) give the humble example of a streetcar motorman, indicating a series of proficiency measures:

1. Number of collisions with pedestrians
2. Number of traffic violations
3. Number of commendations from public
4. Number of complaints from public
5. Number of times company rules broken
6. Number of sleepovers (tardiness)
7. Number of times schedules broken
8. Number of reprimands from inspectors
9. Ratings by inspectors
10. Errors reported by dispatchers

As always with multiple measures such as these, the question comes up of the advisability of combining the various measures into a single composite score. Consider in the list above the problem of weighting each of the ten variables. Ghiselli and Brown suggest multiple cutoffs—establishing a minimum per-

---

[1]For other articles of methodological interest on criteria see Brogden and Taylor (1950), Gordon (1950), Fiske (1951), Bass (1952), Severin (1952), Rush (1953), MacKinney (1960), and Turner (1960).

formance level for each component element of the index. The way in which the variables are combined, and the final score reached, can be disastrously misleading if some minimum standard is not met on each of the tasks of the job. They offer the highly reasonable example that an airline pilot should be able to land a plane as well as take one off—perhaps not so gracefully, but still with an irreducible degree of proficiency (cf. Coombs, 1963).

Another multimeasure study, this one of ship effectiveness in the navy, was conducted by Campbell (1956). Rather than rely solely on ratings by the captain or crew members, Campbell examined the ship records for reports of ship inspections, torpedo firings, reenlistment rates of those aboard, requests for transfer, and disciplinary actions. More recently, and in a similar vein, Grove and Sechrest (1980) have been studying the performance of recruit companies in the U.S. Naval Training Command in relation to characteristics of the company commanders. During training, records are kept and aggregated by company on performance on locker and barracks inspections, performance in marching drill on the parade ground, minor disciplinary infractions known as "street marks," and numbers of recruits set back in training. In addition, at the end of training, all recruits fill out a standard attitude questionnaire. The analysis shows that recruit companies that do well on one of the inspections tend to do well on the other and on marching drill. In addition, these exemplary companies tend to have fewer street marks and fewer setbacks. Moreover, on the attitude measure they report having respect for their company commanders and positive feelings toward boot camp. They also report negative attitudes toward the navy and toward the possibility of making the navy a career!

The Grove and Sechrest data are interesting on one conceptual and one methodological point. Taking the latter first, their data set illustrates especially well the advantage of having multiple data sources. They do not profess to know whether the data really mean that success in boot camp bodes ill for the future of the navy, but the data certainly suggest that it might be worth looking into the impact of boot camp on recruits in a fairly detailed way. The conceptual point has to do with whether official scores on things like locker inspections, close order drill, and street marks are really to be regarded as unobtrusive and nonreactive. They are not unobtrusive, that is clear. They may, however, be less reactive than one might think. Although both company commanders and recruits were certainly aware that scores were given and counts were made, they may have been little aware of any aggregation or any subsequent use of the data. In fact, Grove and Sechrest were not able to determine that any actual use was ever made of the data, despite the fact that data were collected on thousands upon thousands of recruits and hundreds upon hundreds of their company commanders. Furthermore, it can be assumed that in general the recruits and their commanders were trying to do their best, and any residual differences were more likely attributable to real differences in ability and motivation than to artifacts of the measurement process.

Reenlistment rates are a measure of job turnover, and Evan (1963) explored this topic in research on student workers. Personnel records were examined to find a possible relationship between job turnover and departmental placement. He reasoned that a high level of interaction on the job with other student workers would have a stress reducing effect and result in a lower rate of job turnover. He supported this hypothesis by showing that the larger the number of students with whom a worker could interact, the lower the rate of quitting.

Knox (1961) added absenteeism to job turnover and correlated both with age, seniority, and the distance of the worker's home from the factory. Melbin (1961) also used absenteeism and job turnover in research on psychiatric aids. He compared these data to archival reports on work assignments. The correlational methods limited his ability to establish cause-and-effect relationships, but he was able to trace a double-directioned effect between changes in work assignments and absences.

Job turnover is an ambiguous measure—sometimes it is an administrative action, sometimes an action dictated by the individual employee. R. L. Thorndike (1949) holds that administrative actions should be considered as a discrete class of criteria. Along with many others, Guilford (1956) used the record of pay increases as his measure of the firm's appraisal of the individual.

Weitz (1958) suggests the imperfectly correlated measure of promotion within the company, while Jay and Copes (1957) speak of job survival as a criterion. Merely to stay on a job, without being fired, is indicative of an administrative decision that the employee is not too bad. On the other hand, it appears that managers who ranked high in their college classes do not have lower turnover rates in jobs than the lower ranking, and when the high ranking leave, it is not for better pay (Livingston, 1971).

Whisler and Harper (1962) also speak of seniority as a criterion and discuss the implications of this in the union-management struggle over definition of criteria. They state that seniority has appeal because of its qualities of objectivity and precision, and that it is not a simple case of the union wanting seniority and the management fighting it. Promotion from within the management group and the high value placed on experience is evidence of the use of seniority within the management tier.

One could also observe other management actions that reflect the esteem in which an employee is held. The carpet on the floor, the drapes on the window, the second secretary, and the corner office are all salient cues to an employee's success with the firm. Proximity of parking and whether it is reserved or open would be another indicator in many firms. On the other hand, one must determine whether there are bureaucratic restrictions that may produce distortions in individual cases. One of the authors was once told by a colleague from England, who had gone back there for a time, of having an office in what had been a prison cell. One day some workmen came to board off part of it because he had too many square feet of office space for his position.

Nearly all formal organizations have some concern with absenteeism, and industrial organizations perhaps have more than many others. However, industries and other businesses probably have somewhat more capacity to deal with absenteeism than other organizations. Nonetheless, Mann, Indik, and Vroom (1963), in a study of work productivity in a firm engaged nationwide in the delivery of small packages, found absenteeism to correlate −.59 with a measure of productivity (cost per package delivered) for drivers and −.57 for sorters. This study is also of interest because the patterns of relationships among many measured variables were quite different for the two types of jobs. One apparently frequent cause of absenteeism is alcohol abuse, and Bucky, Edwards, and Cohen (1975) found that a navy program to deal with alcoholism was associated with a drop in absenteeism in one unit from about 12,000 days during a pretreatment period to about 2000 days in a post-treatment period of the same length. Note that the program was not designed to reduce absenteeism directly so that the outcome measure was probably minimally reactive.

Another form of absenteeism is failure to keep appointments, and that form is often expensive, too. Kosloski, Schnelle, and Littlepage (1977) examined the records in a mental health center to determine client characteristics related to failure to keep appointments and terminating treatment by merely failing to show up anymore. There were not any relationships. Of course, even being late is partial absenteeism, and when it gets out of hand, something needs to be done about it. Hermann, et al. (1973) studied the effect of bonuses on punctuality, which was evaluated by examining time cards punched daily. Now punching the time clock is neither unobtrusive nor nonreactive, but it is a near perfect measure since it measures what is wanted, time arriving at work. Punching the clock may not be perfect, however, since if too much emphasis is put on it, ways of cheating will be devised, and workers may also learn to retaliate by dawdling after arrival at work. Any single indicator that becomes too important is subject to corruption (Campbell, 1975).

The unions keep books, too, and Stuart (1963) was canny enough to use grievance records in a study of racial conflict. He collected 364 verbatim records of the grievance board of a large union in the textile industry—data extending over a seven-year period. The complaints were analyzed to determine feelings, attitudes, and actions against black and Spanish-speaking workers who comprised a majority of the union. Their complaints are important evidence, but there is the risk of the bias one notes in studies of political speeches. Although the events occurred in the past, and the investigator did not intrude in the production

of the data, the subjects were very much aware that their remarks were "on the record." This perforce limits the degree of
generalization possible.

We have referred previously to Zipf's (1946) hypothesis
about the flow of information being inversely proportional to
distance, and that general notion has been formalized as the
"gravity flow" model. The force of gravity is expressed by $1/d^2$,
that is, if the attraction between two bodies one meter apart is
1.00, the attraction will be .25 at two meters, .11 at three meters, and so on. That model has been applied to a variety of
geographic phenomena and has been shown to predict rather
well the amount of travel between cities, long distance telephone calls between cities, consumer shopping trips, and the
like (Lowe and Moryadas, 1975). Sechrest and Sukstorf (1977)
found that the gravity flow model applied rather well to visitations of institutionalized retarded children by their parents, i.e.,
parents nearby visited disproportionately more often than
those at greater distances.

Unobtrusive measures are likely to be of special value in
the study of issues having to do with conflict between races.
One issue is how people define themselves racially. Smith and
Mazis (1976) investigated the relationship between self-desig-
nated racial label and other variables. Archival data were collected for the 1971–73 period from the tenant files of a low-rent,
public housing authority in a southern state. Usable data were
available for 145 tenants who had identified themselves as ci-
ther black, colored, or Negro. Those designating themselves as
black rather than colored or Negro proved to be different on a
number of dimensions, although it is not clear whether the
differences can be interpreted as a more positive self-image or
as greater flexibility in adopting new language by younger black
persons.

One of the prevalent theories about the effects of racial
prejudice on schools and neighborhoods has been that when the
number of blacks reaches a certain point, a "tipping point,"
there will be a rapid and mass exodus of whites. Stinchcombe,
McDill, and Walker (1969) used school enrollment data for Baltimore to test the tipping point hypothesis and found no evidence for it. The effects of prejudice were continuous: the more

black children who enter a school, the more white children who leave.

Since we are discussing school records, we ought to note that such records may become less and less accessible because they are being protected under the provisions of the Privacy Act. It is difficult to say exactly what the stance of school officials ought to be, and some of them may be being a bit over zealous in protecting school records. One of the authors has had the experience of being denied access to names and addresses of parents whose permission was required before their children could participate in a study. The reason given for refusing access to the information was the confidentiality of school records. It would be unfortunate, in the extreme, if the Privacy Act were to be widely employed to close off school records to any kind of research at all.

McGrath (1962) also used indirect data in his study of friendship and group behavior. The dependent variable was the competitive performance of rifle teams, plotted against whether the team had given favorable or unfavorable ratings to former teammates and how the team had been rated. I.D. Steiner (1964) comments on a possible restriction on generalization: "Additional research is needed to determine whether the individualistic orientation which was a boon to rifle teams would also promote productivity in situations calling for cooperative group action" (p. 434). Steiner's question reminds us that evidence revealed in the study of shooting accuracy of black and white basketball players (Jones and Hochner, 1973) showed that styles of play apparently differed between the National Basketball Association and what was then the American Basketball Association, the latter being characterized by a more individualistic style of play. Even today, fans of the game realize that there are differences between teams in style of play. A new player or manager who might be an improvement for one team may be a disaster for another.

It has long been suspected that the phenomenon of seeking medical attention has a meaning beyond mere illness. In fact, it is often estimated that 60 percent or more of visits to a physician's office are occasioned by psychological rather than physical problems. Mechanic and Volkart (1961) found that the frequency of sick call visits in a population of college students was related to the subject's degree of stress and his or her tendency to play the sick role. In fact, Follette and Cummings (1967) even found that the frequency of use of medical services was reduced by psychotherapy, perhaps even by a single session. On the other hand, Fiedler and his associates (Fiedler et al., 1958; Fiedler, 1962) examined several measures of "adjustment" in army units—sick call frequency, disciplinary offense ratings, and court-martial records—and found little relationship among the measures, underlining the problem of combining pieces of evidence that merely *look* to be similar in reflecting some characteristic.

For a variety of reasons, hospitals keep many and, for the most part, careful records. Such records seem to show that summer is not the best time to have anything serious done at a hospital since that is when experienced residents and interns lose interest, since they are moving, and when new residents and interns do not yet know what they are doing. A review of factors associated with the utilization of medical services, relying on hospital and other medical records such as those from insurance companies, suggests the important role of supply as a determinant of utilization (Health Care Financing Administration, 1980). Where there are lots of hospital beds, lots of physicians, and low bed-occupancy rates, people stay in the hospital longer—apparently unnecessarily. If there are many hospital-based physicians in relation to general practitioners, people tend to get treated in hospitals; not so if there are relatively many general practitioners. Where there are more surgeons, more surgery gets done, but with no evident impact on health. Probably one should try to stay out of hospitals, but Flood et al. (1979) have exploited hospital records in a particularly sophisticated way to show that when other factors are held constant, hospitals that provide more services to a given type of patient have better outcomes. Treatments are often evaluated on the basis of hospital data. For example, Paul and Lentry (1977) used such hospital record data as time to discharge, time out of hospital, and readmission rates to evaluate different treatments for psychiatric patients, all these being far less reactive than either patient or psychiatrist ratings. Similar data from the criminal justice system and schools, for example, police and court contacts, grades, and school attendance, were used to evaluate different interventions with delinquent youngsters. Not all treatment of delinquency may be so good, particularly in terms of long-term effects. McCord (1978) has reported on a 30-year follow-up of men who had been the objects of delinquency interventions in their youth, and in comparison to an untreated group, that they had more often been treated for alcoholism and for serious mental disorder, and that they had also committed a larger number of crimes if they had criminal records.

High-school yearbooks are interesting documents in any number of ways. They record the concerns of students, their interests, reflect some of the social forces and influences impinging upon them, and they display each student's picture and a bit of that student's school history. Barthell and Holmes (1968) examined high-school yearbooks in order to determine whether there might be support for the hypothesis that persons who later become schizophrenic show evidence of earlier social isolation, as had been suggested by more reactive measures that, for example, permitted the possibility that knowledge that a person was schizophrenic might bias memory of, or reports of, earlier behavior. Two groups of patients in a mental hospital were identified, one group composed of persons having been diagnosed as schizophrenic, the other of persons having diagnoses in the psychoneurotic category. The high schools they attended were determined, and investigators then went to the high schools to look at the yearbooks. The data of interest were the social activities listed under each student's picture. Control subjects were those students whose pictures were nearest to those of the psychiatric patients, and who were of the same sex and race, but with a different last name. Sure enough, the schizophrenics had been involved in fewer activities than the control subjects, with the psychoneurotics in between. Additional analysis showed that the difference was specifically attributable to the lower participation of the schizophrenics in "social" activities and not to lower participation in service, performance, or athletic activities. A subsequent study (Napoleon, Chassin, and Young, 1980) has also shown that, as judged by their high school yearbook pictures, psychiatric patients were less attractive as adolescents than their peers.

Church records seem not to have been much explored by social scientists, but many churches keep records of various sorts. Wicker and his associates (Wicker, 1969; Wicker, McGrath, and Armstrong, 1972) were interested in testing some propositions derived from Barker's behavior setting theory about the relationship between the size of a group and participation in its activities. As expected, members of smaller churches participated in more different kinds of activities, spent more time in those activities, were more likely to be in positions of leadership, attended church more often, and contributed more money. Archival data on 104 churches showed a negative relationship between church size and several indexes of support for church activities.

Reverting to military records, Blake (1978) accomplished a study that would surely be impossible by any means other than the study of records. He was interested in Durkheim's theory of suicide as it bears on the concept of altruistic suicide, that is, the deliberate sacrificing of one's life on behalf of others. It is hypothesized that altruistic suicide should be more frequent in highly cohesive than in less cohesive groups. The list of Congressional Medal of Honor winners includes a sizable number of men who voluntarily used their own bodies to shield other men from exploding devices. These deaths, for most did die, could be considered instances of altruistic suicide. Blake thought that "exclusive" combat units, for example, marines, airborne units, special forces, and so on, would be more cohesive than regular units, and, therefore, such units should have had more cases of altruistic suicide. There was, in fact, support for the hypothesis.

WRITTEN DOCUMENTS

The last major class of more or less private archives is personal documents. These have been more the bailiwick of the historiographer than the behavioral scientist, but a number of notable studies have been performed using personal documents. Cox (1926), in Volume 2 of Terman's *Genetic Studies of Genius,* used documentary evidence of all kinds, and, on the history of science side, we have Terman's early (1917) study estimating Galton's IQ. Centering on records of Galton's prowess between the ages of three and eight (he could read any English-language book by five and knew the *Iliad* and *Odyssey* by six), Terman compared them with the ages at which other children are able to accomplish the same or similar achievements and estimated Galton's IQ to be not far from 200.

There have been important methodological works, such as G.W. Allport's (1942) monograph, *The Use of Personal Documents in Psychological Science,* and facilitating method papers, such as Dollard and Mowrer's (1947) system to determine the amount of tension in written documents by a "Discomfort Relief Quotient."

But for all this, written documents have been another of the underdeveloped data resources of social science. In the examples that follow, we cite some of the major studies using written documents and illustrate some of the rival hypotheses coincident with them.

One could not think of letters as a research source without bringing to mind Thomas and Znaniecki's (1918) classic study of the Polish peasant. Letters sent between Poland and the United States were one of the major elements in a data pool that included autobiographies, newspaper accounts, court proceedings, and the records of social agencies. Rather by happenstance, Thomas learned that there was an extensive correspondence between the two countries and that many of the letters were being thrown away. From this lead, advertisements were placed that offered to pay for each letter produced.

There are, to be sure, substantial questions about the population and content restrictions in the letters Thomas and Znaniecki gathered; there are in any body of voluntarily produced (even for pay) research materials. Typically, they only had one side of the exchange, a common and frustrating condition often bemoaned by biographers and historians. In a commentary on this study, Riley (1963) states:

> In all such instances, then, their data refer only to selected members of each group (family) and cover only part of the

> interaction. These gaps illustrate an important potential limitation in the use of available data generally: not having been assembled for the purpose of the investigation, the data may be fragmentary or incomplete, thus depriving the researcher of valuable information.
>
> Another limitation is that such privately owned and spontaneously produced materials may be rare or difficult to obtain. Owners of letters, diaries, or other personal documents may sometimes object to their use for research purposes.... Moreover, situations producing appropriate materials may be rare. The continuing exchange of letters, for example, seems to depend upon long-term or frequent separation of the members, as well as upon a custom of detailed letter writing. Nevertheless, there are no doubt many instances in which similar data are available for further research, as, for instance, when servicemen are separated from their families [pp. 242–243].

Riley thus points out that the dross rate may be high ("situations producing appropriate materials may be rare"), and that population restrictions may be present ("... exchange ... seems to depend upon long-term or frequent separation ... owners may sometimes object to their use"). Specifically for cross-cultural comparison purposes, there is the question of differential literacy rates. How many of the Polish peasants could write? If they could not, and had letters written for them by others, say, village scribes, did the presence of these intervening persons serve to alter the content of the letters? On the voluntary supplying of the letters, did the correspondent give up only a biased sample? A money incentive might have to be prohibitively high to pry loose some love letters, for example, or letters that detailed complaints about the correspondent's frugality in sending money back home.

In Sunday feature articles, one sometimes reads another group of one-way letters: those sent from children in summer camp to their parents. By themselves, they are instructive of a child's perception of the surrounding world. Salzinger (1958) got the other end of this candid correspondence as well, and analyzed the content of mail from children and parents, comparing the letters for similarity on "wants," "demands," and "requests."

Janowitz (1958) dealt with letters and diaries captured from German soldiers. His concern was the impact of propaganda on these troops, and "when these letters dealt with the German writer himself, or his small circle of friends, they contained testimony of considerable value. Many made valuable propaganda documents, especially captured undelivered mail" (p. 734). This last point is of interest, for the undelivered mail is a subset of mail that is most recent and most pertinent for evaluation of propaganda effect. Letters captured on the person of troops may also be particularly valuable, for they contain not only the most recent expressions of feeling, but may also include letters the writer may have been postponing mailing. Such uncertain writings may be prime indicators of attitudes and morale, for the easy stereotypes of "I'm fine Ma and the food's not bad" are more likely to be quickly dispatched.

Letters to political figures are another source of data. For some magnificent examples of these, as well as a general treatment of the topic, one can examine *Dear F.D.R.* (Sussman, 1963, an earlier report of which is in Sussman, 1959. See also Dexter, 1963).

A particularly fine discussion of possible sources of error in letters is presented in Dexter's (1964) chapter on letters to congressmen. He notes that congressmen do not necessarily see any cause for alarm in a barrage of negative mail.

> One "pro-labor" Senator, out of curiosity, had his staff check up the writers of 100 letters he received advocating support of a higher minimum wage. It was found that 75 writers were eligible to register, but of these only 33 actually were registered. Furthermore, the letters were advocating his support of a measure on which he had been particularly active, and the content of the mail showed no realization of the stand he had so publicly taken. The Senator could scarcely get excited about these letter writers as either a source of opposition or of support on the basis of that issue [p. 399].[2]

[2]Reprinted with permission of the Free Press of Glencoe from *People, Society and Mass Communications,* edited by L.A. Dexter and D.M. White. Copyright © 1964 by the Free Press of Glencoe, a division of The Macmillan Company. Based upon "Congressmen and the People They Listen To," Massachusetts Institute of Technology, 1955, and *American Business and Public Policy,* Atherton, New York, 1963.

If the only goal of the senator is to stay in office, the mail from an ineligible voter is only so much dross. His greater concern is the lack of any intelligence from the great mass of eligible voters who do not write.

Dexter goes on to discuss why mail is important, but speaks of the congressman's description of "genuine," "junk," and "stimulated" mail. Of interest is the way in which they are discriminated.

> It [mail] is not believed if "junk" i.e., press releases or other broadcast mailings, nor if it be stimulated. Stimulated mail is not entirely easy to define. In its pure form it consists of virtually identical postcard messages written under the instigation of a single company, union or interest group. (one company even mailed the postcards for its workers, fearing that they would not know who their congressman was.) Congressmen look for signs of stimulation—similarity of phrasing ("They all used the same argument.") or even stationery ("They handed out the paper.") and time of mailing ("You could tell the hour or minute someone pushed the button.") . . . it is hard to fool a congressman as to when mail is stimulated. Some organizations urge their members to write in their own words, on their own stationery, and as personally as possible. Congressional assistants tell us that perhaps one in fifty persons who write such a letter will enclose the original printed notice from the organization urging an individualized apparently spontaneous letter [p. 403].

As for the extent of this false element in spontaneous mail,

> Most of the mail sent on the Reciprocal Trade Act was in some sense stimulated . . . [for] Eastern and Southern congressmen . . . Westinghouse, Dow, Monsanto, and Pittsburgh Plate Glass may have stimulated 40 percent or more of all the mail received on the issue in 1954. . . . Mail in favor of reciprocal trade was equally stimulated and perhaps by even fewer prime movers. Our impression is that three-fourths of all antiprotectionist mail was stimulated directly or indirectly by the League of Women Voters [pp. 403–404].

A check on the true level of protest mail was made by the Xerox Corporation. Flooded with negative letters after sponsorship of a television series on the United Nations, they hired a group of handwriting experts to examine the mail. "A total of

51,279 protests had been received. The handwriting experts determined that the letters were written by 12,785 persons. The latter figures practically equalled the number of favorable letters" (Kupcinet, 1965). No mention is made of an equivalent analysis of the "pro" letters.

This selective bias in the population mailing letters to congressmen or others results in an invalid generalization on the state of public opinion, but it can serve as evidence of how the major pressure groups are responding. The bias itself is not fatal; only not knowing of it is.

Earlier, we mentioned the problem of population-restriction bias in suicide notes, observing that less than 25 percent of all suicides leave final notes. Osgood and Walker (1959) took this into account in their study of motivation and language behavior. Reasoning from behavioral principles, they predicted that the content of suicide notes should differ significantly from control notes and simulated suicide notes. Persons about to take their lives should be highly motivated (something of an understatement), and this motivation should increase the dominant responses in their hierarchies; a higher than normal level of stereotypy should be present. Content analysis by six different stereotypy indexes supported their prediction. This study is a good example of relating "natural phenomena" that exist in the outside world to principles derived from laboratory experimentation. There are many tests for theoretical postulates available in settings other than the laboratory, and joint testing in the laboratory and outside may yield powerful validity checks.

Spiegel and Neuringer (1963) also tested a specific hypothesis by the employment of suicide notes. They examined the proposition that inhibition of the experience of dread ordinarily evoked by suicidal intention is a necessary condition for suicidal action. They drew on the Los Angeles County coroner's office for their material, noting a control of "false" suicide notes. Other suicide-note studies have been conducted by Gottschalk and Gleser (1960) and by Schneidman and Farberow (1957).

Art work is another expressive personal document that may provide data—as is shown by all the clinical psychologists who look at Van Gogh's paintings and say, "Than man was in trouble!" An equally *post hoc* analysis, but with more analytic elegance, has been contributed by Barry (1957). He studied the complexity of art form as related to severity of socialization. From Whiting and Child's (1953) 76 nonliterate societies on which socialization data are available, he found 30 with at least ten extant examples of graphic art—either displays in museums or illustrations in ethnographic reports. There was a low-level association between complexity of art form and degree of severity of socialization. The unknown question is whether a higher or lower level of association would have been detected had the data been available for more than 30 societies. Were those who were more gentle in socialization less likely to produce art work which has survived to the present? Note, too, that there is the selective screen of museum curators and ethnographers. Materials might have survived physically from the other 46 societies but have been defined as of insufficient artistic or scientific worth to display behind glass or on paper.

What might be considered an equally primitive art form was studied by Solley and Haigh (1957) and by Craddick (1961). Both investigations showed that the size of children's drawings of Santa Claus was larger before Christmas than after. Sechrest and Wallace (1964) asked whether the size of the Santa Claus drawing might be traced to a generalized expansive euphoria associated with the excitement of the season, and whether children might be expected to draw almost any object larger during the Christmas season. Their experimentation showed this was not the case, and the Santa Claus was the only one of three objects drawn larger. Craddick (1962) also found that the mean size of drawings of witches decreased at Halloween time. Berger (1954), working from doodles in the notebooks of college students, found a correlation of .75 between graphic constriction in the doodles and neurotic tendency.

A CONCLUDING NOTE

In this review of archival studies, we have seen the versatility of the written record. Not only has the content of study varied, but also the functions these data have served.

The supply of archives is extensive and has only begun to be tapped. Domhoff (1978), for example, is interested in studying "the ruling class" in the United States and has assembled a guide to the sources for such work, so that one may, for example, map the power structure. For information on corporations Domhoff lists among others, the following:

> *Moody's* manuals
> Dun and Bradstreet's *Million Dollar Directory, Middle Market Directory,* and *Directory of Shopping Centers*
> *The New York Times, Wall Street Journal, Business Week*

For information on Foundations:

> *The Foundation Directory*
> *Where America's Foundations Make Their Grants*
> *Trustees of Wealth*

For how to find people and their affiliations:

> *Biographical Dictionaries Master Index* (indexes over 50 Who's Whos)
> *Who's Who in America* (the single most valuable source)
> *Contemporary Authors*
> *New York Times Biographical Service*
> *Who's Who in the West*
> *Who's Who in Colorado*
> *Social Register*
> *Who's Who in World Jewry*
> *Who's Who in Aviation and Astronautics*

Domhoff provides a wide range of suggestions on how to find out who runs things. It would be greatly useful to have a similar diligent effort directed at resources for investigating other kinds of problems.

For some research purposes, there were few alternatives to archives—not a brilliant recommendation, but certainly a compelling one. With suicides, for example, there is no choice but to wait until a population defines itself operationally. Once this happens, one can go to farewell notes, biographical material, and interviews with relatives; but one cannot go to the subject. So, too, for the general student of the past. For one like Terman (1917), who chose to study Galton, there was no easy alternative to consulting the written record.

In a limited content area, the archival record provides *the* dependent variable. Just as votes are the ultimate criterion for the politician, sales and work performance are the ultimate criteria for some applied social scientists. It has been of interest in the history of research in both advertising and personnel that relatively direct criterion variables have been ignored, while less pertinent ones were labored over. (Measuring "willingness to buy" by questionnaire methods is an example, although it does have some utility in prediction studies.)

There are also a few studies in which records were used as a medium through which theoretical principles could be tested. Such studies are too few, but these records offer superb opportunities to validate hypotheses generated in less natural and more reactivity-prone settings. There are restrictions, but it should be recognized that there are restrictions in any single class of information. Berlyne (1964), in commenting on some highly controlled experimental work, wrote:

> Skinner and his associates have concentrated on situations in which an animal can perform a particular kind of response repeatedly at a high rate. The findings yielded by this kind of experiment have been extrapolated without much hesitation, and not always with specific empirical warrant, to a diversity of human activities, including those on which the most important social problems hinge [pp. 115–116].

Osgood and Walker (1959) used suicide notes to study the effect of heightened motivation on response hierarchies. Also using records as a testing medium, Mosteller and Wallace (1963) went to records of 1787–1788 for their comparative study of a Bayesian procedure with a classical statistical approach. They demonstrated that both procedures reached the same conclusion on the disputed authorship of some of *The Federalist Papers*.[3]

The great majority of these studies, however, have used the archives for indirect evidence. Stuart's (1963) study of union grievances and the state of race relations, Parker's (1963) study of library withdrawals to show the effect of television, and the

[3] For an excellent general treatment of "identifying the unknown communicator," see Paisley (1964), where studies in painting, literature, and music are reviewed.

measurement of the size of Santa Clauses (Solley and Haigh, 1957; Craddick, 1961; Sechrest and Wallace, 1964) all reveal the inventive unveiling of valuable evidence. But only partial evidence—for the reasons traced in the preceding chapter show the need for care in generalizing from such analyses. Here, as with the running public records, there is a heavy demand for consideration of possible data transformations and for the construction of multiple indexes. If it is agreed that the archives typically provide only partial evidence, and if the desirable research strategy is to generate multiple displays of overlapping evidence, then the way in which these partial clues are pieced together is critical.

We should recognize that using the archival records frequently means substituting someone else's selective filter for your own. Although the investigator may not himself contaminate the material, he may learn that the producer or repository already has. A thoughtful consideration of the sources of invalidity may provide intelligence on these, either by suggesting astute hedges or new analyses to answer rival hypotheses. In any event, the Chinese proverb still holds:

The palest ink is clearer than the best memory.

CHAPTER 7

Simple Observation

Who could he be? He was evidently reserved, and melancholy. Was he a clergyman?—He danced too well. A barrister?—He was not called. He used very fine words, and said a great deal. Could he be a distinguished foreigner come to England for the purpose of describing the country, its manners and customs; and frequenting city balls and public dinners with the view of becoming acquainted with high life, polished etiquette, and English refinement?—No, he had not a foreign accent. Was he a surgeon, a contributer to the magazines, a writer of fashionable novels or an artist?—No: to each and all of these surmises there existed some valid objection.—"Then," said everybody, "he must be somebody."—"I should think he must be," reasoned Mr. Malderton, with himself, "because he perceives our superiority, and pays us much attention."

(Sketches from Boz)

Charles Dickens displayed a ready touch for observationally scouring the behavior of this mysterious gentleman for evidence with which to classify him—even going so far as to put out the hypothesis that the man was a participant observer. In this chapter, the first of two on observational methods, our interest is focused on situations in which the observer has no control over the behavior or sign in question and plays an unobserved, passive, and nonintrusive role in the research situation. The next chapter details studies in which the observer has played an active role in structuring the situation, but in which he is still unobserved by the actors. Since we have limited our discussion to measures with low risks of reactivity, the visible

197

"research-observer" approach and the participant observation method have been minimized here.[1]

VISIBLE OBSERVERS

The patently visible observer can produce changes in behavior that diminish the validity of comparisons. Arsenian (1943) noted that the simple presence of an adult sitting near a door seemed to lend assurance to a group of nursery school children. The opposite change was noted by Polansky and associates (1949) in studying the effect of the presence of observers among young boys at a summer camp. There the observers were a threat and became objects of active aggression. Not only is change produced that reduces the generalizability of findings, but if one were comparing children in two settings varying in the visibility of observers or the reaction to observers, internal validity would take a blow.

The effect of the observer may erode over time, as Deutsch (1949) has shown, and thereby produce a selective contaminant in observational data series. The defense against this is to permit the effect of the observer contaminant to wear off, and start analysis with data subsequent to the time when the effect is negligible. This is similar to experimental controls for practice effects in learning experiments and presumes that the effect will wear off quickly enough not to waste too much data. And that in turn is based on the researcher's ability to measure the independent effect of observation in the series.

Bales (1950) tested whether different arrangements of observers would selectively bias group behavior. Observers sat with the group, or behind a one-way screen with the group aware they were there, or behind the screen with the group unsure if they were there. He found no difference in group behavior under these conditions. All conditions were applied in a laboratory, however, and all the groups knew they were being

[1]More standard treatments of research methods may be consulted for extensive discussion of observational techniques with the observer visible. See Carlsmith, Ellsworth, and Aronson (1976), Kerlinger (1973), and Weick (1977). The volume edited by Ciminero, Calhoun, and Adams (1977) also has a number of articles pertinent to the methodology of observer studies.

tested. These factors might overpower the possibly weaker effects of the physical position of the observer. Zajonc (1965) has studied the effect of an audience on performance, and to the extent that a visible observer constitutes an audience, his findings indicate the probability of differential effects depending on the response. Specifically, an audience enhances performance of well practiced responses but is harmful to the performance of responses being learned.

No matter how well integrated an observer becomes, we feel he is still an element with potential to bias the production of the critical data substantially. The bias may be a selective one to jeopardize internal validity, or, perhaps more plausibly, it may cripple the ability of the social scientist to generalize her or his findings very far beyond the sample. A number of writers (cf. Bain, 1960; Gullahorn and Strauss, 1960; Gusfield, 1960; Wax, 1960) have argued for the participant observation method as a device to circumvent some of the contaminations of studies employing an "outside" observer. It may do that, but there is still a high risk of contaminants surviving to invalidate comparisons.

Participant Observation

Riley (1963) has suggested that the participant observation studies are subject to two classes of error—"control effect" and "biased-viewpoint effect." The control effect is present when the measurement process itself becomes an agent working for change: "the difficulty with control effect in participant observation, and in many other research designs, is that it is unsystematic . . ." (p. 71). The biased-viewpoint effect includes what we have discussed under the label of intra-instrument processes. The instrument (the human observer) may selectively expose himself to the data, or selectively perceive them, and, worse yet, shift over time the calibration of his observation measures.

This observer bias has been suggested by Naroll and Naroll (1963), who speak of the anthropologist's tendency to be disposed to "exotic data." The observer is more likely to report on phenomena that are different from those of his or her own society or subculture than to report on phenomena common to both. When the participant observer spends an extended period of time in a foreign culture (a year among the Fulani or six months with a city gang), those elements of the culture which first seemed notable because they were alien may later acquire a more homey quality. Increased familiarity with the culture alters the observer as an instrument.

Riley suggests that the control effect may be reduced by the observer assuming an incognito role, even though ethical questions are raised, but,

> on the other hand, the covert observer may find complete immersion in the system, and subsequent likelihood of a biased viewpoint, more difficult to avoid. Limited to his specified role, he may be cut off from valuable channels of information, unable to solicit information not normally accessible to his role without arousing suspicions [p. 72].

Associated with this class of observation is the use of the informant, who is a participant observer one selective screen away from the investigator. Back (1960) writes of the traits of the good informant (knowledgeability, physical exposure, effective exposure, perceptual abilities, availability of information, motivation) and points out some of the difficulties of receiving valid and appropriate data from informants.

Dalton (1964) gives an excellent pro and con analysis of participant observation in his commentary on the methods used in *Men Who Manage*. Dalton's pro list is longer than the con one, and he employs the intriguing terminology of "established circulator" and "peripheral formalist."

It is necessary at this point to comment on the ethical issues germane to participant observation. Some (for example, Erikson, 1967) argue that it is unethical to misrepresent the purpose of research to anyone, but others contend that undercover investigations are acceptable if the target is some group engaged in alleged illegal activities, for example professional criminals and fascist groups (Lofland, 1961). Becker (1964) has stated that clandestine research may be conducted if that is "the only feasible means for reaching important scientific goals." Aside from the complaint of deceiving an innocent public, other issues concerning participant observation cause controversy. Gay Talese, (1980) for example, has recently written a book based on his experiences as a participant observer in what he claims is modern American sexual behavior. Talese informed the people he was writing about of his professional intentions, but many would argue that his project was at best in poor taste. Some things do not bear participation in, even for the purpose of studying them. Alexander Pope explained the risks of participation more elegantly:

> Vice is a monster of so frightful mien
> As to be hated, needs but to be seen.
> And yet having looked too oft on her face
> First we pity, then endure, then embrace.

As a final note on participant observation, we cite Lang and Lang's (1960) report, in which participant observers became participants. Two scientific observers of audience behavior at a Billy Graham Crusade in New York made *their* "Decision for Christ" and left the fold of observers to walk down the aisle. This is in itself an interesting measure. What a testimony to the Reverend Graham's persuasive skills, when sociological observers are so swayed that they leave their posts!

Stephen Leacock said, "Let me hear the jokes of a nation and I will tell you what the people are like, how they are getting along, and what is going to happen to them" (Manago, 1962). This may be too haughty a claim for conclusions possible from one set of observational data, but we note below studies that produce impressive findings from the opportunistic use of observation of events over which the investigator has no control. We could do our readers no better favor, in any case, than to refer them to the fine book by Desmond Morris (1977), *Manwatching: A Field Guide to Human Behavior*. A few items from Morris' index will give the flavor of his work and suggest why we think it an excellent companion piece to this chapter: alternating attention movements, body slump, gesture maps, overkill signals, perfume, Punjab 'snake tongue' sign, shoulder embrace, tic-tac language, and vertical lean. We do urge, however, that *Manwatching* be taken as a source of stimulation and not be treated as a fountain of certain knowledge.

These simple observation studies that follow have been organized into the following categories: exterior physical signs, expressive movement, physical location, language behavior (conversation sampling), and time duration. The breadth of these measures is notable, and they are "simple" only in that the investigator does not intervene in the production of the material.

EXTERIOR PHYSICAL SIGNS

Most of the exterior physical signs discussed are durable ones that have been inferred to be expressive of current or past behavior. A smaller number are portable and short-lived. The bullfighter's beard is a case in point. Conrad (1958) reports that the bullfighter's beard is longer on the day of the fight than on any other day. There are supporting comments among matadors about this phenomenon, yet can one measure the torero's anxiety by noting the length of his beard? The physical task is rather difficult, but not impossible in this day of sophisticated instrumentation. As in all these uncontrolled measures, one must draw inferences about the criterion behavior. Maybe it wasn't the anxiety at all. Perhaps the bullfighter stands farther away from the razor on the morning of the fight, or he may not have shaved that morning at all (like baseball pitchers and boxers). And then there is the possible intersubject contaminant that the more affluent matadors are likely to be shaved, while the less prosperous shave themselves. Perhaps an anonymous report in the highly respected scientific journal *Nature* can lend insight to this apparent phenomenon. In this particular article (1970) a British scientist noted that a man's beard will seem unusually heavy when he is looking forward to a date with an exciting girlfriend or if he has been away from his wife and expects to see her the following day.

A more easily quantified measure is tattoos. Burma (1959) reports on the observation of tattoos among some nine hundred inmates of three different institutions. The research measure was the proportion of inmates with tattoos: "significantly more delinquents than nondelinquents tattoo themselves." Of course, one could hardly reverse the findings and hold that tattooing can be employed as a single measure of delinquency. Although it may be true that delinquents are more likely than nondelinquents to have tattoos, the relationship between number of tattoos and severity of criminal offense is negative (Orten and Bell, 1974). In Orten and Bell's study, 105 inmates at the Tennessee prison for men were interviewed. These researchers found that thieves had the most elaborate sets of tattoos, armed robbers had fewer, and rapists and kidnappers had even fewer. Men convicted of attempted murder displayed only a small number of tattoos and convicted murderers had the least of all. Taylor has also conducted an extensive study of tattoos and the reasons people get them (1970). Among his findings are the following: people are most likely to get tattooed when they are teenagers; psychiatric patients are more likely than other people to have amateur tattoos; females are more likely than males to have tattoos marking homosexual experiences; and girls with tattoos are more likely to have psychological problems than tattooed boys.

More formal classification cues are tribal markings and scars. Doob (1961) reports on a walk he and an African companion took through a Nigerian market.

> I casually pointed to a dozen men, one after the other, who had facial scars. My African friend in all instances named a society; then he and I politely verified the claim by speaking to the person and asking him to tell us the name of his tribe. In eleven instances out of twelve, he was correct. Certainly, however, he may have been responding simultaneously to other cues in the person's appearance, such as his clothing or his skin color [p. 83].

In a report whose authors choose to remain anonymous (Anonymoi, 1953–1960), it was discovered that there is a strong association between the methodological disposition of psychologists and the length of their hair. The authors observed the hair length of psychologists attending professional meetings and coded the meetings by the probable appeal to those of different methodological inclinations. Thus, in one example, the length of hair was compared between those who attended an experimental set of papers and those who attended a series on ego-identity formation. The results are clear cut. The "tough-minded" psychologists have shorter-cut hair than the liberal-minded psychologists. Symptomatic interpretations—psycho-analytic inquiries as to what is cut about the clean-cut young men—are not the only possibilities. The causal ambiguity of the correlation was clarified when the "dehydration hypothesis" (that is, that lack of insulation caused the hard-headedness) was rejected by the "bald-head control," that is, examining the distribution of baldheaded persons (who by the dehydration hypothesis should be most hardheaded of all).

Clothes are an obvious indicator, and A. M. Rosenthal (1962), wrote of "the wide variance between private manners and public behavior" of the Japanese:

> Professor Enright [British lecturer in Japan] and just about every other foreigner who ever visited Japan have noted with varying degrees of astonishment that there is a direct relationship between the politeness of a Japanese and whether or not he is wearing shoes [p. 20].

It is quite likely that this relationship reflects the selective distribution of shoes in the Japanese society more than any causal element, an example of a population restriction. The economically marginal members of the Japanese population should, one would think, be more overt in expressing hostility to foreign visitors than those who are economically stable—and possession of shoes is more probably linked to affluence than it is to xenophobia.

Shoe styles, not their presence, have been used as the unit of discrimination in the United States society where almost everybody does wear shoes. Gearing (1952), in a study of subculture awareness in south Chicago, observed shoe styles, finding features of the shoe to correspond with certain patterns of living. In general, the flashier shoe more often belonged to the more culture-bound individual. Similiar concern with feet was shown by the OSS Assessment Staff (1948) when, because standard uniforms reduced the number of indicators, they paid special attention to shoes and socks as a prime indication "of taste and status." Some years back Sechrest came across a study by Filipino social scientists that attempted to develop an index of social class for use in that country. Several of the items referred to footwear: barefoot, common sandals, shoe material of something other than leather, shoes either brown or black and all of one color, and shoes clean or polished. Other items in the index referred to items of clothing, hairstyle, cleanliness of fingernails, eye contact while speaking, and various linguistic habits or deficiencies. In a sample of 115 males between the ages of 30 and 40 years, the social class index correlated .69 with an English language verbal intelligence test. More direct measures of education and income correlated with the intelligence measure to almost exactly the same degree. An exceptionally interesting effort by Barger and Earl (1971) was directed toward assessing the relative levels of cultural assimilation among Eskimos and Indians in the Great Whale River area in Canada. One evidence of assimilation was taken to be permanent housing: more of the Eskimos lived in permanent housing, and many more of the Indians lived in mobile movable housing of one sort or another. Eskimos also proved to have more of both minor and major possessions characteristic of members of the larger Canadian society.

Despite the general consensus on clothing as an indicator of status, little controlled work has been done on the subject. Flugel (1930) wrote a discursive book on clothing in general, and Webb (1957) reported on class differences in attitudes toward clothes and clothing stores. Another investigation shows many differences between clothing worn by independent and fraternity affiliated college males. Within the fraternity groups, better grades are made by the more neatly dressed (Sechrest, 1971). On the other hand, recently it has been observed that fraternities with lower grade point averages are more likely than those with better grades to dress uniformly at intramural basketball games (Sechrest, Clark, and Grove, 1980). Manner of dress is commonly thought to provide a basis for inferring attitudes, and McGovern and Holmes (1976) offer some confirmation of the stereotype. Students were approached by either a male or female confederate and were asked to sign a noncontroversial petition. Manner of dress of the students was noted, and sloppily dressed students were as likely to sign the petition for the female as the male confederate. Neatly dressed, and by inference conservative, students were less likely to sign the petition if approached by the female confederate. Moreover, neatly dressed females were just as unlikely to cooperate with the female petitioner as the neatly dressed males.

Cialdini has used clothing to study the phenomenon he calls "basking in reflected glory." In one particular study (Cialdini, Borden, Thorne, Walker, Freeman, and Sloan, 1976), he and his colleagues found that university students were more likely to wear school identifying apparel after their school's football team had been victorious than after it had lost. We might wonder whether students would be tempted to wear an identifying jacket when the weather did not call for it at all. At the University of Kansas, there is a specially designed copper manikin that makes it possible to index the insulating value of various items of clothing in a unit called the "clo" (Miller, 1980). A men's jacket has a clo of .22 if light and .49 if heavy; the values for women's jackets are .17 and .37. Heavy skirts clo at .22 and heavy slacks come in at .44. We have a new way of determining who is overdressed, at least in terms of climate.

A number of unobtrusive measures including staff's style of dress were used in a study by Palmer and McGuire (1973) to ascertain descriptors of successful mental health wards at a state hospital. In a similar study, Kane (1958; 1959; 1962) observed the clothing worn by outpatients to their interviews. He has considered pattern, color, texture, and amount of clothing, relating these characteristics to various moods, traits, and personality changes. In a more reactive study, Green and Knapp (1959) associated preferences for different types of tartans with need Achievement. Persons low in need Achievement preferred "warm" colored tartans—reds and yellows—and those with high achievement needs preferred the cooler greens and blues. A similar finding was preported by Sales (1971) who found that a complex set of variables related to introversion-extroversion distinguished between persons who preferred simple to complex tartans. Much needed is a study to determine whether these somewhat reactive preferences are related to clothing actually purchased or worn.

As part of their study of the social status of legislators and their voting, MacRae and MacRae (1961) observed the houses lived in by legislators and rated them along the lines suggested by Warner (Warner, Meeker, and Eells, 1949). This house rating was part of the overall social-class index produced for each legislator. Sechrest, Clark, and Grove (1980) also rated the appearance of houses. In this study several judges rated the overall appearance of fraternity houses on a university campus and these ratings were found to correlate with a number of other measures. For example, the fraternities with the most attractive and well-kept houses were most likely to have a high proportion of female spectators at their intramural basketball games, a relatively greater proportion of intramural players with matching uniforms, a large percentage of cars in their parking lots with university and fraternity bumper stickers and decals, and a small percentage of people leaving the houses for early morning classes.

Wrightsman (1969) also counted bumper stickers, but for a different purpose. He wanted to see if supporters for the three presidential candidates in the 1968 election differed in their tendency to obey the law. By recording presence or absence of county auto tax stickers on cars displaying bumper stickers supporting one of the three candidates, he discovered that Wallace supporters were less likely than Humphrey or Nixon voters to have a tax sticker. This trend apparently could not be attributable to socioeconomic differences between the groups. Bumper stickers are a common method of advertising political loyalty, and Jorgenson, Guardabascio, Higginson, Sutton, and Watkins (1977) found that the proportion of Ford to Carter bumper stickers in the 1976 election was reasonably consistent with the results of two polls on voter preference. The data were collected on a university campus, and a study of graffiti was also consistent with the polls but not as close a match to the values obtained.

Observation of any type of possession can be employed as an index if the investigator knows that there is a clear relationship between possession (ownership) of the object and a second variable. Calluses, for example, can serve as an observable indicator of certain classes of activity. Different sports make selective demands on tissue, for example, and the calluses that result are reliable indicators of whether one is a squash player or a golfer. Undoubtedly some occupations may also be given away by similar physical clues.

With such measures used alone, validity is often tenuous. Phillips (1962) is unusual in giving multiple indicators of the changes in Miami resulting from the influx of a hundred thousand Cubans. Two years following the Castro revolution, he observed:

> Bilingual street signs (No Jaywalking; Cruce por la Zona para Peatones)
> "A visitor hears almost as much Spanish as English."
> Signs in windows saying "Se Habla Espanol"
> Stores with names like "Mi Botanica" and "Carniceria Latina"
> Latin-American foods on restaurant menus
> Supermarkets selling yucca, malanga, and platanos
> The manufacture of a Cuban type of cigarette
> Radio broadcasts in Spanish
> Spanish-language editorials in the English-language newspapers
> Services held in Spanish by 40 Miami churches.

Whatever Phillips' measures might have been taken to mean, they signaled clearly what has happened, for recently it was announced that Hispanics now outnumber both whites and blacks not only in Miami itself but in all of Dade County. It is now necessary to be bilingual to get one of many jobs there. The marshaling of so much, and so diverse, observational evidence should have been persuasive.

There is no visible characteristic of a person that is accorded more importance than general physical appearance, although it must be recognized that appearance is multifaceted. What difference does appearance make? Handsome is as handsome does, and at least some aspects of appearance reflect deliberate behaviors designed to produce that appearance. Other aspects of appearance cannot much be helped, but they may be related to attitudes that people hold about themselves and are quite likely to be related to the impressions people make on others. Although not many people would bluntly say so, there is often likely to be a sizing up of appearance that by some mental calculus results in such conclusions as "too unattractive to make a good salesperson" or "really dynamite appearance should make a good impression on the jury."

It is said that beauty is only skin deep, implying that there is something rather superficial about it and thus devaluing it. The idea probably occurred to someone with no knowledge at all of the great effort required of beautiful people on behalf of their beauty. It is also said that beauty is in the eye of the beholder, implying that there are scarcely any standards at all —unless most beholders are pretty much alike. Morris (1977) suggests, however, that beauty may reside, in part, in the eye of the beheld. Photographs of females with dilated pupils were judged more attractive than photographs of the same persons with smaller pupils. Since work cited elsewhere in this book indicates that pupillary dilation is a sign of interest, perhaps beauty is a reflection of perceived chances of something interesting happening. Huston (1973) found that males tended to choose somewhat less attractive prospective dating partners unless they were assured of acceptance by those more attractive. Beauty is as beauty does—or may do. Dabbs thinks that beauty is power. Stokes and Bickman (1974) found that people in need of help were less likely to ask for help from an attractive person than from a less attractive person, and concluded that beauty is somewhat unapproachable. Dabbs and Stokes (1975) then found that pedestrians on a sidewalk yield more space to an attractive than an unattractive female. In the laboratory, subjects will approach more closely a poster displaying a picture of an attractive person than one with a picture of an unattractive person. In real life, however, it appears that that seemingly natural tendency is overridden. Powell and Dabbs (1976) sent attractive and unattractive interviewers out on the street to ask innocuous questions of passersby and found that interviewees would not approach an attractive male or female more closely than an unattractive one. In real-life social settings it seems that, to quote Powell and Dabbs "beauty will be approached circumspectly, if at all" (p. 64). A relatively nonreactive laboratory study (Nadler, 1980) also suggested that people are more reluctant to ask an attractive person for help, especially if they believe they may have to meet that person face-to-face. A note for the curious: Powell and Dabbs observe that the problem of getting ugly people to pose for photographs or to work as confederates is a matter of "delicacy," and they get around the problem by turning attractive people into unattractive people by means of wigs, makeup, and so on. Another item of some interest is that when attractive females rate the attractiveness of less attractive females, they tend to exaggerate their unattractiveness, whereas attractive males tend to minimize the unattractiveness of less attractive males they rate (Tennis and Dabbs, undated).

EXPRESSIVE MOVEMENT

The more plastic variables of body movement historically have interested many observers. Charles Darwin's (1872) work on the expression of emotions continues to be the landmark commentary. His exposition of the measurement of frowning, the uncovering of teeth, erection of the hair, and the like remains provocative reading. A number of studies on expressive movement and personality measurement are reviewed by Wolff and Precker (1951). Of particular interest in their chapter is the emphasis on consistency among different types of expressive movement. They review the relation between personality and the following measures: facial expression, literary style, artistic style, style of speech, gait, painting and drawing, and handwriting. Not all of these studies are nonreactive, since the central criterion for this is that the subject is not aware of being measured. Harper and Wiens (1979) provide an excellent brief review of recent research using unobtrusively obtained nonverbal indicators, and a more extensive treatment of the subjects appears in Harper, Weins, and Matarazzo (1978). An interesting population restriction on at least some uses of nonverbal cues is that females are better than males at detecting and decoding such cues (Hall, 1978).

Examples of using expressive movement as a response to a particular stimulus—that is, stimulus-linked rather than subject-linked—are provided in the work of Maurice Krout (1933; 1937; 1951; 1954a; 1954b). Although this work was done in a laboratory setting, it was under facade conditions. That is, subjects were unaware of the true purpose of the research, considering the experiment a purely verbal task. There is a good possibility for application of Krout's (1954a) approach in less reactive settings. He elicited autistic gestures through verbal-conflict situations, and his analysis deals primarily with digital-manual responses. An example of his findings is the correlation between an attitude of fear and the gesture of placing hand to nose.

Kinesics as a subject of study is relevant here. Since the first edition of this book, the study of body motion has increased substantially. Birdwhistell (1960; 1963) has defined kinesics as being concerned with the communicational aspects of learned, patterned, body-motion behavior. This system of nonverbal communication is felt to be inextricably linked with the verbal, and the aim of such study is to achieve a quantification of the former which can be related to the latter. Some "motion qualifiers" have been identified, such as intensity, range, and velocity. Ruesch and Kees (1956) have presented a combination text-picture treatment in their book, *Non-Verbal Communication.* An example of the impressionistic style of obervation is provided by Murphy and Murphy (1962), who reported on the differences in facial expression between young and old Russians: "While faces of old people often seemed resigned, tired and sad, generally the children seemed lively, friendly, confident and full of vitality" (p. 12).

Something of the detail possible in such studies is shown in Wolff's (1948; 1951) work on hands. In the first study, Wolff observed the gestures of mental patients at meals and at work, concluding, "I found sufficient evidence that correlations exist (1) between emotional make-up and gesture, (2) between the degree of integration and gesture" (1948, p. 166). The second study was anthropometric, and Wolff compared features of the handprints of schizophrenics, mental defectives, and normals. The hands were divided into three major types: (1) elementary, simple and regressive; (2) motor, fleshy and bony; and (3) small and large. On the basis of an individual's hand type, measurements, nails, crease lines, and type of skin, she delineates the main characteristics of their personality, intelligence, vitality, and temperament.

Without necessarily endorsing her conclusions, we report the finding of a confused crease-line pattern peculiar to the extreme of mental deficiency. Other structural characteristics such as concave primary nails, "appeared to a greater or lesser degree in the hands of mental defectives ... but were completely absent in the hands of the control cases" (Wolff, 1951, p. 105). Certainly the hands can be affected by a wide variety of medical conditions. There is a field of study called *dermatoglyphics,* and a bibliography of work in that field (Mavalwala, 1976) shows that the shape of fingers, the appearance of the nails and nailbeds, fingerprints, lines, creases, and many other features of the hands can be affected by conditions as diverse as those related to heart disorder, thyroid disease, leukemia, mental retardation, and problems with the Y chromosome. It is of interest that the heart and fingerprints develop at about the same time in the fetus.

Schubert (1959) has suggested that overt personal behavior could be used in the study of judicial behavior. In presenting a psychometric model of the Supreme Court, he suggests that the speech, grimaces, and gestures of the judges when hearing oral arguments and when opinions are being delivered are rich sources of data for students of the Court. On the other side of the legal fence, witnesses in Hindu courts are reported to give indications of the truth of their statements by the movement of their toes (Krout, 1951). The eminent American legal scholar J. H. Wigmore, in works on judicial proof and evidence (1935; 1937), speaks of the importance of peripheral expressive movements as clues to the validity of testimony. Of great interest is the finding (Friedman, DiMatteo, and Mertz, 1980) that television news anchormen displayed different facial expressions when pronouncing the names "Ford" and "Carter" during the 1976 campaign. Three had significantly more favorable expressions when saying "Carter," one more favorable when saying "Ford." The sole anchorwoman showed no detectable bias.

A number of studies have been conducted relating nonverbal behaviors to lying and deception. For example, Ekman and Friesen (1969) discuss the relative roles of facial expressions and foot/leg movements in the "leakage" of clues that a person is not telling the truth. That these cues can vary across societies is demonstrated by Sechrest and Flores (1971). They showed that "leg jiggling" is more frequent among Filipino than American males, and held that jiggling is a "nervous" behavior. As evidence of this, they found jiggling more frequent in coffee lounges than in cocktail lounges.

A police officer reported eye movement as a "pickup" clue. A driver who repeatedly glances from side to side, then into the rearview mirror, then again from side to side may be abnormally cautious and perfectly blameless. But he may also be abnormally furtive and guilty of a crime. Another officer, in commenting on auto thefts, said "We . . . look for clean cars with dirty license plates and dirty cars with clean plates," explaining that thieves frequently switch plates (Reddy, 1965). Adams (1963) gives a 19-item list of observable things that should create suspicion in a police officer. Aside from dirty license plates on a clean car, the list includes a person wearing a coat on a hot day and "lovers" parked where they might make good lookouts. Powis (1978), an English police expert, suggests that many thieves have an unreasoning fear of leaving fingerprints and that unnecessary gloves may be a giveaway sign. So, too, are such indicators of unfamiliarity with the operation of a particular automobile as turning on lights in daytime or windscreen wipers when it is not raining. Powis also says of thieves: " . . . I have never known such characters to smoke pipes, or rather to smoke pipes in that slow, reflective way that real smokers do. Some flash confidence thieves may have a pipe in their mouths for effect, but they still will not look like pipe-smokers" (p. 7).

In a validation study of self-reported levels of newspaper readership, eye movement was observed when people were reading newspapers in trains, buses, library reading rooms, and the street (Advertising Service Guild, 1949). Strongman (discussed in *New York Times,* May 20, 1980) has done extensive work on eye movement and has found that when people are interacting socially the person who looks away first is the more dominant. He also claims that aggression, humility, and amorous intent can be inferred from systematic observations of eye contact. In a very interesting study, but one which would probably be considered unethical today, Exline, Thibaut, Brannan, and Gumpert (1966) determined that people scoring high on a

Machiavellianism scale are likely to avert their eyes less than people who score low on the scale after justly being accused of cheating on a test. In fact, these investigators found that Machiavellians actually increase duration of eye contact following accusation. A number of creative eye movement and direction studies have been conducted in controlled laboratory settings. Discussion of them is contained in the following chapter on observational hardware.

There are many cues by which most people recognize their own kind, those who belong to their own group, and distinguish them from outsiders. Some of the cues are ritualistic and obvious, for example, the often elaborate handslap greetings common among black males in many communities. Only those who belong could possibly perform the ritual properly, and few outsiders would even try. Other cues, however, are subtle and may go quite unnoticed except by sensitive insiders. Quick and Farrow (1980) tell, for instance, that Lakota Indians can tell how well-acquainted outsiders are with their culture by the way they shake hands with the Lakota, whose handshake is very soft, scarcely more than touching. LaFrance and Mayo (1976) noted the functions served by gaze, among them regulating the flow of conversation and the possibility that differences in gaze behavior might produce communication difficulties between members of different cultures. Hall (1974), for example, had reported that whites often complain that black working-class persons will not look them in the eye. LaFrance and Mayo filmed black-black and black-white dyads during conversations and studied gaze behavior. Kendon (1967) had reported that whites tend to look at a person who is talking to them and look away while talking to the other person. LaFrance and Mayo found a complete reversal of that pattern in their study of black conversationalists. In both same- and mixed-race dyads, blacks looked at the person to whom they were speaking and looked away while being spoken to. The whites held to the previously noted pattern. A second study showed that black males look least while listening, and white females look most while listening. Some native American tribes also learn early that it is impolite, and even insulting under some circumstances, to look another person directly in the eye (Quick and Farrow, 1980). Those who would be well-regarded by persons of backgrounds different from their own may need to be tutored in the subtleties by which belonging and sensitivity are recognized.

When travelling abroad, one of us enjoys playing a "secret agent" game. The aim of this game is to try to discover subtle social customs that would give an agent away if he or she was unaware of them. Once, for example, a couple observed in a restaurant in Greece studiously employed their knives and forks in the usual European way, the knife being used as a pusher and the fork held upside down (from an American perspective). So far, so good. But the two children with their parents were using their utensils in the correct American way. Sure enough, the family was American rather than European. But then, secret agents do not have children anyway.

PHYSICAL LOCATION

The physical position of animals has been a favored measure of laboratory scientists, as well as of those in the field. Imanishi (1960), for example, described the social structure of Japanese macaques by reporting on their physical grouping patterns. The dominant macaques sit in the center of a series of concentric rings. Menzel (1971) reports a fascinating series of "naturalistic" field studies of primates done in part by introducing strange objects such as scarecrows and dolls into their environment and observing their responses, in some instances by time-sampling photography.

For people, there are the familiar newspaper accounts of who stood next to whom in Red Square reviewing the May Day parade. The proximity of a politician to the leader is a direct clue of his status in the power hierarchy. His physical position is interpreted as symptomatic of other behavior which gave him the status position befitting someone four men away from the premier, and descriptive of that current status position. In this more casual journalistic report of observations, one often finds time-series analysis: Mr. B. has been demoted to the end of the dais, and Mr. L. has moved up close to the middle. Hermann (1980) has, incidentally, reported a fascinating study of the personalities of Soviet Politburo members based on their speeches.

Gromyko is generally like Brezhnev in being low in ethnocentrism, high in conceptual complexity, and high in self-confidence. Kirilenko, on the other hand, is low in conceptual complexity but is the highest of all Politburo members in his belief in his own ability to control events. Andropov, head of the KGB, is high in distrust of others. Does the job make the man?

The clustering of blacks and whites was used by Campbell, Kruskal, and Wallace (1966) in their study of seating aggregation as an index of attitude. Where seating in a classroom is voluntary, the degree to which the blacks and whites present sit by themselves versus mixing randomly may be taken as a presumptive index of the degree to which acquaintance, friendship, and preference are strongly colored by race, as opposed to being distributed without regard to racial considerations. Classes in four schools were studied, and significant aggregation by race was found, varying in degree between schools. Aggregation by age, sex, and race has also been reported for elevated trains and lunch counters (Sechrest, 1971). A systematic study of interracial seating patterns on New Orleans buses, trolleys and streetcars was conducted by Davis, Seibert, and Breed (1966) with interesting results. Seating patterns were more integrated when there was an equal balance of blacks and whites in the vehicle, but absolute number of passengers was not a good predictor of interracial seating. Rubington (1969) speculated that community norms would have reduced force in a psychiatric hospital, particularly if the hospital supported a different behavioral norm. He found, as he expected, that an integrated psychiatric hospital in an otherwise segregated community altered interracial social behavior. Rubington studied commensal behavior—who eats with whom—and found seating patterns in the hospital dining room that were mixed rather than segregated. More interestingly, however, Rubington also found that patients assigned to integrated bedrooms more frequently ate with members of the other race than did patients assigned to bedrooms with only members of their own race.

Feshbach and Feshbach (1963) report on another type of clustering. At a Halloween party, they induced fear in a group of boys, aged nine to twelve, by telling them ghost stories. The boys were then called out of the room and were administered questionnaires. The induction of the fear state was natural, but their dependent-variable measures were potentially reactive. What is of interest to us is a parenthetical statement made by the authors. After describing the ghost-story-telling situation, the Feshbachs offer evidence for the successful induction of fear: "Although the diameter of the circle was about eleven feet at the beginning of the story telling, by the time the last ghost story was completed, it had been spontaneously reduced to approximately three feet" (p. 499).

Sommer initiated a series of studies of social distance in 1959 with the description of the "waltz technique." He learned that as he approached people, they would back away; when he moved backward during a conversation, the other person moved forward (Sommer, 1959). The physical distance between two conversationalists also varies systematically by the nationality of the talkers, and there are substantial differences in distance between two Englishmen talking together and two Frenchmen in conversation. In a cross-cultural study, this would be a response-set characteristic to be accounted for. Aiello and Jones (1971) found differences in social distance even at the first- and second-grade levels. Middle-class white children stood farther apart than lower-class black and Puerto Rican children. Interestingly, white males put much greater distances between themselves and others that did white female children, but the sex differences within the black and Puerto Rican groups were minimal. Sechrest, Flores, and Arellano (1968) studied social distance in a Filipino sample and found considerably greater distance in opposite-sex pairs as compared with same-sex pairs.

Sommer (1965) conducted a series of observations in school cafeterias and libraries, concluding that people prefer to sit across from each other in the former settings and away from each other in the latter. In the same report Sommer notes that casual groups prefer corner seating, cooperating groups to sit side-by-side, co-acting groups in a distant arrangement, and competing groups opposite one another. It appears that initial seating arrangement of a newly formed group is in part determined by the task of the group, and the arrangement, in turn, affects the subsequent communication, friendship, and status differentiation between group members (Sommer, 1967b). Confirming data for the above supposition exists in a report by

Patterson and Sechrest (1970). In an experimental study these researchers systematically varied the distance that a confederate chose to sit from subjects in an interview situation. Subjects rated the confederates who sat farthest away as being the least friendly, aggressive, extraverted, and dominant. Leipold (1963) had found that introverted and anxious subjects chose to sit at a greater distance from an interviewer than did more extraverted and comfortable persons. Powers (1967) discovered in addition that Mexican schizophrenic patients positioned themselves at a greater distance from an experimenter than did nonschizophrenic patients. Worth noting about this study is that Powers used floor tiles as a way of measuring distance.

Dykman and Reis (1979) have also studied personality correlates of seating position, this time in a classroom. In an extention of work by Sommer (1967a), they found that students possessing feelings of vulnerability and inadequacy had a tendency to sit on the sides or in the rear of the classroom, and that students with the most positive self-concepts sat in the front. Also, most classroom participation came from the front and center sections of the room. Another study (Levine, O'Neal, Garwood, and McDonald, 1980) shows that better students tend to sit in the front of a classroom, but when students are assigned seats, scores on examinations are unaffected by seat assignment. On the other hand, participation is affected by seat assignment, since those sitting in the front of a classroom tend to be more active participants.

In many instances involving the relationship between space and human behavior, it is difficult to be certain of the direction of any causal relationship. In research conducted in an experimental prison camp, Grusky (1959) found that even though prisoners were assigned to bunks randomly, those prisoners who became informal leaders were more likely to have lower bunks. Did lower bunks give them status? Provide more opportunities for interaction? Or had they in some manner switched? Studies of juries (Strodtbeck and Hook, 1961) have shown that jurors occupying particular strategically located seats around the table are more likely to be elected foremen, but higher status persons are more likely to occupy those seats in the first place.

Of course, people do not necessarily remain in one place; they can move toward or away from each other, and those movements may be accorded meaning. Moving too close to another person may be considered an invasion of personal space. What happens when personal space is invaded? Murphy-Berman and Berman (1978) report a laboratory study employing male and female confederates who invaded the space of research subjects in a waiting room. Subjects were asked to sit on a table, the only available seating, while waiting for an experiment to begin. The table also had books on it that were arranged in such a way that when the confederate came in, in the guise of a second subject, a manipulation of degree of intent to invade personal space was achieved. In the lowest intent condition, the books left only the space right beside the subject available to sit on; in the minimal choice condition the confederate simply sat next to the subject even though there were no books on the table; in the personal choice condition the confederate sat at a distance initially and then moved to sit next to the subject; finally, in the effortful choice condition, the confederate actually moved some books so as to be able to sit right beside the subject. There was also a counterpart control condition for each of the intent conditions, there being no invasion in the control conditions. (In fact, in one control condition, the confederate actually moved away from the subject during the interaction.) The results? Male space invaders are liked less well with increasing intent to invade, and invaded subjects believe that they are less well liked by the invaders as intent increases. Exactly the opposite is true for female space invaders. With increasing intent, there is a presumption of greater liking by the invader and a corresponding liking for her. Quite interestingly, these findings hold for both male and female subjects. Byrne, Hodges, and Baskett (1971) found that females were likely to sit closer to and beside a person they believed to be similar to themselves than to a dissimilar person. Males, on the other hand, tended to position themselves *across* from a stranger they believed to be similar to themselves.

The physical arrangements of space will determine how it is used and what happens to the people who occupy it. Quite a while ago, it was discovered that the arrangement of an apartment complex determined who would get to know whom and who would become well-known (Festinger, Schachter, and Back, 1950). Specifically, people who lived near each other tended to become friends, and people who lived in apartments that many other people passed by tended to become well-known. Priest and Sawyer (1967) found that in a college dormitory friendships were determined in fairly large measure by propinquity. Such findings are not really surprising, although many of us would scarcely like to think about how much of our behavior might be so casually and externally determined. Consider, for example, the study by Golson and Dabbs (undated) of the behavior of pedestrians in relation to lines on a sidewalk. Although pedestrians generally tend to walk to the right, Golson and Dabbs found that, in an area where the sidewalk was marked by diagonal lines, the lines produced a leftward drift (that having been measured by small, unobtrusive pieces of tape being placed on the sidewalk and a control sidewalk across the street). Females were much more affected by the diagonal lines than males, perhaps a consequence of the oft noted greater field dependence of females. Golson and Dabbs found in another part of their study that females were less likely to stray outside painted crosswalk lines than were males (10 percent versus 23 percent), a finding consistent with another observation that women tend to be more conservative and law-abiding than males.

Barch, Trumbo, and Nangle (1957) used the behavior of automobiles in their observational study of conformity to legal requirements. We are not sure if this is more properly coded under "expressive movement," but the "physical position" category seems more appropriate. They were interested in the degree to which turn signaling was related to the turn signaling behavior of a preceding car. For four weeks, they recorded this information:

1. Presence or absence of a turn signal
2. Direction of turn
3. Presence of another motor vehicle 100 feet or less behind the turning motor vehicle when it begins to turn
4. Sex of drivers.

Observers stood near the side of the road and were not easily visible to the motorists. There was the interesting finding that conforming behavior, as defined by signaling or not, varied with the direction of the turn. Moreover, a sex difference was noted. There was a strong positive correlation if model and follower were females, and also a high correlation if left turns were signaled. But on right turns, the correlation was low and positive. Why there is a high correlation for left turns and a low one for right turns is equivocal. The data, like so many simple observational data, don't offer the "why," but simply establish a relationship. Several of the above findings have been verified and perturbingly elaborated by a finding that signaling is more erratic in bad weather and by drivers of expensive autos (Sechrest, 1971).

Taking a position can involve taking a risk, something done regularly by drivers of automobiles. Ebbeson and Haney (1973) identified one such combination of position and risk in T-shaped intersections at which a driver in the stem of the T must evaluate the risks involved in turning into oncoming traffic. A series of four field studies involved stationing unobtrusive observers at the intersections to time the arrival of the first oncoming cars for drivers who made left hand turns in front of them. The results show that drivers take greater risks when they have been forced to wait for several cars to pass, but risk taking is not affected by the presence of other cars beside or behind the driver. It was also evident that males take more risks than do females, a fact consistent with the higher accident rates for males.

Walls also define space, and one suspects that people are differently affected by them. Dabbs and Wheeler (1976) observed persons as they came down corridors and classified them as "gravitators" (up against the wall) or nongravitators. The two groups were then asked to fill out personality questionnaires as though they had just been selected randomly, and were paid a small amount of money to return the questionnaires. The gravitators turned out to be lower in autonomy and in a measure of willingness to defend oneself against intrusions. A second experiment involving a closeness-of-approach measure suggested that gravitators may also be socially less sensitive than nongravitators, in that they did not approach the experimenter as closely to begin with but also did not move away when she approached them.

OBSERVATION OF LANGUAGE BEHAVIOR: CONVERSATION SAMPLING

Language is a hoary subject for observation, with everything from phonemes to profanity legitimate game. Our interest here is more circumscribed and centers on language samples collected unobtrusively. This means excluding much useful research, Mahl's (1956) study of patients' speech in psychotherapy sessions, for example. The incidence of stuttering, slips of the tongue, and the like are important data, but because the data were collected in a therapist-patient setting, they do not apply here.

Norman (1979) is involved in the study of slips of all kinds, the errors one makes when one intends to do one thing and ends up doing something different. His data may eventually, as he expects, tell us a lot about mental processes, but such slips may also be of value to the unobtrusive measurer, for example, as we noted earlier in connection with Powis' (1977) suggestions about police work. We would be curious to read the findings of a nonreactive study that investigated slips of the typewriter as a measure. The employment of these regularly appearing slips somehow evaded Freud (1920) in his major work on the topic. Sechrest (1971) has demonstrated a higher number of gross errors (skipping lines, poor spacing, and repositioning of hands) when subjects are copying erotic passages than when copying passages from a mineralogy text. Winick (1962) studied some sixty thousand messages written by passersby on a typewriter outside a New York store, but his analysis centered on coding of content. The data are also amenable to study of spelling errors, spacing, and the like.

We have taken one area of language research, conversational sampling, and traced it historically to illustrate the methodological issues. Dittmann and Wynne (1961) demonstrate a modern approach. They coded verbal behavior, with the source of language a radio program—the NBC show "Conversation." To study emotional expression, the authors examined "linguistic" phenomena (junctures, stress, pitch) and "paralinguistic" phenomena (voice set, voice quality, and vocalizations of three types). A problem comes from the possibility that a man's awareness of participation in a radio show—particularly the effects of nervousness on speech—could lead to conditions that bias the production of the critical responses.

Kramer (1963) has reviewed the literature on the nonverbal characteristics of speech, concentrating on personal characteristics and emotional correlates. In a later article (1964), he reports a methodological study of techniques to eliminate verbal cues. The three major methods are: a constant ambiguous set of words for various emotional expressions; filtering out the frequencies which permit word recognition; speech in a language unknown to the listener.

More satisfactory is language analysis which draws its samples from speech of subjects unaware of observation. One of the earliest mentions of conversation as a source of psychological data subject to quantification was made by Tarde (1901). Although he performed no studies on conversation himself, Tarde made several suggestions for potential areas of study, such as variation in speed of talking among cultures and categorization of topics by social-class differences.

For the first reported study of conversations, we can look at H. T. Moore's (1922) work on sex differences in conversation —a canny and delightful research that triggered a whole series of hidden-observer language studies.

Moore sought to prove that there was a definite mental differentiation between the sexes, regardless of what previous studies (to 1922) had shown. To test this, he argued for a content analysis of "easy conversation." Especially at the day's end, he held, conversation should provide significant clues to personal interest.

So Moore slowly walked up Broadway from 33rd Street to 55th Street about 7:30 every night for several weeks. He jotted down every bit of audible conversation and eventually collected 174 fragments. Each was coded by the sex of the speaker and by whether the company was mixed or of the same sex. It is not necessary to cite his findings at length, but one should not pass attention: in male to male conversations Moore found 8 percent in the category "persons of opposite sex"; for female to female conversations, this topic occupied 44 percent of the language specimens.

Some of the limitations of conversation sampling are obvious. Moore could record only intelligible audible conversation. Speech that is muttered, mumbled, or whispered may contain significantly different content than loud and clear speech. The representative character of the speech samples is further questioned by the representatives of the speakers. Walkers on Broadway are probably not even a good sample of Manhattan. In short, there is a strong risk of sampling rigidity in both the talkers and the talk.

We can look, chronologically, at the conversation-sampling studies that followed Moore's and note the efforts of other investigators to reduce error due to data-collecting procedure.

Landis and Burtt (1924) published the first study stimulated by Moore's classic. They were sensitive to positional sampling biases and improved upon Moore's procedure by sampling a wider variety of places and situations. With an experimenter who "wore rubber heels and cultivated an unobtrusive manner," they gathered samples of conversation, adding an estimate of the social status of the speaker. The broadened locations included streetcars, campuses, railroad stations, athletic events, parties, department stores, theater and hotel lobbies, restaurants, barber shops, churches, and streets in both commercial and residential areas. After their analysis, Landis and Burtt concluded that the source of the collection was only a minor factor. Landis (1927) broadened the sampling base even further, reporting in an article entitled "National Differences in Conversation." He sampled conversations in Oxford and Regent streets in London and compared these results to the earlier Landis and Burtt (1924) findings from Columbus, Ohio.

Stoke and West (1931) tried to limit the number of variables in their conversation-sampling study and restricted the sample to undergraduate college students, sampling from random bull sessions held at night in residence halls. The participant observers were 36 college students who worked with a checklist of probable topics and the data and number of people in the conversation. A limitation of this "observe—withdraw—record" approach is that the observer cannot hope to record adequately the duration of responses. The approach is also vulnerable to the criticism that the observers' reports are subject to bias, beyond the initial selective perception one, because of the gap between event and notation.

Moving away from the campus, and more to the Moore approach, Sleeper (1931) sampled conversations in the upper level of Grand Central Terminal in New York, during the rush hour from 5:00 P.M. to 6:30 P.M. Sleeper's procedure reflected the dross-rate problems of such data, as he added a recording variant by excluding all "environmentally stimulated" conversation.

Markets are interesting places to study many behaviors, including conversations. Robert Sommer and his associates have been comparing farmer's markets to supermarkets. Produce in farmer's markets is cheaper (Sommer, Wing, and Aitkens, in press), and at least the bell peppers seem to taste better (in a blind taste testing) than those bought in supermarkets (Sommer, Knight, and Sommer, 1979). Of special interest here, however, are the observations that most people arriving to shop in supermarkets are alone, while most of those who shop in farmer's markets are accompanied by at least one other person. Moreover, there were more friendly conversations in farmer's markets than in supermarkets, which may account for the obviously growing popularity of the former.

Mabie (1931) and McCarthy (1929) employed free-play periods to sample the conversation of children. The visibility of the recorder is a great problem here, and the studies represent reactive methodology. It may be that, as Mabie claims, the children's awareness of her presence had no effect on their conversation. This is uncertain, and our inclination would be to consider that her presence, notebook in hand, would introduce a strong risk of biasing the character of the overheard statements. When asked by the children what she was doing, Mabie told them that she was writing down what the children liked to do during play periods. That response itself could predispose the children to verbalize evaluative comments more frequently.

Cross and Aron (1971) interviewed 40 married couples and later analyzed their verbal behavior, looking for interruptions of one spouse by the other, occasions of simultaneous talking, the ratio of the word "I" to "we", and the duration of speaking. These researchers then correlated the unobtrusive measures of dominance and conflict with responses to a questionnaire concerning the couples' parents.

Surreptitious observation is the only class that fits into what we would call nonreactive testing. Take the studied surreptitiousness of Henle and Hubble (1938). Students were again the subjects, and

> The investigators took special precautions to keep subjects ignorant of the fact that their remarks were being recorded. To this end, they concealed themselves under beds in students' rooms where tea parties were being held, eavesdropped in dormitory smoking rooms and washrooms, and listened to telephone conversations [p. 230].

Without extending their explanation, Henle and Hubble report that "unwitting subjects were pursued in the streets, in department stores, and in the home."

Escaping from under the bed, Carlson, Cook, and Stromberg (1936) studied sex differences in conversation by monitoring lobby conversations at the intermissions of 13 regular concerts of the Minneapolis Symphony and at six University of Minnesota concerts. The self-selection of subjects may be a serious risk to external validity (Who goes to Minneapolis Symphony concerts and who doesn't?), but the whispering problem is not so great in a research setting like a crowded theater, where a premium is placed on loudness.

Cameron (1969) conducted a study in which students eavesdropped on conversations of more than 3000 persons in an attempt to find out who is likely to use profanity. Their results suggest that secretaries swear less than people in other professions, using less than one profane word in 200, and factory and construction workers use an average of one profane word out of every four. Also, college students swear more than most other people (one profane word out of every 14), with there being no differences between female and male students. In a review of sex differences in spoken language, Haas (1979) stated that there were no empirical studies of differences in the use of profanity and obscenity. Another reviewer, Jay (1980), has, however, discovered research quite in accord with common observation. In fact, even male Mojave Indians were found to swear more than females.

Haas did note a considerable number of features of spoken language in which males and females differ, and there is a whole book on the topic soon to appear (Kramarae, 1981, in press) entitled *Women and Men Speaking*. Kramarae does believe that the similarities in speech between the sexes outweigh the differences, but the differences that have been noted include more asking of questions by women, more interrupting by men (especially of women), and a greater tendency for women to utter declarative sentences in an intonation that makes them come out sounding like questions. Incidentally, Hiatt (1977) has found that women also write differently from males, for example, using different similes and making more liberal use of emphasis indicators.

A number of other researchers have investigated usage of profanity and knowledge of various slang words (for example, Gibson, 1964; Gibson, 1966; Kunter and Brogan, 1974; Lerman, 1967). Although these studies used techniques that may have produced reactivity, more unobtrusive methods could be used to investigate knowledge of argot by various groups. Jay (1979) has assembled an extensive bibliography of research on dirty word usage.

The size of the group is a clear influence on the degree to which the experimenter must mask himself. For observing two-person communication, it may well be necessary to hide under a bed. In a large public gathering, the problem of visibility is solved; the individual providing the conversation sample expects to find unfamiliar people close by so the experimenter need not hide. Only the recording of the language need be hidden. But it is not as simple as that. Even though the presence of the observer may cause no surprise, the same situation which permits acceptance of the stranger may also have worked to inhibit a class or classes of verbal behavior. For some experiments this may be unimportant—those in which the difference between public and private utterances is negligible. For other experiments it may be substantial. This is an empirical question for each experimenter to solve. It must be accepted as one of the possible content limitations of conversational sampling.

Watson, Breed, and Posman (1948) displayed their concern about the representativeness of college students by deliberately excluding them from their samples of New York talkers. No campus locations were used, and an attempt was made to eliminate "any one distinguishable as a college student." Working at all times of day and night, they sampled uptown, midtown, and downtown Manhattan, including the following locales: business, amusement and residential streets and parks; subways, buses, ferries, taxis, and railroad stations; lobbies of movie houses and hotels; stores, restaurants, bars, night clubs. Each observer recorded verbatim what he had heard as soon as possible after hearing it. The sampling of respondents was resolved as well by Watson, Breed, and Posman as it has been by anyone.

Contrast this with the participant observation type of approach suggested by Perrine and Wessman (1954). The investigator posed as a stranger to the state, initiated casual conversation with subjects, and then directed conversation to political issues by commenting on recent newspaper headlines and the like. The conversation was recorded as soon as possible after leaving the subject, along with sex, race, location, and estimated age and socioeconomic class. The enormous methodological issue in this type of conversation recording is the 60 to 70 percent rate of refusal. If nothing else, the eavesdropping approach reduces the problem of self-selection of the sample—at least that bias attributable to willingness to participate in a survey. Not everyone will chip into a conversation with some stranger who wants to talk about state politics. To use such data as the basis of inferring the state of public opinion is dubious. The ethics of the approach are not greatly troublesome unless one takes a narrow position that social scientists should never pretend to be what they are not, a position that would rule out most field research, for example, research in which an experimenter approaches someone on a street and asks directions. In principle there seems no great difference between engaging people in conversation to learn whether they are in favor of an incumbent political candidate and asking them directions to learn whether they are helpful types. Both situations involve public behaviors that people are willing to display. In fact, those persons approached for conversation about their attitudes have the option of not responding without any conclusions being implicit in that response; persons approached with a request for help cannot withdraw altogether, and a nonresponse will be interpreted as nonhelpfulness.

Doob (1961) writes of a girl in an African market who "was carefully shadowed in the interest of scholarly research." In an approach described by Doob as "unsystematic eavesdropping," he notes:

> She began talking, and listening, before she entered the market's gate. Within a period of ten minutes—the duration of the research—she spoke with more than twenty people: some she greeted perfunctorily, others she talked to for a few moments concerning relatives and friends. No political or cosmic thoughts were aired [p. 144].

Of interest is his point on a possible ethnocentric bias among foreign observers in Africa:

> ... whereas people in the West ... are likely to keep themselves occupied and to avoid long periods of complete solitude or, in contact with others, of silence, it may be that many Africans are perfectly content to be unoccupied except by their own feelings and thoughts and sense of well being [p. 144].

All the studies of conversation reported here have relied on a content analysis of the conversational samples gathered. The essential problem has been the representativeness of the sample collected. The unobserved observer (secreted under a bed or among a crowd), must be sensitive to the limitations of self-selection of subjects, a problem of external validity, and the limitations of the probable partial character of public conversation samples. Any public conversation may be constrained because of the "danger" of being overheard. Many of the inaudible comments in public are likely to be drawn from a different population of topics than those loudly registered. Moreover, as we noted earlier, the method requires a careful selection of both place- and time-sampling units to increase representativeness, and these controls will not be the same over different geographic locales. Sampling bus conversations in Los Angeles and in Chicago yields a population of very different subjects. Moreover, these data are typically loosely packed, and it takes a substantial investment in time and labor to produce a large enough residual pool of relevant data. For all these limitations, however, there are research problems for which private commentary is not a significant worry, for which the adroit selection of locales and times can circumvent selective population characteristics, and for which the issue is of sufficient currency in the public mind to reduce the dross rate. For these situations, conversational sampling is a sensitive and faithful source of information.

TIME DURATION

The amount of attention paid by a person to an object has long been the source of inferences on interest. For research on infrahuman species, notoriously incompetent at filling out interest questionnaires, visual fixation has been a popular research variable, as in the recent work of Berkson and Fitz-Gerald (1963) on the effect of introducing novel stimuli into the visual world of infant chimps. With humans who can fill out questionnaires, time-duration measures have been less popular, but are not uncommon. Frequently, a duration variable is imbedded in a body of other measures. H. T. Moore (1917) measured anger, fear, and sex interests by giving a subject multiplication tasks and then exposing him to distraction of different types. The time taken to complete the tasks was the measure of interest: the longer the time, the greater the interest in the distracting content.

In a study of museum visitors, Melton (1935) hypothesized a positive relationship between the degree of interest shown by a visitor in the exhibits and the number and quality of the permanent educational results of the museum visit. Melton was very careful to study response-set biases and situational cues which would contaminate his measure of the duration of observed time spent in viewing an exhibit. He demonstrated the "right-turn" bias, and experimented with changing the number of exits and installing directional arrows—all elements which significantly affected the length of a visit.

In one finding, for example, he reports that the closer an exhibit is to an exit, the less time will be spent at it. He posits an "exit gradient." Going further, he talks of the number of paintings in a gallery, the proportion of applied or fine arts in the room, and comes up with findings on "museum satiation." As the number of paintings in a gallery increase, the average total time in the gallery also increases, the total number of paintings visited increases, *and* the time per painting visited does not decrease but increases. Melton's attention to these cues provides a model seldom followed in observational research.

Undoubtedly if one asked, most people would say that they would rather work in esthetically pleasing surroundings, but would it really make any difference? Mintz (1956) had subjects, who were unaware that they were subjects, conduct testing sessions over a considerable period of time in either an attractive or an "ugly" room. Examiners in the ugly room usually finished more quickly than those in the attractive room. They also rated photographs of persons as more attractive when the rating was being done in the attractive room.

Washburne (1928) reported on an experiment conducted in the Russian school system which conceivably could have used time for a measure. Each child in the school was given a garden plot and, at the same time, had joint responsibility for a common garden tended by all the children. It is reported that records were kept to show the relative amount of interest that each child had in the two types of work. Although no mention is made of the measure used to determine amount of interest, time might be an appropriate one. Because it can be assumed that for equal care a greater amount of time would have to be spent on the individual garden, adjustments would have to be made in comparing the times for the two gardens. It has been fairly common for experimental psychologists to provide "free time" in the course of an experiment during which subjects can work on a task if they like, the amount of time spent working being taken as an index of intrinsic interest in the task (Deci,

1975; Lepper, Greene, and Nisbett, 1973). Although not completely nonreactive, such a measure provides a usefully different perspective on self-reported interest. Mischel, Ebbesen, and Zeiss (1973) posted bogus information about desirable and undesirable personality traits purported to characterize subjects who had been exposed either to a success or a failure experience in a laboratory task. Subjects who had succeeded in the task then spent more time studying their presumed desirable traits whereas subjects who had failed divided their time equally between the two sets.

A number of theoretical variables may be linked to time duration and time perception. Cortes (cited in McClelland, 1961, p. 327) has shown that a significantly larger number of high-need achievers have watches that are fast than do low-need achievers. Do the high achievers also perceive time duration differentially?

The lack of general emphasis on time-duration methods is partly due to difficulty of measurement. For accurate observation, the hurly-burly conditions of a natural setting are damaging; the laboratory control over instrumentation is almost necessary if precise observations of small time units are to be reached.

Sometimes this can be circumvented by a measure in which time is scaled in grosser units than microseconds. Jacques (1956) defined "responsibility" by measuring how long a worker is allowed to commit the resources of his task without direct supervision. Observation yields "a time span of responsibility" and a descriptive measure of the worker. For a duration measure like this, it would be foolish to calibrate the measurement in seconds. Many researches demand ultrafine discrimination of time, and for them, natural observation is an awkward method. But where the unit is broader, observation in the natural setting becomes both feasible and desirable. Sometimes it is enough to say, "Professor X's interest in cutaneous sensation extended over a career of 38 years."

TIME SAMPLING AND OBSERVATION

For the permanent physical clues of observation—the scars, tattoos, and houses owned—the timing of when an observation is made may be relatively unimportant. It may be possible to conjure up conditions in which a tattoo may be so placed that it is differentially visible at various points in a day (with or without jacket, for example), but for the most part, the exterior signs are quite invulnerable to time-linked variance.

Many of the other simple observation materials—expressive movement, physical location, and language—are, however, subject to the objection that the critical behavior is variable over a day or some longer time period. The risk, of course, is that the timing of the data collection may be such that a selective population periodically appears before the observer, while another population, equally periodically, engages in the same behavior, but comes along only when the observer is absent. Similarly, the individual's behavior may shift as the hours or days of the week change. The best defense against this source of invalidity is to sample time units randomly.

Time as an index may also distort the nature of activities. State legislators—and many taxpayers—are often distressed by the relatively limited amounts of time that professors spend in their classrooms. Those same legislators would not, however, want to be judged on the amount of time that they spend in the legislative chambers. In both instances what shows is not all of what is. It may be true that police officers spend 80 percent of their time doing things other than crime-related tasks, for example, community service (Reiss, 1971), but it is that other 20 percent that police personnel, and probably most other people, believe is their job.

Working in an industrial setting, Shepard and Blake (1962) observed employees and judged whether they were working or not. By a time-sampling design, they found a strong decline in percentage of workers working between 10:30 and 11:00—the time of a daily supervisors' meeting that drew them away from direct control over employees.

> Hence, the composition of supervisors' meetings was changed so as to ensure continuous supervision in the shop ... thus the managers are correct in their ... conclusions that more consistent control and direction are needed to correct for their tendency to be irresponsible [pp. 88–89].

Note the time originally chosen for the supervisors' meetings. A study of ratings of courses by students done at the University of Oregon (Rankin, personal communication, 1980) showed that students gave systematically higher ratings to 10 o'clock classes no matter who the instructor or what the content.

The greatly discrepant attitudes toward time displayed by different persons and groups may be a source of bias in some observations but may also be of interest in its own right. Quite some time ago it was noted that people high in the motive to achieve tend to have watches either quite on time or set somewhat fast, a fastidiousness about time not so evident in those low in need Achievement. The characteristics of the *Type A* person (Friedman and Rosenman, 1974) are by now well known, and they include a sense of urgency about time. In Latin countries, however, attitudes toward time seem much more casual. Levine, West, and Reis (1980) studied the phenomenon in Brazil. Public clocks in Brazil as well as personal watches proved to be less accurate than in the United States. Moreover, when reporting the time, Brazilians with watches were less exact in their reports, and those without watches were less accurate than their North American counterparts. A variety of survey data fleshed out the findings, but they converged in showing that time and being on time are just not a big deal in Brazil.

The techinque of time sampling has been extensively used in nursery settings, where there is a particular need for it because of the greater periodicity of behavior of infants and young children. Arrington (1943) has pointed out many of the factors that must be considered in assessing the results of time sampling recorded by the observer. The duration of the individual time sample must be chosen in accordance with behavior to be observed. Degree of sophistication, familiarity with the observer, previous experience in being observed, type of situation, and number of individuals in the situation are also thought to be factors contributing to "observation consciousness."

One of the important time-sampling studies of observation in a nursery setting was conducted by Thomas (1929). In recording the activities of the children, Thomas made use of a mapped floor plan and plotted movement against the plan. Olson (1929) used similar procedures but concentrated on oral habits rather than movement patterns.

Barker and Wright (1951; 1954) have adopted an opposite strategy to time sampling. They sought to avoid the problem of selected behavior over time by a saturation method. Rather than sample behavior, they censused it. In their 1951 study, observations were made of one child for an entire day, with minute-by-minute notations. Eight observers were used in turn, each being wholly familiar with the child. For any child under ten, the authors feel the effects of observation are negligible. This may be subject to doubt, however, particularly in view of recorded statements detailing interaction between the observer and the child.

This strategy does solve a problem, but it provides other ones. It is practical for only relatively short periods of time (Imagine following a boy for a year!), and the method is predisposed to measurement of individuals, not groups. This latter point may be important for the probability of reactive effects creeping in, for, as we noted above, the size of the group may be an important factor in the degree of observation consciousness. A person tailing you about all day is quite different from one next to you in a theater lobby.

Yet these limitations are no more punishing than the limitations of other approaches, and the subtlety of links between behaviors can hardly be better described.[2] Either way, sampling or censusuing, a measure of control is added over a usually uncontrolled variable.

Actually there is considerably greater periodicity in human behavior than many think about and perhaps more than others would imagine. We are all creatures of habit, and we tend to do things by the clock. Studies of obese persons show that they are more influenced than persons of normal weight by visible time when it comes to eating. They will eat more or less than normals if the hands of a clock are surreptitiously advanced or retarded

[2]Edmond de Goncourt wrote of the goal of the *Goncourt Journal:* "What we have tried to do, then, is to bring our contemporaries to life for posterity in a speaking likeness, by means of the vivid stenography of a conversation, the physiological spontaneity of a gesture, those little signs of emotion that reveal a personality, those *imponderabilia* that render the intensity of existence, and, last of all, a touch of that fever which is the mark of the heady life of Paris" (p. xi). From *The Goncourt Journals: 1851–1870*, Edmond and Jules de Goncourt, translated by Lewis Galantiere. Copyright 1937 by Doubleday & Company, Inc. Reprinted by permission of the publisher.

(Schachter and Gross, 1968), and they are less bothered by "jet lag" because they eat, and perhaps do other things, when the clock tells them to do so (Goldman, Jaffa, and Schachter, 1968). Jet lag itself is testimony to periodicity, and there are many aspects of our lives that show such effects. A fascinating account is provided by Bryant (1963). Even while writing this a phone call came in from one of our students whose wife had a baby—Andrew, 7 pounds, 2 ounces, for the curious—this morning at 3:21 A.M. We were reminded that the peak time for birth of human infants is around 4:00 A.M. (the stereotype of the anxious father being awakened in the middle of the night is based on fact), whereas the peak time for birthing of some nocturnal animals is around 5:00 P.M. (Kaiser and Halberg, 1962).

Human behavior is seasonal, too, and also cyclic. Suicide is related in rather complex ways to the business cycle, with males in high status occupations being particularly susceptible to hard times. Homicide, however, decreases with downturns in the business cycle and increases with good times as does, perhaps not at all coincidentally, consumption of alcohol (Henry and Short, 1954). Crime is so much a phenomenon of Friday and Saturday nights that crime statistics must take account of the fact that some months have more weekends that others. Crime is also seasonal with peaks of homicide in summer months and of armed robbery toward the Christmas season (Lunden, 1967). Suicide is also seasonal, with a peak in the United States during late winter and early spring. Note that that time is also soon after our major holidays, when bills come due, and so on. We need data from the southern hemisphere to decide whether the effect is one of climatic or social season. The message in all this is clear: data collected and compared without respect to considerations of clock and calendar can lead us astray.

OVERALL COMMENTS ON
SIMPLE OBSERVATION

The emphasis of this chapter has been on research in which the observer is unobserved, and in settings where the investigator has had no part in structuring the situation. The secretive nature of the observer, whether hidden in a crowd or miles

away before a television screen, protects the research from
some of the reactive validity threats. The subject is not aware
of being tested, there is thereby no concomitant role playing
associated with awareness, the measurement does not work as
an agent of change, and the interviewer (observer) effects are
not an issue.

Moreover, there is the great gain that comes from getting
the data at first hand. In studies of archival records and in the
examination of trace and crosion evidence, there is always the
uncertainty that others who came between the data and the
investigator, processing or pawing it, left their own indistin-
guishable marks.

The first-hand collection of the data, usually of a contemporaneous event, also allows the gathering of other information to
reduce alternative hypotheses. One may note characteristics of
the subjects which permit a testing of rival hypotheses about
the selective composition of the sample. To be sure, these are
mostly limited to visual cues, but they can be extremely helpful.
Similarly, the ability to observe the subjects in the act permits
one to designate the indivdual actors, either for follow-up observation, or for study with other instruments like the questionnaire or interview. Such follow-up of individuals is difficult or
impossible with archival and trace measures.

It would be difficult to overestimate the value of this potential for follow-up. One of the singular gains of simple observation is that it is a procedure which allows opportunistic
sampling of important phenomena. Because it is often opportunistic, there is the attendant risk that the population under
observation is an atypical group, one unworthy to produce generalizations. The follow-up studies may protect against this risk,
as can adroit use of locational and time sampling.

Against this impressive list of gains must be balanced some
possible sources of loss. Prime among these is the danger that
the data-gathering instrument, the human observer, will be
variable over the course of his or her observations. He or she
may become less conscientious as boredom sets in or may
become more attentive as he or she learns the task and becomes
involved with it. If there are any ambiguities about how the
behavior is to be coded, the effect of time may be to reduce the

variation of coding (increase intra-observer reliability) as the observer works out operating definitions of which behaviors go with which codes. All of these can work to produce spurious differences in comparisons.

Errors of the observer, however, are not random but show systematic biases that can be predicted, and hence corrected for, from the observer's expectations of the experimental or field situation. Campbell (1959) has inventoried 21 systematic sources of error that apply to the human observer. Albeit in the laboratory, Turner (1974) has studied the differences between persons in their skills at observing and concludes that the most important distinguishing characteristic is that good observers simply "see more to see." For whatever reasons, good observers tend to be female, introverted, and nearsighted! Mitchell (1979) has provided a useful review of problems in interobserver agreement, including appropriate ways of assessing such agreement.

That this may apply to the principal investigator, as well as his or her aides, has been demonstrated by Rosenthal's (1963) "On the Social Psychology of the Psychological Experiment." The implication of these studies is the demand for a greater emphasis on the necessity for saturated training of observers, hopefully under a "blind" condition in which they do not know what a "good" result or behavior will be.

The one other significant issue under the label of reactive threats comes from response sets on those observed. To a large measure, these are knowable—either through application of research conducted in other settings, or through direct observation of behavior under different conditions. Hopefully, there will be enough variation in the settings available for sampling to examine whether any systematic response sets are at work, and whether these can be isolated from other possible sources of variance. This is awkward when one is not actively manipulating the environment and becomes one of the strong arguments for the unobserved observer to alter the research environment surreptitiously and systematically in an undetectable way.

The populations available for observation fluctuate according to both time and location. Thus, some caution should be employed in generalizing from research which gathered observations at one time in one place. If generalizations about the subject matter of conversations are to all people, and content varies by age, then the "place" should be considered as a sampling universe including varying locations which are likely to draw on different populations. When the concern is generalized to more limited settings, say, a study of the effect of different treatment conditions in prisons, then the place sample should be more than one prison for each condition hypothesized to have an effect.

It is not always possible to draw elaborate locational samples, but that should not deter observational research. If the setting is circumscribed by practical conditions, a proper defense is to employ time-sampling methods. Limited to a population of "tour" visitors to a mental hospital, one must bear the cross of a self-selected population unlikely to be representative of much. Imposing a time-sampling design, observing different groups who come on different days or in different months, for example, would markedly improve the solidity of a shaky base.

Both time and locational sampling should be employed if possible, for empirical research and introspection suggest that population variation is a substantial issue in observation. An added gain is that the investigator can also vary his observers over the sampling units and randomly assign them to different times and locations, thus adding a badly needed control. Not all research possibilities afford this chance, but it is a goal to be reached for.

McCarroll and Haddon (1961) took care to ensure that location and time factors would not affect their study of the differences between fatally injured drivers in automobile accidents and noninvolved drivers. At each accident site, a team consisting of the authors, medical students, and from one to eight police stopped noninvolved cars proceeding in the same direction as the accident car on the same day of the week and at the same time of the day.

The same time- and locational-sampling strategy will also help to counteract some of the risks in selective content. The population varies over place and time, and the content of their behavior similarly varies. If one can broaden the sampling base, he can expand the character of material available for study. It is not possible to know all about college students if observations are limited to afternoons in the fall; when these observations fall on Saturday, worse yet.

But all the finesse of the skillful investigator will not solve some content limitations. Much of behavior is precluded from public display and is available only through unethical action, elaborate instrumentation, or some titanic combination of both. This is potentially a variable problem across cultures, as one notes members of certain societies willing to display classes of behavior that are hidden or taboo in others. Cross-cultural observational studies are thereby threatened not only by the ethnocentric attribution of meaning, but also by the lack of equivalence in observable behavior across societies. As one increases the number of societies, of course, the probability is greater that an incomplete set of observations of public behavior will be available over all.

Finally, being on the scene often means a necessary exposure to a large body of irrelevant information. Because one cannot often predict when a critical event will be produced, it is necessary to wait around, observe, and complain about the high dross rate of such a procedure. The payoff is often high, as in the case of one patient observer who knew critical signs and was immortalized in the song, "My Lover Was a Logger." The waitress sings,

> I can tell that you're a logger,
> And not just a common bum,
> 'Cause nobody but a logger
> Stirs his coffee with his thumb.

CHAPTER 8

Contrived Observation:
Hidden Hardware and Control

This chapter discusses the investigator's intervention into the observational setting. In simple observational studies, research is often handicapped by the weaknesses of the human observer, by the unavailability of certain content, and by a cluster of variables over which the investigator has no control. To reduce these threats, a number of workers have elected to vary the setting actively or to substitute hardware devices for human record-keeping observers. We avoid here examples of the "speak clearly into the microphone, please" approach. The emphasis is on those investigations in which the scientist's intervention is not detectable by the subject and the naturalness of the situation is not violated.

HARDWARE:
AVOIDING HUMAN INSTRUMENT ERROR

When the human observer is the recording agent, all the fallibilities of the organism operate to introduce extraneous variance into the data. People are low-fidelity observational instruments. We have already noted how recording and interpretation may be erratic over time, as the observer learns and responds to the research phenomena observed.

The fluctuations of this instrument can be brought under some degree of control by random assignment of observers to locations and time units. Random assignment will not, however, create a capacity in the organism that is not there, nor eliminate response sets characteristic of all members of the society or subcultures from which the observers are drawn.

241

Osgood (1953) illustrates the capacity weakness of the human observer in his comments on studies of language behavior in the first four or five months of a human's life: "... from the total splurge of sounds made by an actively vocal infant, only the small sample that happens to strike the observer is recorded at all" (p. 684).

Not all observable behavior is so complex or so rapid, but there is enough to cause the consideration of a substitute mechanism for the observer. It might not be so bad if there were a random loss of material when the observer's perceptual system got overloaded. Unhappily, the nature of the material noted and not noted is likely to be a function of both the individual's idiosyncracies and the systematic response sets learned in a given society. Again speaking of speech studies of early childhood, Osgood comments,

> The inadequate recording methods employed in most of the early studies make the data of dubious validity. The typical procedure was merely to listen to the spontaneous vocalizations of an infant and write down what was heard. The selective factor of auditory perception—listeners "hear" most readily those sounds that correspond to the phonemes of their own language—was not considered [p. 684].

These same biases are at work with the recording of any language system that is unfamiliar to the observer—whether it be the occult language of a child or the unfamiliar tones of a foreign language. Webb (1963) has noted this in his study of orthographies in African languages. His analysis was based on written records of the languages, many of which had been produced by missionaries, explorers, and other foreign nationals who came to Africa and learned the indigenous speech. In transcribing the sounds of these languages for others, there were selective approximations of the true sound, influenced by the tonal pattern of the characters in the observer's native language. Thus, German observers heard umlauts that evaded the British. There is some possibility of control over this particular bias, since for some of the languages there are written transcriptions of the same words by nationals of various countries; these can be matched against the known tonal characteristics of the

European languages to correct for the selective hearing. When multinational observations are missing, the task is much more difficult, and one must make inferences about the effect of perceptual biases based on the sound characteristics of the observer's native language.

A major gain from hardware recording, of course, is the permanence of this complete record. It is not subject to selective decay and can provide the stuff of reliability checks. Further, the same content can be the base for new hypothesis-testing not considered at the time the data were collected. Or material that was originally viewed as dross may become prime ore. For example, Bryan employed taped interviews in his study of call girls. Among other things, these were coded for the frequency of telephone calls received during the period of the interview. Such information served as a partial check on the girl's self-report of business activity (Bryan, 1965).

Hardware, of varying degrees of flexibility, has been used throughout the history of scientific observation. To reduce the risk of forgetting, if nothing else, permanent records were made of observed behavior. They may have noted less than the total behavior, but they did serve to reduce reliance on human memory. Boring (1961) writes of Galton, "an indefatigable measurer."

> He used to carry a paper cross and a little needle point, arranged so that he could punch holes in the paper to keep count of whatever he was at that time observing. A hole at the head of the cross meant *greater*, on the arm *equal*, and on the bottom, *less* [p. 154].

Galton also contributed to that voluntary, self-descriptive reactive measure, the questionnaire, whose overuse William James anticipated: "Messrs. Darwin and Galton have set the example of circulars of questions sent out by the hundreds to those supposed able to reply. The custom has spread, and it will be well for us in the next generation if such circulars be not ranked among the common pests of life" (James, 1890, p. 194).

Evolving from such simple recording methods was the constriction of communication developed for work in small-group research in laboratory settings. Artificially, the participants were (or are) required to limit all communications to written notes, which are then saved by the investigator to provide a full record of all communication among participants. This is a very low-cost device, much cheaper than tape recording, but its stilted quality suggests a very high risk price for a very low dollar cost. Greenwald (1967) has described a rather elaborate arrangement by which supposedly crumpled up and discarded experimental messages fall through a fake wastebasket into an adjacent cubicle where they may be read by an assistant who then uses them in planning the next steps in the experiment.

Other aids to observers are pieces of apparatus that allow them to record their observations more quickly or more thoroughly. Sometimes the gain comes from forcing observers into using a series of varied codes, sometimes it is just the gain of having a more permanent record of perceptions of the behavior under study. Steiner and Field (1960), for example, timed vocal contributions to a group discussion by means of a polygraph, and a useful supplementary device has been the Interaction Chronograph, one use of which is reported in Chapple (1962). The development in recent years of a wide variety of multifunction watches, calculators, hand-held computers, and so on may greatly enhance the capabilities of observers and limit the magnitude of some human instrument errors.

A big boom exists, and properly, for audio tape recorders. With the development of superior omnidirectional and highly directional microphones, many of the former mechanical limitations have been resolved. The tape becomes the first source of data, and it is often considered the initial input into a hardware system. Thus, Andrew (1963) took tapes of sound patterns from primates (including man) and fed them into a spectrograph for more detailed analyses. More recently, Martin (1980) has used tape-recorded cries of distressed human infants and of an infant chimpanzee to study the effect on newborn infants of exposure to a distress signal. Not totally unexpectedly, newborns are often induced to cry by hearing the cry of another human infant and, to a certain extent, by hearing the cry of the chimpanzee. What was quite unexpected was that the crying newborn babes were quieted by hearing a recording of their own cry.

The spectrograph has been used for a number of purposes, including the detection of stress. Popov (1966), for example, analyzed the speech of fifteen actors and two astronauts through a spectro-analyzer and found that emotional tension is related to frequency and intensity of formant components of speech. Similarly, Williams and Stevens (1969) used spectrograms to detect voice quality changes during maximally stressful situations. These researchers obtained tape recordings of two pilots' conversations with control tower operators during flights that ended in fatal crashes. In one case the fundamental frequency change of the pilot's speech was clearly noticeable and in the other the change was dramatic. Williams and Stevens also used a spectrograph to analyze the tape recording of a radio announcer describing the crash of the Hindenberg. The average fundamental frequency of the announcer's voice was much higher immediately after the zepplin suddenly burst into flames and crashed than just prior to the disaster.

The spectrograph has even been used in lie detection studies. Streeter, Krauss, Geller, Olson, and Apple (1977) used the device to detect pitch changes in subjects instructed to tell the truth or lie. When subjects lied, their voice pitch tended to be higher than when telling the truth.

Another instrument that has aided researchers in recording specific information is the bone conductance microphone. This device is worn on the head and picks up vibrations made by the wearer whenever he or she speaks. Since it only responds to bone vibrations, it is possible to record vocal behavior of a particular person without other noise contaminating the recording. Hayes and Meltzer (1967) were the first researchers to use the bone conductance microphone and have demonstrated its use in the laboratory (Hayes, Meltzer, and Lundberg, 1968).

Although it is often preferable for an experimenter to record speech only from specified people, there are many occasions when overall noise level is the more appropriate phenomenon to be measured. For such purposes, Heusler, Ulett, and their associates (Heusler, Ulett, and Blasques, 1959; Callahan et al., 1960; Heusler, Ulett, and Callahan, 1960; Ulett et al., 1961; Ulett, Heusler, and Callahan, 1961) developed what they termed a noise-level index for hospital wards. Their substantive concern was measuring the effects of drugs on hospital patients, and they planted tape recorders to pick up ward noises. These sounds are meshed in an integrator which provides a numerical total of the activity. Originally, this noise level had been rated by judges; in later work, however, the authors used a direct index of noise level, thus reducing biases, among them the possible confounding due to a judge's recognition of a patient's voice.

A highly opportunistic use of audiotapes was demonstrated by Matarazzo and his associates (Matarazzo et al., 1963) in their study of speech duration. The National Aeronautics and Space Administration made available to these investigators the audiotapes of conversations between astronauts and ground communicators for two orbital flights. These data provided a test of propositions developed in the experimental laboratories. In space, as in the laboratory and as in presidential news conferences, the length of a response is positively correlated with the length of a question. It could hardly be claimed that the astronauts were thinking of Matarazzo's hypotheses at the time they were steering their craft, and the astronaut findings supported the work of the laboratory. This highly imaginative research dipped into archives that were available, archives known not to suffer from intermediary distortions.

Voice-activated tape recorders have extended the usefulness of that recording device since they eliminate the necessity to monitor long silences and waste of tape. Johnson and Bolstad (1975) had found that tape recordings of family interactions did not differ when observers were present or absent, suggesting that family interactions may not be very reactive to observer presence. However, Johnson, Christensen, and Bellamy (1976) greatly enhanced the technology of tape recording interactions by having a target child wear a small radio transmitter that broadcasts to a concealed tape recorder. The tape recorder is devised in such a way that it can be activated at random intervals during the day so that, although the family know they are being monitored, they do not know when. That feature probably reduces reactivity considerably since it would be difficult for most families to maintain a facade for any period of time.

The fidelity and breadth of content of the audiotapes give them an edge over written records for archival analysis. Not only are they uncontaminated by other hands, but they contain more pertinent material physically unavailable on the written record. Matarazzo, for example, could not have conducted so accurate a study had he been limited to transcripts alone. Interested in duration of speech, where the natural unit is a second of time, he would have had to make estimates of duration from word counts, which are pockmarked with substantial individual response-set errors in rate of speech, different levels of noncontent interjections (ummm's), and the like.

There is a weighty mass of research material almost untouched by social scientists, although known and used by historians. It is found in the oral archives of the national radio and television networks, which have kept disc, film, and tape recordings of radio and television shows over the years. The advent of videotape recordings has provided another dimension to these archives.

In recent years the use of videotaping equipment has become so ubiquitous that reactivity to this means of recording behavior should be quite low. Banks and stores, for example, often have cameras for the purpose of controlling thefts, and many buildings use television cameras to monitor entrances. Many schools use videotapes for instruction, and most universities even allow faculty and students to borrow videotaping equipment for use in research. Videotapes have been used in some experimental research to validate the results of paper-and-pencil tests. A student of the effectiveness of television commercials has run some preliminary checks on an advertising exposure test. He called friends and asked them to send their secretaries to his office on the pretext of picking up a package. After arriving, the secretary was asked to wait in a reception room, which contained newspapers, magazines, and a turned-on television set. A hidden television camera monitored her behavior as she turned to the printed material, watched television, or just sat. She left, unsuspecting, and was subsequently interviewed by standard questionnaire methods to determine her exposure to television commercials and magazines and newspapers. This is a more advanced variation of the obvious one-way mirror setting and provides a medium for a good check on observation and self-report data.

A particularly interesting use of videotape has been reported by Ellgring and Clarke (1977; Ellgring, personal communication, 1980). Interviews with depressed patients are conducted and regularly recorded over the period of their treatment. From these interviews, 10 to 15 segments are excerpted, each segment being the response to the same, repeated question: "How do you think things are going to turn out for you in the long run?" What results, then, is a "behavioral time lapse" that is akin to time-lapse photography, and a three-month treatment period is condensed to a tape of about five minutes in duration. The segments can then be arranged in any order for purposes of obtaining judgments concerning the patient's response to treatment.

Still photography is being used in research gradually. In a very early study, Lynn and Lynn (1943) photographed people without their knowing it so they could record involuntary smiles. They found that although most people smile in a balanced way, those who do not tend to smile more on the side of their mouth congruent with their handedness. The people who smiled contralaterally (that is, on the side opposite their dominant hand) tended to be more withdrawn, inadequate, and poor in coping ability than others. Developments in infrared and ultraviolet photography are allowing researchers to do some amazing things. Infrared equipment allows one to see stains on clothing and changes in documents that the naked eye cannot detect.

A fascinating use of still photography is described in a study reported by Ziller and Smith (1977). This researcher gives cameras to students or other persons with varying instructions to use an entire 12 exposure roll to portray themselves and who they are or to characterize their environments, and so on. One of his findings is that good students and books are to be found together in the same photos, but he reports other similarly interesting discoveries, among them that new students portray the university environment primarily in terms of landmarks and buildings, while experienced students are more likely to focus on persons and their activities. The method is scarcely nonreactive; the respondents do know that their pictures will be examined and in relation to what questions. They do not know, however, on what content or dimensions the pictures might be analyzed, and the method has at least the virtue of having *different* sources of bias.

As mentioned earlier, though, photographs can be deceiving. Boring (1953), for example, mentions that "Voliva supported his theory of the flat earth by a photograph of twelve miles of the shore line of Lake Winnebago: you could see, he argued, that the shore is horizontal and bowed."[1] Both still photography and movie films have been used in the study of eye behavior—direction, duration of looking, pupil dilation, and the like.

The physical *location* of eyes was used by Politz (1959) in a study of commercial exposure of advertising posters placed on the outside of buses. Politz' equipment was movie cameras placed in buses and automatically activated in a series of short bursts spread throughout a day. The camera was faced outward, over the poster under study, and a person whose two eyes could be seen in the development film was classified as "in" the advertising audience. This design, which used a random sample of both locations and time, is exemplary for its control of a large number of extraneous variables that could jeopardize external validity. On the other hand, the visibility of the camera, which occupied a bus seat, may nearly have invalidated the measure altogether since people may have been looking at the camera rather than the advertising poster. Moreover, the camera might have attracted more attention to the poster that it would otherwise have received—who looks at posters on buses anyway? The novelty effect of the camera would not even wear off except for regular bus riders, and they would be the very ones who would have extinguished on the poster also. Note, however, that there are places, for example banks and stores, where visible cameras are mostly ignored except by those for whom they were installed in the first place.

Walters, Bowen, and Parke (1963) recorded the eye movements of male undergraduates viewing a series of pictures of nude or almost nude males and females. The men were told that a moving spot of light on the film indicated the eye movements of a previous subject. For about half the subjects, the

---

[1]In the same article, Professor Boring comments on changes in the human observer as an instrument. "I remember how a professor of genetics many years ago showed me published drawings of cell nuclei dated both before and after the discovery and description of chromosomes. Chromosomes kept showing up in the later drawings, not in the earlier" (p. 176).

light roved over the bodies portrayed in the film, while with the other half, the light centered on the background of the pictures. The eye movement of the subjects was influenced, and

> Subjects who had been exposed to a supposedly sexually uninhibited model spent a significantly longer time looking at the nude and semi-nude bodies, and significantly less time looking at the background of the pictures [Walters, Bowen, and Parke, 1963, p. 77].

Another investigation showed that the presence of a female inhibited the interest of male students in "sexy" magazines. The magazines were avoided with a woman present, but upon her leaving, they were quickly retrieved (Sechrest, 1971).

Time spent looking is a measure easily adaptable to laboratory situations since few persons could be expected to be aware that it would be of interest. Zamansky (1956;1959) devised a box into which subjects looked at pairs of pictures displayed on a split screen. Unbeknownst to the subjects, the experimenter could tell which picture was being looked at and for how long. The purpose of Zamansky's research was to test the Freudian theory of paranoia, which is that it stems from homosexual conflict. The paranoids in Zamansky's studies did not look longer at pictures of males, as had been predicted, but they did tend to avoid looking at pictures of females. More recently, Fiske (1980) allowed subjects in a person perception study to control a slide changer switch on a projector and used time spent looking as a measure of attention paid to each slide.

Many feats are performed with mirrors, or at least it often seems that way. Exline (1963;1964) and Exline and Winters (1964) worked behind one-way mirrors to make controlled observations of mutual glances, time spent looking at someone while speaking to him, time spent looking when being spoken to, and the like. Dabbs (1979) has made extensive use of cleverly designed mirror devices that make it possible for two subjects to watch each other while their faces are being videotaped on split-screen for later viewing by judges on such variables as eye contact and facial expression. Some people even watch themselves in mirrors. In fact, Narcissus gave his name to a trait because of his fondness for inspecting his reflected image. Yet another of Dabbs' students (personal communication, 1980) observed people passing by a mirror in a shopping center: 62 percent of females and 46 percent of males checked themselves out while passing. McDonald and Eilenfield (1980) observed undergraduates traversing a walkway adjacent to a wall of reflective windows, in effect a mirrored corridor. Passersby were surreptitiously rated on attractiveness by two experimenters, and another experimenter, concealed and unaware of the hypothesis, recorded time spent in self-examination. For both sexes there was a significant and apparently linear relationship between three levels of attractiveness and time spent gazing at a self image—positive, of course.

Chimpanzees also like to look at themselves in mirrors, and Gallup (1979) has exploited that fact to study self-awareness in chimpanzees. He lets chimpanzees examine themselves in a mirror and then alters their appearance by, for example, putting a dab of red paint on their foreheads. The chimps showed clear evidence of recognizing the change in their appearance, for example, by touching the spot. Monkeys showed no evidence at all of any self-recognition. Wicklund (1975), incidentally, has shown that the mere expedient of putting subjects before mirrors changes their performances on a variety of tasks, a phenomenon that Wicklund calls self-focused awareness.

Our own view of ourselves comes, of course, from gazing into mirrors, while our view of others is usually direct. Mita, Dermer, and Knight (1977) hypothesized that on the basis of mere exposure, people would prefer a photograph of themselves that was actually a mirror image (by reversing the negative), but that for a friend or lover they would prefer a direct photo. Both expectations were supported by the data. Hopper and Dabbs (1980) noted that when we look at another person, the right side of that person's face falls in our left visual field, whereas when we look at ourselves in a mirror, the left side of our own face falls in the left visual field. The processing of information about faces appears to be a predominantly right-hemisphere function. From this, Hopper and Dabbs reasoned that if photographic negatives were carefully cut in half and put together again in such a way as to produce composite photos consisting of right-right or left-left faces, people would prefer photos of their friends that consisted of two right halves, but photos of themselves that consisted of two lefts. These predictions proved quite correct. Moreover, other evidence had indicated that emotions tend to be expressed more intensely on the left side of the face, and since Hopper and Dabbs had asked their subjects to smile while being photographed, they expected the left-left composites to be judged as happier. That prediction was also correct.

Some of the measures discussed in the preceding paragraphs were obtained in potentially reactive settings. In some instances they could not have been obtained without the subject's awareness. Certainly, however, direction of gaze and duration of looking are amenable to naturalistic use. If Politz (1959) was able to solve the technical problems of a jiggling bus, more stable situations should present little difficulty.

Many laboratory experiences could be replicated in natural settings. Landis and Hunt's (1939) method of studying movement responses could easily be applied in nonlaboratory settings. Shooting off a gun, the authors filmed the subject's gestural response pattern, which included such movements as drawing the shoulders forward, contracting the abdomen, and bending the knees. Facial patterns included closing the eyes and widening the mouth. It will be remembered that Krout found that a gesture of placing the hand to the nose was correlated with fear. With the stimulus of an unexpected gunshot, the immediate response may be independent of any contaminants due to the experimental setting.

HARDWARE:
PHYSICAL SUPPLANTING OF THE OBSERVER

The hardware measures mentioned so far have been mainly concerned with reducing the risk associated with the human observer's fallibility as a measuring instrument—selective perceptions and lack of capacity to note all elements in a complex set of behaviors. Another use to which hardware has been put is to obtain research entrée into situations whose study is not amenable to the more usual observational methods. Some of these content areas have been unattainable because of the privacy of the behavior, others because of the prohibitive costs of maintaining observational scrutiny over a substantial enough sample of time. Sitting in for the observer, hardware can help resolve both problems.[2]

"Blind bugging" via audiotapes is one such approach—a controversial one when applied in certain settings, and illegal in many. Jury deliberations are not observable because of standard legal restraints, but Strodtbeck and his colleagues (Strodtbeck and James, 1955; Strodtbeck and Mann, 1956; Strodtbeck, James, and Hawkins, 1957) received the approval of the court and counsel from both sides to place hidden microphones in the jury room. The use of concealed recording devices presents ethical questions that have been underlined by Amrine and Sanford (1956), Burchard (1957), and Shils (1959). Ultimately the recording of jury decisions created such controversy that any further efforts in that direction have been prohibited and

[2]Galton, writing from Africa, sent the following letter to his brother: "I have seen figures that would drive the females of our native land desperate—figures that could afford to scoff at crinoline, nay more, as a scientific man and as a lover of the beautiful I have dexterously even without the knowledge of the parties concerned, resorted to actual measurement. Had I been a proficient in the language, I should have advanced and bowed and smiled like Goldney, I should have explained the dress of the ladies of our country, I should have said that the earth was ransacked for iron to afford steel springs, that the seas were fished with consummate daring to possess ourselves of caoutchou—that these three products were ingeniously wrought by competing artists, to the utmost perfection, that their handiwork was displayed in every street corner and advertised in every periodical but that on the other hand, that great as is European skill, yet it was nothing before the handiwork of a bounteous nature. Here I should have blushed, bowed and smiled again, handed the tape and requested them to make themselves the necessary measurement as I stood by and registered the inches or rather yards. This however I could not do—there were none but Missionaries near to interpret for me, they would never have entered into my feelings and therefore to them I did not apply—but I sat at a distance with my sextant, and as the ladies turned themselves about, as women always do, to be admired. I surveyed them in every way and subsequently measured the distance of the spot where they stood—worked out and tabulated the results at my leisure" (Pearson, 1914, p. 232).

seem unlikly to be permitted any time soon. There is an old saying that if you like sausage and the law, it is better not to watch either one being made. Perhaps that goes for jury decisions also.

We may add as an aside that among the most astute devices for concealed recordings is a microphone rigged in a mock hearing aid. It works extremely well in inducing the subject to lean over and shout directly into the recording apparatus. The presence of a dangling cord does not inhibit response.

Riesman and Watson (1964) met with difficulties in their attempts to record party conversations on tape

> ... losses of comment lasting more than one minute oc-curred at the rate of about seven times per recorded hour ... the critical objection lay ... in the tape's sometimes useful lack of selectivity: the record was a long drawn-out tissue of inanities in which the very diffuseness made analy-sis more difficult than when one was dealing with the more condensed material of recollection [p. 299].[3]

Which are the "better" data—the true conversation or the "condensed material of recollection"—is up to the investigator to decide. The loss of content, however, is a severe limiting condition, demonstrating the selective utility of some hard-ware. In this case, the recorder would be adequate for record-ing sound level, but inadequate for providing a complete record of conversations.

Many pieces of hardware have been developed for measur-ing the level of physical activity, a variable that has been viewed as symptomatic of many things. Perhaps the earliest mention of this type of measure was made by Galton (1884), who was at that time interested in the physical equivalents of metaphorical language. He took as his example the "inclination of one person toward another." This situation is clearly seen when two people are sitting next to each other at a dinner table, according to

[3]Some years later a similar failure of recording devices and abundance of inanities was to plague the investigators of Watergate. High quality equipment currently available should reduce considerably the probability of recording gaps; inanity is an altogether different problem.

Galton. To demonstrate this empirically in quantitative terms (Galton, 1884; Watson, 1959), he suggested a pressure gauge with an index and dial to indicate changes in stress arranged on the legs of the chair on the side nearest the other person. Galton specified three necessary conditions for this type of experiment: the aparatus must be effective; it must not attract notice; and it must be capable of being applied to ordinary furniture. All of these criteria are appropriate for contemporary apparatus studies.

It is obvious that such a device may be a substitute for human observers when their presence might contaminate the situation, and where no convenient hidden observation site is available. Indeed, many of the studies discussed earlier as "simple observation" are amenable to mechanization, provided Galton's criteria can be met.

There is F. Scott Fitzgerald's fictional account in *The Last Tycoon,* of how the title character, a movie executive, evaluated the quality of rushes (preliminary, unedited film "takes") by observing how much they made him wiggle in his chair. The more the wiggles, the poorer the movie scenes. Simple observational measures should be made of twistings by a concealed observer, but they would clearly be inferior to a more mechanical device. There are such devices. An early version by Kretsinger (1952; 1959) was electromagnetic and was employed to study gross bodily movement in theater audiences. The device utilized a concealed copper screen near the head of the subject which enabled the creation of an electrical field that changed every time the subject's head moved. That change could then be detected and recorded for analysis. Other devices utilizing various electrical, electronic, and mechanical principles include modified self-winding wrist watches (*actometers*) for measuring wrist and ankle movements (Johnson, 1971); pedometers (Barkley, 1977), pneumatic floor pads to count footsteps (Montagu and Swarbrick, 1975), motion sensitive chairs (Barkley, 1977; Christensen and Sprague, 1973), and sound-wave generators that can assess movement in a room (McFarland, Peacock, and Watson, 1966). Even the observer can be improved upon by a grid-marked room that requires only counting of lines crossed during a period of time (Barkely, 1977). But we digress.

Galton (1885) suggested a fidget measure based on the amount of body sway among an audience. The greater the sway, the greater the boredom. "Let this suggest to observant philosophers, when the meeting they attend may prove dull, to occupy themselves in estimating the frequency, amplitude and duration of the fidgets of their fellow sufferers" (p. 175). The American playwright Robert Ardrey notes coughing as an audience response to boredom.

> One cougher begins his horrid work in an audience, and the cough spreads until the house is in bedlam, the actors in rage, and the playwright in retreat to the nearest saloon. Yet let the action take a turn for the better, let the play tighten up, and that same audience will sit in a silence unpunctuated by a single tortured throat [p. 85].[4]

Cox and Marley (1959) devised another movement measure in their study of the restlessness of patients as a partial measure of the effect of various drugs. Their rather complex apparatus consists basically of a series of pulleys and springs, set under the springs of the bed, which record the displacement of the mattress. When the patient is perfectly motionless, the relay system does not operate, but the slightest movement will be recorded. A more simple device is possible with baby cribs: the activity level of the child is measured by shaving down one of the four crib legs and attaching a meter which records the frequency of jiggling. This is much less fine a measure than that of Cox and Marley, for the child could move without activating the meter. For studies which don't require such fine calibration, however, the simplicity of the device is appealing.

As beds, cribs, and chairs can be wired, so, too, can desks. Foshee (1958) worked on the hypothesis that a greater general drive state would manifest itself in greater activity. Here is a good theoretical proposition testable by a device appropriate for natural settings away from the laboratory. To measure activity, Foshee used a schoolroom desk which was supported at each corner by rubber stoppers. Attached to the platform that supported the desk was a mechanical lever arrangement that amplified the longitudinal movements of the platform. Through an elaborate transmission system, the amplitude and frequency of the subject's movement could be measured. Foshee does not mention whether the subjects (in this case a group of mental defectives) were aware of the apparatus or not, but it would seem likely that the device could be constructed to evade detection.

To reach into the difficult setting of a darkened movie house for the study of expressive movement, several investigators have employed infrared photography (Siersted and Hansen, 1951; Bloch, 1952; Field, 1954; Greenhill, 1955; Gabriele, 1956). This type of filming eliminates almost entirely the element of subject awareness of the observational apparatus. It is clearly superior to unaided observation because of the advantage of working in the dark; the brighter the light in which to see the subject, the brighter the light for him to see you. This is illustrated in Leroy-Boussion's (1954) visible-observer study of emotional expressions of children during a comedy film. Although Leroy-Boussion claimed to be only a projection aide during the film, she did have to eliminate certain subjects who "seemed to be aware" of her presence as an observer. It would thus seem likely that there were other subjects who did not make their awareness known to the investigator. Putting aside the question of reducing the sample size, the more important issue is whether those who were aware (and discarded as subjects) were a selective group (the more suspicious or paranoid, for example). Infrared photography drastically reduces such selective loss. Further, it is possible to match the infrared camera with the regular projection machine so that in subsequent analysis the photographs of audience reaction can be matched easily to the specific film sequence.

The danger of relying solely on interview or questionnaire self-reports is sharply illustrated in the Siersted and Hansen (1951) study. They supplemented their filming by interviewing the children who had seen the film. There were marked differences between these interview responses and both the filmed reactions and verbal comments made during the film (recorded with hidden tape recorders).

For some reason, the French have been leaders in research on movie hardware. Toulouse and Mourgue (1948) worked with respiratory reactions in order to index reactions to films, and it has even been suggested that the temperature of the room in which a film is viewed might be monitored as an indicator.

Ellis and Pryer (1959) have demonstrated the complexities possible with photoelectric cells in their study of the movements of children with severe neuropathology. Their apparatus consisted of a square plywood enclosure in which the children played. Electronic devices were located on the outside surface of the walls and arranged so that the beams crisscrossed the enclosure at two-foot intervals. Interruption of a beam would be recorded, with each beam recorded separately.

With the light beams visible, the behavior of subjects may be modified—either because they dart back and forth in a playful game with the beam, or because it inhibits their movement to know that they are under observation. Ellis and Pryer suggest modifications of their technique to avoid such risks, among them installing infrared exciter lamps, noiseless relays, and soundproofing. Dabbs and Clower (1973) have reported on the use of an ultrasonic motion detector adapted from a burglar-alarm system, a technique that could easily be made quite unobtrusive.

For some reason, of attendance at an event or an institution can be carried out by planting observers who count heads. Another way is to mechanize and count circuit breaks. The "electric eye," particularly when supplemented by a time recorder, provides a useful record of frequency of attendance and its pacing. The photoelectric cells are typically set up on either side of a doorway so that any break of the current will register a mark on an attached recording device. As Trueswell (1963) shrewdly pointed out, however, this apparatus is not free from mechanical or reactivity contaminants. Particularly when the device is first installed, it is common for people to step back and forth through the light or to wave arms and legs, thus registering three or four marks for a single entry. Another difficulty is the placement of the cells. If they are set too low, it is possible for each leg to register a separate mark as the person walks through. If the doorway is wide enough to admit two people, a couple may walk together and register only one mark.

It is important to note that these are not random errors which balance out, but are constant for the method. Because of this, it is equally important that human observers be there with the mechanical device, particularly in its early period of installation, to study whether any such errors are admitted to the data.

For another example of the use of hardware to get otherwise difficult content, there is Weir's (1963) report of her audiotape recordings of a two-and-a-half-year-old boy falling to sleep. The child practices language, working with noun substitution and articulation. In the evening of the day when he was first offered raspberries, he says, "berries, *not* bayreez, berries." Maccoby (1964), who summarized the study, states: "These observations provide insight into language learning processes which are ordinarily covert and not accessible to observation" (p. 211).

Psychophysiological measures are often of interest for what they can reveal about the reactions of a person to some stimulus. Such measures are difficult to obtain unobtrusively, but they are often not reactive in unwanted ways since they tend to involve involuntary responses. A good review of psychophysiological measures and problems in assessing them is given by Kallman and Feuerstein (1977). Many psychophysiological measures are related to general level of arousal and, hence, are useful in assessing interest and affective state. One frequent physiological response is increased activity of the sweat glands, often manifested by palmar perspiration. Such perspiration can be measured by electrical conductors, but other methods have been devised that may be more adaptable to field use. There is a type of paper that will react to sweat and by obtaining a palm print from time to time, level of arousal may be tracked. One group of investigators (Dabbs, Johnson, and Leventhal, 1968) showed that subjects flying in a small plane doing stunts showed a record of successive palm prints that betrayed heightened arousal just after each stunt as compared with level flying. Another device adaptable for field use relies on ability to detect salt from perspiration in distilled water. Strahan (1974) provides subjects with small tubes of distilled water into which they insert their fingers for controlled periods of time; later the solutions can be analyzed for salt content. Sexual arousal is also often of interest, and specific devices of an obviously intrusive nature have been invented for that purpose. One such device is the penile strain gauge, which measures penile circumference (Freund, 1963). Strain gauge measures have been found to be sensitive to a variety of sexual preferences as represented in auditory and visual stimulation. More recently it has become feasible to measure female sexual arousal in analogous ways (Masters and Johnson, 1966; Sintchak and Geer, 1975).

Then, of course, there are studies of pupil dilation. Gump (1962) reports that Chinese jade dealers were sensitive to this variable and determined a potential buyer's interest in various stones by observing the dilation of his pupils as pieces were shown (astute buyers countered this by wearing dark glasses).

Hess and Polt (1960) measured pupil dilation on 16-millimeter film and related it to stimulus materials. The stimulus objects were a series of pictures—a baby, a mother holding a child, a partially nude woman, a partially nude man, and a landscape. The six pictures elicited clear-cut differences in pupil size, and sex differences were present. Commercial applications of this method have been based on work under the direction of Hess. See Foote (1962); West (1962); Anonymous (1964b); Krugman (1964). Recent studies of pupil-dilation measures (for example, Goldwater, 1972; Juris and Velden, 1977) have cast some doubt on the exact meaning of the measure, and further work will be required before such measures can, with any confidence, be recommended for a specific purpose.

Radio telemetry affords the opportunity to record at a distance the responses of people going about their ordinary, or as in the case of the astronauts their extraordinary, business. Maher (1966), for example, identified a group of people who tended to respond to stress with increased heart rate although they did not all respond to the same situations. He then arranged for them to wear transmitters and to be monitored when they were going to be involved in what they expected to be a personally stressful situation. The specific situations varied widely, for example, from cashing a check in a bank to appearing on stage in a bikini, but there were no persons resistant to stress. Levine and Grinspoon (1971) used telemetry equipment to monitor the GSR (galvanic skin response) and heart rate of a schizophrenic man and were able to relate changes in those measures to apparent hallucinations. It is widely believed that emotional upsets can trigger asthma attacks in victims of that disease, but it has been difficult to establish that theory outside the laboratory. By means of a device slightly larger than a king-size cigarette pack, Miklich, Chai, Purcell, Weiss, and Brady (1974) were able to get telemetered recordings both of verbal behavior and sounds of breathing. Emotional state was judged from verbal behavior and could be associated with disruptions in breathing patterns. Thackray and Orne (1968) monitored GSRs by telemetry in a study of subject awareness and detection of deception. Dabbs (Dabbs and Neuman, 1978), obviously more than a dabbler in instrumentation for behavioral recording, has described a device for telemetry monitoring of human cerebral temperature by way of a device inserted in the ear canal. Dabbs and Moorer (1975) had previously found that temperature is related to arousal. Finally, Rugh (1971; 1972) used radio telemetry to monitor chewing behavior without subject awareness! How? A tiny transmitter in the side frame of eye glasses was sensitive to movement of the temporal muscle. (See Miklich, 1975, for a discussion of many ways in which telemetry may be used in clinical psychology and Rugh and Schwitzgebel, 1977, for a useful discussion of a wide variety of hardware for use in behavioral assessment.)

A general category of assessment problems involves the need for *surveillance,* that is, the monitoring of some ongoing behavior or process. Although the term usually has connotations of surreptitiousness—even of furtiveness—it really means something like "keeping a close watch," and that might or might not need to be surreptitious. Some surveillance techniques are undoubtedly highly reactive, and some are in fact meant to be. For example, when subjects are in substance abuse programs, they may be kept under surveillance as part of the treatment program itself, that is, in the hope that surveillance would have a deterrent effect. Alcohol intake was monitored by Miller, Hersen, Eisler, and Watts (1974) by taking a portable breathalyzer out into the natural environment of a chronic Skid Row alcoholic at random times. After obtaining baseline data, the experimenters administered reinforcements for low readings and demonstrated a decrease in drinking behavior. Alcohol use can also be monitored from urine samples, which can also be obtained at random times (Goldstein and Brown, 1970). A clearer instance of surveillance as treatment was provided by the efforts of the armed forces in Vietnam to suppress drug use by regular urine surveillance. Cigarette smoking can also be brought under potentially reactive surveillance by means of a device to measure carbon monoxide in breath samples (Energetics Science, Elmford, New York). Another instance of surveillance, certainly meant to be reactive but useful in field settings, is the use of "disclosing" tablets to assess thoroughness of toothbrushing behavior (Evans, Rozelle, Lasaster, Demobroski, and Allen, 1970).

In some instances surveillance techniques are employed solely for the purpose of keeping track of the location of the person or object of interest. Use of various signaling devices is common among those who study animals and their movements. Small transmitters can be fastened to turtles or implanted under the skins of mammalian species and tracking then becomes simple. The same could be done for humans. Schwitzgebel (1969) once suggested that as a condition of release into the community some serious and chronic criminal offenders might be required to wear a transmitter that would make it possible for parole supervisors to determine their locations at any time. A small transmitter that could be fitted into the heel of a shoe and that could be used to monitor location was described by Herron and Ramsden (1967). Schwitzgebel's proposal was immediately and strongly attacked on legal and ethical grounds, and the surveillance plan was never implemented. We cite it here not as a recommendation but because it could be used, with free and informed consent, to provide a valuable additional source of data when it is important to know more about locomotion than might be dependably obtained from a self-report. For example, Lee (1980) has interviewed applicants for a driver's license about their driving on the day before (his interest is in gas consumption). An electronic surveillance device might be used quite ethically to obtain more detailed and dependable information than could be obtained from either self-report or odometer readings. Such devices have been used in St. Louis to monitor the locations of police vehicles—without consent of the patrolmen, we might add. The scheme has not been an unqualified success, in part because drivers discover ways to frustrate even sophisticated electronic devices. But at least the cars can be located when their drivers want them to be.

THE INTERVENING OBSERVER

Most of the observation studies reported so far have been ones in which the observer is passive. The observer may take the behavior as it comes or may introduce mechanization to improve the accuracy and span of his or her observations, but he or she has not typically altered the cues in the environment to which the person or group is responding. This passivity has two costs. It is possible that the behavior under study occurs so infrequently that an inordinate amount of effort is expended on gathering large masses of data, only a small segment of which is useful. Or, paying the second cost, the naturally occurring behavior is not stimulated by events of sufficient discriminability. The investigator may want four or five levels of intensity of a condition, say, when the convenient simple observation approach can produce only two.

Rather than pay these costs, many investigators have actively stepped into the research environment and "forced" the data in a way that did not attract attention to the method. In some cases, this has meant grading experimental conditions over equivalent groups, with each group getting a different "natural" treatment. In a smaller number of studies, the conditions have been varied over the individual. The general method has elsewhere been called the method of "contrived situations" (Campbell, 1963). Both classes are illustrated in this section.

Allen Funt of the television show "Candid Camera," perhaps the most visible of the hidden observers, gave up simple observation because of the high dross rate (Flagler, 1960). In the early years of the program, Funt's episodes consisted largely of studies of gestures and conversation (Hamburger, 1950; Martin, 1961). Particularly with conversation, Funt found that a large amount of time was required to obtain a small amount of material, and he turned to introducing confederates who would behave in such a way to direct attention to the topic of study.

In one magnificent sequence of film, Funt prepared a cross-cultural comparison of how men from different countries respond to the request of a female confederate to carry a suitcase to the corner. Filmed abroad, the episodes centered on the girl, indicating she had carried the suitcase for a long time and would like a hand. The critical material is the facial expression and bodily gestures of the men as they attempted to lift the suitcase and sagged under the weight. It was filled with metal. The Frenchman shrugged; the Englishman kept at it. Funt has offered to open his extensive film library to social scientists. For students of response to frustration or unexpected stimuli, this is rich ground.

Obviously, experimental manipulation is not a contaminant. It is only when the manipulation is seen as such that reactivity enters to threaten validity. Some years back, Doob and Gross (1968) used the familiar and mundane situation of a car that does not move when a traffic light changes from red to green to study aggression subsequent to frustration. Their measure of aggression was the latency and frequency of horn honking by blocked cars. They found that a high-status automobile was less likely to be honked at, and not so quickly either, than an older, nonprestigious automobile. There have since been numerous horn-honking studies, for example Deaux (1971), but in two of the more interesting ones, Berkowitz and Alioto (1973) found that people are less likely to honk at a pickup truck if it has a gun hanging in the rear window, and Baron (1976) found that male drivers are more inclined to honk in hot in than cool weather, but less inclined to do so if a sexily attired female had just crossed the intersection in front of them. Feldman (1968) compared the way foreigners versus denizens were treated in various cities by such interventions as overpaying a shopkeeper, asking for directions, and pretending to find money that might be claimed by passersby. In studies such as those cited, the experimental interventions almost certainly were not detected as such by those exposed to them.

Simple observation, mechanized or not, is appropriate to a broad range of imaginative and useful research comparisons. Some of these we have mentioned. The advantage of contrived observation is to extend the base of simple observation and permit more subtle comparisons of the intensity of effect.

The early work of Hartshorne and May yields good examples of the manipulating observer. In *Studies in Service and Self Control* (Hartshorne, May, and Maller, 1929), they report on a long series of experiments—the first behavioral studies of "service." Employing "production methods of measurement," they indexed service or helpfulness by the subject's willingness to produce something—a toy in a shop, or the posting of a picture. Similarly, they employed "self-sacrifice" techniques, measures on which the subject had to give up something.

The subjects were school children, and the active involvement of the experimenter (teacher) in defining alternatives of behavior was both expected and normal. The threat of subjects' awareness of being tested is less an issue in educational research, and the long line of studies on lecture versus discussion methods, as well as the current research on educational television, are a fine source of learning research because the risk of the contaminant is so reduced.

In the same way, it is not a patently false condition for a teacher to present students with the chance to help some other children in hospitals. Hartshorne and May graded the opportunities to help in an "envelope test." The student could put pictures, jokes, or stories in envelopes to give to hospitalized children, could promise to do so, or not do so. In another behavioral measure of sacrifice, one with more artificiality, however, the students were told they would be given some money. They were provided opportunities to bank it, give it to charity, or keep it themselves. In another phase, one that presaged many small-group experiments, the children were given a choice of whether they would work for themselves or for the class in a spelling contest.

In Hartshorne and May's *Studies of Deceit* (1928), children were offered the opportunity not to return all of the coins distributed for arithmetic practice, to cheat by changing original answers in grading their own exam papers (which had previously been collected and then handed back with some excuse), to peek during "eyes-closed" tests and thus perform with unbelievable skill, to exaggerate the number of chin-ups when allowed to make their own records "unobserved." Forty separate opportunities were administered in whole or in part to about eight thousand pupils.

In one of their reports (May and Hartshorne, 1927) is found the first presentation of what is now known as Guttman scale analysis. The experimenters found high unidimensionality for a series of paper regrading opportunities; those students who cheated when an ink eraser was required cheated on *every* easier opportunity.

These studies of Hartshorne and May in the Character Education Inquiry are the classics of contrived observation, and nothing so thorough and ingenious has been done since. It is unfortunate for subsequent measurement efforts that interpretation of the cheating results was viewed as specific to the situation. To be sure, honesty was found to be relative to situation; for example, in one study (May and Hartshorne, 1927), only 2 percent cheated when corrections required an ink eraser, while 80 percent cheated when all that was needed was either erasing or adding a penciled digit. But this is not inconsistent with the six cheating opportunities forming a single-factored test or unidimensional scale. The data show a Guttman reproducibility coefficient of .96. Even though the measure was only six items long, there was a Kuder-Richardson reliability of .72 that becomes .84 when corrected for item-marginal ceiling effects as suggested by Horst (1953). Pooling all their disguised performance tests for a given trait, the experimenters checked the character tests against reputational scores from the so-called Guess Who tests. The validities ranged from .315 to .374. Although very low values in terms of the standards of their day, they are now recognized to be reasonable values typical of those found for personality tests. Of course, the reputational measures contributed their full share of the error in validity.

Contrived observation, then, is observation in which the stimuli or the available responses are varied in an inconspicuous way. For Hartshorne and May, the variation was primarily of the response alternatives. Of critical importance, though, is the fact that respondents do not know that the relevant manipulations are part of an experiment. Once fairly remarkable in psychology, contrived situations have become virtually the hallmark of a large segment of social psychology. So much so, in fact, that we do not need in this edition to do much more than remark on the type of research involved and show how it differs from unobtrusive measurement.

In most instances a contrived situation will involve a non-reactive measure of the dependent variable in that the aim of such research is to render the manipulation nonreactive, with the primary aim of increasing the external validity, the generalizability, of the findings. One can scarcely have an experiment go unrecognized as such if one is forced at the end to request, however apologetically, that the subject fill out a questionnaire. So, in contrived situations, the dependent measure is usually some natural response that flows from the arrangements. In their "damsel in distress" study, Bryan and Test (1967) had an apparently disabled car parked by a highway with a female standing beside it, and the dependent variable was assessed by the number of drivers who stopped to help. Gaertner and Bickman's (1971) study of helping came down to the number of people who would help by making a phone call for a person who had supposedly dialed the wrong number with his last coin. The study by West, Gunn, and Chernicky (1975), of the "Watergate phenomenon," focused on the number of people who agreed to participate in an illegal entry of a business establishment under differing conditions of justification.

Almost any issue of a social psychological journal today will have one or more examples of an experiment with a contrived situation. For instance, the April 1979 issue of the *Journal of Personality and Social Psychology* has an article by Foss and Dempsey (1979) reporting three experiments on blood donating behavior done in such a way that the manipulation was nonreactive and the measure realistic (and reactive, in a sense, since making a blood donation changes the probability of doing so in the future). In the July 1979 issue of the *Personality and Social Psychology Bulletin* is an article by Hastorf, Northcraft, and Picciotto (1979) that is a good illustration of a contrived situation within what appeared to be a quite different kind of experiment. Subjects were asked to monitor and give feedback to another person performing a problem-solving task. That other person was made to appear either normal or physically handicapped (by leg braces), and it was found that subjects behaved according to a "norm to be kind" in giving feedback to the handicapped person. Another article by Kleinke and Singer involved handing out leaflets on the street with either a conciliatory or a commanding suggestion to take one and either looking the respondent directly in the eyes or not. Females were more responsive to a commanding request than were males, and gaze had more effect when the request was conciliatory. There is, in the same issue of the journal, incidentally, a neat example of a natural experiment which came about when a college had to "triple" some freshman students into rooms designed for two and elected to do so by means of a lottery (Karlin, Rosen, and Epstein, 1979). The article, titled "Three into Two Doesn't Go," showed that tripling had a depressing effect on freshman grades and attitudes, but the effects had dissipated by the junior year.

The potential usefulness of contrived situations when combined with relatively nonreactive dependent measures is suggested quite strongly by a recent review (Crosby, Bromley, and Saxe, 1980) of research on behavior of whites toward blacks. Reviews of work on helping, aggression, and nonverbal behaviors pointed toward more prevalent negative attitudes on the part of white subjects than are generally found in more reactive research such as surveys.

The contrived situation is by now well established, and it is not necessary in this volume to urge its more frequent use. In much of the work reported here, there was no manipulation; the research merely involved obtaining an unobtrusive measure of the consequence of some ongoing process. In some of the other work, the interest of the investigator or observer was in getting an unobtrusive measure of what is better thought of as an independent variable, for example, some characteristic of a person that would predict how he or she would respond— the police officer's socks, tattoos, and trouser waist size. Many of the other studies we cited, however, did involve contrived situations of one sort or another and can be considered virtually mainstream research by now, even if they did not always involve control groups. A useful further discussion of the problems and methods may be found in Campbell (1969).

ENTRAPMENT

Jones (1946) provided an excellent summary of early behavioral studies of character development, many of which follow the entrapment strategy of Hartshorne and May. A later example is the work of Freeman and Ataov (1960). They contrived a situation in which the subjects had a chance to cheat by grading their own examinations by a scoring sheet. Using three classes of questions—fill-in blanks, multiple-choice, and true-false—they found the number of changed answers for each class. The three formed a Guttman scale with a reproducibility coefficient of .94.

Stories abound concerning dishonest cab drivers, and many people arriving in a strange city wonder whether a taxi driver will take advantage of their unfamiliarity with the place. A study of taxi drivers in New York City (Brill, 1976) was done by a person pretending to be a foreigner with very limited English and poor knowledge of the taxi system as manifested by asking about zone fares and whether, when he was accompanied, the amount of the fare was "for both of us." The experimenter attempted to overpay the drivers and did so in a way that suggested rather clearly that if the driver wanted to, he could virtually help himself to the money. Two drivers refused to take the experimenter to his destination, going to some lengths to make clear by gesture and words that the address was only a little more than a block away. Twelve cab rides cost about $35, and the experimenter was "cheated" out of 65¢ by one driver and 85¢ by another; both those incidents could be regarded as self-tipping, slightly overgenerously, by drivers who did not expect to receive one otherwise. New York cabbies are not so bad. Contrived situation and unobtrusive simple observation have shown it to be so.

Entrapment studies do raise some difficult ethical issues, and the closer to real life the studies get, the more difficult the issues become. Thus, it may be one thing to provide an easy opportunity for laboratory students to cheat on a laboratory task in order to enhance the favorability of the image they present. It may be something else again to make it tempting to cheat on an actual course exam as was done by Freeman and Ataov (1960). Although that experiment was done in such a way as to ensure that students' grades were not actually influenced by their cheating, nor by the cheating of others, there is cause for discomfort in a research effort that engages people in such realistic dishonesty. It may be somewhat less troublesome to test the honesty of people who are in positions of public trust, for example, taxi drivers, automobile mechanics, physicians, and so on, since their honesty is important to the public welfare. Nonetheless, we think that social scientists should be cautious and sparing in their use of procedures which involve entrapment, able at least to assure themselves that the data they will collect will be worth the ethical jeopardy in which they place their respondents. There are quite enough occasions for dishonesty without social scientists providing them. It goes without saying that in studies of entrapment social scientists should do everything possible to protect the confidentiality of their data and should not report it in any way that would make identification of respondents possible.

Although done in a laboratory, a recent study by Lingle, Brock, and Cialdini (1977) is useful for the light it sheds on when risks of entrapment are likely to be high. Actually the study was done in such a way that subjects did not know that it was their own entrapping behavior that was of interest. Research subjects monitored the performance of a confederate and were given an opportunity to entrap the confederate into cheating. Entrapment tended to occur when the confederate had been observed in previous episodes of cheating, but it was not increased by instructions to be on the lookout for cheating. Entrapment also tended to occur when subjects had a high level of involvement in the surveillance and when they had been criticized by the confederate. These findings may provide clues about circumstances to be guarded against by experimenters whose procedures threaten entrapment.

PETITIONS AND VOLUNTEERING

Petition signing has been the dependent variable in many observational studies, usually being taken as a reflection of tendencies to want to be helpful or as a measure of response to pressures to conform. In earlier studies by Blake, Mouton, and Hain (1956) and Helson, Blake, and Mouton (1958) the interest was in such variables as strength of the plea to sign or in the effect of the behavior of a confederate who might sign readily or refuse. Subsequently other investigators have used petition signing in studies of helping behavior. Solicitation to sign a petition is a common enough event in academic settings, and may be becoming more common outside the cloistered world. Certainly it offers a broad freedom of movement in experimentation and structuring of contrived conditions. Searching for volunteers does, too, and several studies have used observation of the simple "volunteer-not volunteer" alternatives as the behavioral variable.

Rosenbaum and Blake (1955) wanted to test the hypothesis that the act of volunteering is "a special case of conformance with social norms or standards, rather than . . . an individualistic act conditioned by an essentially unidentifiable complex of inner tensions, needs, etc." (p. 193). Subjects were plucked from students studying in the university library, and conditions were varied so that the subject saw either an acceptance or rejection of the request from a confederate. In a third group, the student accepted or rejected the volunteering request in the absence of a model. As predicted, acceptances were high with a conforming confederate, low with a nonconforming confederate, and in between on the control condition.

The University of Texas library was also the site of another study by Rosenbaum (1956). Volunteering was the dependent variable, and stimulus conditions included three request strengths (determined by a pilot study) and three background conditions employing confederates. The confederate entered the library, sat next to an unsuspecting student, and then the volunteer-seeker entered and started with the confederate.

Blake and his associates (Blake et al., 1956) determined the effect on the level of volunteering of varying the attractiveness of alternatives to volunteering. The public or private character of the volunteering was also varied, with conditions altered so that a class might substitute volunteering time for time otherwise devoted to: (1) a pop quiz, (2) released time from class, (3) a control, with no time gained. It might be observed that under the pop-quiz alternative, 98.8 percent of the subjects volunteered under the private-commitment situation and 100.0 percent under public commitment. The 1.2 percent above is accounted for by the single aberrant student who preferred a pop quiz to participation in an experiment.

Volunteering for social action was the subject of a study by Gore and Rotter (1963). The action in this case was the willingness of students in a southern black college to engage in different types of segregation-protest activity. This criterion measure was correlated with previously obtained scores on control of reinforcement and social desirability scales, these scales not specifically dealing with the segregation issue. A generalized attitude toward internal or external control was shown to predict the type and degree of behavior subjects were willing to perform in attempts at social change.

An Overall Appraisal of Hidden Hardware and Control

As the discussion and examples of observational research have progressed over these past two chapters, the reader may have been sensitive to a movement along a passivity-activity dimension. In the studies reported in the chapter on simple observation methods, the observer was a nonintervening passive onlooker of behavior that came before his or her eyes or ears. The observer may have scrambled about in different locations to reduce some population restrictions, but his or her role was a quiet, receptive one. In many ways, this is appropriate for the covert character of the studies we have outlined.

With the hardware employed in the studies cited in this chapter, investigators engaged their data more—actively expanding the possible scope of the content of research and achieving a more faithful record of what behaviors did go on. Yet the hardware varied, too. Some of the hardware devices are static, while others are mobile. To the degree that the hardware is mobile (say, a microphone in a mock hearing aid versus one secreted in a table), the experimenters have flexibility to make more economical forays into locational sampling. They could sample in a number of locations by installing more permanent recording devices, but commonly a more feasible method is to sample occasions and time with mobile equipment. As electronic technology develops, more opportunities arise. It isn't so long ago that television cameras had to be anchored in one spot.

When, through deliberate choice or no realistic alternative, investigators were limited to a fixed instrument, they were forced to depend on the character of the population which flowed past that spot and the content appropriate to it. The waiting game can give accurate and complete measurement of a limited population and limited content, and the decision to use such an approach is posited on two criteria, one "theoretical," one "practical." Are the limitations likely to be selective enough to inhibit the generalizability of the findings? Can investigators absorb the time and money costs of developing material with a low saturation of pertinent data for their comparisons?

In the contrived observation studies, the experimenters took the next step and intervened actively in the production of the data, striding away from passive and critically placed observations. The effect was to produce very dense data, of which a high proportion was pertinent to the research comparisons. Further, a finer graduation of stimuli was then possible, and more subtle shadings of difference could be noted. By active intervention, as the petition and volunteering studies of conformity show, it was also possible to make estimates of the interaction of variables, an extremely difficult matter with passive observation.

As the experimenter's activity increases, and he or she achieves the gains of finer measurement and control, the price paid is the increased risk of being caught—that the subject of the observation will detect the recording device, or will suspect that the confederate is really a "plant." This is a high price, for if the confederate is detected, the experimenter's research is flooded with the reactive measurement errors which the hidden observation approach, regardless of its simplicity or complexity, is designed to avoid. At the extreme end of contrivance, when a confederate is a visible actor in the subject's world, it requires the greatest finesse to protect against detection and against changes in the behavior of the confederate damaging to comparison. The best defense, as always, is knowledge, and almost all of the observational approaches have built into them the capacity to examine whether or not population or instrument contaminants are working to confound the data.

Obviously many of the hardware devices discussed in this chapter raise serious ethical issues that, although they may not prohibit the use of the devices, demand special attention and protection. Some of the devices, for example, radio transmitters in shoe heels, smack more of James Bond than science, but all of them may have quite legitimate uses. Schwitzgebel (1968), for instance, proposes that electronic transmitters might be used to keep track of persons subject to medical emergencies or to disorientation. Some devices do not permit disaggregation of data, for example, counters in door treadles, and hence do not threaten privacy or dignity. We do not propose that the social and behavioral sciences subtract from the array of measurement devices available to them, but that they add only when proper care is taken for ethical—and legal—problems.

CHAPTER 9

Limitations on the Use of Nonreactive Measures

The employment of nonreactive measures is far from being routine in the behavioral and social sciences, but relative infrequency of use is understandable, in part, because of problems with the concept and techniques of nonreactive measurement. Perhaps some problems are inherent in the method; others may, we think, yield to careful conceptual analysis and developmental research. The major problems as we see them are three and are the focus of this chapter. There is, first, very frequently a problem with the potential construct validity of a nonreactive measure. Second, there are troublesome psychometric lacunae for many types of nonreactive measures. And third, there is, as yet, no systematic way of generating nonreactive measures to fit research needs as they arise.

CONSTRUCT VALIDITY OF NONREACTIVE MEASURES

We will not try to hold the concept of nonreactive measurement hostage to any very precise or fancy definition of construct validity. We refer here merely to the fact that if one wishes to use any measure in any but the most naive of empirical ways, it is necessary to know just what it is that is being measured. In the case of many nonreactive measures it is difficult to be certain in any given application what construct may be presumed to underlie the numbers one ends up with. Earlier in this book we used the metaphor of scores as hypotheses with the consequent application of the idea of threats to the validity of those scores. That is what is at issue with respect to the construct validity of nonreactive measures.

An investigator has a measure, let us say, odometer readings from automobiles taken when they are serviced, and the investigator wants to interpret the miles driven as an indicator of concern about energy conservation. Perhaps the study is a comparison of the owners of different makes and models of cars. Whether the investigator realizes it or not, a considerable leap of faith is required to suppose that the odometer readings measure anything at all beyond miles driven, and perhaps not even that with complete accuracy. Some years back, one of the authors read a study in a consumers' magazine on the accuracy of speedometers that indicated that most of them give consistently higher readings than warranted. It was suggested that auto manufacturers deliberately built in such a bias to capitalize on the fascination of the American public with fast cars. Odometer readings are off if a driver uses oversized or undersized tires, some odometers may be disconnected, some are undoubtedly inaccurate, and some may be broken or have been broken in the past. Odometer readings may as well reflect concern for conservation of dollars as of gasoline, and if an auto has multiple drivers, the owner's concerns for conservation may have gone right out the window. So much for the construct validity of odometer readings.

Lost Letters

We choose to illustrate problems of construct validity in the context of what have come to be known as "lost letter" studies (even though studies employing lost keys, lost applications for college, and lost postcards also fall into this category). An advantage of illustrating with lost letter studies is that there have been enough of them to warrant meaningful comparisons and conclusions. In fact, over thirty different studies employing the lost letter technique have come to our attention.

The first lost letter experiment was conducted by Merritt and Fowler (1948) in an attempt to test "the pecuniary honesty of the public at large." These experimenters discreetly dropped sealed, stamped, and addressed envelopes on sidewalks in vari-

ous eastern and midwestern cities. Some of the letters contained a lead slug the dimensions of a fifty-cent piece plus a note
with a trivial message; other letters contained only the message.
As one might expect, significantly fewer letters with slugs than
without were returned. While Merritt and Fowler's results may
not have been very surprising, their method was ingenious and
has since been used extensively.

The most common use of the lost letter technique has been
to assess attitudes, chiefly sentiments of the public toward political candidates (Bouchard and Stuster, 1969; Jacoby and Aranoff,
1971; Milgram, 1969; Shotland, Berger, and Forsyth, 1970;
Weiner and Lurey, 1973; and Wicker, 1969). Additionally, this
method has been implemented in the assessment of racial attitudes (Benson, Karabenick, and Lerner, 1976; Bochner, 1972;
and Montanye, Mulberry and Hardy, 1971). Issues as diverse as
rapid transit (Baskett, Peet, Bradford, and Mulaik, 1973), handicapped children (Cairns and Bochner, 1974), the death penalty
(Sechrest, Grove, and Cosgrove, 1980), the role of pharmacists
in the community (Zelnio and Gagnon, 1977), busing (Bolton,
1974), and the Communist and Nazi parties (Milgram, Mann,
and Garter, 1965) have been investigated using this technique.

These studies demonstrate the wide variety of uses to
which the lost letter technique may be put, but they say little
about the construct validity of the method. Indeed, in light of
the results of some lost letter studies in which the technique
failed to predict election outcomes, factors other than attitudes
must be considered in explaining the return rates. For example,
while Bouchard and Stuster's (1969) study resulted in more
letters addressed to "Citizens for Humphrey" being returned
than letters addressed to "Citizens for Nixon" in a district
where Humphrey did receive more votes, letters addressed to
"Citizens for Wallace" came back at a much higher rate than
would have been expected based on actual election returns. It
is possible that the Wallace supporters felt more strongly about
their candidate than Humphrey or Nixon supporters, and so
were more likely to mail a letter that might help their candidate. Or, people backing Wallace may have realized that their
candidate was a definite underdog and needed every available
manifestation of support.

Jacoby and Aranoff (1971) also conducted a study that failed to predict an election outcome. Here no significant differences in return rates resulted from dropping letters addressed to Citizens for Humphrey-Muskie, Nixon-Agnew, and Wallace-Lemay. The authors suggested that these surprising results were attributable to the higher than average degree of honesty of the citizens in the town where this particular experiment was performed. We question that explanation, however, on the grounds that the overall return rate of letters dropped in that town was similar to rates in other areas. Other explanations offered by the experimenters are more viable (for example, letters were dropped too far ahead of the election) and are worthy of empirical investigation.

After seeing some of the work that has been done using the lost letter technique, it became apparent to one of us (Sechrest) that several factors other than attitudes may be affecting return rates. As an example, Milgram, Mann, and Harter (1965) dropped letters with one of four addressees: "Friends of the Communist Party," "Friends of the Nazi Party," "Medical Research Associates," and "Mr. Walter Carnap." Surely letters with the first two addresses would arouse more curiosity in a finder than would those with the second two. It is possible that curiosity and not attitudes may have produced some of the small return rate for the Communist and Nazi letters. Intrigued by this rival explanation, Sechrest, Grove, and Cosgrove (1980) stuffed a load of envelopes bearing one of the following three addressees: "Education Research Project," "Marijuana Research Project," and "Sex Research Project." As expected, percentages of returns fit a curiosity hypothesis, with most of the returned letters being addressed to "Education Research Project," fewer to the marijuana study, and the least to the sex project. Also supporting this explanation is the fact that raters blind to the hypotheses and conditions judged the backs of sex envelopes to be in poorest condition, followed by the marijuana and then education letters. Several sex letters, a few marijuana letters, and only one education letter came back opened.

Encouraged by the results of the first study, the same investigators attempted to check their curiosity explanation in another way. Specifically, they addressed half the letters to

Education Research Project and half to Sex Research Project. Half the letters were sealed and half merely had the envelope flap tucked. It was predicted that if curiosity can affect the return rate of letters, then fewer Sex Research Project letters would be returned, but only in the sealed condition. It was expected that the same return rate would exist for sex and education letters in the unsealed condition since if a finder were curious he or she could easily read the letter without damaging the envelope. The results were, however, contrary to expectations. For both sealed and unsealed conditions, more education than sex letters were returned, and a much larger percentage of sealed than unsealed letters came back. Two factors probably contributed to these results. First, letter finders did indeed seem to be more curious about the sex letters than the education ones, since four times as many sealed sex as sealed education letters had apparently been opened before being returned. Second, the unsealed letters may not have appeared to be as important as the sealed ones. It was more likely that an unsealed letter would be opened and read, and perhaps readers decided that the message was too trivial to warrant a trip to the mailbox.

Another study in which curiosity was probably aroused was conducted by Barefoot and Strickland (1977). These investigators stamped CONFIDENTIAL across half the envelopes that they dropped. Although there was no significant difference between the two conditions with regard to percentage of returned letters, the confidential letters were returned more quickly and were less likely to have been opened. Perhaps feelings of social responsibility overrode finders' curiosity in this particular experiment. Deaux (1974) manipulated the importance of a message on postcards and found results consistent with a social responsibility explanation since cards with important news were more likely to be returned than those with an unimportant message. Incidentally, she found that people are just as likely to mail a postcard bearing bad news as good. Simon (1971) obtained results that make us hesitate before generalizing about the role of the importance of a letter with regard to return rates. He made up three kinds of envelopes that varied in importance from very important (to Dr. William E. Simon, with "Urgent" displayed on the front of the envelope), to moderately important (to William E. Simon), to unimportant (to Resident). The apparent importance of the letter did not have a statistically significant effect on return rates, but this could very well be due to the small number of letters dropped in the first place. Indeed, the very important-looking letters were returned more often than the others.

In addition to importance of the letter and curiosity of the finder, greed may be a determining factor in differential return rates of lost letters. We mentioned earlier in this section that Merritt and Fowler (1948) got a lower return rate on letters that appeared to contain a fifty-cent piece than those that seemed to hold no money. Similarly, Simon and Gillen (1971) found that letters apparently containing paper money were less likely to be returned than those that did not appear to have money inside. The letters with a "play" ten-dollar bill came back at a rate not significantly different from letters with a one-dollar bill, but had more been dropped the differences may have reached significance, with more one-dollar letters being returned than ten-dollar ones.

Whether or not a lost letter is stamped does seem to affect the likelihood of its being returned. Forbes and Gromoll (1971), Simon (1971), and Simon and Gillen (1971) all lost a number of letters, half stamped and half unstamped, and all obtained a much higher return rate for the stamped letters. Additionally, Forbes, TeVault, and Gromoll (1971) found that although religion does not seem to affect mailing an unstamped letter, it is a factor in determining whether or not the mailer puts a stamp on the letter. Specifically, these investigators found that people from conservative churches were more likely than those from liberal or Catholic churches to send a found letter "postage due." It would be interesting to see what would happen if this study were conducted today, since the postal service will no longer deliver an unstamped letter.

Another factor that may affect return rates is mood. Levin and Isen (1975) dropped letters in telephone booths in which the coin return boxes of half held a dime. As the experimenters predicted, the people who found a dime in the phone booth were more likely than others to mail a "lost" letter. Weyant and

Clark (1977) conducted a study similar to Levin and Isen's, but with a clever addition. They put graphite in the coin return of one fourth of the booths (with the intention of inducing a bad mood), a dime in another fourth, put both graphite and a dime in a fourth, and left the remaining fourth empty. Because no significant return rates resulted from the above manipulations, a finding discrepant with Levin and Isen's work, further investigation is necessary to assess the effect of mood on mailing found letters.

Although a great deal of work has been done with the lost letter technique, we still are not certain just when the method is an accurate assessor of attitudes and when other factors are affecting return rates. The technique is a tempting one for experimenters to use because it has been demonstrated to be an accurate predictor of a wide variety of attitudes and is a measure that can be implemented with relative ease at low expense to the experimenter. However, we caution researchers to question this method's value despite its apparent advantages. The number of explanations for differential return rates may make other research tools appear more useful.

PSYCHOMETRIC PROBLEMS
WITH NONREACTIVE MEASURES

One advantage of traditional questionnaire measures is that one can get a measure of variability across different versions of the same measure, across occasions, over time, and so on—the problem of dependability of measures (Cronbach, Gleser, Rajaratnam, and Nanda, 1972). Unfortunately many unobtrusive measures do not readily lend themselves to such analysis, leading to questions about their usefulness that cannot be answered a priori. For example, suppose one wanted to determine the effectiveness of two types of messages to promote safety and thought of putting each message on the front of a pamphlet and using the proportion of persons choosing each pamphlet when offered one as a measure of the effectiveness of the message. It would be difficult to say ahead of time how dependable the choice behavior involved might be. It might be that the choice behavior involved is so nearly random that no effects could reasonably be expected. Thus, if one failed to find any difference, it might be attributable to unreliability in the choice behavior.

We are not easily accustomed to thinking in terms of random or otherwise unstable response patterns, but they undoubtedly do occur. Consider, for example, the use of guns by police; that is, "shooting incidents," which would probably seem to most people to be a function of certain characteristics of individual officers. That is to say, one might reasonably suppose that some police are more likely than others to become involved in shooting incidents. Yet, one study (Inn and Wheeler, 1977) suggests quite strongly that shooting incidents involving police form exactly the sort of distribution one would expect by chance, given that the event is rare. Note that the problem of potential unreliability, to use the customary psychometric term, disappears if expected results are obtained, for instance, if two groups exposed to different messages make expected choices. The problem is troublesome on those occasions when differences do not exist and one cannot be certain whether the fault is in the theory, the treatment, or the outcome measure. In using traditional measures one capitalizes on both the extensive experience with such measures that makes it relatively simple to find or develop a measure with probable realiability and the characteristics of the measure that make it possible to assess reliability after the fact. Researchers are justifiably hesitant to expend much effort on collecting or to invest too much faith in measures that they and others have had so little previous experience with. Since so often unobtrusive measures are created for specific purposes, the problems are evident.

The problem of reliability with continuous measures is usually reflected in a correlation between two measures, for example, two halves of the same test, the same measure on two occasions, two parallel measures, and so on. Only rarely in assessing the reliability of a continuous measure are questions about comparability of means or variances raised. Two measures are considered reliable to the extent that they order persons in the same way. In measuring height, a meter stick would be considered to give reliable readings even if on a second occasion of measurement it were placed on a baseboard rather than the floor as the beginning point, since people of different heights would be ordered in the same way.

The situation is rather different when categorical measures, for example, binary measures, are employed, for then one wants to know the likelihood of a person ending up in the same category when some other measurement is used. The same problem arises if one is using a measure that has a cutoff point of some sort, for one wants to know not the stability with which people are ordered, but what the probability is that a person who exceeds the cutoff on one occasion will exceed it on another. The statistics required to deal with these problems are not as well worked out as for traditional problems of reliability, a problem clearly detrimental to the case for unobtrusive measures. One of the problems for many categorical measures is that frequencies in the categories are notably uneven, creating the well-known "base rate" problem. If, as an instance, one were interested in the classification of people as caffeinated or decaffeinated coffee drinkers—perhaps as an indicator of health concerns—probably only 10 percent or so of those ordering coffee would order decaffeinated. Therefore, most people would remain correctly classified as caffeinated coffee drinkers even if the decaffeinated coffee drinkers were completely inconsistent from one occasion to another. The statistic *kappa* (Fleiss, 1973) has been developed to deal with this problem, but it is not always completely satisfactory. For example, it might be quite important to know that most persons are obedient to stop signs on two occasions, but if the small proportion disobedient were not consistent, *kappa* could be misleadingly low. Other statistics are currently being developed and tested that may prove more satisfactory (Logsdon, 1979), but for the moment, one simply has to recognize that those favoring some types of nonreactive measures have difficult problems to meet.

A second problem with some nonreactive measures is that they may lack, or at least seem to lack, sensitivity, especially those that involve binary choices. It is commonly noted that binary choices sacrifice information since one cannot take into account the difference between a subject who almost chose A rather than B and a subject who would not have chosen A under any circumstances. Compounding the problem is the fact that statistics for differences between proportions are not very sensitive, a fact often not recognized. For example, most persons would probably regard the difference between 40 percent and 60 percent as fairly remarkable—it is, after all, about the magnitude of the difference that would be regarded as a landslide in an election. Yet, in order to be able to have a .9 probability (power) of detecting a difference of that size at the .05 level, just about 150 subjects would be required for *each* group (Fleiss, 1973). The *t* test or ANOVA for differences between means seem like real bargains.

The more aggregated the data we deal with, the more difficult it is to get meaningful estimates of variability as a basis for statistical testing. The problem even seems worse for many trace measures since one does not know exactly how such measures were created. At the level of one toilet stall, for example, one can only categorize and count graffiti, perhaps calculating proportions within categories. However, when one does not know exactly the population of users, how many "graffitologists" there are, and, often, not even over what time period the graffiti appeared, it is difficult to know for sure what to make of the data. When one has data from several stalls, one can at least calculate a measure of variability, but how meaningful the measure might be is open to question. Most of our statistical procedures are based on the assumption that observations are independent of each other, but data from adjacent toilet stalls involve observations that probably cannot be considered independent. Even across an entire campus graffiti are likely to be more similar than to graffiti in some other locale. Thus, it may often be unclear across just which units a measure of variability might legitimately be calculated.

At least some, probably a good bit, of the advantage of traditional questionnaires comes not from their inherent properties as measures but from the long history of their use and the basis that history gives us for inductive confidence in new applications. We have a sense of the way questions are responded to that makes it possible to write new ones with reasonable expectations about what the response distribution will look like. It is far more difficult to know what to expect when one endeavors to create a nonreactive measure of a type one has had little experience with. If there were a more uniform, perhaps even concerted, effort to devise and employ nonreactive measures, we would rapidly gain the methodological insights into them that we need. For example, from their work with the lost letter technique and from their review of the work of others, Sechrest and Grove (1980) have a reasonably good idea what return rate one might reasonably expect and have some reason to believe that the specific conditions under which letters are dropped may not have much effect on the return rate.

In the meantime, individual researchers can probably be forgiven for a degree of hesistancy in pursuing the development of novel measures, a hazardous enough prospect even for questionnaires. Our hope is, however, that this book will ease the way, in part, by providing a cumulative experience that can be capitalized upon and a source of inspiration and ideas that will prompt the creative process. The psychometric problems are not ineluctable, only challenging.

Metrics for Nonreactive Measures

From the standpoint of metric properties, nonreactive measures may be expressed in various ways. And these ways help to determine the exact form the data will take and the manner in which it may be analyzed and interpreted. The two principal issues have to do with (1) the nature of the observations and the numbers representing them and (2) the units of observation and analysis.

Nonreactive measures may be categorical, numerical counts, or quantities. TV sets are tuned to one channel or another, radios are set at a particular frequency, people do or do not have tattoos—all are categorical measures. A policeman issues a certain number of traffic citations, a household disposes of three liquor bottles, a city has sixteen flower shops, a telephone book lists four pages of "Hernandez." All these are obtained by counting. Quantity measurements include: a city produces 1,200 tons of garbage per week, a newspaper has sixteen column inches of "personals" ads, a drawing by a child is seven inches tall, and a set of records of real estate transactions weighs six pounds. These observations may be transformed in various ways so the final product of an analysis obscures the nature of the original observation, and some observations may produce two or more of the above types of measurement. A study of tuning of TV sets might easily and unobtrusively be carried out in college dormitories. The observations would be categorical but would ultimately be expressed as numerical counts, that is, so many sets tuned to Channel 5, so many to Channel 8, and so on. Numerical counts may be summed and averaged, in fact are likely to be, so that the final number does not look in any way different from an expression of a quantity. It is well to keep in mind the nature of the original observation, however. There is a lot of difference between knowing *whether* a person is tattooed, *how many* tattoos a person has, and *how much* skin is covered by tattoos.

For the most part social scientists are not interested in the behavior of individuals; ordinarily the unit of interest is some aggregation of individuals. However, observations are often made at the individual level and, occasionally, may be retained and analyzed in that way. The behavior of presidents, for example, is often of interest, and nonreactive measures such as content of speeches or speech dysfluencies may be obtained and analyzed by individual president. However, even then, the specific identity of the president is usually of no direct scientific interest. Scientists will usually be interested in generalizations such as that the speech dysfluencies of presidents increase when they are asked about matters that later prove to be especially troublesome or that presidents elected at particular times show a different motivational structure in their speeches. The identities of presidents involved in such analyses may be a bit difficult to conceal but have no bearing on the interpretation of the findings. Rarely, however, will the behavior of an ordinary citizen as represented in a nonreactive measure be of specific scientific interest. That behavior will become interesting only as it can be aggregated along with the behavior of other similar persons.

Many nonreactive measures do involve the aggregation of observations of individuals, and, in principal, the data could be disaggregated. One could associate a particular uniform size with a particular bus driver or one could determine which particular individuals had their TV sets tuned to which stations, even though neither item of information would be of any scien tific interest. When data can, in principal, be disaggregated, then it is appropriate to interpret the data as representing the behavior of individuals. Thus, one could conceivably make some such statement as that owners of expensive automobiles tend not to have their radios tuned to country-western stations. Or one could say that employees who are frequently absent from work are more likely to file grievances against their supervisors. (Neither of the preceding statements is actually supported by any evidence.)

Other nonreactive measures, however, involve aggregates that cannot be disaggregated and that, therefore, do not warrant statements about individual behavior. One cannot know from the quantity of trash picked up in New Orleans after Mardi Gras who strewed it about. We do not know who produced the graffitti in a men's room, how many persons were involved, nor anything else about individual behavior. To the extent that literature is taken to reflect values of society at a particular time, then that reflection is an aggregated measure that cannot be disaggregated and parceled out to individual persons. Seating patterns may give clear evidence of separation along racial lines, but the pattern is the end result of the behavior of perhaps many persons and cannot be taken as an index of the attitudes of any one of them. Care in interpreting aggregate behavior is especially needed when the behaviors of individuals are not independent. There are, after all, only so many seats on a bus, and when a given person occupies one, that limits the options of everyone else who boards; families and friends sit together. (Sometimes it is that very lack of independence that is useful; only one person can be chosen to sit at the right hand of the leader.) Those using nonreactive measures should think carefully about the nature of their data and the implications for their interpretation.

Toward a Generative Taxonomy of Nonreactive Measures

In order to be able to employ nonreactive measures routinely and widely, it is necessary to be able to create them as needed for specific research purposes. At present there is no systematic way in which nonreactive measures may be generated upon demand. The researcher is dependent upon diverse examples of what others have done and his or her own ingenuity. What is needed is a system of some sort that when applied will facilitate the generation of new measures when and where they are needed.

If an investigator wishes to generate a new questionnaire item, say to assess "liking" for some object, person, or idea, there are almost immediately available any number of "armatures" from which new questionnaire items may be generated, with considerable confidence that they will "work." For example, a very simple armature would be:

I like _____ .
Strongly agree   Agree   Disagree   Strongly disagree

The blank could be filled meaningfully with an extraordinarily wide range of nouns and phrases without creating any incredulity in a respondent, for example: this school, peanut butter, overtime work, the CIA, participatory democracy, blind dates, or jogging. One has only to think of what it is one would like to measure feelings or attitudes about, and most likely the proper words will come to mind.

Similarly, if one want to get at a problem in slightly different ways, one may take advantage of armatures of such form as:

I frequently _____ .
I am very good at _____ .
_____ is one of my favorite _____ s.
One of my strongest traits is _____ .
I intend to _____ .

or:

The CIA is _____ .
Participatory democracy is a _____ way of running a group.
Jogging is really very _____ .

and so on.

The idea of nonreactive measures does not lend itself especially well to the armature approach, but a properly developed taxonomy might be useful. A good system of taxonomic description has generative capabilities because it defines and sets limits for categories. Consider, for example, the taxonomic descriptor *dog*. When we hear the descriptor, we can conjur up images of dogs of various sorts, and were we to ask an artist to draw a picture of a dog, we would, unless the artist were an abstractionist, get a representation of a dog that would be recognizable. The picture would not be of any dog we know, but it would surely be recognizable as a dog and different from a cat, a fish, or most any other creature. Were we to ask an imaginative artist to draw us a picture of a Martian dog, that is, a new instance never before encountered, it is still highly likely that the picture of a Martian dog would be recognizable as a dog rather than as a Martian cat.

The categories of nonreactive measures developed so far do not help much since they refer to specific conditions of observation, such as archives, simple observation, hardware, rather than to any purposes of measurement. Bouchard (1976) has also categorized unobtrusive measures, but in a way similar to that in our first edition, and he notes the need for another taxonomy. Sechrest and his associates (Sechrest and Phillips, 1979; Sechrest and Grove, 1980) have done some preliminary work on the development of a taxonomy, and what is presented here is no more than an extension of that work. It should be made clear that what is presented here is not regarded as a definitive effort but is merely the beginnings to which all the authors hope others will make continuing contributions or perhaps even be inspired to different and more productive approaches.

One approach to the development of a taxonomy is to try to construct a matrix representing the conjunctions of those things or conditions which researchers would like to assess and the characteristics of nonreactive measures that might be exploited in that measurement. For example, researchers might want to have an nonreactive measure of the proportion of individuals in a group who fall into a particular category: what proportion of junior high-school students have had experience with drugs; how many new military recruits have histories of delinquent behavior; or how many members of an elitist women's group have had face lifts. One characteristic of people who have had experiences different from those of other persons is that they tend to have knowledge, often of vocabulary, not shared by those who have not had the experience. In the context of lie detection—an individualized identification process with which we are not concerned here—Lykken (1974) has referred to this special knowledge as "guilty knowledge," that is, knowledge of a crime that only one who had participated in it would have. It is also possible, then, that some characteristics of some nonreactive measures might tap the special knowledge that only a person with particular experiences would be likely to have. Lerman (1967) and Gibson (1966), for example, have shown that children who are involved in delinquent behaviors are likely to know the definitions of words that are not known to nondelinquent youth. Persons involved in the drug culture will very likely show similar knowledge of an argot. Probably persons who have had face lifts will know some medical terminology not available to most other persons. One could, then, use an anonymously administered vocabulary test, perhaps with key terms embedded in a disarming context, to make some estimates of the proportions of groups having certain experiences of interest.

Ideally we would like to have a taxonomy that would have mutually exclusive categories on both axes of the matrix, but at present we believe it premature to attempt that degree of elegance. In the first place, our own understanding would probably permit too few distinctions to be of any great help, for the matrix would be of very limited dimensions. Second, for the time being, it seems evident that those who want to generate nonreactive measures are not likely to think in the same terms as fit the theories of social scientists of a particular narrow persuasion. And, if a taxonomy is to be genuinely useful, it has to be couched in the terms employed by those who need it. Therefore, in the taxonomy to be presented, some terms overlap, especially with respect to the things or characteristics to be measured. Moreover, especially with respect to features of nonreactive measures that might be exploited, we are unable to develop a list that has a clear logical structure beyond the first few items; rather the list is derived from common sense and from what has been tried previously. Finally, a consequence of this relative inelegance is that it is possible for the very same nonreactive measure to appear in more than one cell of the matrix, especially on the horizontal axis that has to do with what it is one wants to measure. We do not regard this as a problem uniquely characteristic of nonreactive measures but as one widespread in the social and behavioral sciences.

Characteristics to Be Assessed

Whether explicit or not, when researchers or other persons set out to assess some person, group, or situation, there is usually some one characteristic that is of central concern. Were we to apply reasonably rigorous theoretical terms to concerns about assessment, we would probably find that most such concerns could be reduced to a notion akin to that of "habit strength," in the words of a now nearly forgotten Hullian psychology. By that term we mean, at the risk of some oversimplification, the strength of the relationship between a given stimulus and a particular response. Habit strength was usually assessed in terms of the *probability,* given a stimulus, that the critical response would occur (or the magnitude of the response, or the latency between the occurrence of the stimulus and the occurrence of the response, or the resistance of the response to extinction). From these simple ideas stem a variety of other expectations about indicators of the strength of response tendencies, but these ideas are more likely to be reflected in the folk wisdom of response measurers than in the formal terms of a theory. Consequently, our discussion here will be couched more in terms that reflect everyday measurement concerns and insights than in terms of a theoretical integration which we discern to underlie them.

The list of assessment aims that follows is a distillation of experience and thought, but it is offered tentatively and as a heuristic device. We hope that readers of this volume will comprehend the motive that guided its development and will, themselves, be moved to refine and otherwise improve upon it.

Probability of occurrence.   One of the most frequent aims of assessment seems to be to try to determine in advance the probability that some potentially anticipatable event, response, or behavior will occur. Criminologists want to know the probability that a class of released offenders will stay out of trouble, candidates want to know their chances for election, physicians want to know the likelihood that patients will take medications as prescribed, investors want to know whether a new company is likely to survive, a military organization wants to know the probability that a new group of recruits will enlist. Such interests are related to other categories that follow, for example, capacity, value, and sentiment, but interests in probability of occurrence are often expressed quite directly, and the idea itself is fundamental.

Capacity.   Another frequently encountered aim of assessment is to determine whether a person, group, or institution is capable of performing some response, the level of ability that exists, the degree of strength possessed, and so on. The navy wants to know the capability of its ships to perform in combat, the designers of a defensive driving program want to know how good its driver graduates are, insurance companies want to know survival capabilities (life expectancy), an employer wants to know the job capabilities of potential employees, and a professional sports team owner wants to know the true ability of his or her team. At some level, most of these questions could be reformulated in terms of probabilities, for example, of avoiding accidents or of surviving, but since questions are so often asked directly in terms of capability, and since that concept, too, is fundamental, we include it as a separate category. The question, to take an instance, whether presidents who were effective in office were also good speech makers is translated into probability questions only laboriously and rather tortuously.

Value.   Questions of the value or worth of persons, objects, ideas, and groups are also very frequently posed. It is often alleged, for example, that women in our society are less valued than men. Investigators have tried to assess the value placed on achievement in different societies. Much effort has been devoted to determining the value placed on human life, and one of the pejorative comments one can make about another people is that they "place little value on human life." Such concepts as patriotism, loyalty, and respect all imply a valuing. The mottos "safety first," and "cleanliness is next to Godliness" are value statements that could be assessed in a variety of ways.

Sentiment. We have used the terms *interest* and *cathexis* in the past to refer to this category of measurement aims. It is very often the case that an investigator wishes to measure level of interest in or feeling toward a person, group, institution, or idea. The general concept of an approach-avoidance tendency, or the behavior of attending to something would also be at issue. Investigators have concerned themselves with the interest value of museum exhibits, with career interests, with concern for personal appearance. Attitudes toward political candidates and feelings toward minority group members have been the focus of considerable research activity. It is sometimes difficult to distinguish between value and sentiment; indeed, it seems reasonable that they should be moderately correlated. We value what we like and vice versa. On the other hand, the correlation is not necessarily perfect. It is possible for some males to set a fairly low value on women and yet be highly interested in them. Some persons may set a high value on wealth but have very little interest in earning money. Nearly everyone agrees that good health is of great value, but actual behavior belies interest in pursuing it.

Affective state. The emotional or feeling state of a person or group is often of concern to researchers. Morale of workers, clubs, and organizations of different kinds has often been assessed. Fear, anger, depression, happiness, love, and calmness are all affective states that are frequently of relevance to researchers.

Category membership. Researchers often want to know whether a particular person is a likely member of some category of persons characterized in a special way, or they may want to estimate the number of persons in a category within a larger group. Social class is a category that has been of long-standing and widespread interest, and there have been many suggestions about how social class might be unobtrusively assessed, for example, by observing accent, clothing, or gestures. One of the hazards of streetwalking is the possibility of making a proposition to a plainclothes policeman. Reportedly one good rule is never to proposition a man wearing black socks (Sansing, 1980). All of us are unobtrusive measurers.

Traits. The idea of traits or response dispositions is still prevalent in the social sciences, and one frequent aim of measurement is to determine the standing of some person or group on a trait dimension. Sometimes situations may be assessed according to a trait conception, such as dangerousness or pleasantness. Generally speaking, of course, the rationale for assessing a trait is to enable some further prediction of behavior, and the trait is only intermediary. Traits such as alcoholism, aggressiveness, conservatism, dependability, and efficiency are typical of the assessment efforts that have been made.

Features of Responses to Exploit in Nonreactive Measurement

Any response that is observed is likely to have several features that are discriminable, and those features may provide a basis for inferences about other characteristics of respondents. The list that follows is based partly on derivations from work in experimental psychology on measuring habit strength and partly from examination of the extant literature on nonreactive measures.

Frequency. By frequency is meant how often something occurs or the proportion of time it occurs. The measure is obtained simply by counting things as they occur for a person or a group. A frequency measure will be expressed either in a raw count or as a rate for persons, groups, organizations, or other units. Examples of frequency measures include accidents, disciplinary violations, awards, number of visitations, number of sales, number of graffiti, purchases made, and lost letters returned.

Magnitude. Another feature of some responses is that they reflect differing levels of vigor or size, how much rather than how many. Magnitude measures usually are expressed in terms of an average across some unit of observation but may be the report of a single observation, for instance, pounds of aluminum collected for recycling by a boy scout troop. Examples of magnitude measures are waist-size of uniforms, size of tombstones, inches of advertising space, income tax paid, size of pay raise, amount of space devoted to an activity, size of flag displayed.

Latency. It has been assumed and empirically demonstrated that the more rapidly a response occurs or the less the amount of time between responses, the stronger is some disposition represented by the response. Usually a latency measure will be expressed as an average across a series of observations. Examples of latency measures are time from detection of a malfunction to undertaking of repair, response time to signal, time to first complaint, speed of promotion, time from marriage to first pregnancy, time from finding a lost object to returning it, and time from receiving an application blank to returning it.

Resistance to change. In experimental psychology resistance to extinction was often used as a measure of habit strength. We refer here somewhat more generally to the resistance of responses to change under any particular circumstances, whether pressure, lack of reward, or changing context. Resistance to change measures might be expressed in several different ways: number of responses after a stimulus to change, magnitude of response to pressure for change, number of compensatory responses in other situations. Specific scores might be frequency counts or averages. Examples of resistance to change measures are number of cigarettes smoked per day at the end of an antismoking program, persistence in wearing old clothes beyond style changes, fondness for music of high school days, continuing bad behavior despite disciplinary sanctions, and failure to correct bad grammar despite pressure from associates.

Functional smoothness.   The efficiency or skill with which some response is performed or, conversely, awkwardness in performance, may be taken as an indicator of the value placed on the response or of the strength of the disposition to perform it. A favorite visual gag in many movies has been the seemingly naive bumbler enticed into a card game who then proceeds to dismay his companions by an effortless and dazzling display of card shuffling. Functional smoothness measures may produce either an average or a frequency count. Examples of functional smoothness include number of bills passed per legislative session, inches of self-correcting typewriter ribbon left at the end of a job, number of strikes in bowling, and lines of print scanned per eye retracing. Actually it is somewhat easier to think of examples of functional awkwardness, but note that each of the previous examples implies an inverse measure. Examples of functional awkwardness include verbal dysfluencies, disciplinary violations, employee turnover, glasses of spilled milk, stains on neckties, and square millimeters of marred surface around keyholes.

Association.   There is firm basis in experience for the expectations that similar things are likely to be found together (see Campbell, 1958). An old saw, "Birds of a feather flock together" expresses the idea quite well. Association measures are likely to be reflected in mean distance scores, geographic patterns, and numbers of associates of different types. Examples of association measures are number of delinquent friends, membership in elite societies, proximity to important persons, seating patterns, and "constant companionship." Public figures are often castigated merely for being in the company of gangsters and racketeers, and celebrities can instigate rumors by merely being seen together.

Acquisitions.   People tend to acquire things, or symbols of things, they are interested in. Thus, the extent of a person's acquisitions may be taken as an index of interest. Examples of acquisition measures are bumper stickers, sports team paraphernalia, ownership of drug paraphernalia, "give me my rose and my glove," and religious objects. These measures may result in binary scores or continuous scores based on counting; aggregated scores for groups would probably be expressed in terms of a mean number of objects.

Consumption.   People also use up what they like, and measures of consumption of some good or service may be taken as a measure of liking. Examples of consumption measures are amount of alcohol consumed, number of spare parts used, health services utilized, amount of soap used, and number of haircuts obtained per year. Consumption measures may also reflect other kinds of behavior, for example, amount of typewriter correction fluid used in a typing pool might reflect typing skill. Amounts of goods consumed may be estimated from quantities purchased, but the possibility of waste or other loss would have to be carefully considered. Consumption measures may be expressed in terms of averages or in terms of an aggregated quantity.

Effort.   There is a tradition in experimental psychology to assess strength of motivation by the effort expended to achieve some goal or by the amount of pain that will be endured in the process of achieving a goal. Presumably the amount of work or energy, or the amount of pain, invested in some response either momentarily or over time is a measure of value or interest accorded the goal. In professional sports highly motivated players learn to "play with pain." An old advertising slogan began "I'd walk a mile for . . . ." Other effort measures are volunteering, length of service, amount of work performed, time spent on a task, and risking physical injury. Effort measures may be expressed in terms of means across persons or occasions or in terms of numbers of persons performing some response.

Inappropriateness.   There is a long-standing assumption in psychology that responses that are inappropriate to the context in which they occur are especially meaningful. For example, in his list of assumptions underlying the use of projective techniques, Lindzey (1961) included the notion that responses that do not seem to be called for by the stimulus are likely to be important. Social psychologists have concluded that "out-of-role" responses, those not consonant with the role occupied by a person, are more likely to be diagnostic of individual dispositions (Jones, Davis, and Gergen, 1961). Examples of inappropriateness measures are gratuitous insults, response to minimal cues, deviant responses, unsolicited volunteering, and emotional reactions out of proportion to the situation. Inappropriateness could be characteristic of a group as in a group resolution condemning something or an aggregated measure of the responses of individuals.

Bias.   The degree to which responses depart from standards of accuracy, fairness, or social expectations may be diagnostic of important behavioral characteristics. Examples of bias measures are tendencies to overestimate unfavorable qualities of other persons or groups, selective publication of information, exaggerated linguistic modifiers, favoritism in distribution of resources, and asymmetrical behavior in a triadic interaction. Bias measures could be characteristic of a group or could be aggregated across individuals.

Cognitive articulation.   When people are much interested in or involved in something, they tend to make finer distinctions about that something or to have more detailed knowledge about it. Is there a noncoffee lover, for example, who knows the difference between Tanzanian Peaberry and Jamaican Blue Mountain Supreme? Cognitive articulation measures would be exemplified by brand differentiation, detailed knowledge of grievance procedures, number of distinguishable positions between "liberal" and "conservative," extensiveness of vocabulary for identifying states of intoxication, and ability to identify vintage years for categories of wine. Cognitive articulation measures might reflect aggregate behavior of members of a group or be characteristic of the group itself.

Revelatory. Some behaviors or their traces by their very nature may suggest something important about an individual, or perhaps about a group. Revelatory measures would include such phenomena as tattoos, identifying marks or insignia, guilty knowledge, membership cards, and nicotine stains. There is a legal doctrine, *res ipsa loquitur,* meaning "the thing speaks for itself," that expresses the same idea: one does not have to prove negligence when a pair of surgical scissors are found sewn up in one's body. Ordinarily revelatory responses will be of a binary nature but could involve a frequency count and could be aggregated across units of observation.

A Taxonomic Matrix

The list of aims of assessment and the features of nonreactive measures could be arrayed in such a way as to form a matrix as shown on pages 300–303. Each of the cells represents a potential assessment task with an associated feature of nonreactive measures that might be exploited in accomplishing the assessment. We want to emphasize again that the matrix is meant to have practical heuristic value rather than theoretical elegance. Thus, some of the very same measures can be employed for assessment tasks couched in different terms or can be employed for different features. However, since those involved in assessment may have different preferences about the way in which the task is formulated and since emphasizing different features of nonreactive measures may be variously stimulating for different persons or tasks, we present the matrix in its present form. Perhaps eventually those with an abiding interest in nonreactive measures will develop a simpler and more satisfactory conceptual schema.

We may note, too, that some of the cells are unlikely to be very productive because of the specific relationship between the assessment task and feature involved. We have marked out these cells for the time being although someone may eventually think of some good examples.

The matrix contains references to nonreactive measures that may be found in this text, and readers may determine for themselves whether the examples are apt and instructive. In

Unobtrusive Measure Feature	Assessment Task *Probability*
Frequency	Frequency of broken glue seals and probability of advertisement being read p. 26
Magnitude	The Royal Flush and election probabilities p. 2 Weight of handgun records and gun sales p. 118
Latency	Time to first legitimate birth and premarital sex activity p. 88
Resistance to Change	
Functional Smoothness	Disciplinary lapses and ability of a unit p. 179 Absenteeism and functioning p. 181
Association	Display of bumper stickers and election outcome p. 207
Acquisitions	Possession of political campaign material and probability of voting
Consumption	Water or energy consumption and audience size pp. 112, 174
Effort	
Inappropriateness	
Bias	Differential dust accumulation and machine use p. 20
Cognitive Articulation	
Revelatory	

*Page numbers refer to location in text. Examples without page numbers are hypothetical. Cells without entries represent combinations that do not readily afford examples, but are not necessarily impossible to illustrate.

Capacity	Value
Number of musical compositions and probability of an outstanding one p. 99 Number of errors and ability of bus drivers p. 178	Proportion of last-born males and value of male children p. 86 Frequency of certain art themes and value placed on achievement p. 13
Size of bus drivers' trousers and life expectancy (Morris et al, 1956) Eminence and length of entry in *Who's Who* pp. 96–98	Tombstone size and esteem for females p. 93 Portrayed family size and fertility values p. 87
Time to promotion and ability pp. 180–81 Age of first musical composing and eminence p. 99	
Longevity (resistance to death) and strength pp. 91–92 Resistance of stock prices to bad news p. 173	
Number of errors made by shortstop as (inverse) index of ability	Rifle team performance and attachment to the team p. 184
	Proximity to leader and esteem p. 215
Fraternity paraphernalia and low grades p. 205	University identifying apparel and esteem for winning team p. 206 Possession of religious objects and religious values
Amount of time required to do a task as inverse measure of skill	"I'd walk a mile for a Camel" p. 125 Altruistic suicide p. 187 Fraternity house appearance and identification with fraternity p. 207
	Touching and devaluing (Henley, 1977) Eye contact as insult p. 214
	Nonreporting of membership in Jewish organizations and Jewish identity p. 97 Layout of maps and nationalism p. 171
Dermatoglyphics and disease p. 212	

	Sentiment	Affect State
Frequency	Graffiti and political preferences p. 21 Sales data, e.g., books and literature preferences p. 167	Airline traffic and anxiety about crashes pp. 165–66 Number of priests and happiness of people p. 38
Magnitude	Pupil dilation and interest p. 260 Size of Santa Claus drawings and interest in Christmas p. 193	Size of children's seating circle and fear p. 217 Reported income and tax anxiety p. 117
Latency	Time to repair broken TV and interest p. 125	Alacrity of horn honking and aggression p. 264
Resistance to Change	Time spent looking and interest p. 231	Nonresponse to reassurance and anxiety Refusal to accept apology and anger
Functional Smoothness	Job turnover and interest p. 180 Absenteeism and interest p. 180	Verbal dysfluencies and anxiety p. 286 Grievances and anger p. 182 Pitch changes and stress p. 245
Association	Seating patterns and attitudes p. 216 Membership in an Association (Babchuck & Bates, 1962)	Preference for company and anxiety p. 271 Company and ambience in farmers' markets p. 225
Acquisitions	Lovers' collections "Give me my rose and my glove" p. 76	
Consumption	Nutritional supplement purchases and attitude toward nutrition p. 174	Alcohol consumption and anxiety P. 165 Use of pain medications and pain Use of tranquilizers and anxiety
Effort	Time spent working and attitude toward private vs. communal garden p. 231	
Inappropriateness	Spatial invasion and attitude toward another person p. 219	Overuse of sick call and stress p. 185 Risk taking and impatience p. 221
Bias	Publication of unsmiling pictures and racial attitudes pp. 123–24	
Cognitive Articulation	Sports vocabulary and attitudes p. 128 Women in gynecological textbooks and sex attitudes p. 131	
Revelatory	Don't laugh at my jokes too much" p. 76	Nonverbal clues to lying behavior pp. 212–13

Category Membership	Trait
	Consumption of communion wafers and superstition p. 38 Advertisements and other-directedness p. 177
	Constriction in doodles and neurotic tendencies p. 193 *Actometer* scores and activity level p. 255
	Time to initiate social contact in a new neighborhood and extraversion
"You can take the boy out of the country, but you can't take the country out of the boy"	Persistence in wearing out-of-style clothing and conservatism
The giveaway slickness of the card-shark	
"Birds of a feather flock together" Signature on a letter and group membership p. 123	Entries in Congressional Record and conservatism-liberalism. pp. 102, 105 Association with people and extraversion p. 186
Ownership of burglar tools and identification as a criminal (Powis, 1978)	Types of possessions and degree of cultural assimilation p. 205
Alcohol consumption and diagnosis of alcoholism	
Inappropriate behavior and cultural p.215 or racial/ethnic (p. 214) background	Eye contact while lying and Machiavellianism p. 214
	Setting of watch and motivation p. 232 Wall hugging and autonomy p. 221 Sidewalk gravitation and field dependency p. 220
Extensiveness of drug vocabulary and drug use p. 227	
Signs of criminality p. 213 Tattoos and delinquency p. 202 Handshake and membership in Indian tribe p. 214	Leg jiggling and anxiety p. 213

order to illustrate the use of the matrix, however, we will discuss briefly a few of the examples, identifying the cells by their marginal titles.

Probability-magnitude. The Royal Flush stemmed from the interest of a reporter in knowing the probability of voters voting for different candidates, and the measure was the size of the decrease in water level in the tank. This is a good instance of the fact that probability need not be estimated by a frequency measure, but note also that the probability estimate obtained is only a very general one, not the precise estimate that would be obtained from an opinion poll.

Affect state-frequency. The number of graffiti expressing anger toward a particular establishment might be taken as a measure of the affective state of a group, for example, such graffiti might be produced by the employees of a manufacturing plant.

Sentiment-effort. The continuing interest of parents of institutionalized children may be indexed by the distance they are willing to drive to make a visit. Frequency of visitation is another feature that might be exploited in the same way.

Affect state-consummatory. Consumption of alcohol might be used as a measure of anxiety level under some circumstances.

Capacity-magnitude. Changing health, or a changing capacity to respond to life's challenges, is indexed by changes in the waist size of bus drivers' uniforms. Some might put the question in another way: the probability of sickness or death.

Sentiment-acquisitions. Are the fans at School X as devoted as those at School Y? One might determine the average quantity of goods bearing the school emblem possessed by a sample of fans at each place. One of us is a regular observer of shops in university towns and has noted that some universities seem to generate a much greater variety of such goods than do others.

   Category membership-revelatory. During the years of student demonstrations over the Vietnam war, it was said that undercover police could be identified by their shoes. Later, police working undercover in the drug trade were claimed by some to be obvious because they were even rattier-looking than those they were dealing with. Now it is a policeman's socks that identify him as a dangerous customer. Tattoos may put people in another category altogether.

   The examples just given can only begin to illustrate the matrix, but they do not, of course, demonstrate that the taxonomy is really generative. That remains to be seen. However, let us list a few nonreactive measures potentially generatable by the taxonomy and that we think have never actually been tried. We do not mean to suggest that the following are all *good* ideas, but merely that the taxonomy can be generative.

   Capacity-functional smoothness. The ability of a group of military recruits to organize themselves could be tracked by determining over occasions how many persons have to shift positions when they try to get into formation for some activity.

   Affect-effort. Joy, as upon receiving an award, may be reflected in the amount of effort a person will expend in finding someone to tell about it.

   Value-inappropriateness. The less a person values a group, the less appropriate will be his or her manner of dress while with the group.

   Capacity-acquisitions. Some time back, Robert Ziller told one of us (personal communication, 1978) about a study of his in which he had students take photographs that they thought would be self-descriptive and in which he found that good students more often pictured themselves with books. Perhaps good students would be likely to acquire more books, spend more money on them, and retain rather than sell them back at the end of terms.

Capacity-effort. Incidentally, we note here that capacity and effort are often inversely related since skilled persons function more efficiently.

Probability-latency. Probability of reenlistment in a military unit might be indicated by the earliness of seeking information about the prospects. If reenlistment time is only a month away for one cohort and no one has been in to find out what is involved, prospects are dim.

Trait-cognitive articulation. An authoritarian person should have a keen sense of the authority structure of an organization and should be able to produce a more detailed picture of it than a nonauthoritarian person.

To be truthful, we really do not expect that the taxonomy will be more than modestly helpful in generating new nonreactive measures for specific applications. It may help a bit in organizing one's thoughts and focusing one's attention. Still, there is, and probably always will be, a considerable element of creative ingenuity involved in devising nonreactive measures. We quickly discern the relationship between the magnitude of a response and the probability of occurrence of some event. We confess that we do not know how one gets from there to, let us say, the Royal Flush. To devise the specific measure involves some capabilities that cannot be provided by the taxonomy; at best it can stimulate them. Even that may help.

NONREACTIVE MEASURES AND PUBLIC AND PRIVATE POLICY

The orientation of this book is toward the development of nonreactive measures for use in research. It may occur to some that there might be occasion for their use in implementing some policy, whether in a public or private organization. For example, a particular nonreactive measure might be used to select employees for special training, or to avoid selecting employees likely to be troublemakers, or to decide when to change administrators, or to determine when to hire or lay off employees. We would not argue that nonreactive measures cannot be useful in such circumstances; indeed, they are probably used widely, if unknowingly and unsystematically. We would warn, however, that nonreactive measurement may be easily abused and easily corrupted.

Abuse of nonreactive measures may arise out of their certainly limited validity. It suffices for most research purposes that a measure be able to distinguish, on the average, between fairly sizable groups; errors of one kind are compensated for by their opposites and the group means are unbiased. Errors in decisions about individuals are not so likely to be compensatory. Even if it were shown to be true that, let us say, job applicants wearing a particular style of clothing are likely to have higher rates of absenteeism and to be troublemakers, that relationship would, at best, be weak. Although nonreactive measures are not different from any others in being imperfect, since they are unobtrusive and therefore not so susceptible to the efforts of a person to create a particular impression, their deliberate use to make decisions about people smacks of the unsavory.

If nonreactive measures are used as indicators on the basis of which to make policy decisions important to individuals, there is a good possibility that the indicator will become corrupted. Generally speaking any single indicator that is relied upon too heavily in the making of important decisions will tend to become corrupted (Campbell, 1975), even a nonreactive measure. To begin with, it is difficult to keep a measure nonreactive if it is being used for the making of important decisions. That use almost guarantees that attention will be called to the data-collecting process, but even if it is not, too many people will be likely to know about the measure, and its use will be given away. Suppose, for example, that graffiti in various neighborhoods in large cities were monitored with a view to detecting a level of hostility that should be countered by investment of additional resources, such as new jobs. One imagines that it would not be long before activity in monitoring graffiti would be detected and not much longer before hostile graffiti would be appearing everywhere. If people in a poor community come to believe that various welfare programs are jeopardized by an index of food waste obtained from examining garbage, food will cease to show up as waste in garbage containers.

We do think that nonreactive measures have considerable potential value in monitoring what is going on in organizations, but only to the extent that they are *among* the sources of information available, and in the long run only to the extent that they are insulated from the decision-making process. Otherwise, the value of nonreactive measures in such situations will decline as they prove susceptible to their own characteristic sources of error.

DEMOGRAPHIC AND BIOGRAPHICAL VARIABLES

Correlation is neutral with respect to the direction of its interpretation. If being male, or having blue eyes, or being first-born, or having been reared in a rural area are associated with some characteristic, then that characteristic can be used to "post-dict" history, or perhaps predict the future—I am going to meet the quarterback. I'll bet he has blue eyes. And similarly the variables associated with it can be used to predict the characteristic: he was first-born, so he will probably be very intelligent. Correlation is also neutral with respect to the variables involved, and a correlation of .50 will afford the same degree of precision in predicting between one set of variables as another. If eye color and some type of performance test predict ability on some task equally well, why not use eye color since it is obviously quicker, easier, and cheaper to determine? For research purposes we might very well do just that, but we would be very reluctant to make that recommendation concerning selection in any other setting. Statistically there may be no difference, but conceptually it would concern us if important selection processes were based very heavily on characteristics that people cannot change. The appearance of fairness is important, too.

But even for research purposes there are some types and directions of inference that become worrisome. There are, perhaps, some facts that are best appreciated for what they tell of

human nature and behavior and that are best left out of the
calculus of planning and decision making.

Let us illustrate the point by reference to height, to how
tall people are (the discussion will mostly be confined to data for
males). Good things may come in small packages, but when it
comes to people, big, or at least tall, is better. We have numerous expressions in our language that glorify tallness and dispar-
age shortness: "tall, dark, and handsome," and "shrimp," to
mention two. Good things happen to tall people, too. Deck
(1971) reports that workers who are 6'2" or 6'3" average better
than 10 percent higher pay during their first year on the job
than workers less than 6' tall. Apparently tall workers are believed to be more competent or otherwise deserving than
shorter ones. In the 1960 presidential election, people planning
to vote for Kennedy or for Nixon believed that the candidate
they favored was the taller of the two (Kassajarian, 1963). And
males who liked President Johnson judged him to be taller than
did males who disliked him (Ward, 1967). In a class of nursing
students, estimates of the heights of an instructor and an assistant administrator were taller than they actually were, and
estimates of the heights of two students were shorter than they
actually were (Dannenmaier and Thumin, 1964) (apparently
the effect may obtain for females). Wilson (1968) had the same
man appear before different classes and presented him variously as a student, a demonstrator, a lecturer, a senior lecturer,
and a professor. All the groups actually underestimated the
man's height, but his estimated height went up regularly and
linearly with increase in status. Shorter males tend to underestimate the height of the average American male (Ward, 1967);
and when asked they tend to wish that they were enough taller
to be about 6' in height (they ought to ask for a couple of extra
inches) (Hinkley and Rethlingshafer, 1951).

These data mean that such statements as the following
would be justified:

1. Tall men make more money than short men; therefore,
height can be an unobtrusive index of income.
2. Tall men are better liked than short men.
3. Short men would like to be taller.

Such statements would, other things being equal, be correct, but we would be somewhat loathe to make such statements. From a purely statistical, predictive standpoint there would be nothing wrong with such statements, and we admit that our objections to them are conditioned more on esthetics than statistics.

Height might correlate as well with popularity as the number of birthday cards received last birthday, but we would prefer the latter as an unobtrusive indicator. The conceptual clarity of the link between popularity and receiving of birthday cards makes the case for the measure relatively much more attractive. Part of the problem is that many biographical variables, physical variables, and so on have many correlates, and we cannot be sure which ones we may be picking up in using the measures at any given time. We may be using height as an index of popularity in relation to frequency of dating, and the relevant correlate of height may be income; or perhaps taller men are also more aggressive in seeking dates. True, the number of birthday cards one receives also has a number of correlates other than popularity, but most of those correlates are likely to be related in one way or another to how many friends one has and how attentive they are.

We hasten to add that we would discourage any inferences at all about individual persons on the basis of most of the measures we discuss in this book. Most of the relationships that are likely to be found are of at best modest size and not a sufficient basis for making individual decisions. A young woman had better find another reason for preferring a tall young man than the expectation that he will make more money than a similarly attractive and shorter counterpart. One more word about height. Osborn (1973) used height rather unobtrusively in a laboratory study and found that short people think that attractive people are *shorter* than they actually are.

CHAPTER 10

A Final Note

In the dialectic between impulsivity and restraint, the scientific superego became too harsh—a development that was particularly effective in intimidating adventurous research, because the young were learning more about methodological pitfalls than had their elders.

(Riesman, 1959, p. 11)

David Riesman's remarks on the evolution of communications research apply equally well to the broader panoply of the study of social behavior. As social scientists, we have learned much of the labyrinth that is research on human behavior, and in so doing discovered an abundance of cul-de-sacs. Learning the complexities of the maze shortened our stride through it and often led to a pattern of timid steps, frequently retraced. No more can the knowledgeable person enjoy the casual bravura that marked the sweeping and easy generalizations of an earlier day.

The facile promulgation of "truth," backed by a few observations massaged by introspection, properly met its end—flattened by a more questioning and sophisticated rigor. The blackballing of verification by introspection was a positive advance, but an advance by subtraction. Partly as a reaction to the grandiosities of the past, partly as a result of a growing sophistication about the opportunities for error, the scope of individual research studies shrank, both in the range of content considered and in the diversity of procedures.

The shrinkage was understandable and desirable, for certainly no science can develop until a base is reached from which reliable and consistent empirical findings can be produced.[1] But if reliability is the initial step of a science, validity is its necessary stride. The primary effect of improved methodological practices has been to further what we earlier called the internal validity of a comparison—the confidence that a true difference is being observed. Unfortunately, practices have not advanced so far in improving external validity—the confidence with which the findings can be generalized to populations and measures beyond those immediately studied.

Slowing this advance in ability to generalize was the laissez-faire intellectualism of the operational definition. Operational definitionalism (to use a ponderously cumbersome term) provided a methodological justification for the scientist not to stray beyond a highly narrow, if reliable, base. One could follow a single method in developing data and be "pure," even if this purity were more associated with sterility than virtue.

The corkscrew convolutions of the maze of behavior were ironed, by definitional fiat, into a two-dimensional T maze. To define a social attitude, for example, solely by the character of responses to a list of questionnaire items is eminently legitimate —so much so that almost everything we know about attitudes comes from such research. Almost everything we know about attitudes is also suspect because the findings are saturated with the inherent risks of self-report information. One swallow does not make a summer; nor do two "strongly agrees," one "disagree," and an "I don't know" make an attitude or social value.

Questionnaires and interviews are probably the most flexible and generally useful devices we have for gathering information. Our criticism is not against them, but against the tradition that allowed them to become the methodological sanctuary to which the myopia of operational definitionalism permitted a

[1]"Almost all experiments on the effects of persuasion communications, including those reported in the present volume, have been limited to investigating changes in opinion. The reason, of course, is that such changes can readily be assessed in a highly reliable way, whereas other components of verbalizable attitudes, although of considerable theoretical interest, are much more difficult to measure" (Janis and Hovland, 1959, p. 3).

retreat. If one were going to be limited to a single method, then certainly the verbal report from a respondent would be the choice. With no other device can an investigator swing his or her attention into so many different areas of substantive content, often simultaneously, and also gather intelligence on the extent to which his or her findings are hampered by population restrictions.

The power of the questionnaire and interview has been enormously enhanced, as have all methods, by the development of sensitive sampling procedures. With the early impetus provided by the Census Bureau to locational sampling, particularly to the theory and practice of stratification, concern about the population restrictions of a research sample has been radically diminished. Less well developed is the random sampling of time units—either over long periods such as months, or within a shorter period such as a day. There is no theoretical reason why time sampling is scarce, for it is a simple question of substituting time for location in a sampling design. Time sampling is of interest not only for its control over population fluctuations which might confound comparisons, but also because it permits control over the possibility of variable content at different times of the day or different months of the year. One study that did involve time sampling was William Bieck's study of time required to reach a police dispatcher by means of various telephone numbers (Van Kirk, 1977). Since telephone circuits, operators, and dispatchers are busy at different times of the day and different days of the week, it was necessary to schedule the mock telephone calls to sample time periods. (The study was done with the consent of the telephone company and with the knowledge of the dispatchers, although there would have been no way for operators or dispatchers to know that they were handling a mock call until it was over.)

The cost of research that requires systematic sampling in the community is high, and for that reason government and commercial research organizations have led in the area, while academic research continues to limp along with conscripted sophomores. The controlled laboratory setting makes for excellent internal validity, as one has tight control over the conditions of administration and the internal structure of the questionnaire, but the specter of low generalizability is ever present.

That same specter is present, however, even if one has a national probability sample and the most carefully prepared questionnaire form or interview schedule. So long as one has only a single class of data collection, and that class is the questionnaire or interview, one has inadequate knowledge of the rival hypotheses grouped under the term "reactive measurement effects." These potential sources of error, some stemming from an individual's awareness of being tested, others from the nature of the investigator, must be accounted for by some other class of measurement than the verbal self-report.

It is too much to ask of any single class that it eliminate all the rival hypotheses subsumed under the population-, content-, and reactive-effects groupings. As long as the research strategy is based on a single measurement class, some flanks will be exposed, and even if fewer are exposed with the choice of the questionnaire method, there is still insufficient justification for its use as the only approach. Recently, Cialdini and Baumann (1980) have shown that a straightforward survey question ("For whom did you vote?" "Should the coach be fired?") gave results in good accord with a more expensive and cumbersome nonreactive measure. The latter involved distributing "fliers" for or against a candidate or issue in an area "seeded" with fliers apparently thrown away (littered) by previous recipients. With a more sensitive question, however (for example, "Do you favor ERA?" asked by females dressed in such a manner as to convey their feminist position), the survey question and the litter measure produced different findings, the latter suggesting a less favorable attitude than the former. We will likely be better off if we can avoid being limited to a single measure; if we are to be limited, the choice must be made carefully.

If no single measurement class is perfect, neither is any scientifically useless. Many studies and many novel sources of data have been mentioned in these pages. The reader may indeed have wondered which turn of the page would provide a commentary on some Ouija-board investigation. It would have been there had we known of one and had it met some reasonable criteria of scientific worth. These "oddball" studies have been discussed because they demonstrate ways in which the investigator may shore up reactive infirmities of the interview and questionnaire. As a group, these classes of measurement are themselves infirm and individually contain more risk (more rival plausible hypotheses) than does a well-constructed interview.

This does not trouble us, nor does it argue against their use, for the most fertile search for validity comes from a combined series of different measures, each with its idiosyncratic weaknesses, each pointed to a single hypothesis. When a hypothesis can survive the confrontation of a series of complementary methods of testing, it contains a degree of validity unattainable by one tested within the more constricted framework of a single method (Campbell and Fiske, 1959). Findings from this latter approach must always be subject to the suspicion that they are method-bound: Will the comparison totter when exposed to an equally prudent but different testing method? There must be a multiple operationalism. E. G. Boring (1963) put it this way:

> ... as long as a new construct has only the single operational definition that it received at birth, it is just a construct. When it gets two alternative operational definitions, it is beginning to be validated. When the defining operations, because of proven correlations, are many, then it becomes reified [p. 222].

This means, obviously, that the notion of a single "critical experiment" is erroneous. *There must be a series of linked critical experiments, each testing a different outcropping of the hypothesis.* It is through triangulation of data procured from different measurement classes that the investigator can most effectively strip of plausibility rival explanations for his comparison. The usual procedural question asked is: Which of the several available data-collection methods will be best for my research problem? We suggest the alternative question: Which set of methods will be best?—with "best" defined as a series that provides data to test the most significant threats to a comparison with a reasonable expenditure of resources.

There are a number of research conditions in which the sole use of the interview or questionnaire leaves unanswerable rival explanations. The purpose of those less popular measurement classes emphasized here is to bolster these weak spots and provide intelligence to evaluate threats to validity. The payout for using these measures is high, but the approach is more demanding of the investigator. In their discussion of statistical records, Selltiz and her associates (Selltiz et al., 1959) note:

> The use of such data demands a capacity to ask many different questions related to the research problem.... The guiding principle for the use of available statistics consists in keeping oneself flexible with respect to the form in which research questions are asked [p. 318].

This flexibility of thought is required to handle reactive measurement effects, which are the most systematic weakness of all interview and questionnaire studies. These error threats are also systematically present in all observation studies in which the presence of an observer is known to those under study. To varying degrees, measurements conducted in natural settings, without the individual's knowledge, control this type of error possibility. In all of them—hidden observation, contrived observation, trace analysis, and secondary records—the individual is not aware of being tested, and there is little danger that the act of measurement will itself serve as a force for change in behavior or elicit role playing that confounds the data. There is also minimal risk that biases coming from the physical appearance or other cues provided by the investigator will contaminate the results.

In the observational studies, however, hiding observers does not eliminate the risk that they will change as data-collecting instruments over time. Any change, for the better or worse, will introduce shifts that might be erroneously interpreted as stemming from the causal variable. This source of error must be guarded against in the same way that it is in other measurement classes—by careful training of the observer (interviewer), by permitting practice effects to take place before the critical data are collected, and by "blinding" the observer to the hypothesis. There is no way of knowing, of course, whether all reasonable precautions have worked. For this, the only solution is an internal longitudinal analysis of data from a single observer and cross-analysis of data from different observers at various times during the data collection.

Finally, none of the methods emphasized here, by themselves, can eliminate response sets, which might strongly influence the character of the data. These must be brought under
experimental control by manipulation of the setting itself (as in
contrived field experimentation) or by statistical operations
with the data if the character of the response sets is known well
enough to permit adjustments. With archival records, it may be
extremely difficult to know if response sets were operating at
the time the data were produced.

These methods also may counter a necessary weakness of
the interview and questionnaire—dependence upon language.
When one is working within a single society, there is always the
question whether the differential verbal skills of various subcultures will mislead the investigator. It is possible, if groups vary
in articulateness, to overgeneralize the behavior or attitudes of
the group or individuals with the greater verbal fluency. This
risk is particularly marked for the interpretation of research
reports that employ quotations liberally. The natural tendency
of the writer is to choose illustrative quotations that are fluent,
dramatic, or engaging. If the pool of good quotations is variable
across the subcultures, the reader may mistakenly overvalue
the ideas in the quotations, even though the writer does not.
This is a question of presentation, but an important one because
of the disproportionate weight that may be placed on population segments.

The differential capacity to use the language artfully is one
source of error, while the absolute capacity of the language to
convey ideas is another.[2] This is an issue strongly present in
cross-cultural comparisons, where different languages may vary
radically as a medium of information transfer. The effect of this
is to limit the content possible for study with questionnaires or
interviews. If one worked in New Guinea, for example, and had
to depend upon the *lingua franca* pidgin widely spoken there,
one would find it adequate to indicate an answer to "Where do
you keep your fishing nets?" but too gross a filter to study the
ethnocentricism of a tribe. Pidgin simply does not possess the

---

[2]In a similar note on observers, Heyns and Lippitt (1954) ask if the "observer lacks the sensitivity or the vocabulary which the particular observation
requires" (p. 372).

subtle gradients required to yield textured responses to questions on attitudes toward neighboring tribes or one's own tribe. Although it is theoretically possible to learn all the regional dialects well enough to be competent in a language, in practice this does not occur. A more pragmatic approach is to search for observational or trace evidence that will document aspects of ethnocentrism (for example, reactions to outsiders, disposition and use of weapons) and then relate it to the verbal responses in the inadequate pidgin. Mention should be made, though, of the strategy employed by Brewer and Campbell (1976) in their study of ethnocentrism among 30 ethnic groups in East Africa. They capitalized on the fact that there were field workers in each group who did know the local language and who were willing to collaborate in a large-scale data-collecting effort.

One more weakness of the dependence on language is that sometimes there is silence. So long as a respondent talks, glibly or not, in a rich language or not, checks and controls can be worked on the reported content.[3] There are, however, situations in which refusals to cooperate preclude any chance of correcting distorted information. This usually results in a biased research population and not a rejection of all findings, because it is almost always possible to find some people who will discuss any topic. But it can also result in a complete stalemate if only the verbal report is considered as the research instrument.

An amusing example of this inability to get data by verbal report, and a nonreactive circumvention, is provided by Shadegg (1964). In his book on political campaign methods, Shadegg writes of a campaign manager who used every available means to learn the plans of his opponent, who, reasonably enough, was unwilling to grant a revealing interview. One method arranged for procuring the contents of his opponent's wastebasket: "He came into possession of carbon copies of letters . . . memos in the handwriting of his opponent's mamager." Admittedly a less efficient method than the interview, it admirably met the criterion of being workable: "It took a lot of digging through the trash to come up with the nuggets. But . . .

---

[3]For an extended discussion of this issue, see Hyman et al. (1954) and Kahn and Cannell (1957).

daily panning produced some very fine gold." The "investigator" did not limit himself to inferences drawn from observations of his opponent's public acts but was able to develop ingeniously (although perhaps not ethically for a politician, and certainly not ethically for a social scientist) a trace measure to complement the observation. Each aided the other, for the observations give a validity check on the nuggets among the trash (Was misleading material being planted?), and the nuggets gave a more accurate means of interpreting the meaning of the public acts.

Evidence of how others are sensitive to wastebaskets is seen in the practice in diplomatic embassies of burning refuse under guard, the discussion of refuse purchase by industrial spies (Anonymous, 1964c), and the development of an electric wastebasket that shreds discarded paper into unreadable bits.

Generally speaking, then, observational and trace methods are indicated as supplementary or primary when language may serve as a poor medium of information—either because of its differential use, its absolute capacity for transfer, or when significant elements of the research population are silent.

The verbal methods are necessarily weak along another dimension, the study of past behavior or of change. For historical studies, there is no alternative but to rely mainly on records of the past time. Behavioral research on the distant past is rare, however; more common are studies which center on experiences within the lifetime of respondents. For example, there is a large literature on child-rearing practices, in which mothers recollect their behavior of years past. We now know that such data should be interpreted only with great caution, for time warps memories. It may be enough to cite Mark Twain, who in his autobiography asserted, "For many years I believed that I remembered helping my grandfather drink his whiskey toddy when I was six weeks old, but I do not tell about that any more now.... When I was younger I could remember anything, whether it had happened or not" (Neider, 1959, p. 3).

For more current evidence on the fallibility of such recall data, see Pyles, Stolz, and Macfarlane, 1935; McGraw and Molloy, 1941; Smith, 1958; Weiss and Dawis, 1960 all of whom comment on, or test, the validity of mothers' recall of child-rearing practices. Weiss and Dawis wrote, "It is indefensible to assume the validity of purportedly factual data obtained by interview" (p. 384). The work of Haggard, Brekstad, and Skard (1960) and Robbins (1963) suggests that it is a problem of differentially accurate recall. In Haggard's phrase, the interviews "did not reflect the mothers' earlier experiences and attitudes so much as their current picture of the past" (p. 317). Adler (1931) believed that one's earliest recollections express crucial personality factors and that they are selectively retained because they are consistent with one's life style. Those memories are recalled that serve to justify the person's specific approach to life at the time of recall (Brodsky, 1952).

When, through death or refusal, reports of past behavior are unavailable, a proper contingent strategy is to interview others who have had access to the same information, or who can report at second hand. This may be very shaky information, but useful if other intelligence is available as a check. For many investigations, of course, the nature of the distortion is itself an important datum and can become a central topic of study when a reliable baseline is possible.[4] If other materials are present, and they usually are in a record-keeping society, the best way to estimate past behavior is to combine methods of study of archival records, available traces, and verbal reports, even if secondhand. Clearly, direct observational methods are useless for past events.

With studies of social change, the most practical method is to rely on available records, supplemented by verbal recall. If one wanted more control over the data, it would be possible to conduct a continuing series of field experiments extending over a long period of years. But the difficulty of such an approach is evidenced by the scarcity of such longitudinal, original-data studies in social science. Forgetting the number of years required, there is the problem of unstable populations over time,

[4]The courts have handled secondary information by excluding it under the "hearsay" rule (Wigmore, 1935; Morgan, 1963). Epically put, "Pouring rumored scandal into the bent ear of blabbering busybodies in a pool room or gambling house is no more disreputable than pronouncing it with clipped accents in a courtroom" (Donnelly, Goldstein, and Schwartz, 1962, p. 277). The case from which this is cited is *Holmes,* 379 Pa. 599 (1954).

a growing problem as the society becomes more mobile. Potential errors lie in both directions as one moves forward or backward in time, and the more practical approach of the two is to analyze data already collected—making the ever-present assumption that such are available.

A more integrative approach for studying change is to develop two discrete time series—one based on available records, the other freshy developed by the investigator. With this strategy, it is necessary to have an overlap period in which the relationships between the two series are established. Given knowledge of the relationships, the available records can be studied retrospectively, thereby providing more intelligence than would be possible if they existed alone. Again, there is a necessary assumption: one must be able to reject the plausibility of an interaction between time and the method. If there is any content or population fluctuation beyond chance, such a method is invalid. Diagrammatically, where O is an observation and the subscript n equals new data and a available data:

$$O_{a1}O_{a2}O_{a3}O_{a4}O_{a5}O_{a6}O_{a7}O_{a8}O_{a9}O_{a10}$$

$$O_{n6}O_{n7}O_{n8}O_{n9}O_{n10}$$

A final gain from the less reactive methods is frequently the lower cost of data collection. Many scholars know how to conduct massive surveys that effectively control major sources of error; few do so. This knowledge is an underdeveloped resource. With survey interviews often costing as much as $100 apiece, the failure is understandable, however regrettable. When the interview or questionnaire is viewed as the only method, the researcher is doomed either to frustration or a studied avoidance of thoughts on external validity. Peace of mind will come if the investigator breaks the single-method mold and examines the extent to which other measurement classes can substitute for verbal reports. The price of collecting each unit of data is low for most of the methods we have stressed. In some cases, the dross rate is high, and it may be necessary to observe a hundred cases before one meets the research specifications. Nonetheless, even under these high dross-rate conditions, the cost per usable response is often lower than that of a completed interview or returned questionnaire. The lower cost permits flexibility to expand into content and population areas otherwise precluded, and the result of this is to increase the confidence one has in generalizing findings. Just as in the case of studying social change, it may be possible to generate different data series, some based on verbal reports, others based on secondary or observational data. Providing for enough cases of the more expensive procedures to yield a broad base for linkage, the larger number of cases can be allocated to the usually less expensive observational or secondary methods. It is important to note that we add "usually" before "less expensive." The savings are centered in data-collection costs, and it may be that all the savings are vitiated by the elaborate corrections or transformations that a particular data series may require. The cost of materials and analysis is an equivocal area indeed.

In the multimethod pattern of testing, the primary gains coming from the less popular methods are protection against reactive measurement threats, auxiliary data in content areas where verbal reports are unreliable, an easier method of determining long-term change, and a potentially lower cost substitute for some standard survey practices.

Offsetting these gains, there are associated problems for each of the less popular measurement classes—indeed, if they were less problematic, we would be writing an argument in favor of an increased use of the interview.

The most powerful aspect of the verbal methods—their ability to reach into all content areas—is a soft spot in the hidden-observation, trace, and archival analysis procedures. We have noted remarkably adept and nonobvious applications of data from these sources, but for some content areas, the most imaginative of investigators will have trouble finding pertinent material. Individually, those methods are simply not as broad gauged.

Often missing, too, is complete knowledge of the conditions under which the data were collected, the definitions of important terms used in classification, and the control or lack of it over error risks that may be salient. This is particularly disturbing when dealing with comparisons of public records from different areas or from widely different times. The variation in definitions of "suicide" versus "accidental death," or the differential thoroughness with which marriages are entered in official records are examples of this issue. In general, for trace evidence and archival records, a dominant concern is the possibility of selective deposit and selective survival of the research data. Through supporting research designed to learn of these errors, it is sometimes possible to apply corrections to what is available. At other times, researchers must remain in ignorance and make assumptions. If they restrict themselves to working with *only* such data, they remain helpless before their vagaries. If they use other measurement classes, the process of triangulating all the different data may provide tests of their assumptions and reveal the presence or extent of error. The comparison of data from the different classes can always add intelligence unavailable from comparisons of data from within the single class.

Because of the risks of error and the danger of unknown biases, we have stressed the importance of careful data sampling. Wherever feasible, locational sampling should be employed, extending over regions as well as areas within a single locality. Similarly, time sampling should be considered not only as a device employed within a single day or week, but applied over months and years. By such effort, we are able to protect against both population and content restrictions and very often produce interesting data from comparisons of results from different locations or times.[5] The need for time and location sampling is no less for observational or archival data than it is for interviews or questionnaires, for sampling is a problem that transcends the class of measurement.

Another common demand, this one not so applicable to the verbal-report approaches, is for data adjustment and conversion. The need comes from the experimenter's decreased control over the production of his or her materials. The exception

[5]Studies of the prestige of universities over time are of interest, showing changes over time with some gainers and some losers (see Gourman, 1977 for a listing of 55 top institutions).

to this is the contrived field experiment, where the investigator can have full control, but the data from archives, trace sources, and observations are frequently too raw to be used as is. The need is underlined because of one of the major advantages of the secondary data—their ability to produce fine time-series information. In time series, it is usually necessary to account for extraneous sources of variation, such as secular trends or cyclical patterns. Thus, the "score," which is the basis of comparison, is some transformed measure that is a residual of the total "score." In other studies, the absolute number of cases varies from unit time to unit time, and the only reasonable comparison score is one which is related in some way, through an average or percentage, for example, to the variable baseline. Investigators may have no control over the flow of an observed population, but they can obtain a count of that flow and use this intelligence as the basis for modifying their comparison scores.

The more sophisticated forms of transformation, such as index numbers based on multiple components, demand more information, particularly as one assigns relative weights to components collected into a single score. This is not as awesome as it sounds, and if investigators are sensitive to the potential usefulness of index numbers, they often find enough secondary data available for the task, or may obtain new information without extraordinarily high marginal costs. Insofar as these transformations demand time and labor to make the raw data more precise, they are disadvantageous compared with standard questionnaire procedures. There are, however, as we have suggested in various points in the text, indications that index numbers and more simple transformations could be used properly in all classes of measurement. The *Zeitgeist* may as yet be inappropriate, but an important work will someday link index-number theory and literature to social science measurement theory and practice.

These, then, are the gains; these the losses. There are no rewards for ingenuity as such, and the payoff comes only when ingenuity leads to new means of making more valid comparisons. In the available grab bag of imperfect research methods, there is room for new uses of the old.

ETHICS OF NONREACTIVE
MEASUREMENT: A CODA

We have raised frequent questions about ethical issues involved in nonreactive measurement during the course of our
discussions in this book, and we even devoted one entire chapter to the matter. We do not, however, consider this book to be
a treatise on ethics, nor do we intend for it to be considered a
definitive source. The pervasiveness of the issues and the frequency of their mention may have led some readers to infer a
pessimism about ethics that we do not share. Most nonreactive
measures—most unobtrusive measures, for that matter—should
raise no ethical concerns even among those most sensitive on
the issues. Analysis of archives, for example, unless they involve
private papers, is almost always permissible, especially if proper
attention is paid to preserving confidentiality by one or more
of what are now established procedures. Most simple observations are, perhaps by their very simplicity, innocuous and
not offending. If privacy must be invaded, as in garbage studies, or if anonymity cannot be assured, as in obtaining physiological measures, informed consent provides a mechanism
for minimizing the prospect of later concern for an ethical
breach.

As suggested earlier, there are, however unfortunately, no
clear-cut principles of ethics to be followed; at some point one
gets to the level of judgment and individual sensitivity. The
forthcoming ethical statement of the National Commission for
the Protection of Human Subjects of Biomedical and Behavioral
Research (see *The Belmont Report*, 1978, for an early draft) will
establish some limits and guidelines, but the very conception of
Institutional Review Boards involves the notions of local standards and judgments. At present the whole area is inchoate, but
it is well to remember that widespread public concern for the
ethics of behavioral research began scarcely more than a
decade ago. In the meantime, Campbell and Cecil (1978) have
provided a potentially helpful beginning to the codifying of
ethical principles for the areas of "program evaluation, social
experimentation, social indicators, survey research, secondary

analysis of research data, and statistical analyses of data from administrative records." Those areas include much of what falls under the rubric of nonreactive measurement, and their principles can be used as a guide to the edge of the territory where judgment then is called for. Such books as those by Diener and Crandall (1978) and Reynolds (1979) help to inform judgment. The book by Klockars and O'Connor (1979) is of special interest since it focuses on the ethics of research on rule-breaking behavior, a type of problem especially vulnerable to ethical concerns.

We call here for alertness of investigators to potential ethical problems but not for paralysis induced by either pessimism or anxiety. What is wanted is that each investigator consider a proposed research plan that calls for the use of nonreactive measures to determine whether those measures will be considered ethically acceptable. Not everyone will come to the same conclusion, but science, our respondents, and the public will be better off if the decision to proceed is at least thoughtful.

Since the central issues in nonreactive measurement are likely to revolve around potential invasion of privacy, it may be helpful to formulate questions in relation to four considerations, all alluded to earlier. Judgments concerning privacy invasion are aided by distinctions derived from the legal system and the general culture. Tapping these sources, we bring to the reader's attention some dimensions that regularly enter into determining the privacy interest.

A first consideration is the element of publicness in the location of the behavior. A person observed in the marketplace, a public restaurant, a public square, or a thoroughfare can lay less claim to privacy than can a person in his or her own dwelling. The value of privacy in the home is recognized in doctrines of the common law. For example, in establishing self-defense as a justification for homicide, a defendant must meet a requirement in most circumstances of reasonable effort to avoid the attacker by retreating. Where the attack occurs in the home, however, no obligation to retreat is imposed (*People* v. *Tomlins* 213 N.Y. Reports 496). Similarly, the constitutional provisions against unreasonable searches and seizures express a particular concern for security from public authority in the sanctity of the home (*Mapp* v. *Ohio* 367 U.S. 643). (The ethical standard for social scientific research clearly differs from the legal, which is here introduced only to illustrate the commitment of the society to the value of privacy.)

The distinction between public and private places is not always clear. Even when a person moves beyond the permanent residence, some special right may accrue to a place that serves some of the functions of home: a hotel room, an automobile, a compartment on a train, a restaurant booth, and so forth. Werthman and Piliavin (1967) suggest that the touchiness of youth gangs about police observance is exacerbated by their own perception of the corner where they hang out as their home, a place where their privacy should be accordingly protected.

A second consideration is the publicness of the person. Again, a legal doctrine suggests a cultural attitude. When a person has become a public official, he or she sacrifices some of the legal protections accorded an ordinary citizen. The public person, for example, must make a stronger case, including a showing of actual malice, to obtain damages for libel than is necessary for a private citizen (*New York Times* v. *Sullivan* 376 U.S. 254). Public persons are regularly subject to what would otherwise be considered invasions of privacy and come to expect that their every move may be observed and reported. Even the home appears to be less sacrosanct, although many celebrities have learned to defend its privacy.

A third consideration is the explicit identification of the person with particular information. If the connection is completely severed between the individual and the information, privacy is clearly preserved. By contrast, identification of a single individual with the information poses the maximum danger to privacy. Intermediate degrees of identification may also impose harm, as when the information pertains to an individual whose identity, though not given, is obtainable. Some ethical problems may arise even if the individual cannot be singled out, as when some unpleasant information is attributed to one or more members of a family, a club, or a company. To the extent of the members' attachment to such a group, even a group identification may be damaging or disfavored.

Finally, the nature of the information disclosed is a factor in the privacy question. In American society, sexual information has long been a sensitive subject. With a relaxation of the sexual mores, such information seems to be somewhat less a problem than before. Even so, the researcher must not equate voluntary disclosure with a generalized indifference concerning what is known. (It is one thing for Gay Talese to publish extensive disclosures concerning his sexual adventures. It is quite another matter for the mayor of New York to publish in the newspaper, over their objections, the names of men who have visited prostitutes.) In recent years, information concerning income seems to have become very sensitive, perhaps surpassing sexual information in this regard. It is important to recognize that such sensitivities vary by individual and group. In making ethical judgments, one must recognize the possibility that any information associated with a person, if disclosed or publicized more widely than before, may be perceived as an unwelcome invasion of privacy.

These four considerations interact in complicated ways. In making ethical judgments, social scientists must bear in mind the potential affront and harm to the subject, as well as the damage that unethical behavior might inflict on the field. These considerations must also be balanced against the value for science and society of the scientific investigation of social behavior. All of this means that wise judgments may be difficult, especially for the individual whose research project is at stake.

Max Eastman once suggested that books should start with a first section consisting of a few sentences, the second section a few pages, and so on. He even wrote one like that—*The Enjoyment of Laughter.* Since this has been an unconventional monograph on unconventional research procedures, it is proper that it should have an unconventional close. We reverse Eastman's formula and offer a one-phrase final chapter and a one-paragraph penultimate chapter. We have not, in the fifteen years since the first publication of this book, found a better way to bring it to a close.

CHAPTER 11

A Statistician on Method

We must use all available weapons of attack, face our problems realistically and not retreat to the land of fashionable sterility, learn to sweat over our data with an admixture of judgment and intuitive rumination, and accept the usefulness of particular data even when the level of analysis available for them is markedly below that available for other data in the empirical area.

(Binder, 1964, p. 294)

CHAPTER 12

Cardinal Newman's Epitaph

From symbols and shadows to the truth

References

Adams, T. F. Field interrogation. *Police,* 1963, March–April, 28.

Adler, A. *What life should mean to you.* Boston: Little, Brown, 1931

Advertising Service Guild. *The press and its readers.* London: Art & Technics, 1949.

Aiello, J. R., and Jones, S. E. Field study of the proxemic behavior of young school children in three subcultural groups. *Journal of Personality and Social Psychology,* 1971, *19,* 351–356.

Alderson, M. Relationship between month of birth and month of death in the elderly. *British Journal of Preventive and Social Medicine,* 1975, *29,* 151–156.

Allport, G. W. *The use of personal documents in psychological science.* New York: Social Science Research Council, 1942.

American Anthropology Association. *Ethical Principles for Conducting Fieldwork.* Washington, D.C., 1980.

American Association of Public Opinion Research. *Code of Professional Ethics and Practices.* 1979.

American Psychological Association. *Ethical principles in the conduct of research with human subjects.* Washington, D.C.: Ad hoc Committee on Ethical Standards in Psychological Research, American Psychological Association, 1973.

American Sociological Association, *Code of ethics.* Washington, D.C.: American Sociological Association, 1971.

Amrine, M. & Sanford, F. In the matter of juries, democracy, science, truth, senators, and bugs. *American Psychologist,* 1056, *11,* 54–60.

Anastasi, A. *Differential psychology.* (3rd ed.) New York: Macmillan, 1958.

Andrew, R. J. The origin and evolution of the cells and facial expressions of the primates. *Behavior,* 1963, *20,* 1–109.

Angell, R. C. The moral integration of American cities. *American Journal of Sociology,* 1951, *57,* 123–126.

Anonymoi. Hair style as a function of hard-headedness *vs.* long-hairedness in psychological research, a study in the personology of science. Unprepared manuscript, Northwestern Univer. & Univers. of Chicago, 1953–1960.

331

Anonymous. Z-*Frank stresses radio to build big Chevy dealership.* *Advertising Age,* 1962, *33,* 83.

Anonymous. Litter bugged. *Advertising Age,* November 2, 1964, *35,* 74.

Anonymous. In the eye of the beholder. *Sponsor,* December 28, 1964, *18,* 25–29.

Anonymous. Effects of sexual activity on beard growth in man. *Nature,* 1970, *226,* 869–870.

Archer, D., and Erlich, L. Weighing the evidence: A new method for research on restricted information. Unpublished manuscript, 1980.

Ardrey, R. *African genesis.* New York: Delta, 1961.

Arrington, R. Time sampling in studies of social behavior: a critical review of techniques and results with research suggestions. *Psychological Bulletin,* 1943, *40,* 81–124.

Arsenian, J. M. Young children in an insecure situation. *Journal of Abnormal and Social Psychology,* 1943, *38,* 225–249.

Ashley, J. W. Stock prices and changes in earnings and dividends: Some empirical results. *Journal of Political Economy,* 1962, *70,* 82–85.

Athey, K. R., Coleman, J. E., Reitman, A. P., & Tang, J. Two experiments showing the effect of the interviewer's racial background on responses to questionnaires concerning racial issues. *Journal of Applied Psychology,* 1960, *44,* 244–246.

Babchuk, N., & Bates, A. P. Professor or producer: the two faces of academic man. *Social Forces,* 1962, *40,* 341–348.

Back, K. W. The well-informed informant. In R. N. Adams & J. J. Preiss (Eds.), *Human organization research.* Homewood, Ill.: Dorsey Press, 1960. Pp. 179–187.

Bain, H. M., & Hecock, D. S. *Ballot position and voter's choice: the arrangement of names on the ballot and its effect on the voter.* Detroit: Wayne State Univer. Press, 1957.

Bain, R. K. The researcher's role: a case study. In R. N. Adams & J. J. Preiss (Eds.), *Human organization research.* Homewood, Ill.: Dorsey Press, 1960. Pp. 140–152.

Bales, R. F. *Interaction process analysis.* Cambridge: Addison-Wesley, 1950.

Barber, J. D. *The presidential character: Predicting performance in the White House.* Englewood Cliffs, New Jersey: Prentice-Hall, 1972.

Barch, A. M., Trumbo, D., & Nangle, J. Social setting and conformity to a legal requirement. *Journal of Abnormal and Social Psychology,* 1957, *55,* 396–398.

Barefoot, J. C., and Strickland, L. H. The confidentiality of "confidential" lost letters. *Journal of Social Psychology,* 1977, *101,* 123–126.

Barger, K., and Earl, D. Differential adaptation to northern town life by the Eskimos and Indians of Great Whale River. *Human Organization,* 1971, *30,* 25–30.

Barker, R. G., & Wright, H. F. *One boy's day: a specimen record of behavior.* New York: Harper & Bros., 1951.

Barker, R. G., & Wright, H. F. *Midwest and its children: the psychological ecology of an American town.* Evanston, Ill.: Row, Peterson, 1954.

Barkley, R. A. The effects of methylphenidate on various measures of activity level and attention in hyperkinetic children. *Journal of Abnormal Child Psychology,* 1977, *5,* 351–369.

Barmack, J. E., and Payne, D. E. The Lackland accident countermeasure experiment. *Highway Research Board Proceedings,* 1961, *40,* 513–522. Published by the National Research Council, Washington, D.C.

Baron, R. A. The reduction of human aggression: A field study of the influence of incompatible reactions. *Journal of Applied Social Psychology,* 1976, *6,* 260–274.

Baron, R. A., and Ransberger, V. M. Ambient temperature and the occurrence of collective violence: The "long, hot summer" revisited. *Journal of Personality and Social Psychology,* 1978, *36,* 351–360.

Barry, H. Relationships between child training and the pictorial arts. *Journal of Abnormal and Social Psychology,* 1957, *54,* 380–383.

Barthell, C. N., and Holmes, D. S. High school yearbooks: A nonreactive measure of social isolation in graduates who later became schizophrenic. *Journal of Abnormal Psychology,* 1968, *73,* 313–316.

Barzum, J. *The delights of detection,* New York: Criterion Books, 1961.

Baskett, G. D., Peet, J. G., Bradford, D., and Mulaik, S. A. An examination of the lost-letter technique. *Journal of Applied Social Psychology,* 1973, *3,* 165–173.

Bass, B. M. Ultimate criteria of organizational worth. *Personnel Psychology, 1952, 5,* 157–173.

Baumrind, D. Some thoughts on ethics of research: after reading Milgram's "Behavioral Study of Obedience," *American Psychologist,* 1964, *19,* 421–423.

Becker, H. A. Problems in the publication of field studies. In A. J. Vidich, J. Bensman, and M. R. Stein. *Reflections on Community Studies.* New York: Wiley, 1964.

Becker, H. Do photographs tell the truth? *Afterimage,* February, 1978.

Belmont report: The ethical principles and guidelines for the protection of human subjects of research. The National Commission for the Protection of Human Subjects of Biomedical and Behavioral Research. Washington, D. C.: U. S. Government Printing Office, DHEW publication (OS), 78–0012, 0013, 0014, September 30, 1978.

Benney, M., Riesman, D., & Star, S. Age and sex in the interview. *American Journal of Sociology,* 1956, *62,* 143–152.

Benson, P. L., Karabenick, S. A., and Lerner, R. M. Pretty pleases: The effects of physical attractiveness, race, and sex on receiving help. *Journal of Experimental Social Psychology*, 1976, *12*, 409–415.

Berelson, B. *Content analysis in communication research.* Glencoe, Ill.: Free Press, 1952.

Berger, C. S. An experimental study of doodles. *Psychological Newsletter*, 1954, *6*, 138–141.

Berkowitz, L., and Alioto, J. T. The meaning of an observed event as a determinant of its aggressive consequences. *Journal of Personality and Social Psychology*, 1973, *28*, 206–217.

Berkson, G., & Fitz-Gerald, F. L. Eye fixation aspect of attention to visual stimuli in infant chimpanzees. *Science*, 1963, *139*, 586–587.

Berkun, M., Bialek, H. M., Kern, P. R., and Yagi, K. Experimental studies of psychological stress in man. Psychological Monographs: *General and Applied*, 1962, *76*, (15), 1–39.

Berlyne, D. E. Emotional aspects of learning. In P. R. Farnsworth, O. McNemar, & Q. McNemar (Eds.), *Annual Review of Psychology*, 1964, *15*, 115–142.

Bernstein, E. M. *Money and the economic system.* Chapel Hill.: Univer. of North Carolina Press, 1935.

Berreman, J. V. M. Factors affecting the sale of modern books of fiction: A study of social psychology. Unpublished doctoral dissertation, Stanford University, 1940.

Binder, A. Statistical theory. In P. R. Farnsworth, O. McNemar, & Q. McNemar (Eds.), *Annual Review of Psychology*, 1964, *15*, 277–310.

Birdwhistell, R. Kinesics and communication. In E. Carpenter (Ed.), *Exploration in communication.* Boston: Beacon Hill, 1960, Pp. 54–64.

Birdwhistell, R. The kinesic level in the investigations of emotions. In P. Knapp (Ed.), *The expression of emotions in man.* New York: International Universities Press, 1963. Pp. 123–140.

Blake, J. A. Death by hand grenade: Altruistic suicide in combat. *Suicide and Life-Threatening Behavior*, 1978, *8*, 46–59.

Blake, R. R., Berkowitz, H., Bellamy, R. Q., & Mouton, J. S. Volunteering as an avoidance act. *Journal of Abnormal and Social Psychology*, 1956, *53*, 154–156.

Blake, R. R., Mouton, J. S., & Hain, J. D. Social forces in petition signing. *Southwest Social Science Quarterly*, 1956, *36*, 385–390.

Blau, P. M. *The dynamics of bureaucracy.* Chicago: Univer. of Chicago Press, 1955.

Bloch, V. L'étude objective du comportement des spectateurs. *Revue Internationale de Filmologie*, 1952, *3*, 221–222.

Block, J. *The challenge of response sets.* New York: Appleton-Century-Crofts, 1965.

Blomgren, G. W., & Scheuneman, T. W. Psychological resistance to seat belts. Research Project RR-115. Northwestern Univer., Traffic Institute. 1961.

Blumstein, A., Cohen, J., and Nagin, D. *Deterrence and incapacitation: Estimating the effects of criminal sanctions on crime rates.* Washington, D.C.: National Academy of Sciences, 1978.

Bochner, S. An unobtrusive approach to the study of housing discrimination against Aborigines. *Australian Journal of Psychology,* 1972, *24,* 335–337.

Bolton, G. M. The lost letter technique as a measure of community attitudes towards a major social issue. *Sociological Quarterly,* 1974, *15,* 567–570.

Bolton, R. Child holding patterns. *Current Anthropology,* 1978, *19,* 134–135.

Boring, E. G. The role of theory in experimental psychology. *American Journal of Psychology,* 1953, *66,* 169–184. (Reprinted in E. G. Boring, *History, psychology, and science.* Ed. R. I. Watson & D. T. Campbell. New York: Wiley, 1963. Pp. 210–225.)

Boring, E. G. The beginning and growth of measurement in psychology. *Isis,* 1961, *52,* 238–257. (Reprinted in E. G. Boring, *History, psychology, and science.* Ed. R. I. Watson & D. T. Campbell. New York: Wiley, 1963, Pp. 140–158.)

Boring, E. G. *History, psychology and science.* Ed. R. I. Watson & D. T. Campbell. New York: Wiley, 1963.

Boring, E. G., & Boring, M. D. Masters and pupils among the American psychologists. *American Journal of Psychology,* 1948, *61,* 527–534. (Reprinted in E. G. Boring, *History, psychology, and science.* Ed., R. I. Watson & D. T. Campbell, New York: Wiley, 1963. Pp. 132–139.)

Boruch, R. F., and Cecil, J. S. *Assuring the confidentiality of social research data.* Philadelphia: University of Pennsylvania Press, 1979.

Bouchard, T. J., Jr, and Stuctor, J. The lost-letter technique: Predicting elections. *Psychological Reports,* 1969, *25,* 231–234.

Bouchard, T. J., Jr. Unobtrusive measures: An inventory of uses. *Sociological Methods and Research,* 1976, *4,* 267–300.

Bradshaw, D. Sister, can you spare a smile? *New York,* 1980, *13* (8), 7.

Brenner, M. H. *Mental illness and the economy.* Cambridge, Massachusetts: Harvard University Press, 1973.

Brenner, M. H. Aggression, justice, and the economy. Cambridge: Harvard University Press, 1975.

Brewer, M. B., and Campbell, D. T. *Ethnocentrism and intergroup attitudes: East African evidence.* New York: Sage, 1976.

Brill, S. A New York cabby story you won't believe. *New York,* 1976 (July 19), *8,* 10.

Brodsky, P. The diagnostic importance of early recollections *American Journal of Psychotherapy,* 1952, *6,* 484–483.

Brogden, H., & Taylor, E. The dollar criterion—applying the cost accounting concept to criterion construction. *Personnel Psychology*, 1950, *3*, 133–154.

Brookover, L., and Back, K. W. Time sampling as a field technique. *Human Organization*, 1966, *25*, 64–70.

Brown, B. W. Wife-employment and the emergence of egalitarian marital role prescriptions: 1900–1974. *Family Studies*, 1978, *9*, (1), 5–17.

Brown, J. W. A new approach to the assessment of psychiatric therapies. Unpublished manuscript, 1960.

Bryan, J. Personal communication, 1965.

Bryan, J. H., and Test, M. A. Models and helping: Naturalistic studies in aiding behavior. *Journal of Personality and Social Psychology*, 1967, *6*, 400–407.

Bryant, S. W. What jet travel does to your metabolic clock. *Fortune*, 1963, *68*, 160–163, 183–186.

Bucky, S. F., Edwards, D., and Cohen, P. Primary and secondary benefits from treatment of alcoholism. Naval Health Research Center, San Diego. Report No. 75–44, 1975.

Burchard, W. W. A study of attitudes towards the use of concealed devices in social science research. *Social Forces*, 1957, *36*, 111.

Burchinal, L. G., & Chancellor. L. E. Ages at marriage, occupations of grooms and interreligious marriage rates. *Social Forces*, 1962, *40*, 348–354.

Burchinal, L. G., & Chancellor, L. E. Survival rates among religious homogamous and interreligious marriages. *Social Forces*, 1963, *41*, 353–362.

Burchinal, L. G., & Kenkel, W. F. Religious identification and occupational status of Iowa grooms. *American Sociological Review*, 1962, *27*, 526–532.

Burgess, R. L., Clark, R. M., and Hendee, J. C. An experimental analysis of antilitter procedures. *Journal of Applied Behavior Analysis*, 1971, *4*, 71–75.

Burma, J. H. Self-tattooing among delinquents: a research note. *Sociology and Social Research*, 1959, *43*, 341–345.

Burstein, P., and Freudenburg, W. Changing public policy: The impact of public opinion, antiwar demonstrations, and war costs on Senate voting on Vietnam war motions. *American Journal of Sociology*, 1978, *84*, 99–122.

Burwen, L., & Campbell, D. T. The generality of attitudes toward authority and nonauthority figures. *Journal of Abnormal and Social Psychology*, 1957, *54*, 24–31.

Butler, J. S. Inequality in the military: An examination of promotion time for black and white enlisted men. *American Sociological Review*, 1976, *41*, 807–818.

Byrne, D., Baskett, G. D., and Hodges, L. Behavioral Indicators of interpersonal attraction. *Journal of Applied Social Psychology*, 1971, *1*, 137–149.

Cairns, L. G., and Bochner, S. Measuring sympathy toward handicapped children with the "lost-letter" technique. *Australian Journal of Psychology*, 1974, *26*, 89–91.

Callahan, J. D., Morris, J. C., Seifried, S., Ulett, G. A., & Heusler, A. F. Objective measures in psychopharmacology: baseline observations. *Missouri Medicine*, 1960, *57*, 714–718.

Cameron, P. Frequency and kinds of words in various social settings, or what the hell's going on? *Pacific Sociological Review*, 1969, *12*, 101–104.

Campbell, D. E., and Beets, J. L. Lunacy and the moon. *Psychological Bulletin*, 1978, *85*, 1123–1129.

Campbell, D. T. Leadership and its effects upon the group *Ohio Studies in Personnel*, Research Monograph 83. Columbus: Ohio State Univer., Bureau of Business Research, 1956.

Campbell, D. T. Factors relevant to the validity of experiments in social settings. *Psychological Bulletin*, 1957, *54*, 297–312.

Campbell, D. T. Common fate, similarity, and other indices of the status of aggregates of persons as social entities. *Behavioral Science*, 1958, *3*, 14–25.

Campbell, D. T. Systematic error on the part of human links in communication systems. *Information and Control*, 1959, *1*, 334–369.

Campbell, D. T. Recommendations for APA test standards regarding construct trait or discriminant validity. *American Psychologist*, 1960, *15*, 546–553.

Campbell, D. T. The mutual methodological relevance of anthropology and psychology. In F. L. K. Hsu (Ed.), *Psychological anthropology approaches to culture and personality*. Homewood, Ill.: Dorsey Press, 1961. Pp. 333–352.

Campbell, D. T. Social attitudes and other acquired behavioral dispositions. In S. Koch (Ed.), *Psychology: a study of a science*, Vol. 6, *Investigations of man as socius*. New York: McGraw-Hill, 1963, pp. 94–176.

Campbell, D. T. Pattern matching as an essential in distal knowing. In K. R. Hammond (Ed.), *The psychology of Egon Brunswik*. New York: Holt, Rinehart, 1966.

Campbell, D. T. Administrative experimentation, institutional records, and nonreactive measures. In J. C. Stanley (Ed.), *Improving experimental design and statistical analysis*. Chicago: Rand McNally, 1967.

Campbell, D. T. Prospective: Artifact and control. In R. Rosenthal and R. L. Rosnow (Eds.), *Artifact in Behavioral Research*. New York: Academic Press, 1969.

Campbell, D. T. Evolutionary epistemology. In P. A. Schilpp (Ed.), *The philosophy of Karl Popper* (Vol. 14, 1 and 2). The *library of living philosophers* (Vol. 14, 1). La Salle, Illinois: Open Court Publishing, 1974.

Campbell, D. T. "Degrees of freedom" and the case study. *Comparative Political Studies,* 1975 (September), 178–193.

Campbell, D. T. Assessing the impact of planned social change. In G. M. Lyons (Ed.) *Social research and public policies: The Dartmouth / OECD Conference.* Hanover, New Hampshire: University Press of New England, 1975. Also in (with minor revisions and additions) *Evaluation and Program Planning,* 1979, *2,* 67–90.

Campbell, D. T., Boruch, R. F., Schwartz, R. D., and Steinberg, J. Confidentiality-preserving modes of access to files and to interfile exchange for useful statistical analysis. *Evaluation Quarterly,* 1977, *1,* 269–300.

Campbell, D. T., and Cecil, J. S. Protection of the rights and interests of human subjects in the areas of program evaluation, social experimentation, social indicators, survey research, secondary analysis of research data, and statistical analysis of data from administrative records. In *the Belmont Report: The ethical principles and guidelines for the protection of human subjects of research.* The National Commission for the Protection of Human Subjects of Biomedical and Behavioral Research. Washington, D. C.: U. S. Government Printing Office, DHEW publication (OS), 78–0012, 0013, 0014, September 30, 1978, Appendix II pp. 12–1 —12–23.

Campbell, D. T., & Fiske, D. W. Convergent and discriminant validation by the multitrait-multimethod matrix. *Psychological Bulletin,* 1959, *56,* 81–105.

Campbell, D. T., Kruskal, W. H., & Wallace, W. P. Seating aggregation as an index of attitude. *Sociometry,* 1966, *29,* 1–15.

Campbell, D. T., and Mack, R. W. The steepness of interracial boundaries as a function of the locus of social interaction. Unpublished manuscript.

Campbell, D. T., & McCormack, T. H. Military experience and attitudes toward authority. *American Journal of Sociology,* 1957, *62,* 482–490.

Campbell, D. T., Siegman, C. R., and Rees, M. B. Direction-of-wording effects in the relationships between scales. *Psychological Bulletin,* 1967, *68,* 293–303.

Campbell, D. T., and Stanley, J. C. *Experimental and quasi-experimental designs for research.* Chicago: Rand McNally College Publishing Company, 1966. Also as Experimental and quasiexperimental designs for research on teaching, in N. L. Gage (Ed.), *Handbook of research on teaching,* Chicago: Rand McNally and Company, 1963.

Cane, V. R., & Heim, A. W. The effects of repeated testing: III. further experiments and general conclusions. *Quarterly Journal of Experimental Psychology,* 1950, *2,* 182–195.

Cannell, C. F., Oksenberg, L., and Converse, J. M. Striving for response accuracy: Experiments in new interviewing techniques. *Journal of Marketing Research,* 1977, *14,* 306–315.

Cantril, H. *Gauging Public opinion.* Princeton: Princeton Univer. Press, 1944.

Capra, P. C., & Dittes, J. E. Birth order as a selective factor among volunteer subjects. *Journal of Abnormal and Social Psychology,* 1962, *64,* 302.

Carlsmith, J. M., Ellsworth, P. C., and Aronson, E. *Methods of research in social psychology.* Reading, MA: Addison-Wesley, 1976.

Carlson, J., Cook, S. W., & Stromberg, E. L. Sex differences in conversation. *Journal of Applied Psychology,* 1936, *20,* 727–735.

Cartter, A. M. *An Assessment of Quality in Graduate Education.* Washington: American Council on Education, 1966.

Chai, T. R. A content analysis of the obituary notices on Mao Tse-Tung. *Public Opinion Quarterly,* 1977–1978, *41,* 475–487.

Chapman, C., and Risley, T. R. Anti-litter procedures in an urban high-density area. *Journal of Applied Behavior Analysis,* 1974, *7,* 377–383.

Chapple, E. D. Quantitative analysis of complex organizational systems. *Human Organization,* 1962, *21,* 67–80.

Chicago Tribune Task Force. Auto repairs: Proceed with caution. In T. D. Cook, M. L. Del Rosario, K. M. Hennigan, M. M. Mark, and W. M. K. Trochim (Eds.), *Evaluation Studies Review Annual,* 1978, *3,* 716–734.

Christensen, D., and Sprague, R. Reduction of hyperactive behavior by conditioning procedures alone and combined with methylphenidate. *Behavior Research and Therapy,* 1973, *11,* 331–343.

Christensen, H. T. Cultural relativism and premarital sex norms. *American Sociological Review,* 1960, *25,* 31–39.

Church, T. W., Jr. Plea bargains, concessions and the courts: Analysis of a quasi-experiment. *Law and Society,* 1976, *10,* 377–401.

Cialdini, R. B., and Baumann, D. J. Littering. A new unobtrusive measure of attitude. Unpublished manuscript, 1980.

Cialdini, R. B., Borden, R. J., Thorne, A., Walker, R. M., Freeman, S., and Sloan, R. E. Basking in reflected glory: Three football field studies. *Journal of Personality and Social Psychology,* 1976, *34,* 366–375.

Cialdini, R. B., Vincent, J. E., Lewis, S. K., Catalan, T., Wheeler, D., and Darby, B. L. Reciprocal concession procedure for inducing compliance: The door-in-the-face technique. *Journal of Personality and Social Psychology,* 1975, *31,* 206–215.

Ciminero, A. R., Calhoun, K. S., and Adams, H. E. (Eds.) *Handbook of behavioral assessment,* New York: John Wiley and Sons, 1977.

Clark, G. K. *The critical historian.* London: Heinemann Educational Books, Ltd., 1967.

Clark, K. *America's psychologists.* Washington, D. C.: American Psychological Association, 1957.

Clark, R. D. III. Automobile purchases during the energy crisis: Trading up and down in size. Unpublished manuscript, Florida State University, 1980.

Clark, R. D., III, Grove, J. B., and Sechrest, L. Wedding and engagement announcements: Some unexpected uses. Unpublished manuscript, 1980.

Clark, W. H. A study of some of the factors leading to achievement and creativity with special reference to religious skepticism and belief. *Journal of Social Psychology*, 1955, *41*, 57–69. (Abstracted in M. I. Stein & S. J. Heinze [Eds.], *Creativity and the individual.* Glencoe, Ill.: Free Press, 1960. Pp. 147–148.)

Cogley, J. Cited in D. McCahill, Parleys to evaluate Catholics. *Chicago Sun-Times,* June 8, 1963, *16*, 12.

Coleman, J., Katz, E. & Menzel, H. The diffusion of an innovation among physicians. *Sociometry,* 1957, *20*, 253–270.

Conrad, B. *The death of Manolete.* Cambridge: Houghton Mifflin, 1958.

Cook, S. W., & Sellitz, C. A multiple-indicator approach to attitude measurement. *Psychological Bulletin,* 1964, *62*, 36–55.

Cook, T. D., and Campbell, D. T. *Quasi-experimentation: Design and analysis issues for field settings.* Chicago: Rand McNally College Publishing Company, 1979.

Coombs, C. *A theory of data.* New York: Wiley, 1963.

Cooper, H. J. Occupation and season of birth. *Journal of Social Psychology,* 1973, *89*, 109–114.

Cooper, S. L. Random sampling by telephone: a new and improved method. *Journal of Marketing Research,* 1964, *1*, 45–48.

Cox, C. M. *The early mental traits of three hundred geniuses.* Stanford, Calif.: Stanford Univer. Press, 1926.

Cox, G. H., & Marley, E. The estimation of motility during rest or sleep. *Journal of Neurology, Neurosurgery and Psychiatry,* 1959, *22*, 57–60.

Craddick, R. A. Size of Santa Claus drawings as a function of time before and after Christmas. *Journal of Psychological Studies,* 1961, *12*, 121–125.

Craddick, R. A. Size of witch drawings as a function of time before, on, and after Halloween. *American Psychologist,* 1962, *17*, 307. (Abstr.)

Crespi, L. P. The interview effect on polling. *Public Opinion Quarterly,* 1948, *12*, 99–111.

Cronbach, L. J. Response sets and test validity. *Educational and Psychological Measurement,* 1946, *6*, 475–494.

Cronbach, L. J. Proposals leading to analytic treatment of social perception scores. In R. Tagiuri & L. Petrullo (Eds.), *Person perception and interpersonal behavior,* Stanford, Calif.: Stanford Univer. Press, 1958. Pp. 353–379.

Cronbach, L. J.; Glesser, G. C., Nanda, H., and Rajaratnam, N. *The dependability of behavioral measurements: Theory of generalizability for scores and profiles.* New York: Wiley, 1972.

Crosby, F., Bromley, S., and Saxe, L. Recent unobtrusive studies of black and white discrimination and prejudice: A literature review. *Psychological Bulletin,* 1980, *87,* 546–563.

Cross, H. J., and Aron, R. D. The relationship of unobtrusive measures of marital conflict to remembered differences between parents. *Proceedings of the 79th Annual Convention of the American Psychological Association,* 1971, *6,* 365–366.

Crowald, R. H. Soviet grave markers indicate how buried rated with regime. *El Universal* (Mexico City), August 15, 1964, *196,* 12.

Cunningham, M. R. Weather, mood, and helping behavior: Quasi experiments with the sunshine Samaritan. *Journal of Personality and Social Psychology,* 1979, *37,* 1947–1956.

Dabbs, J. M. Jr. Portable apparatus for recording direct frontal views of conversing subjects' faces. *Behavior Research Methods and Instrumentation,* 1979, *11,* 531–532.

Dabbs, J. M. Jr. Personal communication, July, 1980.

Dabbs, J. M. Jr. Personal communication, August 1980.

Dabbs, J. M. Jr., and Clower, B. J. An ultrasonic motion detector, with data on stare, restriction of movement, and startle. *Behavior Research Methods, and Instrumentation,* 1973, *5,* 475–476.

Dabbs, J. M. Jr., Johnson, J. E., and Leventhal, H. Palmar sweating: A quick and simple measure. *Journal of Experimental Psychology,* 1968, *78,* 347–350.

Dabbs, J. M. Jr., and Moorer, J. P. Jr. Core body temperature and social arousal. *Personality and Social Psychology Bulletin,* 1975, *1,* 517–520.

Dabbs, J. M. Jr., and Neuman, M. R. Telemetry of human cerebral temperature. *Psychophysiology,* 1978, *15,* 599–603.

Dabbs, J. M. Jr., and Stokes, N. A. III. Beauty is power: The use of space on the sidewalk. *Sociometry,* 1975, *38,* 551–557.

Dabbs, J. M. Jr., and Wheeler, P. A. Gravitation toward walls among human subjects. *Social Behavior and Personality,* 1976, *4,* 121–125.

Dalton, M. Preconceptions and methods in *Men Who Manage.* In P. E. Hammond (Ed.), *Sociologists at work.* New York: Basic Books, 1964. Pp. 50–95.

Daly, M., and Wilson, M. *Sex, evolution, and behavior.* North Scituate, MA: Duxbury Press, 1978.

Dannenmaier, W., and Thumin, F. J. Authority status as a factor in perceptual distortion of size. *Journal of Social Psychology,* 1964, *63,* 361–365.

Darwin, C. *The expression of the emotions in man and animals.* London: Murray, 1872.

Davis, F. J. Crime news in Colorado newspapers. *American Journal of Sociology,* 1952, *57,* 325–330.

Davis, M., Seibert, R., and Breed, W. Interracial seating patterns on New Orleans public transit. *Social Problems,* 1966, *13,* 298–306.

Deaux, K. K. Honking at the intersection: A replication and extension. *Journal of Social Psychology,* 1971, *84,* 159–160.

Deaux, K. Anonymous altruism: Extending the lost letter technique. *Journal of Social Psychology,* 1974, *92,* 61–66.

DeCharms, R., & Moeller, G. Values expressed in American children's readers: 1800–1950. *Journal of Abnormal and Social Psychology,* 1962, *64,* 136–142.

Deci, E. L. *Intrinsic motivation.* New York: Plenum Press, 1975.

Deck, L. D. Short workers of the world, unite! In Tie Line, *Psychology Today,* 1971, *5,* 102.

Dempsey, P. Liberalism-conservatism and party loyalty in the U. S. Senate. *Journal of Social Psychology,* 1962, *56,* 159–170.

Deutsch, M. An experimental study of the effects of cooperation and competition upon group process. *Human Relations,* 1949, *2,* 199–231.

Dexter, E. G. Weather influences. New York: The Macmillan Company, 1904.

Dexter, L. A. What do congressmen hear? In N. Polsby, R. Dentler, & P. Smith (Eds.), *Politics and social life.* Boston: Houghton Mifflin, 1963. Pp. 485–495.

Dexter, L. A. Communications—pressure, influence or education? In L. A. Dexter & D. M. White (Eds.), *People, society and mass communications.* New York: Free Press, 1964. Pp. 394–409.

Diener, E., and Crandall, R. *Ethics in social and behavioral research.* Chicago: University of Chicago Press, 1978.

Digon, E., and Bock, H. Suicides and climatology. *Archives of Environmental Health,* 1966, *12,* 279–286.

Dittman, A. T., & Wynne, L. C. Linguistic techniques and the analysis of emotionality in interviews. *Journal of Abnormal and Social Psychology,* 1961, *63,* 201–204.

Dollard, J., & Mowrer, O. H. A method for measuring tension in written documents. *Journal of Abnormal and Social Psychology,* 1947, *42,* 3–32.

Domhoff, G. W. Researching the ruling class in America: A guide to published sources. Unpublished paper, University of California at Santa Cruz, 1978.

Donley, R. E., and Winter, D. G. Measuring the motives of public officials at a distance: An exploratory study of American presidents. *Behavioral Science,* 1970, *15,* 227–236.

Donnelly, R. C., Goldstein, J., & Schwartz, R. D. *Criminal law.* New York: Free Press, 1962.

Doob, A. N., and Gross, A. E. Status of frustrator as an inhibitor of horn-honking responses. *Journal of Social Psychology,* 1968, *76,* 213–218.

Doob, L. W. *Communication in Africa.* New Haven: Yale Univer. Press, 1961.

Dornbusch, S., & Hickman, L. Other-directedness in consumer goods advertising: a test of Riesman's historical theory. *Social Forces,* 1959, *38,* 99–102.

DuBois, C. N. Time Magazine's fingerprints' study. *Proceedings: 9th Conference, Advertising Research Foundation.* New York: Advertising Research Foundation, 1963.

Duncan, C. P. Personal communication, 1963.

Durand, J. Mortality estimates from Roman tombstone inscriptions. *American Journal of Sociology,* 1960, *65,* 365–373.

Durkheim, E. *Suicide.* Trans. J. A. Spaulding & G. Simpson. Glencoe, Ill.: Free Press, 1951.

Dykman, B. M., and Reis, H. T. Personality correlates of classroom seating position. *Journal of Educational Psychology,* 1979, *71,* 346–354.

Ebbesen, E. B. and Haney, M. Flirting with death: Variables affecting risk taking at intersections. *Journal of Applied Social Psychology,* 1973, *3,* 303–324.

Eck, J. E., and Riccio, L. J. Relationship between reported crime rates and victimization survey results: An empirical and analytical study. *Journal of Criminal Justice,* 1979, *7,* 293–308.

Ehrle, R. A., & Johnson, B. G. Psychologists and cartoonists. *American Psychologist,* 1961, *16,* 693–695.

Eisenstadt, M. Parental loss and genius. *American Psychologist,* 1978, *33,* 211–223.

Ekelblad, F. A. *The statistical method in business.* New York: Wiley, 1962.

Ekman, P., and Friesen, W. V. Nonverbal leakage and clues to deception. *Psychiatry,* 1969, *32,* 88–106.

Ellgring, J. II. Personal communication, July 24, 1980.

Ellgring, J. II., and Clarke, A. H. Kommunikative verhaltensweisen des menschen. Unpublished manuscript. Max Planck Institute for Psychiatry, Munich, Germany, 1977.

Ellis, N. R., & Pryer, R. S. Quantification of gross bodily activity in children with severe neuropathology. *American Journal of Mental Deficiency,* 1959, *63,* 1034–1037.

Enciso, J. *Design motifs of ancient Mexico.* New York: Dover, 1953.

Endler, N. S., Rushton, J. P., and Roediger, H. L., III. Productivity and scholarly impact (citations) of British, Canadian, and U.S. departments of psychology (1975). *American Psychologist,* 1978, *33,* 1064–1082.

Erikson, K. T. A comment on disguised observation in sociology. *Social Problems,* 1967, *14,* 366–373.

Ettlie, J. E. Validation of an unobtrusive measure of technological utilization. *Psychological Reports,* 1977, *40,* 123–128.

Evans, W. M. Peer-group interaction and organizational socialization: a study of employee turnover. *American Sociological Review,* 1963, *28,* 429–435.

Evans, R. I., Rozelle, R. M., Lasater, T. M., Demobroski, T. M., and Allen, B. P. Fear arousal, persuasion, and actual versus implied behavioral change: New perspective utilizing a real life dental hygiene program. *Journal of Personality and Social Psychology,* 1970, *16,* 220–227.

Exline, R. V. Explorations in the process of person perception: visual interaction in relation to competition, sex and affiliation. *Journal of Personality,* 1963, *31,* 1–20.

Exline, R. V. *Affective phenomena and the mutual glance: effects of evaluative feedback and social reinforcement upon visual interaction with an interviewer.* Technical Report No. 12, Office of Naval Research Contract No. Nonr-2285(02), 1964.

Exline, R. V., Thibout, J., Brannan, C., and Gumpert, P. Visual interaction in relation to Machiavellianism and an unethical act. Technical Report No. 16, Office of Naval Research, Washington, D.C., 1966.

Exline, R. V., & Winters, L. C. *Interpersonal preference and the mutual glance.* Technical Report No. 13, Office of Naval Research Contract No. Nonr-2285(02), 1964.

Eyer, J. Review of mental illness and the economy. *International Journal of Health Services,* 1976, *6,* 139–148.

Feldman, R. E. Response to compatriot and foreigner who seek assistance. *Journal of Personality and Social Psychology,* 1968, *10,* 202–214.

Feshbach, S., & Feshbach, N. Influence of the stimulus object upon the complementary and supplementary projection of fear. *Journal of Abnormal and Social Psychology,* 1963, *66,* 498–502.

Festinger, L., Schachter, S., and Back, K. *Social pressures in informal groups: A study of human factors in housing.* Stanford, CA: Stanford University Press, 1950.

Fidler, D. S., and Kleinknecht, R. E. Randomized response versus direct questioning: Two data-collection methods for sensitive information. *Psychological Bulletin,* 1977, *84,* 1045–1049.

Fiedler, F. E. The nature of teamwork. *Discovery,* February 1962.

Fiedler, F. E., Dodge, J. S., Jones, R. E., & Hutchins, E. B. Interrelations among measures of personality adjustment in nonclinical populations. *Journal of Abnormal and Social Psychology,* 1958, *56,* 345–351.

Field, M. *Children and films: a study of boys and girls in the cinema.* Dunfermline, Fife: Carnegie United Kingdom Trust, 1954.

Fischer, H. K., and Dlin, B. M. Psychogenic determination of time of illness or death by anniversary reactions and emotional deadlines. *Psychometrics,* 1972, *32,* 170–173.

Fisher, I. *The making of index numbers.* Boston: Houghton Mifflin, 1923.

Fiske, D. W. Values, theory and the criterion problem. *Personnel Psychology,* 1951, *4,* 93–98.

Fiske, S. T. Attention and weight in person perception: The impact of negative and extreme behavior. *Journal of Personality and Social Psychology,* 1980, *38,* 889–906.

Flagler, J. M. Profiles: student of the spontaneous. *New Yorker,* December 10, 1960, *36,* 59–92.

Fleiss, J. L. *Statistical methods for rates and proportions.* New York: John Wiley and Sons, 1973.

Flood, B., Ewy, W., Scott, W. R., Forrest, W. H., and Brown, B. W. The relationship between intensity and duration of medical services and outcomes for hospitalized patients. *Medical Care,* 1979, *17,* 1088–1102.

Flugel, J. C. *Psychology of clothes.* London: Hogarth, 1930.

Follette, W. T., and Cummings, N. A. Psychiatric services and medical utilization in a prepaid health plan setting. *Medical Care,* 1967, *5,* 25–35.

Foote, E. Pupil dilation—new measurement of ad's effictiveness. *Advertising Age,* March 5, 1962, *33,* 12.

Forbes, G. B., and Gromoll, H. F. The lost letter technique as a measure of social variables: some exploratory findings. *Social Forces,* 1971, *50,* 113–115.

Forbes, G. B., TeVault, R. K., and Gromoll, H. F. Willingness to help strangers as a function of liberal, conservative, or Catholic church membership: a field study with the lost-letter technique. *Psychological Reports,* 1971, *28,* 947–949.

Foshee, J. G. Studies in activity level: I. simple and complex task performances in defectives. *American Journal of Mental Deficiency,* 1958, *62,* 882–886.

Foss, R. D., and Dempsey, C. B. Blood donation and the foot-in-the door technique: A limiting case. *Journal of Personality and Social Psychology,* 1979, *37,* 580–590.

Fowler, E. M. Help-wanted ads show sharp rise. *New York Times,* May 13, 1962, *III,* 1.

Foxx, R. M., and Hake, D. F. Gasoline conservation: A procedure for measuring and reducing the driving of college students. *Journal of Applied Behavior Analysis,* 1977, *10,* 61–74.

Fraser, S. Food choice preferences in obese and normal weight children: Teasing the fat eye. Paper presented at meeting of the Western Psychological Association, Portland, Ore., 1972.

Freedom of Information Act. *United States Statutes at Large,* 1974, *88,* 1561–1565.

Freeman, L. C., & Ataov, T. Invalidity of indirect and direct measures of attitude toward cheating. *Journal of Personality,* 1960, *28,* 443–447.

Freire-Maia, N. Inbreeding levels in American and Canadian populations: A comparison with Latin America. *Eugenics Quarterly*, 1968, *15*, 22–33.

French, E. G. Some characteristics of achievement motivation. *Journal of Experimental Psychology*, 1955, *50*, 232–236.

Freud, S. *Psychopathology of everyday life*. London: Unwin, 1920.

Freund, K. A laboratory method for diagnosing the predominance of homo- or hetero-erotic interest in the male. *Behaviour Research and Therapy*, 1963, *1*, 85–93.

Friedman, H. S., DiMatteo, M. R., and Hertz, T. I. Nonverbal communication on television news: the facial expressions of broadcasters during coverage of a presidential election campaign. *Personality and Social Psychology Bulletin*, 1980, *6*, 427–435.

Friedman, M., and Rosenman, R. H. *Type A Behavior and Your Heart* New York: Alfred A. Knopf, 1974.

Fry, C. L. The religious affiliations of American leaders. *Scientific Monthly*, 1933, *36*, 241–249. (Abstracted in M. I. Stein & S. J. Heinze [Eds.], *Creativity and the individual*. Glencoe, Ill.: Free Press, 1960. Pp. 148–149.)

Gabriele, C. T. *The recording of audience reactions by infrared photography*. Technical Report, NAVTRADEVCEN 269-7-56, 1956.

Gaetner, S., and Bickman, L. Effects of race on the elicitation of helping behavior: The wrong number technique. *Journal of Personality and Social Psychology*, 1971, *20*, 218–222.

Gage, N. L., & Shimberg, B. Measuring senatorial progressivism. *Journal of Abnormal and Social Psychology*, 1949, *44*, 112–117.

Gallup, G. G. Self-awareness in primates. *American Scientist*, 1979, *67*, 417–421.

Galton, F. *Hereditary genius*. New York: D. Appleton, 1870. (Abstracted in M. I. Stein, & S. J. Heinze [Eds.], *Creativity and the individual*. Glencoe, Ill.: Free Press, 1960. Pp. 85–90.)

Galton, F. Statistical inquiries into the efficacy of prayer. *Fortnightly Review*, 1872, *12*, 125–135.

Galton, F. Measurement of character. *Fortnightly Review*, 1884, *36*, 179–185.

Galton, F. The measure of fidget. *Nature*, 1885, *32*, 174–175.

Garner, W. R. Context effects and the validity of loudness scales. *Journal of Experimental Psychology*, 1954, *48*, 218–224.

Garner, W. R., Hake, H. W., & Eriksen, C. W. Operationism and the concept of perception. *Psychological Review*, 1956, *63*, 149–159.

Gary, A. L., & Glover, J. *Eye color, sex, and children's behavior.* Chicago: Nelson-Hall Publishers, 1976.

Gastil, R. D. The relationship of regional cultures to educational performance. *Sociology of Education*, 1972, *45*, 408–425.

Gastil, R. D. *Cultural regions of the United States.* Seattle and London: University of Washington Press, 1976.

Gearing, F. The response to a cultural precept among migrants from Bronzeville to Hyde Park. Unpublished master's thesis, Univer. of Chicago, June, 1952.

Ghiselli, E. E., & Brown, C. W. *Personnel and industrial psychology,* (2nd ed.) New York: McGraw-Hill, 1955.

Gibson, H. B. A slang vocabulary test as an indicator of delinquent association. *British Journal of Social and Clinical Psychology,* 1964, *3,* 50–55.

Gibson, H. B. The validation of a technique for measuring delinquent association by means of vocabulary. *British Journal of Social and Clinical Psychology,* 1966, *5,* 190–195.

Ginsburg, H. J., Fling, S., Hope, M. L., Musgrove, D., and Andrews, C. Maternal holding preferences: A consequence of newborn head-turning response. *Child Development,* 1979, *50,* 280–281.

Goffman, E. *The presentation of self in everyday life.* Garden City, New York: Doubleday, 1959.

Goldman, R., Jaffa, M., and Schachter, S. Yom Kippur, Air France, dormitory food, and the eating behavior of obese and normal persons. *Journal of Personality and Social Psychology,* 1968, *10,* 117–123.

Goldstein, A., and Brown, B. W. Urine testing schedules in methadone maintenance treatment of heroin addiction. *Journal of the American Medical Association,* 1970, *214,* 311–315.

Goldstein, R. S., Minkin, B. L., Minkin, N., and Baer, D. M. Finders, keepers?: An analysis and validation of a free-found-ad policy. *Journal of Applied Behavior Analysis,* 1978, *11,* 465–473;and in *Evaluation Studies Review Annual,* Vol. 4. Beverly Hills: Sage Publications, 1979.

Goldwater, B. C. Psychological significance of pupillary movements. *Psychological Bulletin,* 1972, *77,* 340–355.

Golson, H. L., and Dabbs, J. M. Jr. Line-following tendencies among pedestrians: A sex difference. Unpublished manuscript, Georgia State University, Atlanta, GA.

Goncourt, E. de, and J. de *The Goncourt Journals 1851–1870* New York: Doubleday & Co., 1937.

Gordon, T. The development of a method of evaluating flying skill. *Personnel Psychology,* 1950, *3,* 71–84.

Gore, P. M., & Rotter, J. B. A personality correlate of social action. *Journal of Personality,* 1963, *31,* 58–64.

Gosnell, H. F. *Getting out the vote: an experiment in the stimulation of voting.* Chicago: Univer. of Chicago Press, 1927.

Gottschalk, L. A., & Gleser, G. C. An analysis of the verbal content of suicide notes. *British Journal of Medical Psychology,* 1960, *33,* 195–204.

Goulden, J. C. Sex, the press, and Ted Kennedy: Does he or doesn't he? Should anybody care? *Washingtonian,* 1979 (December), *15,* (3), 9–11.

Gourman, J. *The Gourman report: A rating of American and international universities.* Los Angeles: National Election Standards, 1977.

Grace, H., & Tandy, M. Delegate communication as an index of group tension. *Journal of Social Psychology,* 1957, *45,* 93–97.

Grauer, F. L. On deadline effects: Intra-day trading volume on the New York Stock Exchange. In E. J. Webb (Ed.), *Papers for the March, 1973 Deadline Conference.* Unpublished manuscript, Graduate School of Business, Stanford University, 1973.

Green, H. B., & Knapp, R. H. Time judgment, aesthetic preference, and need for achievement. *Journal of Abnormal and Social Psychology,* 1959, *58,* 140–142.

Greenhill, L. P. The recording of audience reactions by infrared photography. Technical report from Pennsylvania State Univer. to U.S. Navy, Special Devices Center, SPECDEVCEN 269-7-56, September 20, 1955, pp. 1–11.

Greenwald, H. J. A disguise for obtaining self-report data. *Psychological Reports,* 1967, *21,* 400.

Grey, D. L., and Brown, T. R. Letters to the editor: Hazy reflections of public opinion. *Journalism Quarterly,* 1970, *47,* 450–456, 471

Griffith, R. M. Odds adjustments by American horse race bettors. *American Journal of Psychology,* 1949, *62,* 290–294.

Grove, J. B., and Sechrest, L. Nonreactive and attitude measures of Navy recruit companies. Unpublished manuscript, Florida State University, 1980.

Groves, R., and Kahn, R. *Surveys by telephone.* New York: Academic Press, 1979.

Grusky, O. Organizational goals and the behavior of informal leaders. *American Journal of Sociology,* 1959, *65,* 59–67.

Grusky, O. The effects of formal structure on managerial recruitment: a study of baseball organization. *Sociometry,* 1963, *26,* 345–353. (a)

Grusky, O. Managerial succession and organizational effectiveness. *American Journal of Sociology,* 1963, *69,* 21–31. (b)

Guion, R. M. Criterion measurement and personnel judgments. *Personnel Psychology,* 1961, *14,* 141–149.

Guilford, J. P. The relation of intellectual factors to creative thinking in science. In C. Taylor (Ed.), *The 1955 University of Utah research conference on the identification of creative scientific talent.* Salt Lake City: Univer. of Utah Press, 1956. Pp. 69–95.

Gullahorn, J., & Strauss, G. The field worker in union research. In R. N. Adams & J. J. Preiss (Eds.), *Human organization research.* Homewood, Ill.: Dorsey Press, 1960. Pp. 153–165.

Gump, R. *Jade: stone of heaven.* New York: Doubleday, 1962.

Gusfield, J. R. Fund work reciprocities in studying a social movement. In R. N. Adams & J. J. Preiss (Eds.), *Human organization research.* Homewood, Ill.: Dorsey Press, 1960. Pp. 99–108.

Haas, A. Male and female spoken language differences: Stereotypes and evidence. *Psychological Bulletin,* 1979, *86,* 616–626.

Hafner, E. M., & Presswood, S. Strong inference and weak interactions. *Science,* 1965, *149,* 503–510.

Haggard, E. A., Brekstad, A., & Skard, A. G. On the reliability of the anamnestic interview. *Journal of Abnormal and Social Psychology,* 1960, *61,* 311–318.

Halbwachs, M. *Les causes de suicide.* Paris: Felix Alcan, 1930.

Hale, W. B. *The Story of a Style.* New York: B. W. Huebsch, 1920.

Hall, E. T. Silent assumption in social communication. *Disorders of Communication,* 1964, *42,* 41–55.

Hall, J. A. Gender effects in decoding nonverbal cues. *Phychological Bulletin,* 1978, *85,* 845–857.

Hake, D. F., and Foxx, R. M. Promoting gasoline conservation: The effects of reinforcement schedule, a leader, and self-recording. *Behavior Modification,* 1978, *2,* 339–369.

Hamburger, P. Peeping Funt. *New Yorker,* January 7, 1950, *25,* 72–73.

Hamilton, C. *The book of autographs.* New York: Simon and Schuster, 1978.

Hamilton, T. Social optimism in American protestanism. *Public Opinion Quarterly,* 1942, *6,* 280–283.

Hansen, A. H. Cycles of prosperity and depression in the United States. *Univ. of Wisconsin Studies in Social Sciences and History.* Madison, 1921.

Hanson, N. R. *Patterns of discovery.* Cambridge: Cambridge Univer. Press, 1958.

Harper, R. G., and Wiens, A. N. Nonverbal behaviors as unobtrusive measures. In L. Sechrest (Ed.), *Unobtrusive measurement today.* San Francisco: Jossey Bass, 1979, pp. 59–73.

Harper, R. G., Wiens, A. N., and Matarazzo, J. D. *Nonverbal communication: State of the art.* New York: Wiley, 1978.

Hartmann, G. W. A field experiment on the comparative effectiveness of "emotional" and "rational" political leaflets in determining election results *Journal of Abnormal and Social Psychology,* 1936, *31,* 99–114.

Hartshorne, H., & May, M. A. *Studies in the nature of character.* Vol. 1. *Studies in deceit.* New York: Macmillan, 1928.

Hartshorne, H., May, M. A., & Maller, J. B. *Studies in the nature of character.* Vol. 2. *Studies in service and self control.* New York: Macmillan, 1929.

Hastorf, A. H., Northcraft, G. B., and Picciotto, S. R. Helping the handicapped: How realistic is the performance feedback received by the physically handicapped. *Personality and Social Psychology Bulletin*, 1979, *5*, 373–376.

Hayes, D. P., and Meltzer, L. Bone-conducting microphones. *American Journal of Psychology*, 1967, *80*, 619–624.

Hayes, D. P., Meltzer, L., and Lundberg, S. Information distribution, interdependence, and activity levels. *Sociometry*, 1968, *31*, 162–179.

Health Care Financing Administration. *Research report: Professional standards review organization 1980 program evaluation.* Baltimore, MD: Health Care Financing Administration, 1980.

Helson, H., Blake, R. R., & Mouton, J. S. Petition-signing as adjustment to situational and personal factors. *Journal of Social Psychology*, 1958, *48*, 3–10.

Henle, M., & Hubble, M. B. "Egocentricity" in adult conversation. *Journal of Social Psychology*, 1938, *9*, 227–234.

Henley, N. *Body politics: Power, sex, and nonverbal communication.* Englewood Cliffs, N.J.: Prentice-Hall, Inc., 1977.

Henry, A. F. and Short, J. F. Jr. *Suicide and homicide: some economic, sociological, and psychological aspects of aggression.* New York: The Free Press, 1954.

Henry, H. *Motivation research: its practice and uses for advertising, marketing, and other business purposes.* London: Crosby Lockwood, 1958.

Herbert-Jackson, E., and Risley, T. R. Behavioral nutrition: Consumption of foods of the future by toddlers. *Journal of Applied Behavior Analysis*, 1977, *10*, 407–413.

Hermann, J. A., deMontes, A. I., Dominguez, B., Montes, F., and Hopkins, B. L. Effects of bonuses for punctuality on the tardiness of industrial workers. *Journal of Applied Behavior Analysts*, 1973, *6*, 563–570.

Hermann, M. G. Assessing the personalities of Soviet Politburo members. *Personality and Social Psychology Bulletin*, 1980, *6*, 332–352.

Herron, R. E., and Ramsden, R. W. A telepedometer for the remote measurement of human locomotor activity. *Psychophysiology*, 1967, *4*, 112–115.

Hess, E. H., & Polt, J. M. Pupil size as related to interest value of visual stimuli. *Science*, 1960, *132*, 349–350.

Heumann, M. A note on plea bargaining and case pressure. *Law and Society*, 1975, *9*, 515–528.

Heusler, A., Ulett, G., & Blasques, J. Noise-level index: an objective measurement of the effect of drugs on the psychomotor activity of patients. *Journal of Neuropsychiatry*, 1959, *1*, 23–25.

Heusler, A. F., Ulett, G. A., & Callahan, J. D. Comparative EEG studies of tranquilizing drugs. Research Laboratories of the St. Louis State Hospital, St. Louis, Mo. Paper read at Pan-American Medical Congress, Mexico City, May 3, 1960.

Heyns, R., & Lippitt, R. Systematic observational techniques. In G. Lindzey (Ed.), *Handbook of social psychology.* Vol. 1. Cambridge: Addison-Wesley, 1954. Pp. 370–404.

Hiatt, M. *The way women write.* New York: Teachers College Press, 1977.

Hildum, D. C., & Brown, R. W. Verbal reinforcement and interviewer bias. *Journal of Abnormal and Social Psychology,* 1956, *53,* 108–111.

Hillebrandt, R. H. Panel design and time-series analysis. Unpublished master's thesis, Northwestern Univer., 1962.

Hinkley, E. D., and Rethlingshafer, D. Value judgments of height of men by college students. *Journal of Psychology,* 1951, *31,* 257–262.

Hodgkinson, H. Cited in Human factors: Unobtrusive measures. *Behavior Today,* 1971, (November 22), *2,* 3.

Holahan, C. Seating patterns and patient behavior in an experimental dayroom. *Journal of Abnormal Psychology,* 1972, *80,* 115–124.

Holmes, D. S., Curtright, C. A., McCaul, K. D., and Thissen, D. Biorhythms: Their utility for predicting postoperative recuperative time, death, and athletic performance. *Journal of Applied Psychology,* 1980, *65,* 233–236.

Holmes, L. D. *Ta'u: Stability and change in a Samoan village.* Reprint No. 7. Wellington, N.Z.: Polynesian Society, 1958.

Hoover, E. D. Index numbers: Practical applications. In W. H. Kruskal and J. M. Tanur (Eds.), *International encyclopedia of statistics.* New York: Free Press/Macmillan, 1978, *5,* 456–463.

Hooper, C. H., and Dabbs, J. M. Jr. Self and friend's views of the asymmetry of the face. Paper presented at the Annual Meeting of the American Psychological Association, Montreal, Canada, September, 1980.

Horst, P. Correcting the Kuder-Richardson reliability for dispersion of item difficulties. *Psychological Bulletin,* 1953, *50,* 371–374.

Hovland, C. I., and Sears, R. R. Minor studies of aggression: VI. Correlation of lynchings with economic indices. *Journal of Psychology,* 1940, *9,* 301–310.

Hughes, E. C. *Men and their work.* Glencoe, Ill.: Free Press, 1958.

Humphrey, R. Personal communication, May 2, 1980.

Humphreys, L. G. Note on the multitrait-multimethod matrix. *Psychological Bulletin,* 1960, *57,* 86–88.

Humphreys, L. *Tearoom trade.* Chicago: Aldine, 1970.

Huston, T. L. Ambiguity of acceptance, social desirability, and dating choice. *Journal of Experimental Social Psychology,* 1973, *9,* 32–42.

Hyman, H. H., Cobb, W. J., Feldman, J. J., Hart, C. W., & Stember, C. H. *Interviewing in social research.* Chicago: Univer. of Chicago Press, 1954.

Ianni, F. A. Residential and occupational mobility as indices of the acculturation of an ethnic group. *Social Forces*, 1957–58, *36*, 65–72.

Imanishi, K. Social organization of subhuman primates in their natural habitat. *Current Anthropology*, 1960, *1*, 393–407.

Inn, A. and Wheeler, A. C. Individual differences, situational constraints, and police shooting incidents. *Journal of Applied Social Psychology*, 1977, *7*, 19–26.

Jackson, B. Documentary truth: Working notes. *Afterimage*, 1978, (Summer), *8*, 40.

Jacoby, J., and Aranoff, D. Political polling and the lost-letter technique. *Journal of Social Psychology*, 1971, *83*, 209–212.

Jacques, E. Measurement of responsibility. Cambridge: Harvard Univer. Press, 1956.

Jaffe, A. J., & Stewart, C. D. *Manpower, resources and utilizations.* New York: Wiley, 1951.

Jahoda-Lazarsfeld, M., and Zeisel, H. *Die Arbeitslösen von Marienthal.* Leipzig: Hirzel, 1932.

James, J. A preliminary study of the size determinant in small group interaction. *American Sociological Review*, 1951, *16*, 474–477.

James, R. W. A technique for describing community structure through newspaper analysis. *Social Forces*, 1958, *37*, 102–109.

James, W. *The principles of psychology.* New York: Holt, 1890.

Janis, I. L., & Hovland, C. I. An overview of persuasibility research. In I. L. Janis & C. I. Hovland (Eds.), *Personality and persuasibility.* New Haven: Yale Univer. Press, 1959. Pp. 1–26.

Janowitz, M. Inferences about propaganda impact from textual and documentary analysis. In W. E. Daugherty & M. Janowitz (Eds.), *A psychological warfare casebook.* Baltimore: Johns Hopkins Press, 1958. Pp. 732–735.

Jay, R., & Copes, J. Seniority and criterion measures of job proficiency. *Journal of Applied Psychology*, 1957, *41*, 58–60.

Jay, T. B. A bibliography of research on dirty word usage. *Journal Supplement Abstract Service: Catalog of Selected Documents in Psychology*, 1979, *9*, 77.

Jay, T. B. Sex roles and dirty word usage: A review of the literature and a reply to Haas. *Psychological Bulletin*, 1980, *88*, 614–621.

Jelenko, C., III The "rock syndrome": A newly discovered environmental hazard. *The Journal of Irreproducible Results*, 1980, *26*, 14.

Johnson, C. F. Hyperactivity and the machine: The acometer. *Child Development*, 1971, *42*, 2105–2110.

Johnson, S. M., and Bolstad, O. D. Reactivity to home observation: A comparison of audio recorded behavior with observers present or absent. *Journal of Applied Behavior Analysis*, 1975, *8*, 181–185.

Johnson, S. M., Christensen, A., and Bellamy, G. T. Evaluations of family interventions through unobtrusive audio recordings: Experiences in "bugging" children. *Journal of Applied Behavior Analysis,* 1976, *9,* 213–219.

Joint Committee on New York Drug Law Evaluation. *The nation's toughest drug law: Evaluating the New York experience: Final report.* Washington, D.C.: National Institute of Law Enforcement and Criminal Justice, LEAA, 1978.

Jones, E. E., Davis, K. E., and Gergen, K. J. Role playing variations and their informational value for person perception. *Journal of Abnormal and Social Psychology,* 1961, *63,* 302–310.

Jones, J. M., and Hochner, A. R. Racial differences in sports activities: A look at the self-paced versus reactive hypothesis. *Journal of Personality and Social Psychology,* 1973, *27,* 86–96.

Jones, V. Character development in children: an objective approach. In L. Carmichael (Ed.), *Manual of child psychology.* New York: Wiley, 1946. Pp. 707–751.

Jorgenson, D. O., Guardabascio, P., Higginson, C., Sutton, D., and Watkins, J. Contents of graffiti and bumper stickers as measures of political behavior. *Perceptual and Motor Skills,* 1977, *45,* 630.

Jorgenson, D. O., and Lange, C. Graffiti content as an index of political interest. *Perceptual and Motor Skills,* 1975, *40,* 616–618.

Joyce, C. R. B., and Welldon, R. M. C. The objective efficacy of prayer: A double-blind clinical trial. *Journal of Chronic Diseases,* 1965, *18,* 367–377.

Juris, M. and Velden, M. The pupillary response to mental overload. *Physiological Psychology,* 1977, *5,* 421–424.

Kadish, S. On the tactics of police-prosecution oriented critics of the courts. *Cornell Law Quarterly,* 1964, *49,* 436–477.

Kahn, R. L., & Cannell, C. F. *The dynamics of interviewing: theory, technique and cases.* New York: Wiley, 1957.

Kaiser, E. H. and Halberg, F. Circadian periodic aspects of birth. *Annals of the New York Academy of Science,* 1962, *98,* 1056–1000.

Kallman, W. M., and Feuerstein, M. Psychophysiological procedures. In A. R. Ciminero, K. S. Calhoun, and H. E. Adams (Eds.), *Handbook of behavioral assessment.* New York: John Wiley and Sons, 1977

Kane, F Clothing worn by out-patients to interviews. *Psychiatric Communications,* 1958, *1,* (2).

Kane, F. Clothing worn by an out-patient: a case study. *Psychiatric communications,* 1959, *2,* (2).

Kane, F. The meaning of the form of clothing. *Psychiatric Communications,* 1962, *5,* (1).

Karlin, R. A., Rosen, L. S., and Epstein, Y. M. Three into two doesn't go: A follow-up on the effects of overcrowded dormitory rooms. *Personality and Social Psychology Bulletin,* 1979, *5,* 391–395.

Kassajarian, H. H. Voting intentions and political perception. *Journal of Psychology,* 1963, *56,* 85–88.

Katz, D. Do interviewers bias poll results? *Public Opinion Quarterly*, 1942, *6*, 248–268.

Kelly, G. A. *The psychology of personal constructs*. New York: Norton, 1955.

Kendall, L. M. The hidden variance: What does it measure? *American Psychologist*, 1963, *18*, 452.

Kerlinger, F. N. *Foundations of behavioral research: educational, psychological, and sociological inquiry.* 2nd edition. New York: Holt, Rinehart, and Winston, 1973.

Kendon, A. Some functions of gaze direction in social interaction. *Acta Psychologica*, 1967, *26*, 22–63.

Kinsey, A. C., Pomeroy, W. B., Martin, C. E., & Gebhard, P. H. *Sexual behavior in the human female.* Philadelphia: W. B. Saunders, 1953.

Kitsuse, J. I., & Cicourel, A. V. A note on the uses of official statistics. *Social Problems*, 1963, *11*, 131–139.

Kleinke, C. L., and Singer, D. A. Influence of gaze on compliance with demanding and conciliatory requests in a field setting. *Personality and Social Psychology Bulletin*, 1979, *5*, 386–390.

Klockars, C. B., and O'Connor, F. W. *Deviance and decency: The ethics of research with human subjects.* Beverly Hills, Calif.: Sage, 1979.

Knox, J. B. Absenteeism and turnover in an Argentine factory. *American Sociological Review*, 1961, *26*, 424–428.

Kopelman, R. E., and Pantaleno, J. J. Rejection, motivation and athletic performance: Is there a traded player syndrome? *Perceptual and Motor Skills*, 1977, *45*, 827–834.

Kosloski, K., Schnelle, J., and Littlepage, G. Relationships between descriptive client characteristics and absenteeism from a mental health center. *Journal of Community Psychology*, 1977, *5*, 238–240.

Krajick, K. Seattle: Sifting through the ashes. *Police Magazine*, 1979 (July), 10–11.

Kramarae, C. *Women and men speaking.* Rowley, MA: Newburg House, in press.

Kramer, E. Judgment of personal characteristics and emotions from nonverbal properties of speech. *Psychological Bulletin*, 1963, *60*, 408–420.

Kramer, E. Elimination of verbal cues in judgments of emotion from voice. *Journal of Abnormal and Social Psychology*, 1964, *68*, 390–396.

Krasner, L. Studies of the conditioning of verbal behavior. *Psychological Bulletin*, 1958, *55*, 148–170.

Kretsinger, E. A. An experimental study of gross bodily movement as an index to audience interest. *Speech Monographs*, 1952, *19*, 244–148.

Kretsinger, E. A. An experimental study of restiveness in preschool educational television audiences. *Speech Monographs*, 1959, *26*, 72–77.

Krout, M. H. Further studies on the relation of personality and gestures: A nosological analysis of autistic gestures. *Journal of Experimental Psychology*, 1937, *20*, 279–287.

Krout, M. H. *Major aspects of personality*. Chicago: College Press, 1933.

Krout, M. H. Gestures and attitudes: an experimental study of the verbal equivalents and other characteristics of a selected group of manual autistic gestures. Unpublished doctoral dissertation, Univer. of Chicago, 1951.

Krout, M. H. An experimental attempt to determine the significance of unconscious manual symbolic movements. *Journal of General Psychology*, 1954, *51*, 121–152. (a)

Krout, M. H. An experimental attempt to produce unconscious manual symbolic movements. *Journal of General Psychology*, 1954, *51*, 93–120. (b)

Krueger, L. E. & Ramond, C. K. References. In M. Mayer, *The intelligent man's guide to sales measures of advertising*. New York: Advertising Research Foundation, 1965. Pp. 29–71.

Krugman, H. E. Some applications of pupil measurement. *Journal of Marketing Research*, 1964, *1*, 15–19.

Kuhn, T. *The structure of scientific revolutions*. Chicago Univer. of Chicago Press, 1962.

Kunter, N. G., and Brogan, D. An investigation of sex-related slang vocabulary and sex-role orientation among male and female university students. *Journal of Marriage and the Family*, 1974, *36*, 474–484.

Kupcinet, I. Kup's column. *Chicago Sun-Times*, March 9, 1965. *18*, 46.

Kutchinsky, B. The effect of easy availability of pornography on the incidence of sex crimes: The Danish experience. *Journal of Social Issues*, 1973, *29*, 163–181.

LaFrance, M., and Mayo, C. Racial differences in gaze behavior: Two systematic observational studies. *Journal of Personality and Social Psychology*, 1976, *33*, 547–552.

Landis, C. National differences in conversation. *Journal of Abnormal and Social Psychology*, 1927, *21*, 354–357.

Landis, M. H., & Burtt, H. E. A study of conversations. *Journal of Comparative Psychology*, 1924, *4*, 81–89.

Landis, C., & Hunt, W. A. *The startle pattern*. New York: Farrar & Rinehart, 1939.

Lang, K., & Lang, G. E. Decisions for Christ: Billy Graham in New York City. In M. Stein, A. J. Vidich, & D. M. White (Eds.), *Identity and anxiety* Glencoe, Ill.: Free Press, 1960 Pp. 415–427.

Larwood, L., Zalkind, D., and Legault, J. The bank job: A field study of sexually discriminatory performance on a neutral-role task. *Journal of Applied Social Psychology,* 1975, *5,* 68–74.

Lasswell, H. D. The world attention survey. *Public Opinion Quarterly,* 1941, *5,* 456–462.

Lau, R. R. and Russell, D. Attributions in the sports pages. *Journal of Personality and Social Psychology,* 1980, *39,* 29–38.

Law Enforcement Assistance Administration. *Criminal victimization surveys in thirteen American cities.* Washington, D.C.: U.S. Department of Justice, 1975.

Lee, M. Patterns of gasoline consumption in Michigan and their implications for rationing and alternative conservation policies: A disaggregate analysis. Unpublished doctoral dissertation, University of Michigan, 1980.

Lehman, H. C., & Witty, P. A. Scientific eminence and church membership. *Scientific Monthly,* 1931, *36,* 544–549. (Abstracted in M. I. Stein, & S. J. Heinze, *Creativity and the individual.* Glencoe, Ill.: Free Press, 1960. Pp. 149–50.)

Leipold, W. D. Psychological distance in a dyadic interview as a function of introversion-extraversion, anxiety, social desirability and stress. Unpublished doctoral dissertation, Univer. of North Dakota, 1963.

Lenski, G. E., & Leggett, J. C. Caste, class, and deference in the research interview. *American Journal of Sociology,* 1960, *65,* 463–467.

Lepper, M. R., Greene, D., and Nisbett, R. E. Undermining children's intrinsic interest with extrinsic reward: A test of the "oversufficient justification" hypothesis. *Journal of Personality and Social Psychology,* 1973, *28,* 129–137.

Lerman, P. Argot, symbolic deviance, and subcultural delinquency. *American Sociological Review,* 1967, *32,* 209–224.

Leroy-Boussion, A. Etude du comportement émotional enfantin au cours de la projection d'un film comique. *Revue Internationale de Filmologie,* 1954, *5,* 105–123.

Lester, K. Effect of suicide prevention centers on suicide rates in the United States. *Health Services Reports,* 1974, *89,* 37–39.

Levin, P. F., and Isen, A. M. Further studies on the effect of feeling good on helping. *Sociometry,* 1975, *38,* 141–147.

Levine, D. W., O'Neal, E. C., Garwood, S. G., and McDonald, P. J. Classroom ecology: The effects of seating position on grades and participation. *Personality and Social Psychology Bulletin,* 1980, *6,* 409–412.

Levine, F. M., and Grinspoon, L. Telemetered heart rate and skin potential of a chronic schizophrenic patient especially during periods of hallucinations and periods of talking. *Journal of Consulting and Clinical Psychology,* 1971, *37,* 345–350.

Levine, R. V., West, L. J., and Reis, H. T. Perceptions of time and punctuality in the United States and Brazil. *Journal of Personality and Social Psychology*, 1980, *38*, 541–550.

Levy, S. Getting in: The rules of the game. *New York*, 1980 (June 30), *13*, 24.

Lewin, H. S. Hitler youth and the Boys Scouts of America. *Human Relations*, 1947, *1*, 206–227.

Lewis, O. *The children of Sanchez*. New York: Random House, 1961.

Libby, W. I. Accuracy of radio-carbon dates. *Science*, 1963, *140*, 278–280.

Lincoln, Y. S. Documentary analysis and record utilization: New uses for old methods. Paper prepared for presentation at the Annual Meeting, American Educational Research Association, Boston, MA, April, 1980.

Lindzey, G. *Projective techniques and cross-cultural research*. New York: Appleton-Century-Crofts, 1961.

Lingle, J. H., Brock, T. C., and Cialdini, R. B. Surveillance instigates entrapment when violations are observed, when personal involvement is high, and when sanctions are severe. *Journal of Personality and Social Psychology*, 1977, *35*, 419–429.

Link, A. S. Personal communication, November 26, 1980.

Lippmann, W. *The public philosophy*. New York: New American Library, 1955.

Livingston, J. S. Myth of the well-educated manager. *Harvard Business Review*, 1971 (January–February), 79–89.

Lockard, J. S., McDonald, L. L., Clifford, D. A., and Martiniz, R. Panhandling: Sharing of resources. *Science*, 1976, *191*, 406–408.

Lodge, G. T. Pilot stature in relation to cockpit size: a hidden factor in Navy jet aircraft accidents. *American Psychologist*, 1963, *17*, 468. (Abstr.)

Lofland, J. Comment on "Initial interaction of newcomers in Alcoholics Anonymous." *Social Problems*, 1961, *8*, 365–367.

Logsdon, D. M. A study of the meaningfulness of criterion and norm-referenced reliability indices in assessing the validity of mastery rates. Unpublished doctoral dissertation, Florida State University, 1979.

Lombroso, C. *The man of genius*. London: Walter Scott, 1891. (Abstracted in M. I. Stein, & S. J. Heinze, *Creativity and the individual*. Glencoe, Ill.: Free Press, 1960. Pp. 350–353.)

Long, S. B. The continuing debate over the use of ratio variables: Facts and fiction. In K. F. Schuessler (Ed.), *Sociological methodology 1980*. San Francisco: Jossey-Bass, 1980, 37–67.

Los Angeles Times. April 20, 1980, Part VII, p. 2.

Louis, A. M. The worst American city: A scientific study to confirm or deny your prejudices. *Harper's Magazine*, 1975, January, 67–71.

Lowe, J. C. and Moryadas, S. *Spatial interaction: The geography of movement.* New York: Houghton Mifflin, 1975.

Lucas, D. B., & Britt, S. H. *Advertising psychology and research.* New York: McGraw-Hill, 1950.

Lucas, D. B., & Britt, S. H. *Measuring advertising effectiveness.* New York: McGraw-Hill, 1963.

Lunden, W. A. *Crime and Criminals.* Ames: Iowa State Univ. Press, 1967.

Lykken, D. T. Psychology and the lie detector industry. *American Psychologist,* 1974, *29,* 725–739.

Lynn, J. G., and Lynn, D. R. Smile and hand dominance in relation to basic modes of adaptation. *Journal of Abnormal and Social Psychology,* 1943, *38,* 250–276.

Mabie, E. A study of the conversion of first-grade pupils during free play periods. *Journal of Educational Research,* 1931, *24,* 135–138.

Mabley, J. Mabley's report. *Chicago American,* January 22, 1963, *62,* 3.

Macaulay, D. A. *Motel of the mysteries.* Boston: Houghton Mifflin, 1979.

Maccoby, E. E. Developmental psychology. In P. R. Farnsworth, O. McNemar, & Q. McNemar (Eds.), *Annual Review of Psychology,* 1964, *15,* 203–250.

MacKinney, A. C. What should ratings rate? *Personnel,* 1960, *37,* 75–78.

MacRae, D. The role of the state legislator in Massachusetts. *American Sociological Review,* 1954, *19,* 185–194. (a)

MacRae, D. Some underlying variables in legislative roll call votes. *Public Opinion Quarterly,* 1954, *18,* 191–196. (b)

MacRae, D., & MacRae, E. Legislators' social status and their votes. *American Journal of Sociology,* 1961, *66,* 599–603.

Maher, B. A. *Principles of psychopathology: An experimental approach.* New York: McGraw-Hill, 1966.

Mahl, G. Disturbances and silences in the patient's speech in psychotherapy. *Journal of Abnormal and Social Psychology,* 1956, *53,* 1–15.

Manago, B. R. Mad: Out of the comics rack and into satire. *Add One,* 1962, *1,* 41–46.

Mankoff, M. Studying the invisible hand behind the writings on the wall: Towards the demystification of graffitists and graffiti. Unpublished manuscript.

Mann, F. C., Indik, B. P., and Vroom, V. H. *The productivity of work groups.* Ann Arbor, MI: Institute for Social Research, 1963.

Markle, G. E. Sex ratio at birth: Values, variance, and some determinants. *Demography,* 1974, *11,* 131–142.

Marsh, R. M. Formal organization and promotion in a pre-industrial society. *American Sociological Review,* 1961, *26,* 547–556.

Martin, G. B. Responsive distress in human neonates. Unpublished doctoral dissertation, Florida State University, 1980.

Martin, P. I call on the Candid Camera man. *Saturday Evening Post,* May 27, 1961, *234,* 26–27.

Masters, W., and Johnson, V. E. *Human sexual response.* Boston: Little, Brown, 1966.

Matarazzo, J. D. Control of interview bahavior. Paper read at American Psychological Association, St. Louis, September, 1962.

Matarazzo, J. D., Weitman, M., Saslow, G., & Wiens, A. N. Interviewer influence on duration of interviewee speech. *Journal of Verbal Learning and Verbal Behavior,* 1963, *1,* 451–458.

Matarazzo, J. D., Wiens, A. N., Saslow, G., Dunham, R. M., & Voas, R. B. Speech durations of astronaut and ground communicator. *Science,* 1964, *143,* 148–150.

Matejcek, Z. Report from Prague: Studies of unwanted and wanted children. In H. P. David and J. Bernheim (Eds.) *Proceedings of the conference on psychosocial factors in transnational family planning research.* Washington: American Institutes for Research, 1970.

Matthews, T. S. *The sugar pill.* New York: Simon & Schuster, 1957.

Mavalwala, J. Dermatoglyphics: An international bibliography. The Hague: Mouton Publishers, 1077.

May, M. A., & Hartshorne, H. First steps toward a scale for measuring attitude. *Journal of Educational Psychology,* 1927, *17,* 145–162.

Mazur-Hart, S. F., and Berman, J. J. Changing from fault to no-fault divorce: An interrupted time series analysis. In L. Sechrest, S. G. West, M. A. Phillips, R. Redner, and W. Yeaton (Eds.), *Evaluation studies review annual* (Vol. 4). Beverly Hills; Sage Publications, 1979. Also in *Journal of Applied Psychology,* 1977, *1,* 300–312.

McCarroll, J. R., & Haddon, W. A controlled study of fatal accidents in New York City. *Journal of Chronic Diseases,* 1961. *15,* 811–826.

McCarthy, D. A comparison of children's language in different situations and its relation to personality traits. *Journal of Genetic Psychology,* 1929, *36,* 583–591.

McCarthy, P. J. Index numbers. Sampling. In W. H. Kruskal and J. M. Tanur (Eds.), *International encyclopedia of statistics.* New York: Free Press/Macmillan, 1978, *5,* 463–467.

McClelland, D. C. *The achieving society.* Princeton: Van Nostrand, 1961.

McClelland, D. C. Love and power: The psychological signals of war. *Psychology Today,* 1975, *8,* 44–48.

McCord, J. A thirty-year follow-up of treatment effects. *American Psychologist,* 1978, *33,* 284–289.

McDonald, P. J., and Eilenfield, V. C. Physical attractiveness and the approach/avoidance of self-awareness. *Personality and Social Psychology Bulletin.* 1980, *6,* 391–395.

McFarland, J. N., Peacock, L. J., and Watson, J. A. Mental retardation and activity level in rats and children. *American Journal of Mental Deficiency,* 166, *71,* 376–380.

McGovern, J. L., and Holmes, D. S. Influence of sex and dress on cooperation: An instance of "person" chauvinism. *Journal of Applied Social Psychology,* 1976, *6,* 206–20.

McGranahan, D., & Wayne, I. German and American traits reflected in popular drama. *Human Relations,* 1948, *1,* 429–455.

McGrath, J. E. The influence of positive interpersonal relations on adjustment and effectiveness in rifle teams. *Journal of Abnormal and Social Psychology,* 1962, *65,* 365–375.

McGraw, M., & Molloy, L. B. The pediatric anamnesis: inaccuracies in eliciting developmental data. *Child Development,* 1941, *12,* 255–265.

McKendry, J. M., and Parco, S. A. A community development rating scale for Philippine poblaciones. Technical Report 857-R-4. State College: HRB-Singer, Inc., 1967.

Mechanic, D., & Volkart, E. H. Stress, Illness behavior and the sick role. *American Sociological Review,* 1961, *26,* 51–58.

Mednick, S., and Christiansen, K. O. (Eds.) *Biosocial bases of criminal behavior.* New York: Gardner Press, Inc., 1977.

Mednick, S. A., Schulsinger, F., Higgins, J., and Bell, B. *Genetics, environment and psychopathology.* Amsterdam: North Holland/Elsevier, 1974.

Meier, P. & Zabell, S. Benjamin Pierce and the Howland will. *Journal of the American Statistical Association,* 1980, *75,* 497–506.

Melbin, M. Organization practice and individual behavior: absenteeism among psychiatric aides. *American Sociological Review,* 1961, *26,* 14–23.

Melton, A. W. Some behavior characteristics of museum visitors. *Psychological Bulletin,* 1933, *30,* 720–721. (a)

Melton, A. W. Studies of installation at the Pennsylvania Museum of Art. *Museum News,* 1933, *11,* 508. (b)

Melton, A. W. Problems of installation in museums of art. *Studies in museum education.* Washington, D. C.: American Association of Museums, 1935.

Melton, A. W. Distribution of attention in galleries in a museum of science and industry. *Museum News,* 1936, *13,* 3, 5–8.

Melton, A. W., Feldman, N. G., & Mason, C. W. Experimental studies of the education of children in a museum of science. *Publications of the American Association of Museums,* New Series, No. 15, 1936.

Menzel, E. W. Jr. Naturalistic and experimental approaches to primate behavior. In E. P. Willems and H. L. Raush (Eds.), *Naturalistic viewpoints in psychological research.* New York: Holt, Rinehart, and Winston, 1969.

Merritt, C. B., & Fowler, R. G. The pecuniary honesty of the public at large. *Journal of Abnormal and Social Psychology,* 1948, *43,* 90–93.

Michigan Daily. Watered down. October 31, 1980.

Middlemist, D., Knowles, E. S., and Matter, C. F. Personal space invasions in the lavatory: Suggestive evidence for arousal. *Journal of Personality and Social Psychology,* 1976, *33,* 541–546.

Middleton, R. Fertility values in American magazine fiction: 1916–1956. *Public Opinion Quarterly,* 1960, *24,* 139–143.

Midwest Research Institute. *Quality of life indicators in the U.S. metropolitan areas.* Kansas City, Missouri, 1970.

Miklich, D. R. Radio telemetry in clinical psychology and related areas. *American Psychologist,* 1975, *30,* 419–425.

Miklich, D. R., Chai, H., Purcell, K., Weiss, J. H., and Brady, K. Naturalistic observation of emotions preceding low pulmonary flow rates. *Journal of Allergy and Clinical Immunology,* 1974, *53,* 102 (abstract)

Milgram, S. Behavioral study of obedience. *Journal of Abnormal and Social Psychology,* 1963, *67,* 371–378.

Milgram, S. The lost letter technique. *Psychology* Today, 1969 (June), *3,* 30,ff.

Milgram, S., Mann, L., and Harter, S. The lost letter technique: A tool of social research. *Public Opinion Quarterly,* 1965, *29,* 437–438.

Miller, G. A. Population, distance and the circulation of information. *American Journal of Psychology,* 1947, *60,* 276–284.

Miller, J. A. Wearing the right clos. *Science News,* 1980 (June 21), *117,* 396–397.

Miller, N. A study of the number of persons with records of arrest or conviction in the labor force. Springfield, Virginia: National Technical Information Service, 1979.

Miller, P. M., Hersen, M., Eisler, R. M., and Watts, J. G. Contingent reinforcement of lowered blood/alcohol levels in an outpatient chronic alcoholic. *Behavior Research and Therapy,* 1974, *12,* 261–263.

Mills, F. C. *The behavior of prices.* New York: National Bureau of Economic Research, 1927.

Mindak, W. A., Neibergs, A., & Anderson, A. Economic effects of the Minneapolis newspaper strike. *Journalism Quarterly,* 1963, *40,* 213–218.

Minneapolis Star, Drummond, B. Statistics mislead: Black illegitimacy not rising. May 22, 1978, 2–A.

Mintz, A. A re-examination of correlations between lynchings and economic indices. *Journal of Abnormal and Social Psychology,* 1946, *41,* 154–160.

Mintz, N. L. Effects of esthetic surroundings: II. Prolonged and repeated experience in a "beautiful" and an "ugly" room. *The Journal of Psychology,* 1956, *41,* 459–466.

Mischel, W., Ebbesen, E. B. and Zeiss, A. R. Selective attention to the self: Situational and dispositional determinants. *Journal of Personality and Social Psychology,* 1973, *27,* 129–142.

Mita, T. H., Dermer, M., and Knight, J. Reversed facial images and the mere-exposure hypothesis. *Journal of Personality and Social Psychology,* 1977, *35,* 597–601.

Mitchell, S. K. Interobserver agreement, reliability, and generalizability of data collected in observational studies. *Psychological Bulletin,* 1979, *86,* 376–390.

Mitchell, W. C. *Index numbers of wholesale prices in the U.S. and foreign countries: I. the making and using of index numbers.* Bulletin No. 284. Washington, D.C.: U.S. Department of Labor, Bureau of Labor Statistics, 1921.

Mockridge, N. *The scrawl of the wild: What people write on walls— and why.* Cleveland: The World Publishing Company, 1968.

Montagu, J. D., and Swarbick, L. Effect of amphetamines in hyperkinetic children: Stimulant or sedative? A pilot study. *Developmental Medicine and Child Neurology,* 1975, *15,* 293–298.

Montanye, T., II, Mulberry, R. F., and Hardy, K. R. Assessing prejudice toward Negroes at three universities using the lost-letter technique. *Psychological Reports,* 1971, *29,* 531–537.

Moody, D. Campsite litter: Tagging the culprit. *The Seattle Times,* November 11, 1974, 4A.

Moore, H. T. Laboratory tests of anger, fear, and sex interest. *American Journal of Psychology,* 1917, *28,* 390–395.

Moore, H. T. Further data concerning sex differences. *Journal of Abnormal and Social Psychology,* 1922, *17,* 210–214.

Moore, W. E. The exploitability of the "labor force" concept. *American Sociological Review,* 1953, *18,* 68–72.

Morgan, E. M. *Basic problems of evidence.* New York: Joint Committee on Continuing Legal Education of the American Law Institute and the American Bar Association, 1963.

Morgenstern, O. *On the accuracy of economic observations.* (2nd ed.) Princeton: Princeton Univer. Press, 1963.

Morisey, M. Linear bookings rise in wake of skyjackings. *Washington Post,* September 16, 1970, D-8.

Morris, D. *Manwatching: A field guide to human behavior.* New York: Harry N. Abrams, Inc., 1977.

Morris, J. N., Heady, J. A., and Raffle, P. A. B. Physique of London busmen: epidemiology of uniforms. *Lancet,* 1966 (Sept.), 569–570.

Mosteller, F. Use as evidenced by an examination of wear and tear on selected sets of EES. In K. Davis *et al.,* A study of the need for a new encyclopedic treatment of the social sciences. Unpublished manuscript, 1955. Pp. 167–174.

Mosteller, F., & Wallace, O. L. Inference in an authorship problem: a comparative study of discrimination methods applied to the authorship of *The Federalist Papers. Journal of the American Statistical Association.* 1963. *58*, 275–309.

Mudgett, B. D. *Index numbers.* New York: Wiley, 1951.

Murphy, G., & Murphy, L. Soviet life and Soviet psychology. In R. A. Bauer (Ed.), *Some views on Soviet psychology.* Washington, D.C.: American Psychological Association, 1962. Pp. 253–276.

Murphy-Berman, V., and Berman, J. The importance of choice and sex in invasions of interpersonal space. *Personality and Social Psychology Bulletin,* 1978, *4*, 424–428.

Nadler, A. "Good looks do not help:" effects of helper's physical attractiveness and expectations for future interaction on help-seeking behavior. *Personality and Social Psychology Bulletin,* 1980, *6*, 378–383.

Nagel, S. Ethic affiliations and judicial propensities. *Journal of Politics,* 1962, *24*, 92.

Napolean, T., Chassin, L., and Young, R. A replication and extension of "physical attractiveness." *Journal of Abnormal Psychology,* 1980, *89*, 250–253.

Naroll, R. The preliminary index of social development. *American Anthropologist,* 1956, *58*, 687–715.

Naroll, R. Controlling data quality. In Series Research in Social Psychology. *Symposia Studies Series,* No. 4, September, 1960. Pp. 7–12.

Naroll, R. Two solutions to Galton's problems. *Philosophy of Science,* 1961, *28*, 15–39.

Naroll, R. *Data quality control.* Glencoe, Ill.: Free Press, 1962.

Naroll, R., & Naroll, F. On bias of exotic data. *Man,* 1963, *25*, 24–26.

National Advertising Company. *Shopping center research study.* Bedford Park, Ill.: Author, 1963.

Neider, C. (Ed.) *The autobiography of Mark Twain.* New York: Harper Bros., 1959, p. 3.

New Orleans States, February 11, 1970.

New York Times, Researchers find people's glances tell whole story. May 20, 1970.

New York Times, April 1980.

Newsweek. Senator Salinger? August 10, 1964, *63*, 28.

Nisbett, R. E. and Wilson, T. D. Telling more than we can know: Verbal reports on mental processes. *Psychological Review,* 1977, *84*, 231–259.

Nobile, P. Garbage collector trashes Nixon. *New York,* 1980, *13* (June 30), 12.

Norman, D. A. Slips of the mind and an outline for a theory of action. Technical report No. 7905, Office of Naval Research, 1979.

North, R. C., Holsti, O. R., Zaninovich, M. G., & Zinnes, D. A. *Content analysis.* Evanston, Ill.: Northwestern University Press, 1963.

Olson, W. C. *The measurement of nervous habits in normal children.* Minneapolis: Univer. of Minnesota Press, 1929.

Orne, M. T. The nature of hypnosis: artifact and essence. *Journal of Abnormal and Social Psychology,* 1959, *58,* 277–299.

Orne, M. T. On the social psychology of the psychological experiment: with particular reference to demand characteristics and their implications. *American Psychologist,* 1962, *17,* 776–783.

Orne, M. T. & Evans, F. J. Social control in the psychological experiment: antisocial behavior and hypnosis. *Journal of Personality and Social Psychology,* 1965, *1,* 189–200.

Orne, M. T., & Scheibe, K. E. The contribution of nondeprivation factors in the production of sensory deprivation effects: the psychology of the "panic button." *Journal of Abnormal and Social Psychology,* 1964, *68,* 3–12.

Orten, J. D., and Bell, W. J. Study described in P. Horn, Personal graffiti: The rogue's tatoo. *Psychology Today,* 1974, *7*(8), 26, 90.

Osborn, D. Own height, similarity to other, and judgment of other's height. Unpublished doctoral dissertation, Northwestern University, 1973.

Osgood, C. E. *Method and theory in experimental psychology.* New York: Oxford Univer. Press, 1953.

Osgood, C. E. & Walker, E. Motivation and language behavior: a content analysis of suicide notes. *Journal of Abnormal and Social Psychology,* 1959, *59,* 58–67.

OSS Assessment Staff. *Assessment of men.* New York: Rinehart, 1948.

Paisley, W. J. Identifying the unknown communicator in painting, literature and music: the significance of minor encoding habits. *Journal of Communication,* 1964, *14,* 219–237.

Palmer, J., and McGuire, F. L. The use of unobtrusive measures in mental health research. *Journal of Consulting and Clinical Psychology,* 1973, *40,* 431–436.

Parker, E. B. The effects of television on public library circulation. *Public Opinion Quarterly,* 1963, *27,* 578–589.

Participant. Recent longevity studies. 1972 (November), p. 4.

Patterson, M. L., and Sechrest, L. Interpersonal distance and impression formation. *Journal of Personality,* 1970, *38,* 161–166.

Paul, G. L. and Lentz, R. J. *Psychosocial treatment of chronic mental patients: Milieu versus social-learning programs.* Cambridge, MA: Harvard University Press, 1978.

Pearson, K. *The life, letters and labours of Francis Galton.* Vol. 1. Cambridge: Cambridge Univer. Press, 1914.

Perrine, M., & Wessman, A. W. Disguised public opinion interviewing with small samples. *Public Opinion Quarterly,* 1954, *18,* 92–96.

Persinger, M. S. Lag response in mood reports to changes in the weather matrix. *International Journal of Biometeorology,* 1975, *19,* 108–114.

Phillips, D. P. Deathday and birthday: An unexpected connection. In J. M. Tanur, F. Mosteller, W. H. Kruskal, R. F. Link, R. S. Pieters, and G. R. Rising (Eds.), *Statistics: A guide to the unknown.* San Francisco: Holden-Day, Inc., 1972.

Phillips, D. P. Motor vehicle fatalities increase just after publicized suicide stories. *Science,* 1977, *196,* 1464–1465.

Phillips, D. P. Airplane accident fatalities increase just after newspaper stories about murder and suicide. *Science,* 1978, *201,* 748–750.

Phillips, D. P., and Feldman, K. A. A dip in deaths before ceremonial occasions: Some new relationships between social integration and mortality. *American Sociological Review,* 1973, *38,* 678–696.

Phillips, R. H. Miami goes Latin under Cuban tide. *New York Times,* March 18, 1962, *111,* 85.

Pileggi, N. Secrets of a private eye. *New York,* 1976 (October 4), 38–45.

Platt, J. R. Strong inference. *Science,* 1964, *146,* 347–353.

Polansky, N., Freeman, W., Horowitz, M., Irwin, L., Paponia, N., Rapaport, D., & Whaley, F. Problems of interpersonal relations in research on groups. *Human Relations,* 1949, *2,* 281–291.

Politz Media Studies. *The readers of "The Saturday Evening Post."* Philadelphia: Curtis Publishing Co., 1958.

Politz Media Studies. *A study of outside transit poster exposure.* New York: Alfred Politz, 1959.

Pool, Ithiel de Sola (Ed.). *Trends in content analysis.* Urbana: Univer. of Illinois Press, 1959.

Popov, V. A. Analysis of intonational characteristics of speech as an index of the emotional state of man under conditions of flight in space. *Zhurnal Vysshei Nervnoi Deyatel'nosti,* 1966, *16,* 964–983.

Popper, K. *Logic der Forschung.* Wien: Springer, 1935.

Popper, K. *The logic of scientific discovery.* New York: Basic Books, 1959.

Popper, K. *Conjectures and refutations.* New York: Basic Books, 1962.

Powell, P. H., and Dabbs, J. M., Jr. Physical attractiveness and personal space. *Journal of Social Psychology,* 1976, *100,* 59–64.

Powers, J. Physical distance: A non-reactive measure of social distance among Mexican mental patients. Unpublished thesis, Northwestern University, 1967.

Powis, D. *The signs of crime: A field manual for police.* New York: John Jay Press, 1978.

Priest, R. F., and Sawyer, J. Proximity and peership: Bases of balance in interpersonal attraction. *The American Journal of Sociology,* 1967, *72,* 633–649.

Press, R. M. You can tell a lot about a person by looking at his garbage. *Christian Science Monitor,* May *13,* 1980.

Privacy Act of 1974. *United States Statutes at Large,* 1974, *88.* Washington, D.C.: United States Government Printing Office, 1976.

Prosser, W. L. *Handbook of the law of torts.* (3rd ed.) St. Paul: West, 1964.

Pyles, M. K., Stolz, H. R., & Macfarlane, J. W. The accuracy of mothers' reports on birth and developmental data. *Child Development,* 1935, *6,* 165–176.

Quick, E. L., and Farrow, J. M. An annotated bibliography for initiating research on psychology of native American women. *Journal Supplement Abstract Service: Catalog of Selected Documents in Psychology,* 1980, *10,* 86.

Quine, W. V. *From a logical point of view.* Cambridge: Harvard Univ. Press, 1953.

Rabkin, S. W., Matthewson, F. A. L., and Tate, R. B. Chronobiology of cardiac sudden death in men. *Journal of the American Medical Association,* 1980, *244,* 1357–1358.

Rahe, R. H., and Lind, E. Psychosocial factors and sudden cardiac death: A pilot study. *Journal of Psychosomatic Research,* 1971, *15,* 19–24.

Rankin, R. Personal communication, Dec. 3, 1980.

Rathje, W. L. Trace measures. In L. Sechrest (Ed.) *Unobtrusive measurement today.* San Francisco: Jossey-Bass, 1979.

Rathje, W. L. personal communication, May 28, 1980.

Rathje, W. L., and Hughes, W. W. The garbage project as a nonreactive approach: Garbage in . . . Garbage out? In H. W. Sinaiko and L. A. Broedling (Eds.) *Perspectives on attitude assessment: Surveys and their alternatives.* Washington: Smithsonian Institution, 1975.

Ray, M. L. Cross-cultural content analysis: its promise and its problems. Unpublished manuscript, Northwestern Univ., 1965.

Ray, M. L. and Webb, E. J. Speech duration effects in the Kennedy news conferences. *Science,* 1966, *153,* 899–901.

Reddy, J. Heady thieves find Wheeling their Waterloo. *Chicago Sun-Times,* February 28, 1965, *18,* 66.

Reed, S. J. The heart of dixie: An essay in folk geography. *Social Forces,* 1976, *54,* 925–939.

Reiss, A. J. Jr. *Police and the public.* New Haven, CT: Yale Univ. Press, 1971.

Report of the Advisory Committee to the Surgeon General of the Public Health Service. *Smoking and health.* Washington, D.C.: U.S. Government Printing Office, 1959, p. 177.

Reynolds, P. D. *Ethical dilemmas and social science research: An analysis of moral issues confronting investigators in research using human participants.* San Francisco: Jossey-Bass, 1979.

Rhyne, L. D., and Ullmann, L. P. Graffiti: A nonreactive measure? *The Psychological Record,* 1972, *22,* 255–258.

Richards, J. L., and Finger, S. Mother-child holding patterns: A cross-cultural photographic survey. *Child Development,* 1975, *46,* 1001–1004.

Riesman, D. Orbits of tolerance, interviewers and elites. *Public Opinion Quarterly*, 1956, *20*, 49–73.

Riesman, D. Comment on "The State of Communication Research." *Public Opinion Quarterly*, 1959, *23*, 10–13.

Riesman, D., & Ehrlich, J. Age and authority in the interview. *Public Opinion Quarterly*, 1961, *25*, 39–56.

Riesman, D., & Watson, J. The sociability project: a chronicle of frustration and achievement. In P. E. Hammond (Ed.), *Sociologists at work*. New York: Basic Books, 1964. Pp. 235–321.

Riker, W., & Niemi, D. The stability of coalitions on roll calls in the House of Representatives. *American Political Science Review*, 1962, *56*, 58–65.

Riley, M. W. *Sociological research: I. a case approach*. New York: Harcourt, Brace & World, 1963.

Robbins, L. C. The accuracy of parental recall of aspects of child development and of child rearing practices. *Journal of Abnormal and Social Psychology*, 1963, *66*, 261–270.

Robinson, D., & Rohde, S. Two experiments with an anti-semitism poll. *Journal of Abnormal and Social Psychology*, 1946, *41*, 136–144.

Robinson, E. S. The behavior of the museum visitor. *Publications of the American Association of Museums*, New Series, No. 5, 1928.

Roens, B. B. New findings from Scott's special advertising research study. In *Proceedings: 7th Annual Conference, Advertising Research Foundation*. New York: Advertising Research Foundation, 1961. Pp. 65–70.

Roose, K. D., & Andersen, C. J. *A rating of graduate programs*. Washington, D.C.: American Council on Education, 1970.

Rorer, L. G. The great response-style myth. *Psychological Bulletin*, 1965, *63*, 129–156.

Rosenbaum, M. E. The effect of stimulus and background factors on the volunteering response. *Journal of Abnormal and Social Psychology*, 1956, *53*, 118–121.

Rosenbaum, M. E., & Blake, R. R. Volunteering as a function of field structure. *Journal of Abnormal and Social Psychology*, 1955, *50*, 193–196.

Rosenthal, A. M. Japan, famous for politeness, has a less courteous side, too. *New York Times*, February 25, 1962, *111*, 20.

Rosenthal, R. On the social psychology of the psychological experiment: the experimenter's hypothesis as unintended determinant of experimental results. *American Scientist*, 1963, *51*, 268–283.

Rosenthal, R. *Experimenter effects in behavioral research*. (Enlarged edition.) Halsted/Wiley, 1976.

Rosenthal, R., and Rosnow, R. L. *The volunteer subjects*. New York: Wiley-Interscience, 1975.

Ross, H. L. The inaccessible respondent: a note on privacy in city and country. *Public Opinion Quarterly*, 1963, *27*, 269–275.

Ross, H. L. The neutralization of severe penalties: Some traffic law studies. *Law and Society,* 1976, *10,* 403–413.

Rubenstein, E. A. Television and the young viewer. *American Scientist,* 1978, *66,* 685–693.

Rubington, E. Race relations in a psychiatric hospital. *Human Organization,* 1969, *28,* 128–132.

Ruesch, J., & Kees, W. *Nonverbal communication: notes on the visual perception of human relations.* Berkeley: University of California Press, 1956.

Rugh, J. D. A telemetry system for measuring chewing behavior in humans. *Behavior Research Methods and Instrumentation,* 1971, *3,* 73–77.

Rugh, J. D. Variation in human masticatory behavior under temporal constraints. *Journal of Comparative and Physiological Psychology,* 1972, *80,* 169–174.

Rugh, J. D., and Schwitzgebel, R. L. Variability in commerical electromyographic biofeedback devices. *Behavior Research Methods and Instrumentation,* 1977, *9,* 281–285.

Ruist, E. Index numbers: Theoretical aspects. In W. H. Kruskal and J. M. Tanur (Eds.), *International encyclopedia of statistics.* New York: Free Press/Macmillan, 1978, *5,* 451–456.

Runion, H. L. An objective study of the speech style of Woodrow Wilson. *Speech Monographs,* 1936, *3,* 75–94.

Rush, C. A factorial study of sales criteria. *Personnel Psychology,* 1953, *6,* 9–24.

Russell, G. W., and Drewry, B. R. Crowd size and competitive aspects of aggression in ice hockey: An archival study. *Human Relations,* 1976, *29,* 723–735.

Sansing, J. Speedball and the pimp. *Washingtonian,* 1980, *15* (9), 101–105, 217, 218.

Saks, M., Jr., and Ostrom, T. Anonymity in letters to the editor. *Public Opinion Quarterly,* 1973, *37,* 417–422.

Sales, S. M. Need for stimulation as a factor in social behavior. *Journal of Personality and Social Psychology,* 1971, *19,* 124–134.

Sales, S. M. Threat as a factor in authoritarianism: An analysis of archival data. *Journal of Personality and Social Psychology,* 1973, *28,* 44–57.

Salk, L. The role of the heartbeat in relations between mother and infant. *Scientific American,* 1973, *229,* 24–29.

Salzinger, K. A method of analysis of the process of verbal communication between a group of emotionally disturbed adolescents and their friends and relatives. *Journal of Social Psychology,* 1958, *47,* 39–53.

Sawyer, H. G. The meaning of numbers. Speech before the American Association of Advertising Agencies, 1961.

Schachter, S., and Gross, L. Manipulated time and eating behavior. *Journal of Personality and Social Psychology*, 1968, *10*, 98–106.

Schanck, R. L., & Goodman, C. Reactions to propaganda on both sides of a controversial issue. *Public Opinion Quarterly*, 1939, *3*, 107–112.

Schneidman, E. S., & Farberow, N. L. Some comparisons between genuine and stimulated suicide notes in terms of Mowrer's concepts of discomfort and relief. *Journal of General Psychology*, 1957, *56*, 251–256.

Schriesheim, C. A. Job satisfaction, attitudes toward unions, and voting in a union representation election. *Journal of Applied Psychology*, 1978, *63*, 548–552.

Schubert, G. *Quantitative analysis of judicial behavior*. Glencoe, Ill.: Free Press, 1959.

Schubert, G. *Judicial decision-making*. New York: Free Press, 1963.

Schuman, H. and Converse, J. M. The effect of black and white interviewers on black responses in 1968. *Public Opinion Quarterly*, 1971, *35*, 44–68.

Schutz, R., and Bazerman, M. Ceremonial occasions and mortality: A second look. *American Psychologist*, 1980, *35*, 253–261.

Schwartz, B., and Barsky, S. F. The home advantage. *Social Forces*, 1977, *55*, 641–661.

Schwartz, R. D. Field experimentation in sociolegal research. *Journal of Legal Education*, 1961, *13*, 401–410.

Schwartz, R. D., and Orleans, S. On legal sanctions. *University of Chicago Law Review*, 1967, *34*, 274–300.

Schwitzgebel, R. L. Survey of electromechanical devices for behavior modification. *Psychological Bulletin*, 1968, 70, 444–459.

Schwitzgebel, R. L. A belt from big brother. *Psychology Today*, 1969, *2*, 45–47, 65.

Scully, D., and Bart, R. A funny thing happened on the way to the orifice: Women in gynecology textbooks. *American Journal of Sociology*, 1973, *78*, 283–288.

Seaver, W. B., and Patterson, A. H. Decreasing fuel-oil consumption through feedback and social commendation. *Journal of Applied Behavior Analysis*, 1976, *9*, 147–152.

Sebald, H. Studying national character through comparative content analysis. *Social Forces*, 1962, *40*, 318–322.

Sechrest, L. Situational sampling and contrived situations in assessment of behavior. *Pakistan Journal of Psychology*, 1971, *4*, 3–19.

Sechrest, L., and Flores, L. The handwriting on the wall: Homosexuality in the Philippines and the U.S. *Journal of Social Psychology*, 1969, *79*, 3–12.

Sechrest, L., and Flores, L. The occurrence of a nervous mannerism in two cultures. *Asian Studies,* 1971, *9,* 55–63.

Sechrest, L., Flores, L., and Arellano, L. Language and social interaction in a bilingual culture. *Journal of Social Psychology,* 1968, *76,* 155–161.

Sechrest, L., and Grove, J. B. The lost letter technique: the role of curiosity. Unpublished manuscript, Florida State University, 1980.

Sechrest, L., Grove, J. B., and Clark, R. D. III Aggregate nonreactive performance measures of fraternities. Unpublished manuscript, Florida State University, 1980.

Sechrest, L., Grove, J. B., and Cosgrove, R. Validation of the lost letter technique. Unpublished manuscript, 1980.

Sechrest, L., Grove, J. B., and Cosgrove, R. Lost letters and attitudes toward the death penalty. Unpublished manuscript, Florida State University, 1980.

Sechrest, L., and Olson, A. K. Graffiti in four types of institutions of higher education. *Journal of Sex Research,* 1971, *7,* 62–71.

Sechrest, L. and Phillips, M. Unobtrusive measures: An overview. In L. Sechrest (Ed.), *Unobtrusive Measurement today,* San Francisco: Jossey-Bass, 1979, pp. 1–17.

Sechrest, L., and Sukstorf, S. Parental visitation of the institutionalized retarded. *Journal of Applied Social Psychology,* 1977, *7,* 286–294.

Sechrest, L., & Wallace, J. Figure drawing and naturally occurring events: elimination of the expansive euphoria hypothesis. *Journal of Educational Psychology,* 1964, *55,* 42–44.

Segal, J. Child abuse: A review of research. In E. Corfman (Ed.), *Families today: A research sampler on families and children.* Rockville, Maryland: National Institute of Mental Health, 1979.

Seligman, C. and Darley, J. M. Feedback as a means of decreasing residential energy consumption. *Journal of Applied Psychology,* 1977, *62,* 363–368.

Selltiz, C., Jahoda, M., Deutsch, M., & Cook, S. W. *Research methods in social relations.* New York: Holt, Rinehart & Winston, 1959.

Severin, D. The predictability of various kinds of criteria. *Personnel Psychology,* 1952, *5,* 93–104.

Shadegg, S. C. *How to win an election.* New York: Toplinger, 1964.

Shaver, P., Schurtman, R., and Blank, T. O. Conflict between firemen and ghetto dwellers: Environmental and attitudinal factors. *Journal of Applied Social Psychology,* 1975, *5,* 240–261.

Shepard, H. R., & Blake, R. R. Changing behavior through cognitive change. *Human Organization,* 1962, *21,* 88–92. Published by the Society for Applied Anthropology.

Shils, E. A. Social inquiry and the autonomy of the individual. In D. Lerner (Ed.), *The human meaning of the social sciences.* Cleveland: Meridian, 1959. Pp. 114–157.

Shotland, R. L., Berger, W. G., and Forsythe, R. A validation of the lost-letter technique. *Public Opinion Quarterly*, 1970, *34*, 278–281.

Shulman, A. D. Exploratory literary analysis of interracial behaviors. *Journal of Social Psychology*, 1974, *92*, 127–132.

Siersted, E., & Hansen, H. L. Réaction des petits enfants au cinema: resumé d'une serie d'observations faites au Danemark. *Review Internationale de Filmologie*, 1951, *2*, 241–245.

Sikorski, L. A., Roberts, D. F., and Paisley, W. J. Analyzing letters in mass magazines as "outcroppings" of public concern. Unpublished manuscript, 1967.

Simón, A. Violence in the mass media: A case of modeling. *Perceptual and Motor Skills*, 1979, *48*, 1081–1082.

Simon, W. E. Return rates of "lost" letters as a function of whether the letter is stamped and the apparent importance of the letter. *Psychological Reports*, 1971, *29*, 937–938.

Simon, W. E., and Gillen, M. J. Return rates of "lost" letters as a function of whether the letter is stamped and amount of money apparently in the letter. *Psychological Reports*, 1971, *29*, 141–142.

Simonton, D. K. Sociocultural context of individual creativity: A transhistorical time-series analysis. *Journal of Personality and Social Psychology*, 1975, *32*, 1119–1133.

Simonton, D. K. Biographical determinants of achieved eminence: A multivariate approach to the Cox data. *Journal of Personality and Social Psychology*, 1976, *33*, 218–226.

Simonton, D. K. Eminence, creativity, and geographic marginality: A recursive structural equation model. *Journal of Personality and Social Psychology*, 1977, *35*, 805–16. (a)

Simonton, D. K. Creative productivity, age, and stress: A biographical time series analysis of ten classical composers. *Journal of Personality and Social Psychology*, 1977, *35*, 791–804. (b)

Simonton, D. K. Land Battles, generals, and armies: Individual and situational determinants of victory and casualties. *Journal of Personality and Social Psychology*, 1980, *38*, 110–119.

Singh, P. H., & Huang, S. C. Some socio-cultural and psychological determinants of advertising in India: a comparative study. *Journal of Social Psychology*, 1962, *57*, 113–121.

Sintchak, G., and Geer, J. H. A vaginal plethysmograph system. *Psychophysiology*, 1975, *12*, 113–115.

Sleeper, C B. Samplings of leisure-time conversations to find sex differences in drives. Unpublished, cited in G. Murphy & S. L. Murphy, *Experimental social psychology*. New York: Harper, 1931.

Sletto, R. F. *A construction of personality scales by the criterion of internal consistency*. Hanover, N. H.: Sociological Press, 1937.

Smith, D. M., and Mazis, M. B. Racial self-identification and self-concept by means of unobtrusive measures. *Journal of Social Psychology*, 1976, *98*, 221–228.

Smith, H. T. A comparison of interview and observation methods of mother behavior. *Journal of Abnormal and Social Psychology*, 1958, *57*, 278–282.

Smith, H. *The Russians*. New York: Quadrangle/New York Times Book Company, 1976.

Smolensky, M. To everything there is a season. In *Science News*, 1980 (Sept. 6.), *118*, 150–151.

Solley, C. M., & Haigh, G. A. A note to Santa Claus. *Topeka Research Papers, The Menninger Foundation*, 1957, *18*, 4–5.

Sommer, R. Studies in personal space. *Sociometry*, 1959, *22*, 247–260.

Sommer, R. Further studies of small group ecology. *Sociometry*, 1965, *28*, 337–348.

Sommer, R. Classroom ecology. *Journal of Applied Behavioral Science*, 1967, *3*, 489–503. (a)

Sommer, R. Small group ecology. *Psychological Bulletin*, 1967, *67*, 145–152. (b)

Sommer, R., Knight, H., and Sommer, B. A. Comparison of farmers' market and supermarket produce: Tomatoes and bell peppers. *Journal of Food Science*, 1979, *44*, 1474–1477, 1482.

Sommer, R., Wing, M., and Aitkens, S. Price savings to consumers at farmers' markets. *Journal of Consumer Affairs*, in press.

Spiegel, D. E., & Neuringer, C. Role of dread in suicidal behavior. *Journal of Abnormal and Social Psychology*, 1963, *66*, 507–511.

Stamp, J. *Some economic factors in modern life*. London: P. S. King & Son, Ltd., 1929, 258–259

Stein, J. In "Capitol Comment," *Washingtonian*, 1980 (July), 11.

Stein, M. I., & Heinze, S. J. *Creativity and the individual*. Glencoe, Ill.: Free Press, 1960.

Steiner, I. D. Group dynamics. In P. R. Farnsworth, O. McNemar, & Q. McNemar (Eds.), *Annual Review of Psychology*, 1964, *15*, 421–446.

Steiner, I. D., & Field, W. L. Role assignment and interpersonal influence. *Journal of Abnormal and Social Psychology*, 1960, *61*, 239–245.

Stephan, F. F., & McCarthy, P. J. *Sampling opinions*. New York: Wiley, 1958.

Stewart, J. Q. Empirical mathematical rules concerning the distinction and equilibrium of population. *Geographical Review*, 1947, *37*, 461–485.

Stinchcombe, A. L., McDill, M., and Walker, D. Is there a racial tipping point in changing schools? *Journal of Social Issues*, 1969, *25*, 127–136.

Stoke, S. M., & West, E. D. Sex differences in conversational interests. *Journal of Social Psychology*, 1931, *2*, 120–126.

Stokes, S. J., and Bickman, L. The effect of the physical attractiveness and role of helper on help seeking. *Journal of Applied Social Psychology,* 1974, *4,* 286–294.

Strahan, R. F., Todd, J. B., and Inglis, G. B. A palmar sweat measure particularly suited for naturalistic research. *Psychophysiology,* 1974, *2,* 715–719.

Streeter, L. A., Krauss, R. M., Geller, V., Olson, C., and Apple, W. Pitch changes during attempted deception. *Journal of Personality and Social Psychology,* 1977, *35,* 345–350.

Strodtbeck, F. L. and Hook, L. H. The social dimensions of a twelve man jury table. *Sociometry,* 1961, *24,* 397–415.

Strodtbeck, F. L., & James, R. M. Social process in jury deliberations. Paper read at American Sociological Society, 1955.

Strodtbeck, F. L., James, R. M., & Hawkins, C. Social status in jury deliberations. *American Sociological Review,* 1957, *22,* 713–719.

Strodtbeck, F. L., & Mann, R. D. Sex role differentiation in jury deliberations. *Sociometry,* 1956, *19,* 3–11.

Stuart, I. R. Minorities vs. minorities: cognitive, affective and conative components of Puerto Rican and Negro acceptance and rejection. *Journal of Social Psychology,* 1963, *59,* 93–99.

Sudman, S. and Bradburn, N. M. *Response effects in surveys: A review and synthesis.* Chicago: Aldine Publishing Co., 1974.

Suedfeld, P., and Rank, A. D. Revolutionary leaders: Long-term success as a function of changes in conceptual complexity. *Journal of Personality and Social Psychology,* 1976, *34,* 169–178.

Sullivan, J. L., and Uslaner, E. M. Congressional behavior and electoral marginality. *American Journal of Political Science,* 1978, *22,* 536–553.

Sussman, L. Mass political letter writing in America. *Public Opinion Quarterly,* 1959, *23,* 203–212.

Sussman, L. *Dear F. D. R.* New York: Bedminster, 1963.

Talese, G. *Thy neighbor's wife.* New York: Doubleday, 1980.

Tannenbaum, P. H., and Noah, J. E. Sportugese: A study of sports page communication. *Journalism Quarterly,* 1959, *36,* 163–170.

Tarde, G. *L'Opinion et la foule.* Paris: Felix Alcan, 1901.

Taylor, A. J. W. Tattooing among male and female offenders of different ages in different types of institutions. *Genetic Psychology Monographs,* 1970, *81,* 81–119.

Taylor, R. John Doe, Jr.: A study of his distribution in space, time, and the social structure. *Social Forces,* 1974, *53,* 11–21.

Tedford, W. H., Jr., Hill, W. R., and Hensley, L. Human eye color and reaction time. *Perceptual and Motor Skills,* 1978, *47,* 503–506.

Templer, D. I., Austin, R. K., and Veleber, D. M. Eminent men and women in psychology as manifested by photographs in introductory psychology textbooks. *Journal Supplement Abstract Service,* 1980, *10,* 79.

Tennis, G. H., and Dabbs, J. M. Jr. Judging physical attractiveness: Effects of judges' own attractiveness. Unpublished manuscript, Georgia State University, Atlanta, GA.

Terman, L. M. The intelligence quotients of Francis Galton in childhood. *American Journal of Psychology,* 1917, *28,* 209–215.

Thackray, R. I., and Orne, M. T. Effects of the type of stimulus employed and the level of subjects' awareness on the detection of deception. *Journal of Applied Psychology,* 1968, *52,* 234–239.

Thomas, D. S. *Some new techniques for studying social behavior.* New York: Columbia Univ. Press, 1929.

Thomas, W. I., & Znaniecki, F. *The Polish peasant in Europe and America: monograph of an immigrant group.* Vol. 1. Chicago: Univ. of Chicago Press, 1918.

Thorndike, E. L. *Your City.* New York: Harcourt, Brace, 1939.

Thorndike, R. L. *Personnel selection.* New York: Wiley, 1949.

Toulouse, M. M., & Mourgue, R. Des réactions respiratoires au cours de projections cinématographiques. *Revuew Internationale de Filmologie,* 1948, *2,* 77–83.

Trivers, R. L. Parental investment and sexual selection. In B. Campbell (Ed.) *Sexual selection and the descent of man 1871–1971.* Chicago: Aldine Publishing Company, 1972.

Trueswell, R. W. A survey of library users' needs and behavior as related to the application of data processing and computer technique. Unpublished doctoral dissertation, Northwestern Univ., 1963.

Tuchfarber, A. J., and Klecka, W. R. Measuring crime victimization: An efficient method. Washington, D.C.: The Police Foundation, 1976.

Turner, C. F., and Krauss, E. Fallible indicators of the subjective state of the nation. *American Psychologist,* 1978, *33,* 456–470.

Turner, J. L. Powers of observation: The measurement and correlates of observational ability. *Dissertation Abstracts International,* 1974, *35* (2-B), 1031–1032.

Turner, W. Dimensions of foreman performance: a factor analysis of criterion measures. *Journal of Applied Psychology,* 1960, *44,* 216–223.

Udy, S. H. Cross-cultural analysis: a case study. In P. E. Hammond (Ed.), *Sociologists at work.* New York: Basic Books, 1964. Pp. 161–183.

Ulett, G. A., Heusler, A., Callahan, J. Objective measures in psychopharmacology (methodology). In E. Rothlin (Ed.), *Neuro-psychopharmacology,* 1961, *2,* 401–409.

Ulett, G. A., Heusler, A., Ives-Word, V., Word, T., & Quick, R. Influence of chlordiozepoxide on drug-altered EEG patterns and behavior. *Medicina Experimentalis,* 1961, *5,* 386–390.

Ulmer, S. S. Quantitative processes: some practical and theoretical applications. In Hans W. Baade (Ed.), *Jurimetrics*. New York: Basic Books, 1963.

Underwood, B. J. *Psychological research*. New York: Appleton-Century-Crofts, 1957.

VanKirk, M. L. *Response Time Analysis*. Vol. II. *Results*. Kansas City, Missouri, Board of Police Commissioners, 1977.

Vera Institute of Justice. *Felony arrests: Their prosecution and dispositions in New York City's courts*. New York: A Vera Institute of Justice Monograph, 1977.

Vidich, A. J., & Shapiro, G. A. A comparison of participant observation and survey data. *American Sociological Review*, 1955, *20*, 28–33.

Vincent, C. E. Socioeconomic status and familial variables in mail questionnaire responses. *American Journal of Sociology*, 1864, *69*, 647–653.

Walbeck, N. H. Precepts, paragons, and practice: The effects of various methods of nutrition instruction on attitudes, knowledge, and behavior. *Journal of Social Psychology*, 1973, *91*, 197–205.

Wales, E., and Brewer, B. Graffiti in the 1970's. *The Journal of Social Psychology*, 1976, *99*, 115–123.

Wall Street Journal. Shave and a haircut, four towels—by the Tax Court's count of a barber's income. May 20, 1970, p. 1.

Walters, R. H., Bowen, Norma V., & Parke, R. D. Experimentally induced disinhibition of sexual responses. Unpublished manuscript, Univ. of Waterloo, 1963. Cited in A. Bandura & R. H. Walters, *Social learning and personality development*. New York: Holt, Rinehart & Winston, 1964. Pp. 76–79.

Walters, E., Markley, R. P., and Tiffany, D. W. Lunacy: A type 1 error? *Journal of Abnormal Psychology*, 1975, *84*, 715–717.

Ward, C. D. Own height, sex, and liking in the judgment of the height of others. *Journal of Personality*, 1967, *35*, 381–401.

Warner, W. L. *The living and the dead*. New Haven: Yale Univ. Press, 1959.

Warner, W. L., Meeker, M., & Eells, K. *Social class in America*. Chicago: Science Research Associates, 1949.

Washburne, C. The good and bad in Russian education. *New Era*, 1928, *9*, 8–12.

Washingtonian. June 1979, *14* (9), 15.

Watson, J., Breed, W., & Posman, H. A study in urban conversation: sample of 1001 remarks overheard in Manhattan. *Journal of Social Psychology*, 1948, *28*, 121–123.

Watson, R. I. Historical review of objective personality testing: the search for objectivity. In B. M. Bass & I. A. Berg (Eds.), *Objective approaches to personality assessment*. Princeton: Van Nostrand, 1959. Pp. 1–23.

Wax, R. H. Reciprocity in field work. In R. N. Adams & J. J. Preiss (Eds.), *Human organization research.* Homewood, Ill.: Dorsey Press, 1960. Pp. 90–98.

Weaver, K. F. The mystery of the shroud. *National Geographic Magazine,* 1980, *157,* 730–753.

Webb, E. J. *Men's clothing study.* Chicago: Chicago Tribune Co., 1957.

Webb, E. J. How to tell a columinst: I. *Columbia Journalism Review,* 1962, *1,* 23–25.

Webb, E. J. How to tell a columnist: II. *Columbia Journalism Review,* 1963, *2,* 20. (a)

Webb. E. J. The orthographics of seven African languages. Technical report, U.S. Army, 1963. (b)

Weick, K. E. Systematic observational methods. In G. Lindzey and E. Aronson (Eds.), *The handbook of social psychology: Volume II Research methods.* Reading, MA: Addison-Wesley, 1968, 357–451.

Weiner, B., Heckhausen, H., and Meyer, W. Causal ascriptions and achievement behavior: A conceptual analysis of effort and reanalysis of locus of control. *Journal of Personality and Social Psychology,* 1972, *21,* 239–248.

Weiner, M. J., and Lurey, E. The "lost letter technique" as a predictor of the 1972 presidential election. *Journal of Psychology,* 1973, *84,* 195–197.

Weir, R. H. *Language in the crib* The Hague: Mouton, 1963.

Weiss, D. J., and Dawis, R. V. An objective validation of interview data. *Journal of Applied Psychology,* 1960, *44,* 381–385.

Weitz, J. Selecting supervisors with peer ratings. *Personnel Psychology,* 1958, *11,* 25–35.

Welch, M. S. Where do they love you most? *Redbook,* 1978, *151,* (3), 86–95.

Werthman, C., and Piliavin, I. Gang members and the police. In D. J. Bordua (Ed.), *The police: six sociological essays.* New York: John Wiley, 1967.

West, D. Y. In the eye of the beholder. *Television Magazine,* 1962, *19,* 60–63.

West, S. G., Gunn, S. P., and Chernicky, P. Ubiquitous Watergate: An attributional analysis. *Journal of Personality and Social Psychology,* 1975, *32,* 55–65.

Westley, B. H., Higbie, C. E., Burke, T., Lippert, P. J., Maurer, L., and Stone, V. A. The news magazines and the 1960 convention. *Journalism Quarterly,* 1963, *42,* 591–595.

Westoff, C. F., and Rindfuss, R. R. Sex preselection in the United States: Some implications. *Science,* 1974, *184,* 633–636.

Weyant, J., and Clark, R. D., III. Dimes and helping: The other side of the coin. *Personality and Social Psychology Bulletin,* 1977, *3,* 107–110.

Whisler, T. L., & Harper, S. F. *Performance appraisal: research and practice.* New York: Holt, Rinehart & Winston, 1962.

White, R. K. Hitler, Roosevelt and the nature of war propaganda. *Journal of Abnormal and Social Psychology,* 1949, *44,* 157–174.

Whiting, J. W., and Child, I. L. *Child training and personality: A cross-cultural study.* New Haven, CT: Yale Univ. Press, 1953.

Wicker, A. W. Size of church membership and members' support of church behavior settings. *Journal of Personality and Social Psychology,* 1969, *13,* 278–288. (a)

Wicker, A. W. A failure to validate the lost-letter technique. *Public Opinion Quarterly,* 1969, *32,* 260–262. (b)

Wicker, A. W., McGrath, J. E., and Armstrong, G. E. Organization size and behavior setting capacity as determinants of member participation. *Behavioral Science,* 1972, *17,* 499–513.

Wicklund, R. A. Objective self-awareness. In L. Berkowitz (Ed.) *Advances in experimental social psychology* (Vol. 8). New York: Academic Press, 1975. Pp. 233–275.

Wiggins, J. S. *Personality and prediction: Principles of personality assessment.* Reading, Massachusetts: Addison-Wesley, 1973.

Wigmore, J. H. *A student's textbook of the law of evidence.* Brooklyn: Foundation Press, 1935.

Wigmore, J. H. *The science of judicial proof as given by logic, psychology, and general experience and illustrated in judicial trials.* (3rd ed.) Boston: Little, Brown, 1937.

Will, G. *Tallahassee Democrat,* May 11, 1980, 2B.

Williams, C. E., and Stevens, K. N. On determining the emotional state of pilots during flight: An exploratory study. *Aerospace Medicine,* 1969, *12,* 1369–1372.

Williams, R. Probability sampling in the field: a case history. *Public Opinion Quarterly,* 1950, *14,* 316–330.

Wills, G. *Inventing America: Jefferson's Declaration of Independence.* Garden City, New York: Doubleday, 1978.

Wilson, E. B. *An introduction to scientific research.* New York: McGraw-Hill, 1952.

Wilson, M., and Mather, L. Life expectancy. *Journal of the American Medical Association,* 1974, *229,* 1421–1422.

Wilson, P. R. Perceptual distortion of height as a function of ascribed academic status. *Journal of Social Psychology,* 1968, *74,* 97–102.

Windle, C. Test-retest effect on personality questionnaires. *Educational and Psychological Measurement,* 1954, *14,* 617–633.

Winick, C. Thoughts and feelings of the general population as expressed in free association typing. *The American Imago,* 1962, *19,* 67–84.

Winship, E. C., & Allport, G. W. Do rosy headlines sell newspapers? *Public Opinion Quarterly,* 1943, *7,* 205–210.

Winston, S. Birth control and the sex-ratio at birth. *American Journal of Sociology,* 1932, *38,* 225–231.

Withey, S. Personal Communication, November 18, 1980.

Wolfenstein, M., and Leites, N. *Movies: A psychological study.* New York: Atheneum, 1970.

Wolff, C. *A psychology of gesture.* London: Methuen, 1948.

Wolff. C. *The hand in psychological diagnosis.* London: Metheun, 1951.

Wolff, W., & Precker, J. A. Expressive movement and themethods of experimental depth psychology. In H. H. Anderson & G. L. Anderson (Eds.), *An introduction to projection techniques.* New York: Prentice-Hall, 1951. Pp. 457–397.

Woodhouse, J. G. Self-serving biases in causal attributions for success and failure in a natural setting. Unpublished doctoral dissertation, Florida State Univer., 1978.

Worthy, M. *Eye color, race and sex: Keys to human and animal behavior.* Anderson, South Carolina: Droke House/Hallux, 1974.

Wrightsman, L. S. Wallace supporters and adherence to "law and order." *Journal of Personality and Social Psychology,* 1969, *13,* 17–22.

Yule, G. U., & Kendall, M. G. *An introduction to the theory of statistics.* (14th ed.) New York: Hafner, 1950.

Zajonc, R. Social facilitation. *Science,* 1965, *149,* 269–274.

Zamansky, H. S. A technique for assessing homosexual tendencies. *Journal of Personality,* 1956, *24,* 436–448.

Zamansky, H. S. An investigation of the psychoanalytic theory of paranoid delusions. *Journal of Personality,* 1958, *26,* 410–425.

Zeisel, H. *Say it with figures.* (4th ed.) New York: Harper, 1957.

Zeisel, H. The FBI's biased sampling. *Bulletin of the Atomic Scientist,* 1973, *29* (1), 38–42.

Zelnio, R. N., and Gagnon, J. P. The viability of the lost letter technique. *Journal of Psychology,* 1977, *95,* 51–53.

Ziller, R. C. Personal communication, 1978.

Ziller, R. C. and Smith, D. E. A phenomenological utilization of photographs. *Journal of Phenomenological Psychology.* 1977, *7,* 172–182.

Zipf, G. K. Some determinants of the circulation of information. *American Journal of Psychology,* 1946, *59,* 401–421.

Zipf, G. K. *Human behavior and the principle of least effort.* Cambridge: Addison-Wesley, 1949.

Zweigenhaft, R. L. Signature size: A key to status awareness. *Journal of Social Psychology,* 1970, *81,* 49–54.

Zweigenhaft, R. L. The empirical study of signature size. *Social Behavior and Personality,* 1977, *5,* 177–185.

Zweigenhaft, R. L. American Jews: In or out of the upper class? In G. W. Domhoff (Ed.), *Power structure research.* Beverly Hills: Sage Publications, 1980.

Name Index

Subject Index